Gre

Green Bay's Greatest
Profiles of the Packers in the Pro Football Hall of Fame

MICHAEL JACQUART

Foreword by Jerry Kramer

McFarland & Company, Inc., Publishers
Jefferson, North Carolina

Library of Congress Cataloguing-in-Publication Data

Names: Jacquart, Michael, 1959– author.
Title: Green Bay's greatest : profiles of the Packers in the Pro Football Hall of Fame / Michael Jacquart ; foreword by Jerry Kramer.
Description: Jefferson, North Carolina : McFarland & Company, Inc., Publishers, 2022 | Includes bibliographical references and index.
Identifiers: LCCN 2021062282 | ISBN 9781476686097 (paperback : acid free paper) ISBN 9781476645094 (eBook) ∞
Subjects: LCSH: Green Bay Packers (Football team)—History. | Football players—Wisconsin—Green Bay—History. | Football players—Rating of—United States. | Football—Wisconsin—Green Bay—History. | BISAC: SPORTS & RECREATION / Football
Classification: LCC GV956.G7 .J53 2022 | DDC 796.332/640977561—dc23/eng/20220114
LC record available at https://lccn.loc.gov/2021062282

British Library cataloguing data are available

ISBN (print) 978-1-4766-8609-7
ISBN (ebook) 978-1-4766-4509-4

© 2022 Michael Jacquart. All rights reserved

No part of this book may be reproduced or transmitted in any form or by any means, electronic or mechanical, including photocopying or recording, or by any information storage and retrieval system, without permission in writing from the publisher.

Bronze statue of Vince Lombardi outside Lambeau Field (Mark Palczewski); (inset, left to right) Curly Lambeau (University of Notre Dame), Bart Starr (Green Bay Packers), and Brett Favre (Mark Palczewski)

Printed in the United States of America

McFarland & Company, Inc., Publishers
Box 611, Jefferson, North Carolina 28640
www.mcfarlandpub.com

To my loving wife, Debra,
who has always been there for me through thick and thin,
including some tough Packers losses over the years!

Acknowledgments

I wish to thank Joe Zagorski, whose excellent book for McFarland, *The Year the Packers Came Back: Green Bay's 1972 Resurgence*, inspired and challenged me during my research and writing. Joe also referred me to McFarland editor Gary Mitchem, whose support and timely responses to my seemingly endless queries made this project a reality.

Second, I want to recognize Hall of Fame guard Jerry Kramer, who offered quips on his own career and also fondly shared stories about the strong bond he shared with his teammates and with their legendary coach Vince Lombardi. They will remain special memories.

I also need to acknowledge my "Iola, Wisconsin, connections." When I wondered if I had come up with enough material for such an ambitious writing project, librarians Lisa Bauer and Robyn Grove repeatedly came through with numerous Packers books, articles, and clippings, which made me realize I could do this! Thanks, Lisa and Robyn.

Ted Willems of Iola provided another personal touch. Ted grew up in DePere, a Green Bay suburb, and he vividly retold his memories of Mike Michalske, whom he remembered as more of a gentleman and friend than as a former Packers great. I also need to recognize Mark Forseth, a friend in the Iola Lions Club, who was a key photo contributor, as he was for my first book, *A Century of Excellence: 100 Greatest Packers of All Time*.

No book on the green and gold would be complete without consulting *the* authority on the subject, Green Bay Packers historian Cliff Christl, a fellow UW–Oshkosh journalism grad, who generously offered both photos and his considerable expertise. I also need to acknowledge author David Zimmerman, who assisted with permissions for not just one, or even two, but *three* excellent Packers books!

Finally, I thank God for the writing talents He's given me that I am only too happy to share with others.

Table of Contents

Acknowledgments — vi

Foreword by Jerry Kramer — 1

Introduction — 3

Packers Inducted into the Pro Football Hall of Fame in the 1960s

1. Arnie Herber (1966): First of the Great Long-Ball Throwers (*Packers Years 1930–1940*) — 7
2. Clarke Hinkle (1964): A "Hunk of Steel" (*Packers Years 1932–1941*) — 14
3. Robert "Cal" Hubbard (1963): A Mountain of a Man (*Packers Years 1929–1933, 1935*) — 21
4. Don Hutson (1963): A Revolutionary Receiver (*Packers Years 1935–1945*) — 28
5. Earl "Curly" Lambeau (1963): A Man of Historic Achievements (*Packers Years 1919–1949*) — 36
6. Johnny "Blood" McNally (1963): Clearly One of a Kind (*Packers Years 1929–1933, 1935–1936*) — 44
7. Mike Michalske (1964): A Quarterback Playing Guard (*Packers Years 1929–1935, 1937*) — 52

Packers Inducted into the Pro Football Hall of Fame in the 1970s

8. Tony Canadeo (1974): The 50-Year Packer (*Packers Years 1941–1944, 1946–1952*) — 61
9. Forrest Gregg (1977): Flawless Execution (*Packers Years 1956, 1958–1970*) — 68

10. Vince Lombardi (1971): Much More Than a Stern Taskmaster
 (*Packers Years 1959–1967*) 76
11. Ray Nitschke (1978): Meaner Than a Junkyard Dog … but
 Only on the Gridiron (*Packers Years 1958–1972*) 85
12. Bart Starr (1977): Role Model for the Ages (*Packers Years
 1956–1971*) 94
13. Jim Taylor (1976): Fierce Fullback Fueled Packers Ground
 Game (*Packers Years 1958–1966*) 103

Packers Inducted into the Pro Football Hall of Fame in the 1980s–1990s

14. Herb Adderley (1980): Shutdown Corner and Kick Returner
 (*Packers Years 1961–1969*) 111
15. Willie Davis (1981): Stalwart on Outstanding Defenses
 (*Packers Years 1960–1969*) 119
16. Paul Hornung (1986): Mr. Versatility (*Packers Years
 1957–1962, 1964–1966*) 127
17. Henry Jordan (1995): Tenacious … and Quick-Witted
 (*Packers Years 1959–1969*) 134
18. Jim Ringo (1981): Undersized, but Perfect for Packers Offense
 (*Packers Years 1953–1963*) 141
19. Willie Wood (1989): Overcoming Long Odds (*Packers Years
 1960–1971*) 148

Packers Inducted into the Pro Football Hall of Fame in the 21st Century

20. Bobby Dillon (2020): One-Eyed Ballhawking Safety
 (*Packers Years 1952–1959*) 157
21. Brett Favre (2016): Unpredictable, but Always Entertaining
 (*Packers Years 1992–2007*) 164
22. Jerry Kramer (2018): Overcoming Adversity; "You Can If
 You Will" (*Packers Years 1958–1968*) 172
23. James Lofton (2003): Shining Light in Dim Era (*Packers Years
 1978–1986*) 180
24. Dave Robinson (2013): Trailblazing Linebacker (*Packers Years
 1963–1972*) 188

25. Reggie White (2006): Leaving a Legacy On and Off the Field (*Packers Years 1993–1998*)	196
26. Ron Wolf (2015): Savior of a Franchise (*Packers Years 1991–2001*)	204
27. Charles Woodson (2021): Takeaway Machine (*Packers Years 2006–2012*)	212
Appendix A. Packers Who Should Be (or Will Be) in the Pro Football Hall of Fame	221
Appendix B. Player Statistics, Biographies and Fast Facts	230
Chapter Notes	257
Bibliography	271
Index	279

Foreword
by Jerry Kramer

People have often wondered why the Green Bay Packers were so successful in the 1960s. There are a number of reasons. While we had great individual talent, ability alone doesn't win football games. It takes a *team* effort. It is a characteristic that often separates the champions from the also-rans.

Coach Lombardi told us repeatedly that you don't do things right some of the time, you do them right *all* of the time. That is an important lesson not only in football, but in life, and it's a key reason why many of us became successful after our football careers. Willie Davis served on 17 boards of directors at one time while he was in the business community. Dave Robinson was an engineer and started his own beer distributorship.

I was involved in a number of business endeavors following my retirement, one of which was in coal mining. It started out simply enough in western Kentucky when I asked American Electric Power if they'd buy my coal. Between specs, permits, trucks, buyers, I learned everything I could about the business, and the business grew. It was no accident—it involved a lot of hard work, just like football.

I also got involved in the commercial diving business, motivational speaking, and other ventures. The point is, whatever you do, it boils down to common sense, treating people fairly, and *doing things the right way all the time.*

Mike Jacquart's book describes the special qualities of the 1960s Packers—not only teamwork, but also our lack of prejudice and the special friendships we forged, many of which lasted well past our playing years. Whatever the era, whether Lombardi years or otherwise, a commitment to excellence, doing things the right way is crucial to success.

Packers guard **Jerry Kramer** *was inducted into the Pro Football Hall of Fame in 2018. He was a five-time first-team All-Pro and was named to the NFL 50th Anniversary All-Time Team. He wrote* Instant Replay *(with Dick Schaap), which chronicled the Packers' 1967 championship season. He is also the subject of a 2021 documentary (and CD),* You Can if You Will: The Jerry Kramer Story.

Introduction

No franchise in the National Football League is more iconic than the Green Bay Packers. Tiny Green Bay has a population just over 100,000—little more than a suburb in any other NFL city. Packers team historian Cliff Christl has said that the Packers "are the greatest story in sports." And he is right. The Packers offer an incredible lesson in perseverance. How did a city that size manage not only to remain in professional sports but take center stage as a 13-time world champion? It's a tale hard to believe.

The Packers nearly went bankrupt any number of times, as it took many decades before they finally reached financial solvency. Their first stock sale to raise money took place as early as 1923.[1] Additional tough times and much-needed fundraising efforts occurred in 1933 and as recently as 1950.[2,3]

Not only did the Packers survive, an accomplishment in and of itself, they *thrived* on the gridiron, claiming more titles than any other NFL team.

In terms of the Pro Football Hall of Fame, Packers faithful take great pride in the fact that only the Chicago Bears have had more players enshrined in Canton. Perhaps no team is represented by quite so many legendary figures—Vince Lombardi, Curly Lambeau, Don Hutson, and Bart Starr, to name a few.

Recalling not only Packers but NFL giants was but one reason for writing this book. There were plenty of others. In poring over information about the Packers who have been enshrined in Canton, it became increasingly clear what a caring, even loving bond the Lombardi-era greats in particular had for their teammates. As I was researching the chapter about Ray Nitschke, for instance, it came as no surprise that Jerry Kramer and Dave Robinson had spoken in glowing terms about him, or that Kramer had likewise praised Willie Davis. Toward the end of their careers, ex-Packers Forrest Gregg and Herb Adderley commented on how this strong bond was missing from their new team (the Dallas Cowboys)—how business-like the Cowboys appeared compared with the emotional Packers. One has to believe that when the chips were down, it was that love for one another these men learned under Lombardi that often made the difference between victory and defeat. In today's Not-For-Long era of pro football, it's rare that a player spends his entire career with any one franchise, and so demonstrating what a *team* these Packers were—how strong their bond was—became one of my goals for the book.

Even race proved not to be as divisive as it was for other franchises. First and foremost, a Packers player wasn't white or black; he was green and gold. Period. Willie Davis said as much when he told roommate Jerry Kramer he believed in green power. Race is a difficult issue everywhere in America, but the Packers have a reputation, one that began under Lombardi, for handling race relations better than many other teams in spite of the heavily white local population.

Another reason for writing this book was to illustrate the strong contributions of the Hall of Famers from the Curly Lambeau era. There have been many lists naming the greatest Packers of all time, including my own, published as a book with the title *A Century of Excellence: 100 Greatest Packers of All Time*. It seems that in virtually all of them, the abilities of the standout players from the Packers' earliest years are grossly underestimated, with the possible exception of Don Hutson.

It's true that it's difficult to compare players and statistics from different eras—the best one can do is to establish what stars they were relative to other great players from that time. But with five championships in the 1920s and 1930s, and a sixth in the 1940s, one could make a decent case that Lambeau's Packers were comparable in their dominance to Lombardi's teams. The tough-nosed Clarke Hinkle was essentially the Jim Taylor of his era. Robert "Cal" Hubbard was as dominant a tackle as Forrest Gregg, only in Hubbard's day he had to play defense, too. Would Gregg have fared as well on the "d-line"? We'll never know. And don't forget the versatile Johnny Blood, who was the Lambeau-years equivalent of Paul Hornung. Athletic guard Mike Michalske was his generation's version of Jerry Kramer, but in this case paving the way for Hinkle, as opposed to Hornung and Taylor.

The point here is not to try to take *any* of the luster off any of the great players from the Lombardi years. First, it's fun to compare eras. Second, it's worth noting that even the Lombardi years are getting to be a long time ago. The number of 1960s greats who have passed away since I began writing this book is a reflection of this stark fact. It should come as no big surprise that some Packers fans have never heard of, say, Henry Jordan or Dave Robinson. The point: Since even wide-receiving great James Lofton is an "old-timer" to some, this book will make younger readers aware of the terrific players from other eras. Even older Packers fans who remember some of the greats of the 1960s may have overlooked the number of talented

Introduction 5

Packers that won six championships long before Vince Lombardi arrived on the scene.

Any writer worth his salt enjoys reading the work of his peers, and that served as an important source of inspiration when it came time to put fingers to a keyboard. Pro football writers the author delved into for this project included Bob Fox, a prolific online Packers writer familiar with legends from yesteryear; Joe Zagorski, who has published two books about the NFL in the 1970s, one of them on the Packers; Ralph Hickok, author of *Vagabond Halfback: The Saga of Johnny Blood McNally*; David Zimmerman, author of two exceptional biographies, *Curly Lambeau: The Man and the Mystique* and *In Search of a Hero: Life and Times of Tony Canadeo, Green Bay Packers Gray Ghost*; and Christl, longtime sportswriter and Packers team historian.

I pored over many other books as well, including Jim Taylor and Kristine Setting Clark's *The Fire Within*; Forrest Gregg and Andrew O'Toole's *Winning in the Trenches*; Paul Hornung and Chuck Carlson's *The Paul Hornung Scrapbook*; Willie Davis's *Closing the Gap*; and Herb Adderly, Dave Robinson, and Royce Boyles's *Lombardi's Left Side*.

For a writer passionate about Packers and NFL history, reliving these stories was like discovering an attic full of lost treasures—a time warp of sorts into the past—as I researched players who starred at a time when the NFL was struggling to establish itself and other greats who commanded center stage when football emerged as the number one sport in America in the 1960s.

Since many of these players have had stories—if not books—written about them, a key idea was to focus on lesser-known aspects of the person or his playing career. In the case of Jerry Kramer, so much has been said and written about his famous Ice Bowl block and lengthy wait for HOF enshrinement that I dug into other aspects of his career, including the health issues and surgeries he overcame in even playing professional football for 11 seasons.

Most everyone is familiar with Vince Lombardi as a stern taskmaster who drove the Packers to five world championships in the 1960s. But did you know that he was deeply religious? Or that the traits he instilled in his team extended beyond the gridiron to life lessons that led to post-football success for many of his former players? Those are but two examples, but the story of each enshrinee is special, one of a kind, and that was a key point the author wished to make.

I also elected to forgo a strict chronological approach within the chapters, my goal being less to present mini biographies than to give emphasis to unique achievements and challenges, or to memorable moments. As a result, readers first learn about the important role that Tony Canadeo, as a Packers administrator, played in Green Bay's hiring Vince Lombardi well before learning about his great playing career. Instead of simply diving into the background of Jim Ringo, I began that chapter by describing important characteristics of his position, the idea being to offer insights into what it takes to play center.

Those are just for starters. There are plenty of other stories that go beyond statistics, accolades, and simple biography. I take up questions, for instance: What made Ray Nitschke so mean on the gridiron? As the leading rushers of their era, how does Jim Taylor compare to Browns legend Jim Brown? Why was Dave Robinson considered a trailblazer? What Packers great retired and unretired long before Brett Favre made such flip-flopping famous? What are some of the important games and individual plays that these standouts participated in? These facts and stories are all here, and more.

The criteria for inclusion in this book are also worth mentioning. Each player profiled suited up for the Packers for at least six seasons. In a few cases, this was fewer than the number of years they played for another team (Reggie White, for example, and Charles Woodson), but the impact they had while in Green Bay was plenty sufficient for inclusion as a Packer enshrined in Canton.

Hall of Famers who made *shorter* stops in Titletown, and hence are not profiled in this book but still worth mentioning briefly, are Len Ford, DE, Los Angeles Dons, Cleveland Browns, and Packers (1958); Walt Kiesling, guard, Eskimos, Maroons, Cardinals, Bears, Packers (1935–1936) and Pirates; Ted Hendricks, LB, Colts, Packers (1974) and Raiders; Jan Stenerud, K, Chiefs, Packers (1980–1983) and Vikings; and Emlen Tunnell, DB, Giants and Packers (1959–1961).

Finally, one can't discuss the Packers, and their great players, without mentioning the team being "owned" by its stockholder fans and not by a rich businessman. It's a bond unique to the smallest NFL franchise, and while it still is, I dare say this bond was even stronger decades ago when the Packers were common, everyday people just like the fans who came to see them play, not the multimillionaires of today who are more distant from the crowds and who often charge for their autographs. A former Green Bay area resident interviewed for this book fondly recalls the era of fan-friendly Packers and former Packers.

In short, reading about great Packers players enshrined in Canton provides a glimpse into a rich history of players, teams, and championships unlike any other. For older Packers fans, it's the author's sincerest hope is that these stories will allow the reader to relive some great memories. It's also a wish that younger "Packer backers" discover terrific players they may have never even heard of given Green Bay's long, storied football history. Happy reading.

Packers Inducted into the Pro Football Hall of Fame in the 1960s

1

Arnie Herber (1966)

*First of the Great Long-Ball Throwers
(Packers Years 1930–1940)*

It's fascinating to study NFL quarterbacks. Arm strength IS important, but so are other characteristics like reading defenses, knowing when to call an audible, instinctive traits like understanding when to step up in the pocket to elude a pass rusher, and of course, accuracy. Yet arm strength will always rate high on the list of important quarterback traits for the simple reason that it takes a certain amount of velocity to make all of the necessary throws in the NFL. Take too much off a QB's "fastball" and it goes from a crisp, quick throw that zips to a receiver with time to spare before the defender breaks on the ball, to a softer pitch that takes too long to get where it needs to be, giving the defensive back an opportunity to time the route and intercept the throw, or at the very least, break it up.

What about the arm strength of Packers signal callers? While not possessing the "howitzer" arm of prestigious peers like Joe Namath and Sonny Jurgensen, it was said that Bart Starr threw the ball just hard enough to get where it needed to be. And accuracy, a specialty of Starr's, is of course vital.

In the late 1970s and 1980s, Lynn Dickey threw about as "pretty" a deep pass as anyone. Teammate Larry McCarren used to say that Dickey was the best long-ball thrower he had ever seen. A decade later, along came Brett Favre, whose throws looked more like they were shot out of a cannon than a right arm. "Whish!" as a ball would zip by. "What was that? Was the ball going THAT fast?" A different adjective seemed in order to gauge the velocity of a Favre throw, and that was the first time the author ever heard an announcer use the word "laser" to describe one of his "rocket shots."

It might surprise many a Packers fan to learn that neither Favre nor Dickey was the team's first great long-ball thrower. That honor would belong to Arnie Herber, the Packers' principal passer in the Curly Lambeau era. Born in Green Bay, Herber starred in basketball and football at Green Bay West High School, where he was known as the "Flash" for his running ability. He was an all-around athlete, the first 10-letter man in West High's history. As well as captaining both the football and basketball teams, he also starred in track and broke conference records in the javelin throw, discus, and shot.[1]

Arnie Herber, considered one of the first of the great long-ball throwers in the NFL, could supposedly heave a football 80 yards. Inducted in the Pro Football HOF in 1966, he is undoubtedly one of the unsung stars of the Curly Lambeau era (courtesy Neville Public Museum of Brown County).

1. Arnie Herber (1966)

Herber played two years of college football, first on the freshman team at University of Wisconsin–Madison, then for his sophomore season at Regis College in Denver, which dropped football after the 1929 season following the stock market crash.

Arnie Herber Highlights

4× NFL champion (1930, 1931, 1936, 1939)
NFL All-Star (1939)
3× First-team All-Pro (1932, 1935, 1936)
3× NFL passing yards leader (1932, 1934, 1936)
3× NFL touchdown leader (1932, 1934, 1936)
NFL passer rating leader (1936)
NFL 1930s All-Decade Team
Green Bay Packers Hall of Fame (1972)
Pro Football HOF (1966)

Playing career:
Green Bay Packers (1930–1940)
New York Giants (1944–1945)

Already a Packers fan, Herber moved back to Green Bay and took a job as a handyman in the team's clubhouse. It was fortuitous timing. A late-season victory over the big city New Yorkers in 1929 basically secured the Packers' first NFL championship with a 12–0–1 record. Only a scoreless tie against the Frankford Yellow Jackets kept Green Bay from an undefeated season.

Even with a loaded team, Lambeau was never one to stand pat. He gave Herber a tryout and added the talented local boy to the 1930 roster. Besides, the shrewd Packers coach knew the hometown Herber could be a drawing card, which was an important consideration in the early days of the NFL when gate receipts were crucial.

It's important to point out why Herber has been referred to as a "passer" and "long-ball thrower" as opposed to "quarterback." Pro offenses differed in the early days of the NFL, and coach Curly Lambeau liked running the Notre Dame Box, which he had learned from his Notre Dame mentor, Knute Rockne. The offense differed from the single-wing formation commonly used at the time in three principal areas:

The line was balanced.

The two tight ends were split from the line of scrimmage.

The wingback, who lined up outside the tight end in the single wing, was brought in more tightly.

The wingback now lined up behind the tackle, with the quarterback next to him, the fullback behind him, and the tailback set diagonally behind him. The placement of the four players resembled a box, hence the name.

Unlike the single-wing, deception and not power was what made the Notre Dame Box so successful. The constant shifting of the backs was designed to keep opposing defenses off-balance. Additionally, the backs often switched positions on any given play, causing even more confusion on the other side of the ball.[2]

The offense was perfect for the Packers, who featured a number of talented, versatile backs who could both run and throw the ball. Herber actually did most of his passing from the right halfback position. When quarterback Red Dunn retired after leading the Packers to three straight championships from 1929–1931, Lambeau tweaked his Box offense. "He put Herber at right halfback, making him his primary passer while turning the Packers' quarterback into a blocking back. Herber also called signals from the halfback position."[3]

In fact, while Herber was inducted into the Pro Football Hall of Fame as a quarterback, Packers team historian Cliff Christl noted that Herber actually started only two games there during his 11 seasons with the Packers, both in his rookie year.[4]

Regardless of the position, there was no questioning that Herber was gifted with a powerful right arm. "Arnie Herber could throw the ball 80 yards," former teammate Harold Van Every said. "Greatest arm I've ever seen. The man was a terrific, terrific passer."[5]

Van Every would not have been alone in his assessment. Later in Herber's career, the Packers made a short film during a post-season visit to California. He was asked to throw the ball at a three-foot-square pane of glass from 50 yards away.[6] On his first attempt, he hit the bullseye. But the director wasn't ready and didn't get the cameras rolling. "He told Herber he would have to do it again. Calmly on his very next toss, Herber duplicated the feat."[7]

What's more, Herber had an unusual grip, which made his powerful throws all the more amazing. At the time, the ball was still rounder than the modern football, which was introduced in the NFL in 1933.

Writer Rob Reischel described his grip like this: "Herber had extremely small hands, so instead of using the laces, he learned to palm the ball. That style certainly worked."[8]

Indeed it did, and it was no accident. With short fingers, using his thumb on the laces kept the ball from wobbling, ensuring a spiraling pass. Actually, Herber's unique throwing style went beyond his hand. In what can only be described as a signature "jump-throw," he held the ball far above his head, with his right knee bent and elevated to his waist.[9]

In Herber's first year, 1930, the Packers continued their success and won another title with him playing tailback. In 1931, with Herber throwing more than usual for that time to early greats like Johnny "Blood" McNally,

1. Arnie Herber (1966)

the Packers reeled off nine straight victories to start the season and won a third straight title. (Until the playoff system was implemented in 1933, championships were determined by regular season winning percentages.) No other team in NFL history, other than the Packers themselves in the 1960s, has won three consecutive titles.

But Herber did more than throw the ball. The Packers won the championship in each of his first two seasons, and while his passing certainly played a factor, Herber could also run, catch passes, and punt with the best. Such versatility was important in that era compared to today's specialty-driven NFL.

His multiple skills were on display in a 1932 contest against the Staten Island Stapletons. Herber did all of the punting, ran for 85- and 45-yard touchdowns, and completed nine of 11 passes for three additional scores. That was the first year the NFL kept statistics, and Herber finished as the top passer in the league with 639 yards and nine touchdowns.

He won the passing title again in 1934 with 799 yards and eight touchdowns. But Herber would not reach his peak until Don Hutson, a fleet receiver from Alabama, joined the Packers the following year. Hutson admitted that Herber's passing was a main reason he wanted to play in Green Bay. "I remember Curly Lambeau telling me over the telephone that Green Bay had the best long passer in football," he said.[10]

Fans didn't have to wait long for the pass-catch tandem to make its mark when the Packers matched up against the archrival Chicago Bears on September 22, 1935. On the Packers' first play, Herber called for Johnny Blood to line up on the right side, with the Alabama rookie on the opposite side of the field. Blood raced up the sideline, drawing Bears defenders with him, while Herber saw that the gazelle-like Hutson was open. Herber launched a pass the rookie snared on the Chicago 43-yard-line and bolted untouched for a breathtaking 83-yard touchdown. It was the game's only score in a 7–0 Packers victory.

The Herber-to-Hutson touchdown against the Bears was the first of many such scores as the combination soon began terrorizing the league. "He has the uncanny knack of arching a long pass so that the receiver simply races to the spot, makes the catch and speeds on without breaking stride," said veteran coach Clark Shaughnessy, about Herber's long-range accuracy.[11]

Curly Lambeau concurred. "He [Herber] completes a greater percentage of his passes beyond 40 yards than many recognized passers complete within 30 yards of the line of scrimmage," he stated.[12]

In 1935 alone, the Herber-to-Hutson tandem connected on 18 completions for 420 yards and seven touchdowns. From 1935 onward, "Herber-to-Hutson always spelled double-trouble for NFL defenses."[13]

It's worth pointing out that Herber played at a time when *toughness* was critical. In those brutal days, there were few rules protecting the quarterback (or anyone for that matter), which meant the passer was "fair game" to be hit by a defender, even after he threw the ball. Combine this common occurrence with the extra time needed for his receivers to get downfield for one of his long passes, "meant that he took many fierce beatings. Yet in his early years with the Packers he never wore a helmet."[14]

With Herber solidly built at six-foot and 200 pounds, the roughhouse play didn't stop the pair. In 1936, Hutson's second in the NFL, Herber and his star receiver rewrote the NFL record book. Herber tossed 177 passes for a record 1,239 yards and 11 touchdowns. Hutson set new records with 34 catches, 526 yards receiving, and eight touchdowns, all marks he would soon improve upon. Green Bay finished 10-1-1 and advanced to the 1936 NFL title game, which they won, 21-6, over the Boston Redskins at the Polo Grounds in New York. In that contest, Herber tossed two touchdowns, one to Hutson.

Some say that Herber was the fortunate beneficiary of playing with Hutson, the game's first great receiver. There is no question that the legendary wideout transformed the game, but he still needed someone capable of launching the ball to him far down the field. What's more, Herber achieved remarkable statistics (for that era) and success before Hutson's arrival (although admittedly not at the level he attained with his mercurial wideout).

With a 7-4 record, the Packers slipped to second place in 1937, but they returned to the NFL championship game in each of the next two years. The 1938 season marked the first with tailback Cecil Isbell, who was selected in the first round of the 1938 draft by the Packers—the seventh overall pick out of Purdue. Since the Packers already had Herber, Lambeau alternated Isbell and Herber and occasionally used them in the same backfield, with Isbell at halfback. Platooning gave Isbell time to learn Lambeau's offense, the Notre Dame Box. However, it should also be noted that a leg injury Herber sustained during the 1937 season began reducing his effectiveness.

In the 1938 championship game, Green Bay lost to the New York Giants, 23-17, at the Polo Grounds despite another touchdown pass by Herber. In 1939, the Packers avenged the loss with a 27-0 walloping of the Giants in Milwaukee. Herber threw for another score in the 1939 title contest.[15] (Isbell also threw a 27-yard TD pass.)

All told, Herber threw four touchdowns in his three career post-season games with the Packers, but his versatility deserves another mention. In 1939, he blocked two punts, and in 1940, he intercepted two passes. He kicked two successful extra points in his career, scored a defensive touchdown, and launched 37 punts for the Packers, with the longest going a whopping 74 yards.[16]

Isbell began to get more playing time in 1940, and Herber was waived at the end of training camp in 1941. He retired after 11 seasons with the Packers.[17] While alternating with Herber early in his career, Isbell eventually blossomed as a passer in his own right. His streak of 23 straight games with a touchdown pass was an NFL record until broken by the Colts' Johnny Unitas in 1957.

This is not to diminish Herber's accomplishments with the Packers. Three times each he led the NFL in completions, passing yards, passing touchdowns, longest pass, and passer rating. Herber's 14.5 touchdowns per pass attempt are, by far, the highest in team history (obviously a different era), but not once did he lead the league in interceptions. Twice he led the NFL in completion percentage. To this day, no Packers quarterback has led the league in passing yards or completions more often than Herber.[18]

He placed in the top five in touchdown passes in eight of the nine seasons in which official stats were kept. And in 1936 he led the league in touchdown percentage and just about every other statistic on the way to a championship season.[19]

Four years later, the Giants, overwhelmed by the player shortages of World War II, talked Herber out of retirement. He was 34 and overweight but worked hard and was down to his playing weight of 210 pounds by the start of the season.[20]

While past his prime, Herber still had his moments. In a game against the Eagles in 1944, he completed five of six passes for 114 yards and two touchdowns in the last six minutes of the game to forge a 21–21 tie. The surprising Giants advanced to the NFL title game against his old team, losing to the Packers, 14–7.

New York slipped dismally in 1945, but Herber still occasionally shined even in his last season. The Giants were trailing Philadelphia, 21–0, when he entered the game in the third quarter. In just under five minutes, Herber tossed four touchdown passes to give the New Yorkers a 28–21 triumph.[21]

Even at the time of his initial retirement in 1940, Herber was regarded as the best long-distance passer in NFL history. His 66 TDs were tied for the most all-time. "Herber helped steer the league in a direction that would allow Sammy Baugh, Sid Luckman, Bob Waterfield, Otto Graham, and even his teammate [Isbell]" to dominate opponents by throwing the ball downfield. An easy argument could be made that Herber is one of the most underrated players in league annals.[22]

2

Clarke Hinkle (1964)

A *"Hunk of Steel"*
(Packers Years 1932–1941)

Between shattered bones, busted teeth, split lips, and concussions—better known in the day as "getting your bell rung"—football has never been a game for the faint of heart. Vince Lombardi once famously said that dancing was a "contact" sport—football was a *collision* sport. All too true. No doubt today's football players are bigger, stronger, and faster than ever. With modern medicine, players and coaches are even more aware of the health risks associated with playing a dangerous sport.

Players from the prewar era may not have been as big as today's behemoth linemen, but remember they also had little protection from violent hits. They wore leather helmets, simple pads—not very good ones at that—and they *didn't* wear face masks or guards. Whatever the time frame, hitting is still hitting. Collisions still bust ribs, cause concussions, and worse. Football is a rough, sometimes barbaric sport regardless of the era.

One of the toughest players from the NFL's early days was Packers fullback and linebacker Clarke Hinkle. He was a contemporary of Chicago Bears legend Bronko Nagurski, another bruising fullback/linebacker whose toughness and chiseled physique made him another back that no one was interested in tackling on their own. No one, that is, except the rough-and-tumble Hinkle! Nagurski was taller and 35–40 pounds heavier than the 5'11", 202-pound Packers star, but Hinkle was every bit as tough, something he proved when he gained the unique distinction of being the only man ever to knock "the Bronk" out of a game in 1934, Hinkle's third year in the NFL.

Since they played the same positions, the pair met head-on many times. On one particularly memorable encounter, Nagurski left the contest with multiple injuries. David Zimmerman described how the action in this Bears-Packers contest unfolded in his book, *Curly Lambeau: The Man Behind the Mystique*.

2. Clarke Hinkle (1964)

Clarke Hinkle was one tough hombre, even knocking out Chicago Bears great Bronko Nagurski in one memorable contest (courtesy Neville Public Museum of Brown County).

Clarke Hinkle Highlights

2× NFL champion (1936, 1939)
3× NFL All-Star (1938–1940)
7× First-team All-Pro (1932, 1935–1938, 1940–1941)
NFL rushing touchdowns co-leader (1937)
NFL 1930s All-Decade Team
College Football Hall of Fame (1971)
Green Bay Packers Hall of Fame (1972)
Pro Football HOF (1964)
Packers practice field across Oneida Avenue from Lambeau
    Field dedicated as "Clarke Hinkle Field" (1997)

In that largely run-first era, it was not unusual to punt the ball away on third down if gaining a first down was unlikely. On 3rd and 14, Hinkle went back to punt, but instead of kicking he ran to his right, and the Bears star ran up to meet him. Football players are taught to wrap up ball carriers with their arms, but the powerful Nagurski was often able to get the man down simply by blocking him with a shoulder, forearm, etc.

Then all hell broke loose.

Hinkle was running near the sideline when Nagurski tried to block him out of bounds, but the Packers back lowered his shoulder and crashed it into Nagurski's face. "Hinkle ran into Nagurski and over him, stayed inbounds and reached midfield for a first down before he was brought down from behind."[1] The Bears great had to be helped from the field with a broken nose, bruised ribs, fractured hip, and injured shoulder.

In recalling the brutal hit, Hinkle said that when encountering a foe as powerful as Nagurski, it was either hit him first or *get hit*. Before Hinkle went out of bounds at the sideline, he cut back and caught Nagurski square with his shoulder and head. In the bone-jarring collision, it should be noted that Hinkle also absorbed punishment. "He knocked me back pretty near five yards. I sat there for a few seconds, because it really shook me up. Then I looked over at old Bronk and his nose was all over his face."[2]

According to Hinkle, "[Bears coach] George Halas was really mad about it, and he said I played Bronk dirty. I don't know how he got that. I was carrying the ball. I couldn't be doing anything dirty."[3]

It's also worth pointing out the play because Hinkle never got the publicity or notoriety that Nagurski did. The late *Sports Illustrated* writer Paul Zimmerman said as much. "My impression was that Hinkle was a lot better than people gave him credit for," he stated. "He was a well-kept secret in Green Bay. … So, yeah, I think he was every bit as good."[4]

In any case, no matter the opponent, Hinkle's reputation as a *tough* ball carrier and *physical* tackler was well deserved. "I vividly remember Russ Winnie—a very dramatic play-by-play announcer in his day—describe Hinkle as a 'hunk of steel,'" recalled former team historian Lee Remmel.[5]

"I think he liked to hit people any chance he could," said Herm Schneidman, who played in the Packers backfield with Hinkle from 1935–1939.[6]

Opponents agreed. "When he hit you, you knew you were hit," recalled Ken Strong, another Hall of Fame back from that era. "Bells rang and you felt it all the way to your toes."[7]

In *Pain Gang: Pro Football's Fifty Toughest Players*, Neil Reynolds included both Hinkle and Nagurski on his list of the toughest players in the history of the game. Another back, Johnny Sisk, testified to Hinkle's physicality in the 2006 book. "No one in the whole league ever bruised me as much as Hinkle did," Sisk stated. "Hinkle had a lot of leg action. I broke my shoulder twice tackling Mr. Hinkle."[8]

According to another account, "Clark [sic] Hinkle loved contact. It didn't matter which side of the ball he was coming from. Hinkle loved delivering blows."[9]

Off the field was a different story, as Nagurski and the mild-mannered Hinkle remained friends long after their playing careers were over. In fact, Nagurski was Hinkle's presenter when the Packers great was inducted into the Pro Football Hall of Fame. "They said I was hard to tackle, but here was a guy who didn't have too much trouble," quipped Nagurski at Hinkle's induction in Canton in 1964.[10] (Nagurski was one of 17 charter members of the Hall in 1963.)

Hinkle was born in Toronto, Ohio, located on the Ohio River roughly 40 miles west of Pittsburgh. He was the son of Ohio natives Charles Hinkle and Lillian Ault Clark. His father was an engineer and later worked as a forger at a steel mill. Hinkle attended Toronto High School.

He played football at Bucknell University in Lewisburg, Pennsylvania, where he set records for the Bucknell Bisons as a defensive halfback and fullback on offense. In a contest against Dickinson on Thanksgiving Day 1929, Hinkle, nicknamed the "Lackawanna Express," tallied *eight* touchdowns and scored 50 points. With the incredible game, he became the leading scorer in the nation. "The national football individual scoring crown seems destined to rest on the head of Clarke Hinkle.... Hinkle broke loose for 50 points against Dickinson on Thanksgiving Day to boost his season's total to 128, thus superseding Al Marsters, injured Dartmouth star, as the national, as well as eastern, leader."[11]

In 1931, Hinkle helped lead Bucknell to a 6–0–3 record, the only undefeated record by an Eastern school that year. In an era when players lined up on both sides of the line of scrimmage, Hinkle was also outstanding on defense. His college coach, Carl Snavely, called him "Without a doubt, the greatest defensive back I have ever seen or coached."[12]

Hinkle played for the East in the East-West Shrine Game in San Francisco on New Year's Day 1932. He was the leading ground gainer in the game, and a *United Press* correspondent wrote: "If there was a single star in the long-drawn battle of line plunges and punting it was Clark Hinkle of Bucknell whose stabs through tackle were a revelation in driving power."[13]

This was four years prior to the NFL draft, so college players were free to sign with any team they wished. Hinkle was debating his future and having a drink with an All-American roommate after the East-West game when who knocked on the hotel door but Curly Lambeau, with a contract in his hand. In those days, it was not unusual for Lambeau to scout, recruit, and sign a player to a Packers contract.

"He scouted games every year and often picked up players from the East-West game," Hinkle said. "So, I signed a contract, $125 a game."[14] (This was a typical salary for a Packer in that day, which equaled roughly $1,700 a year. Some of the top players in the NFL earned between $300 and $500 a game, while star Packers made "as much as $200 a game." This was largely due to the Packers' financial problems and Lambeau's tight-fistedness.)[15]

Not that Hinkle was complaining. Coming from a small town in Ohio, it was only natural that he wanted to play in a smaller city that was more like a college town than, say, New York or Chicago. The Packers were a perfect fit. "I thought Green Bay would be like a college town with a lot of college spirit, and it was," Hinkle said. "They took their football seriously in Green Bay. If we won a game, we were in all the bars that night and never bought any drinks. We had a ball! But if we lost a ball game, we never left the hotel. People were mad. If we had to leave the hotel, we would go down the alleys," Hinkle recalled.[16]

A blend of bulldozing power and terrific speed, Hinkle led the Packers with 331 yards rushing on 95 carries as a rookie in 1932. Green Bay posted a 10–3–1 record, good for second place behind the Chicago Bears. (The Packers had won the championship the previous season.)

He quickly gained a reputation for his two-way play on both offense and defense, where he might have been even better than he was as a runner. "Backing up the Packers line, he was a vicious tackler against the run and terrific on pass defense." In fact, Hinkle proudly claimed later in his career that he let only one receiver get behind him during his decade of pro football.[17] Moreover, in an era when versatility was much more prized than today's specialized game, Hinkle also excelled as a punter and kicker.

A newspaper clipping from that year alluded to Hinkle's skills, especially as a rookie. "Red Grange, the greatest ball carrier the game has known, was a 'washout' during his first year in 'pro' ball, but not Clarke Hinkle. ... Hinkle is not only a great ball carrier and defensive player but is leading the league in punting."[18] The article added that Lambeau had found a worthy successor to their great punter, Vern Lewellen, who had been handling that task for eight seasons.

There was no facet of the game in which Hinkle didn't shine. This included something that the typical fan often misses—faking. While he ran with brute power, Hinkle was tremendous at pretending he had the ball. "He frequently hit the line without the ball and drew the defense to himself, while Arnie Herber, and later, Cecil Isbell gained time to fade back for a long pass to Don Hutson."[19]

After spending the offseason working for a steel construction company in his hometown, Hinkle returned to Green Bay in September 1933.[20] In his second NFL season, he again led the team in rushing with 413 yards,

2. Clarke Hinkle (1964)

but the Packers' record slipped to 5-7-1, a rare losing season. Despite the team's poor record, Hinkle was still selected as a Second-team All-Pro by the *United Press*, *Chicago Daily News*, and *Green Bay Press-Gazette*.

Hinkle continued to display his rare combination of power, speed, and accurate kicking in 1934 and 1935, helping lead Green Bay to winning records in both seasons (7-6, third place; and 8-4, second place, respectively).

While always a versatile player throughout his career, the "hunk of steel" broke through with 476 yards on only 100 carries, as he helped lead the Packers to the 1936 title over the Boston Redskins at New York's Polo Grounds, 21-6.

In 1937, Hinkle led the NFL with seven touchdowns and ranked second with 552 yards rushing. In 1938, he paced the NFL in scoring with 58 points on seven touchdowns, seven extra points, and three field goals.[21]

The following campaign marked another championship, this time 27-0 over the New York Giants in a contest played at State Fair Park in Milwaukee. "So rugged was the Green Bay defense that the Giants gained only 70 yards rushing all afternoon.... The crowd braved a cold, cloudy, blustery day to attend the game, giving the Packers a record gate of more than $80,000 as Green Bay recorded the first shutout in an NFL championship game."[22] Hinkle picked up 23 yards rushing in the title contest, third on the team.

He again played a major role in the 1939 regular season, amassing 381 yards rushing, nearly 100 more than he had in 1938. He also scored five TDs, matching his total from 1937, although not registering a touchdown receiving, as he had two years prior.

The well-rounded Hinkle continued to display his talented kicking, leading the NFL in field goals and field goal percentage in both 1940 and 1941.[23] He also excelled as a punter, ranking second in punting yards in 1939 and averaging 44.5 yards per boot in 1941.

The only thing Hinkle wasn't good at was losing, as his emotions and dedication to the game would get the best of him. "After the game," a teammate said, "if we lost, he'd sit at his locker and cry like a baby. He didn't know how to lose."[24]

Hinkle's playing career was cut short after the 1941 season by wartime military service. Tough until the very end, on November 2, 1941, in his final game against the Chicago Bears, Hinkle had his leg torn open by an opponent's spike. It opened a gash on his shin that exposed the bone. He stayed on field for a few plays but then called a timeout and ran to the sideline to get the wound dressed. Lambeau was not happy that Hinkle spent a timeout to get an injury looked at. He responded, "I came over to get a bandage on it because you know it kind of makes me sick to look at my shinbone."

20 Packers Inducted into the Pro Football Hall of Fame in the 1960s

Hinkle not only went back into the game, but he kicked a 38-yard field goal to give the Packers a 16–14 win.[25]

In May 1942, following the United States entry into World War II, Hinkle enlisted in the United States Coast Guard and received the rank of lieutenant.[26] Hinkle was discharged from the Coast Guard in 1946 and began working at Kimberly-Clark in Neenah, Wisconsin.

With 3,860 yards, Hinkle is still the seventh-leading rusher in Packers history. In 1994, the versatile back was named to the NFL's 75th Anniversary All-Time Two-Way Team. Three years later, the Packers' practice field on Oneida Avenue across from Lambeau Field was dedicated as "Clarke Hinkle Field."

3

Robert "Cal" Hubbard (1963)

A Mountain of a Man
(Packers Years 1929–1933, 1935)

Football is a game that has always been played by big men, but they weren't always so "gi-normous" like they are today. Of the 159 players who have started at least four games as an offensive lineman since the start of the 2014 season, only 23 weigh less than 300 pounds, and 39 are at least 320 pounds.[1]

Let's make some comparisons throughout NFL history. In the 1920s, the average lineman was the size of today's smaller wide receivers, 6-foot, 211 pounds. In the 1930s, a typical lineman had roughly the same frame as today's bigger wide receivers, 6-foot-1, 220 pounds. In the 1940s, the usual lineman measured about the same as today's taller running backs, 6-foot-1, 221 pounds. By the 1990s, linemen had bulked up to the size of today's larger defensive ends, 6–4, 300 pounds.[2]

Of course, there have always been exceptions. At 6'9", San Francisco 49ers great Bob St. Clair essentially was Ed "Too Tall" Jones decades before Jones arrived on the scene in Dallas. (St. Clair, a 1940s–1950s star tackle, weighed 263.) Among Packers, Gilbert "Gravedigger" Brown, their mammoth nose tackle in the 1990s and early 2000s, measured 6'2", 340 (some would say more than that). For those keeping track, St. Clair was roughly 40 pounds larger than the typical tackle of his era, and Brown about the same, at 340 compared to 300.

Pro Football Hall of Famer and Packers great Robert "Cal" Hubbard, likewise, was a large player for his day. Just how big was he? That is subject to debate. The Pro Football HOF lists him as standing 6-foot-2 and weighing 250 pounds, while Ralph Hickok, a leading authority on sports history, describes Hubbard as 6'5", 265, in his book, *Vagabond Halfback: The Saga of Johnny Blood McNally*. Hickok doesn't believe there is any way of knowing for sure, but this much is certain: Like St. Clair and Brown,

Hubbard weighed at least 40 pounds more than the majority of tackles in his era.

Robert "Cal" Hubbard Highlights

4× NFL champion (1927, 1929–1931)
4× First-team All-Pro (1927, 1931–1933)
NFL 1920s All-Decade Team
Charter member Pro Football Hall of Fame (1963)
Charter member Green Bay Packers HOF (1970)
College Football Hall of Fame (1962)
NFL 50th, 75th, 100th Anniversary All-Time Teams
(75th was all-time two-way team; Don Hutson was the only other Packer on all three teams)

Professional playing career:
New York Giants (1927–1928)
Green Bay Packers (1929–1933, 1935)
New York Giants, Pittsburgh Pirates (1936)

Coaching career:
Geneva (1942)
Major League Baseball umpire (1936–1951)
Baseball Hall of Fame (1976)
Only person enshrined in Pro and College Football and Baseball Halls of Fame

Maybe a better approach would be to see how Hubbard measured against some other great linemen of his era. Wilbur "Fats" Henry, a fellow 1963 enshrinee, went 5'11", 245; Giants center Mel Hein, another charter member of the HOF, measured 6'2", 225; Chicago Bears great Ed Healey, 6'0", 207; fellow Bears standout George Trafton, 6'2", 230; William Roy "Link" Lyman, 6'2", 233; Dan Fortmann, 6'0", 210; and guard Walt Kiesling, who played two seasons with the Packers toward the end of his career, went 6'2", 249.

Thus, with no one on that list tipping the scales at even Hubbard's lesser weight of 250, and no one taller, he definitely stacks up as a mountain of a man of that day and age. Of course, reputation means something, too, and a bio on Hubbard on the Pro Football HOF website describes the Packers great as the "most feared lineman of his time."[3]

Russ Winnie, noted broadcaster and radio voice of the Packers, offered a more colorful description of the tackle's size, as he used to say that Cal Hubbard weighed between 265 and 280 pounds, depending on what he ate for breakfast.

It seems Hubbard was always on the large side. The son of a farmer,

3. Robert "Cal" Hubbard (1963)

Robert "Cal" Hubbard grew up in Missouri. He graduated from Keytesville High School, but because the school did not have a football team, he also attended one year in nearby Glasgow, which *did* offer the sport. Already tall and weighing 200 pounds as a 14-year-old, Hubbard displayed natural athletic talents. He aspired to attend the U.S. Military Academy at West Point, but a physical revealed he had flat feet, which rendered him ineligible.[4]

Since he could not attend West Point, he looked for a college with a promising football program. After a chance meeting with Alvin "Bo" McMillan, "a college All-American quarterback and coach at Centenary College in Shreveport, Louisiana" he accepted McMillan's invitation to enroll there. "He played at the school from 1922 to 1924 and was a star player."[5]

Hubbard was the school's first All-American, but when McMillan moved on to Geneva in Beaver Falls, Pennsylvania, he decided to join him there. Hubbard played at Geneva in 1926 after being declared ineligible in 1925 due to transferring to a new school.

Hubbard moved on to the NFL in 1927, signing with the New York Giants for a salary of $150 per game (typical at that time). He helped the Giants' defense limit opponents to an incredibly low 20 points on the entire season in capturing the league championship. The talented lineman garnered all-league honors, but he disliked big cities, and a game in Green Bay the following year convinced him that he liked the smaller city and would be much happier there. So Hubbard told his team, "Trade me to the Packers or I quit."[6]

"Good players make good coaches better, and [Curly] Lambeau added three excellent members to his 1929 team of already solid athletes—men who would make the Packers dominating champions. The three he came up with are well known in Packer lore: the flamboyant Johnny [Blood] McNally, Cal Hubbard, an incredible two-way athlete, and 'Iron Mike' Michalske, one of the finest linemen of his day."[7] Lambeau moved Hubbard, an end with the Giants, to tackle.

Gaining three future Hall of Famers in a single year put the Packers over the top, since Green Bay already had a good team. As well as these talented newcomers, returning standouts in 1929 included Bo Molenda, Jug Earp, back Joseph "Red" Dunn, end Laverne "Lavvie" Dilweg, and back/punter Vern Lewellen. Many believe Dilweg and Lewellen also belong in Canton.

Ironically, it was a late-season victory over Hubbard's former team, the Giants, that basically secured the Packers' first NFL championship with a 12–0–1 record in 1929. It needs to be pointed out that before the NFL playoff system was implemented in 1933, regular season standings determined the league champion.

In spite of their success, not all of the Packers got along with Lambeau. Hubbard was among those whose relationships with his coach was contentious. "To be frank," Hubbard would say, "Curly really didn't know that much about football. After all, he just spent one year at Notre Dame, how much did he learn? Most of us knew more, because we had spent more time learning during four years of college and then, for most of us, some professional experience, too. Hell, sometimes Curly would design a new play, draw it up on the blackboard and we just knew it wouldn't work the way he drew it."[8]

In fact, the uneasy association got downright ugly at times. "The two had no fondness for another," wrote David Zimmerman in his book, *Curly Lambeau: The Man Behind the Mystique*. "'They won't be able to find six men to bury the so and so,' Hubbard was once quoted as saying about his coach, although he also admitted, 'He was a hard driver, but he got the job done.'"[9]

The mammoth Green Bay tackle certainly "got the job done," too—a major understatement. Giants star center Mel Hein, a future Hall of Famer himself, said Hubbard "was probably the greatest tackle I ever played against."[10]

The following story illustrates how the Packers great could dominate a game. "Hubbard was the left defensive tackle, and he stopped everything," Hein recalled about the contest. "We used to like to run to our right from the single wing, running to the strong side of the line—that was our normal tactic out of that formation. But against the Packers that meant we would be running into Cal Hubbard's side of the line."[11]

The Giants began making yardage once they started running plays on the opposite side. Lambeau had seen enough. He pulled Hubbard out of the line "and let him roam around behind it, along with the fullback and the roving center, to spot and bump any receivers coming through and to plug up whatever holes might open."[12] (Indeed, Hubbard is credited as being one of the first linebackers in the NFL.)

"From that position," said Hein about Hubbard's responsibilities, "the son of a gun made tackles all over the field and they ... beat us."[13]

It was a role that Hubbard relished. "When a crowd of blockers came roaring around end, as they often did in those power days, Cal would dump the whole herd of them into the lap of the ball carrier," Zimmerman stated. "Or he might single out the lonely ball carrier, collar him with one sweep of his paw, and then splash him on the sod."[14]

Another description of his duties went like this: "On offense, he played very wide on the line and swept in ... knocking down multiple players like dominoes. On defense, he chose to step back from his tackle position on the line of scrimmage so that he could better see what the offense was doing. This allowed him to react quickly to the play."[15] Again, he was essentially one of the first linebackers.

While strength and brute power are important in football, quickness is

Robert "Cal" Hubbard was a large player for his day, measuring 6'2" and tipping the scales at more than 250 pounds, according to records. Despite his size, he was also quick enough to roam from sideline to sideline, chasing down ball carriers. As such, he was considered one of the first "linebackers" in the NFL (courtesy Neville Public Museum of Brown County).

another factor crucial to success, and Hubbard shined in that department as well. "He could run the 100-yard dash in close to 11 seconds. It was an awesome combination for a tackle—size and speed."[16]

In 1930, the Packers posted a 10–3–1 record, while the Giants ended up 13–4–0. Despite the Giants having more wins, league championships were decided by percentage at the time, so Green Bay eked out its second straight title.

In 1931, Michalske, Hubbard, Dilweg, and McNally were all named First-Team All-Pro, as the Packers rolled to another title, earning a *rare* "three-peat" with a 12–2 mark. The Packers posted an incredible 34–5–1 record from 1929–1931, but because the titles occurred before the playoff system, these early teams often don't get the recognition they deserve. One could make a case that these Packers squads were every bit as dominant as their 1960s counterparts.

Like their Lombardi successors, the early Packers were as close off the field as they were on the gridiron. "During the late 1930s and early 1940s, the Packer players were a tight knit group. Many of the players and their wives spent time together and would often recall they 'were just like a big family.'"[17]

While the Packers, and Hubbard, were often dominant, that doesn't mean no one ever got the best of them. On one occasion, Green Bay was playing the Chicago Bears, with stars Harold "Red" Grange and bruising fullback Bronko Nagurski. As Chicago prepared to punt, Hubbard allegedly told Grange, "I promise not to try to block the kick, Red, but get out of the way so I can get a shot at that Polack."[18]

Grange was more than happy not to have to block the massive Hubbard, so he gladly agreed. "Cal tore through the line, slammed into Nagurski and bounced off." Getting slowly off the turf, "he turned to Grange and said: 'Hey, Red, don't do me any more favors.'"[19]

The Packers came close to a fourth straight title in 1932. This time not counting ties in the standings hurt the Packers as it had helped them in 1930. Green Bay finished 10–3–1 in 1932 (.769), while the Chicago Bears went 7–1–6 (.875).

The 1933 Packers posted a 5–7–1 record, the first losing season in team history. Perhaps in part due to the subpar campaign, Hubbard left the Packers following the 1933 season to take a job as the line coach at Texas A&M. However, Green Bay convinced him to come back in 1935, but his return was short-lived. The Giants wooed him back in 1936, but he played only six games the entire season, five for the Giants and a final game for the Pirates.

"I've taken enough beatings for one man," said Hubbard when he hung up his cleats for good. "Not that I couldn't take some more. It's not fat nor age that's driving me out. ... I've just had enough shoving and kicking around."[20]

It was more than enough to convince McMillan, his college coach, of his greatness, calling Hubbard "The greatest football player who ever lived, lineman or back, college or pro."[21]

Hubbard returned to football coaching briefly, serving as head coach of his alma mater, Geneva College, in 1941 and 1942. Yet football wasn't his only love. In the days before fat contracts, football players had to take jobs in the offseason as well as considering possible careers for their post–NFL lives. For Hubbard, who said he loved to "be in the middle of the action," that extracurricular job was the national pastime, which back then was baseball.

Even while Hubbard's football career was going full-bore, he began focusing on a second career in baseball officiating. Starting in 1928, he spent his football off-season umpiring in minor league baseball. "By 1936 Hubbard had been called up to the major leagues, umpiring in the American League from 1936 to 1951. Soon recognized as one of the game's best officials, he was selected to work in the 1938 World Series, followed by Series appearances in 1942, 1946, and 1949."[22] He also umpired in three midsummer classics, otherwise known as All-Star Games. "His 20-10 vision and imposing size made him very effective as an umpire."[23]

As well as awe-inspiring, Hubbard was also innovative. At the time, umpires moved around to different positions on the field through the course of a game. This led to inconsistencies in which an umpire might move to a certain spot, others would move to a different spot, and some would stand still, all to call the same play. Hubbard found this both confusing as well as reducing accuracy while making calls.

He discovered a solution when he became an umpire supervisor in 1952. "He devised a system where each official had clearly defined duties and also added an additional official to the crew. This was the foundation on which Major League Baseball established new officiating standards"[24] that same year.

Then disaster struck. While Hubbard was hunting during the off-season in 1951, a pellet from a friend's shotgun ricocheted and accidentally struck Hubbard in the right eye. The damage was severe enough to force Hubbard to retire as an umpire. "However, the American League soon hired him as an assistant supervisor for league officiating crews, and in 1954 he became the top supervisor, a position he would hold until retiring for good in 1969."[25]

Hubbard developed emphysema in the last few years of his life, so doctors suggested that he move away from the cold weather in Missouri. He relocated to St. Petersburg, Florida, in 1976. That same year, in recognition of his accomplishments on the diamond, Hubbard was elected to the Baseball Hall of Fame in 1976. He was only the fifth umpire so honored up to that time.

That isn't to say anyone ever forgot about his skills on the gridiron. Seven years earlier, in a 1969 poll by the Pro Football Hall of Fame, Hubbard was voted the NFL's greatest tackle of all time. Bears coaching legend George Halas referred to him as the "Big Umpire."

4

Don Hutson (1963)

A Revolutionary Receiver (Packers Years 1935–1945)

There aren't many immortals in professional sports—athletes whose feats were so extraordinary that they left an imprint for decades. In baseball, Babe Ruth and Ty Cobb come to mind. Wilt Chamberlain in basketball would be a third, while a fourth would be hockey's Wayne Gretzky. While not as well-known as this quartet, Don Hutson also belongs on any such short list. Hutson, a standout pass-catcher and route-runner at a time when running the ball was *far* more popular, was light-years ahead of his time as an NFL wide receiver. Consider the following:

His single-season record of 17 touchdown receptions in 1942 stood as an NFL record for more than 40 years until broken by Miami Dolphins wide receiver Mark Clayton in 1984. Hutson's record of 99 career receiving touchdowns was another long-standing league mark until finally surpassed when the Seattle Seahawks' Steve Largent scored his 100th career TD in 1989. Yet Hutson, never a vain man, was happy to see his records fall. "I love to see my records broken, I really do," he said when Largent broke his touchdown mark in 1989. "You get a chance to relive [a part of] your life, the whole experience."[1]

With his lightning speed (he reportedly ran 9.7 100-yard dashes at a time when 9.5 was the world record) and clear, precise routes that made him nearly impossible to cover, Hutson made the passing game look easy. Many NFL pundits have sung of Hutson's praises over the years. The following are but a few of them.

"I don't know if there is such a thing as royalty in professional football, but this is the closest I've ever come to it," said Packers General Manager Ron Wolf, when the team christened their new indoor football facility the "Don Hutson Center" in 1994.[2] "He most certainly was the greatest player in the history of this franchise," Wolf added. "In the era he played, he was the dominant player in the game."[3]

Don Hutson Highlights

- 3× NFL champion (1936, 1939, 1944)
- 2× NFL Most Valuable Player (1941, 1942)
- 7× NFL receiving yards leader (1936, 1938, 1939, 1941–1944)
- 9× NFL touchdown receiving leader (1935–1938, 1940–1944)
- NFL interceptions leader (1940)
- His "14" was first number retired by Packers (1951)
- Charter member, Pro Football HOF (1963)
- Charter member, College Football HOF (1951)
- Green Bay Packers HOF (1972)
- NFL 100th, 75th and 50th Anniversary Teams
- Coaching career (Packers assistant, 1944–1948)
- Served on Green Bay Packers Board of Directors (1952–1980)
- State-of-the-art indoor practice facility, Don Hutson Center, named in his honor (1994)

"Hutson was football's Copernicus, proving that the universe did not revolve around the run," quipped writer David Whitley.[4]

In 2012, the NFL Network named Hutson the greatest Green Bay Packer of all time.

"I don't think there's any doubt that Don Hutson was the greatest receiver ever," Washington Redskins coach George Allen wrote in 1982. "He improvised moves and devised patterns that have been copied ever since."[5]

Only San Francisco 49ers great Jerry Rice has dominated the wide receiver position like Hutson—and some would question whether even Rice had the same impact. Hutson was such a dominating football presence that by the 1940s, he held *14* of the league's *15* pass-catching records.[6] The league now has 31 officially recognized pass-catching records—and Hutson's name *still* appears 14 times.[7]

Yet Don Hutson was a long-shot to become a sports legend, at least in football. While he was quick and agile as a youth, his tall, thin frame was better suited for baseball and basketball than it was for football. As a teenager, he played baseball for the community team in his hometown of Pine Bluff, Arkansas. He was also an all-state basketball player as a senior at Pine Bluff High School. Hutson once said that basketball was his favorite sport.

But when he finally did take to the gridiron, the athletic Hutson turned heads. Paul Bryant, a future college teammate of Hutson's, remarked, "He was something to see even then." Bryant, who also hailed from Arkansas, used to hitchhike to Pine Bluff to watch Hutson play, and he saw the young phenom catch five touchdown passes in a single high school game.[8] (Yes, *that* Paul "Bear" Bryant, the future legendary coach at Kentucky and later Alabama.)

30   Packers Inducted into the Pro Football Hall of Fame, 1960s

© Neville Public Museum of Brown County

Packers legend Don Hutson poses with nine footballs, the number of touchdown passes he caught in 1938, which set a record. Hutson was the most dominant player of his day, setting receiving records that lasted for decades—and in some cases, like his 105 touchdowns as a Packer, even to this day (courtesy Neville Public Museum of Brown County).

Despite Hutson's heroics, it was Bryant who was the more recruited player. It took the owner of a local pool hall to arrange a scholarship for Hutson to attend Alabama—and it was in baseball! "I didn't even think about pro football," he told *the SI Vault* years later. "They didn't even write about it in the newspapers."[9]

4. Don Hutson (1963)

Even with competing interests, Hutson's itch for the gridiron proved to be enough for him to walk onto the team. At first, the spindly Pine Bluff native had a difficult time competing against much larger ends such as Ralph Gandy, Jimmy Walker, and of course, Bryant. It was no big surprise that Hutson spent most of his first three years at Alabama on the bench.[10]

As in his last year in high school, the late-blooming Hutson really came on in his senior season at Alabama in 1934. Alabama stood at 3–0 going into a key game against rival Tennessee that proved to be Hutson's coming-out party. Now weighing 191 pounds, Hutson caught a 33-yard pass to set up the Crimson Tide's first touchdown. In the third quarter, with the score tied, 6–6, Hutson scored on an end around for what proved to be the game's winning score.[11]

That started a string of dominating performances by Hutson as Alabama breezed through their SEC schedule, easily beating Georgia, Clemson, and Georgia Tech. Hutson starred in each contest as the tall, lean, and elusive receiver now known as the "Alabama Antelope"—a moniker that stuck with him over the years—recorded eight touchdowns during that stretch.

Bryant had this to say about his dazzling teammate. "Don had the most fluid motion you had ever seen when he was running," said the "other end" at Alabama. "It looked like he was going just as fast as possible when all of a sudden he would put on an extra burst of speed and be gone."[12]

The question becomes why did it take so long for coaches to recognize Hutson's great talent as a receiver? Alabama assistant coach Harold "Red" Drew explained, "I guess the main reason was that he played so effortlessly and with such grace, the coaches thought he was loafing. It turned out he could catch any ball thrown near him. He had big hands and was relaxed at all times."[13]

In the weeks leading up to the 1935 Rose Bowl, it was clear that Hutson was no longer a player on the bench that nobody paid attention to. He dominated every sports headline and was seen as the key to unbeaten Alabama defeating Stanford, which they did handily, 29–13, for the Tide's fourth national championship.

If 1934 was a watershed year for Don Hutson, 1935 would be even more monumental. First came the matter of what he wanted to do with his life. A budding businessman, Hutson had started a laundromat with Bryant in college that failed, but it whet his entrepreneurial spirit to do more in business. As mentioned, pursuing a gridiron career wasn't really on young Hutson's mind in spite of his awesome senior season as an All-American split end on a national championship team.

The idea of a college star *not* moving on to the NFL seems almost impossible to fathom given the quick riches that come with a professional sports career today. But the 1930s weren't like that. Fame was often fleeting in the NFL, and fortune most assuredly was. Major League Baseball was still America's pastime, and Hutson still held out hope for a career in the big leagues. He played in the Cincinnati Reds organization for several years before being released.

Besides, the issue of whether his 6'1", 190-frame would hold up in a rough-and-tumble sport had not gone away. (Unlike today's NFL, defenders weren't limited to a five-yard zone where they could legally hit receivers.) What's more, a professional draft was still a year away, and budding pros were free to sign with anyone they wanted to after college.

Green Bay Packers head coach Curly Lambeau was ahead of his time in his strong interest in the passing game, and Lambeau saw the fleet Hutson as a perfect complement to strong-armed passer Arnie Herber and end Johnny "Blood" McNally, a terrific talent, but in the twilight of a stellar career. Meanwhile, Hutson was also being pursued by Brooklyn Dodgers owner John Simms "Shipwreck" Kelly, who had promised to match any offer that Hutson received. When the NFL office received both contracts, NFL President Joseph Carr, in noting the earlier signing date on the Packers' contract, declared that Hutson should go to Green Bay.

A brief note about how Hutson nearly ended up in Brooklyn. As opposed to the much more successful baseball team of the same name, the football Dodgers, later the Tigers, were founded in 1930 and disbanded in 1945—an afterthought today in NFL history. In addition, since the Dodgers, like other NFL teams at the time, stressed running the ball over passing, it's unlikely the name "Don Hutson" would have meant anything in pro football history, at least as a receiver.

While it took Hutson a while to catch on in high school and college, no such breaking-in period would be needed in the pros. Hutson's first catch as a professional was an 83-yard touchdown pass from Herber on the first play from scrimmage against the archrival Chicago Bears in the second game of the 1935 season. It was the only score of the game as the Packers won, 7–0. Hutson caught six touchdowns in his rookie campaign, which led the league. In December, he married Julia Richards, his college sweetheart at Alabama. A monumental year indeed.

The following year also proved to be special. Following a second place, 8–4 record in 1935, the Packers improved to 10–1–1 and captured their fourth NFL title in 1936 with a 21–6 victory over the Boston Redskins. Hutson scored the first touchdown of the game on a 48-yard pass from Herber in the first quarter. Hutson finished the season with 34 receptions and eight touchdowns.

In 1938, Hutson had nine touchdown receptions, again setting a league record, as he led the Packers to another NFL Championship Game, this

4. Don Hutson (1963)

time against the New York Giants. But a knee injury sustained a month earlier kept him out of the starting lineup. Hutson played, but he did not catch any passes as the Giants claimed the title, 23–17.

In 1939, Hutson snared 34 passes for 846 yards, an unbelievable 24.9 yards per catch. More importantly, the Packers earned a title rematch against the Giants, this time winning easily, 27–0.[14]

Hutson became the first receiver to catch 50 passes in a season in 1941 and was awarded the Joe F. Carr trophy as the league's Most Valuable Player.

DON HUTSON CLASS OF 1963 (CHARTER) ENSHRINEE
PRO FOOTBALL HALL OF FAME

Don Hutson was one of 17 charter members of the Pro Football Hall of Fame in 1963. Many consider him a revolutionary receiver and perhaps the greatest Packer of all time (courtesy Mark Forseth Collection).

Hutson repeated as league MVP in 1942 as he *shattered* most of his own records with 74 catches for 1,211 yards and 17 touchdowns.

Roughly *60 years* before Brett Favre would drive Packers fans crazy by retiring and unretiring, it might surprise the Packers faithful to learn that Don Hutson did the same thing in the 1940s! In February 1943, Hutson announced his retirement from football due to a lingering chest injury. He changed his mind and returned for the 1943 season, snaring 47 passes for 776 yards and 11 touchdowns, leading the league in all three categories.

After the season, Hutson again announced his plans to retire, this time to become an assistant coach with the Packers. He *did* become an assistant, but he returned in 1944 as a *player*/coach. "I was trying to quit before I got killed," Hutson later quipped about his multiple retirements.[15]

Despite holding down a dual role, he led the team with 58 receptions and nine scores as Green Bay advanced to the 1944 title game, again versus the Giants. He caught two passes in the contest as the Packers beat the Giants, 14–7, for their third and last championship with Hutson on the roster.

For the third time in as many years, Hutson announced his retirement, and for the third time he returned as a player (and coach) in 1945. While the Packers, as a team, dipped to a 6–4, third-place finish, Hutson was still on top of his game. In perhaps the best quarter of football anyone has ever played, and in his last season no less, Hutson tallied an astounding 29 points on four touchdowns and five kicked PATs) in the second quarter in the Packers' 51–27 blowout win over the Detroit Lions.[16] (As a team, the Packers scored six TDs against the hapless Lions in the quarter, which accounts for Hutson's additional PAT.) Four touchdowns and a total of 29 points in not just a game or even a half, but a single *quarter* of football. It's a league mark that remains to this day.

Yes, with five PATs in the second quarter, the sterling pass catcher also doubled as the team's kicker, which he did for many of his 11 seasons as a Packer. In fact, Hutson led the league in field goals made in 1943. As did almost all players in that era, Hutson played both offense and defense. It's easy to overlook that he excelled on that side of the ball as well. He played safety and intercepted 30 passes over the final six seasons of his career.

In 2012, the NFL Network named Don Hutson the greatest Green Bay Packer of all time. He was also listed #1 in the book, *A Century of Excellence: 100 Greatest Packers of All Time*. Some would question whether the gifted receiver deserved *that* high a distinction, noting that his most productive seasons were from 1942 to 1945, when the NFL was depleted with many talented players serving in the military during World War II. (Hutson had three daughters, so he was not drafted.) It is a point well taken, and clearly naming the number-one all-time Packer is no easy task!

However, Green Bay Packers great Paul Hornung was among those who rebuked the idea that Hutson took advantage of watered-down defenses. "I'm a believer. Am I a believer! You know what Hutson would do in this league today? The same things he did when he played."[17]

There are others who agree with Hornung's assessment. "His impact of the game was of such power that it could legitimately be compared to the influence Babe Ruth spun on baseball," wrote sports columnist Rick Joslin when Hutson passed away in 1997.[18]

"Ruth was an elite star as a pitcher *and* hitter, that is part of his lore, his legend," said Tom Andrews on Packers History.com. "Don Hutson was, literally, the exact same on the football field. He was an elite star as a wide receiver on offense and a star safety on defense. And Hutson had the burden of having to reinvent the game of football and become a star receiver when there had never been one before."

"Many people outside of Wisconsin, even hardcore NFL fans, haven't heard of Hutson," Andrews added. "Some people only know his name and that he was an old-time Green Bay Packer. In fact, he was the best Packer there has ever been."[19]

Whether or not one agrees, it is certainly clear that Don Hutson revolutionized the game.

5

Earl "Curly" Lambeau (1963)

A Man of Historic Achievements (Packers Years 1919–1949)

Vince Lombardi and Ron Wolf deserve a ton of credit for rejuvenating the Green Bay Packers, but without Earl "Curly" Lambeau, they would not have had a Packers franchise to resurrect. Part innovator, motivator, promoter, and fundraiser, Lambeau was all those things and more, vital at a time in the National Football League's infancy when wearing different hats was much more important than in today's highly specialized era. While NFL and Chicago Bears founder George Halas was a bitter rival, he admitted that pro football would not have survived without men like Lambeau.

The Packers' longtime coach was also an enigma of sorts. He was considered a pioneer of the passing game at a time when running was considered safe while passing was risky. Yet, while an innovative thinker, Lambeau was not considered a good X's and O's strategist. He ran the team with an iron fist but was willing to settle for less than exemplary integrity in his own life, which included plenty of womanizing, according to *Curly Lambeau: The Man Behind the Mystique* and other publications.

Since he coached for more than three decades, it's easy to overlook that Lambeau was a great player in his own right and starred at Green Bay East High School from 1914–1917. His interest in playing football at the University of Wisconsin in 1917 caught the attention of *Green Bay Press-Gazette* sportswriter George Calhoun, who wrote in his "Cal's Comment" column that the star "has been heralded with joy by the university papers as the majority of football critics consider the Green Bay boy one of the best gridiron prospects that has ever been turned out of a high school."[1]

For reasons lost to history, Lambeau reportedly never even enrolled at Wisconsin, let alone played for the Badgers. The following year, he attended the University of Notre Dame and played for first-year coach Knute Rockne, making the Fighting Irish varsity squad. (As a player, Rockne had put the

Irish on the map with a 35–13 upset of Navy in 1913. Rockne would go on to post 105 victories and three national championships at Notre Dame.)

However, infected tonsils forced Lambeau to miss the 1919 spring semester, and he returned home. No one knew at the time that Notre Dame's and Wisconsin's loss would be Green Bay's gain.

Curly Lambeau Highlights

Co-founded Green Bay Packers August 11, 1919, after packing company put up $500 for uniforms
6× NFL champion (1929–1931, 1936, 1939, 1944)
2× Second-team All-Pro (1922, 1924)
NFL 1920s All-Decade Team
NFL 100th Anniversary All-Time Team
Wisconsin Athletic Hall of Fame (1961)
Charter member Pro Football HOF (1963)
Charter member Green Bay Packers HOF (1970)

Playing career:
Green Bay Packers (1919–1929)

Coaching career:
Green Bay Packers (1919–1949)
Chicago Cardinals (1950–1951)
Washington Redskins (1952–1953)
Career coaching record (226–132–22)
Shares distinction, with George Halas and Bill Belichick, of coaching his team to most NFL championships

Roughly 300 miles from his girlfriend, Marquerite, Lambeau was likely homesick for Green Bay, something alluded to in *Curly Lambeau: The Man Behind the Mystique*. His parents and Marguerite's parents pleaded with him to return to South Bend when he had recovered from tonsillitis. But he felt he was getting too far behind in his studies, and when he landed a job as a shipping clerk at the Indian (later Acme) Packing Company that paid him $250 a month—big money at the time—that was basically that. Lambeau was staying put in Green Bay.

The next chapter in Lambeau's life—co-founding a Packers team with George Calhoun of the *Press-Gazette* in 1919—is well documented. While he did not pony up the money, it is still surprising that he elected to try that undertaking. Professional football was an incredibly risky enterprise at that time, but Lambeau had a strong itch to return to the gridiron in spite of the uncertain venture.

After forming the Packers with Calhoun, Lambeau starred for the team for ten seasons, including the first eight years after Green Bay joined the newly formed National Football League in 1921. (It was previously known as the American Professional Football Association.) As a fledgling operation, the Packers nearly ran out of money on multiple occasions; Lambeau and city leaders held fund-raising events that got the team out of serious financial trouble. Once the team was sued when a fan fell out of the stands in old City Stadium. The Packers had to file bankruptcy to gain the necessary time to pay off the settlement and keep the team afloat.

Other small- and mid-sized towns like Akron, Canton, Rock Island, Dayton, Pottsville, and others came and went. Unlike today's NFL, with lucrative TV revenue sharing packages, teams' fortunes were strongly tied to gate receipts, which meant that poor attendance hurt significantly. The Packers drew well on the road, but it was hard to convince other teams to come to small Green Bay, where sparser crowds were likely.

After Cleveland joined Chicago and New York in the NFL, and the Portsmouth Spartans moved to Detroit to become the Lions, it became even more difficult for a team in a community like Green Bay to compete against larger cities. This meant it wasn't enough for Lambeau to coach; he had to be a P.T. Barnum of sorts, continually selling Green Bay and the Packers. In fact, barnstorming exhibition games on top of the regular schedule were sometimes held to raise much-needed cash.

"It was Lambeau's persistence that kept the Packers alive," wrote sportswriter Bud Lea.[2] Sportswriter Lloyd Larson lauded the coach's keen eye for talent. "Lambeau has a great knack of spotting potential stars and selling them on coming to Green Bay."[3]

It didn't hurt that Lambeau was handsome and always well-dressed, with a charming personality.

Although often overshadowed by Lambeau, the role of leading Green Bay businessmen like Andrew Turnbull, Lee Joannes, and Calhoun in particular should not be overlooked. Utilizing his influence at the *Press-Gazette*, Calhoun became the team's first publicity director, helping establish local support and interest.

Still, the bottom line is that one must have a good team worth watching, and there, too. Lambeau played an important part. Playing halfback in the then-popular single wing offensive formation, he was both the main runner and principal passer. He threw 24 touchdown passes, rushed for eight touchdowns, and caught three touchdowns in 77 games. He was named to the NFL's 1920s All-Decade Team. After retiring as a player in 1929, he remained as head coach and general manager for 20 more years. For most of that time, he had near-complete control over the team's day-to-day operations and represented the Packers at owners' meetings. "Lambeau dominated his teams, bent them to his will," said Oliver Kuechle,

5. Earl "Curly" Lambeau (1963)

Curly Lambeau gets ready to launch a punt. Lambeau played for the Packers for 10 years before coaching them for 30 years, during which time he led Green Bay to six world championships, one more than even the fabled Vince Lombardi (courtesy Neville Public Museum of Brown County).

former sports editor of the *Milwaukee Journal*. "He was a genius in the way he inspired and led his teams."[4]

Possessing a keen eye for talent and then knowing how to sell players on playing for the Packers were two of Lambeau's key attributes, and by 1929, he had put together a powerhouse team featuring a threesome who would end up in the Pro Football HOF: Robert "Cal" Hubbard, a large (for that era), 250-pound tackle who Lambeau had acquired from the New York Giants; back Johnny "Blood" McNally; and guard August "Mike" Michalske, who formerly played for the Pottsville Maroons and New York (football) Yankees, respectively. As well as these talented newcomers, returning standouts in 1929 included back Joseph "Red" Dunn, end Laverne "Lavvie" Dilweg, and back/punter Vern Lewellen.

A late-season victory over the "big city" New Yorkers in 1929 basically secured the Packers' first NFL championship with a 12–0–1 record. Only a scoreless tie against the Frankford Yellow Jackets kept Green Bay from an undefeated season. The Packers outscored the opposition by an incredible 198 points to just 22 allowed. Green Bay pitched eight shutouts that season, and no one scored more than six points against their stingy defense.

But Lambeau was never one to stand pat and added talented local boy, Green Bay native Arnie Herber, to the 1930 roster. Herber, who played collegiately at Regis College in Colorado, had a cannon of an arm and eventually wound up in Canton as well. It's said that sometimes it's better to be lucky than good, and that's how the Packers ended up defending their title. The Packers posted a 10–3–1 record, while the Giants ended up 13–4–0. Despite the Giants having more wins, league championships were decided by percentage at the time, so Green Bay eked out its second straight title.

In 1931, Michalske, Hubbard, Dilweg, and Johnny McNally were all named First-Team All-Pro as the Packers rolled to another title, earning a *rare* "three-peat" with a 12–2 mark. The Packers posted an incredible 34–5–1 record from 1929–1931, but because the titles occurred before the playoff system, these early teams often don't get the recognition they deserve. One could make a case that these Packers squads were every bit as dominant as their 1960s counterparts.

In any case, it's a myth that the Lombardi Packers were the first and only team to win three straight championships.

Even less widely known is how close the Packers came to a fourth straight title in 1932. This time the quirky fact that ties didn't count in the standings hurt, rather than helped, the Packers. Green Bay finished 10–3–1 in 1932 (.769), while the Chicago Bears went 7–1–6 (.875). "As it is, those Packers did amazing things, and set the bar fantastically high for all Green Bay teams to come."[5]

Does a great coach make his players even better? Or do terrific players make their coach look good? While Lambeau was ahead of his time as a proponent of the passing game, that didn't necessarily make him a game planning strategist.

"Curly really didn't know that much about football," Cal Hubbard stated. "After all, he just spent one year at Notre Dame, how much did he learn? Most of us knew more, because we had spent more time learning during four years of college and then, for most of us, some professional experience, too. Hell, sometimes Curly would design a new play, draw it up on the blackboard and we just knew it wouldn't work the way he drew it. He'd have impossible blocking assignments, or the play would just take too long to develop."6

Michalske offered a different view. "I will say that Curly was willing to learn from us. He really learned football from his players, and after a few years I think he knew as much as any coach in the game. He just had to have that learning experience for a while."7

While game planning and well-designed plays are important, sometimes improvisation also works, especially when you have talented players. According to *The Pro Football Chronicle* by Dan Daly and Bob O'Donnell, Johnny McNally once entered the huddle with a pass play from Lambeau. He made the call, as the halfback did in those days, turned to Herber, and said, "Arnie, throw it in the direction of Mother Pierre's whorehouse." No stranger to the Green Bay nightlife himself, Herber knew McNally was

Curly Lambeau diagrams a play for Don Hutson (left) and Cecil Isbell. Xs and Os were not his strong suit at first, but he got better at it over time, according to Packers great Mike Michalske (Photofest).

heading for the goal post at the northeast end of the stadium. The pass was there, and so was McNally.[8]

McNally and Lambeau had an often-adversarial relationship. Though supremely talented, the star halfback, known for his love of liquor and the ladies, was always up to crazy hijinks that drove his coach nuts. Lambeau would often comment "how he couldn't understand how such an irresponsible character off the field could be such a fine strategist on the field."[9] (McNally called all the plays.)

With his penchant for off-the-field antics, McNally was a notorious spender, so much that Lambeau would pay him $25 a week and hold the rest of the money until the end of the season. Even that tactic met with mixed results.

At the end of the 1931 season, Lambeau congratulated McNally on the Packers' third straight title and gave him the rest of his salary—several thousand dollars. Several weeks later, the Packers were staying at the Biltmore in Los Angeles before an exhibition game.

Lambeau's phone rang. It was McNally telling his coach he was broke. "Johnny, I just gave you a few thousand two weeks ago. How could you have spent it so fast?" "Curly," he said, "I've never had any money at Christmas before, so this time I bought everybody in my family ... presents.... But I'm broke. Could you let me have ten?"[10]

A contentious relationship usually has its limits, and Lambeau eventually had enough and dealt McNally to the Pittsburgh (football) Pirates in 1934, before welcoming him back the following season.

Thanks to the additions of fullback Clarke Hinkle (1932) and receiver Don Hutson (1935), the Packers' most successful period under Lambeau came in the 1930s, when they won two more championships for a total of four in the decade (1930–31, 1936, 1939).

After the playoff system was instituted in 1933, the Packers' first *post-season* contest finally occurred in 1936, when they beat the Boston Redskins, 21–6, for the NFL title at the Polo Grounds in New York. After the Packers lost the championship to the Giants in 1938 (Hutson was injured), they avenged the loss the following year, shutting out New York, 27–0, for the title in a game played at Milwaukee's State Fair Park. (Due to the Packers' small venues and unattractive gate receipts, it wasn't until 1961 that Green Bay finally hosted a championship contest.) Lambeau led the Packers to their sixth and last title under his guidance in 1944, when they upended the Giants, 14–7, at the Polo Grounds. In the nine-year period from 1936–1944, the Packers posted an impressive 67–21–4 record.

But any coach needs great players, and by 1944, Herber, Hubbard, Blood, Michalske, and Hinkle were all retired, and the great Hutson would play just one more season. The Packers could only manage third-place finishes in 1945, 1946, and 1947, and then plummeted to 3–9 and 2–10 records to conclude the 1940s.

The retirement of these stars, a reduced roster due to players who were away defending their country in World War II, and competition for talent from the upstart All-America Football Conference were just part of Lambeau's problems. He was frequently at odds with the team's Executive Committee over his off-field philandering and extravagant spending, which included the ill-fated Rockwood Lodge training facility that cost $32,000 (nearly $400,000 today; it burned to the ground in 1950). He had also married Grace Garland, a rich California socialite, and conservative Green Bay saw Lambeau as having "gone Hollywood." The game also appeared to be passing him by, as he resisted scrapping the Notre Dame box offense (basically the single wing) while the rest of pro football had moved on to the far more versatile T-formation.

The decline was striking. Between 1936–1944, Lambeau's Packers won 75 percent of their regular season games. The 1948 and 1949 teams, while bad, marked just his second and third losing seasons. The Packers' finances were also in rough shape, as they "began to see their profits slip away to the point that midway through the 1949 season the club was on the verge of bankruptcy."[11]

The small-market Packers barely survived being ousted by the NFL when the league absorbed three teams from the defunct All-America Football Conference—Cleveland, San Francisco, and Baltimore—that same year. "The Packers were very, very close to going away for good," said former Packers president Bob Harlan.[12]

Lambeau's resignation was announced on January 30, 1950. Most didn't care that he had already accepted the head coaching job with the Chicago Cardinals.

Perhaps it didn't really matter, as Lambeau's legacy was assured. "Few men anywhere have ever done as much for their hometown as Lambeau has for his," Kuechle stated.[13] "His vision and foresight made the Packers and the National Football League what they are today," said Charles "Buckets" Goldenberg, who played for Lambeau from 1933–1945.[14]

Lambeau's 209–104–21 (.668) record tops Packers coaching annals in terms of wins by a wide margin, and his overall mark of 226–132–22 still ranks 5th all-time in NFL history. He shares the distinction with rival George Halas of the Chicago Bears, and later Bill Belichick of the New England Patriots, of coaching his team to the most NFL championships.

6

Johnny "Blood" McNally (1963)

Clearly One of a Kind
(Packers Years 1929–1933, 1935–1936)

There are many different personalities on a football team. Some players are quiet, while others are friendly, good teammates but not necessarily memorable people. Then there are colorful characters, hell-raisers and eccentric types whose exploits on and off the field become legendary for decades—some more fiction than fact, but fun tales nonetheless. John Victor McNally, more commonly known as "Johnny Blood," was one such character.

The fourth of six surviving children born to Mary and John McNally Sr., John was born and raised in New Richmond, a small community in northwestern Wisconsin, a short drive from the Twin Cities. He came from a well-to-do family, and his mother exposed him to mythology and to poets William Shakespeare and Rudyard Kipling while he was quite young. McNally's life was one of paradoxes. On the one hand, the scholarly lad impressed teachers, was a persuasive debater, and graduated from high school at age 14.

"His first-grade teacher, Mrs. W.T. Doar, often described young John McNally as 'far and away the smartest student' she'd ever taught." At age eight, John recited Rudyard Kipling's "Gunga Din" in "a public performance at Hagan's Opera House on Main Street in downtown New Richmond."[1]

The precocious McNally also had an adventurous side. While not particularly athletic as a youth (he never played high school sports), he loved to climb. As a young boy, he climbed out of his bedroom window to the peak of their three-story house, where he became frightened. He stayed there until his father got home from work and used a ladder to bring him down.

On a dare at age 12, he jumped 30 feet into a river directly below. He also enjoyed the dangerous practice of jumping on and off moving trains.

"It was part of growing up in a small town in Wisconsin back then," he said. "Hitching rides on these trains was a sport to all of us."[2]

While most youth outgrow such risky stunts, McNally never really did, even his love of climbing.

Johnny "Blood" McNally Highlights

4× NFL champion (1929, 1930, 1931, 1936)
NFL 1930s All-Decade Team
Charter member Pro Football Hall of Fame (1963)
Charter member Green Bay Packers HOF (1970)

Professional playing career:
Milwaukee Badgers (1925–1926)
Duluth Eskimos (1926–1927)
Pottsville Maroons (1928)
Green Bay Packers (1929–1933)
Pittsburgh Pirates (1934)
Green Bay Packers (1935–1936)
Pittsburgh Pirates (1937–1938)
Buffalo Tigers (1941)

Coaching career:
Pittsburgh Pirates (1937–1939)
Kenosha Cardinals (1940–1941)
St. John's, MN (1950–1952)

A ladies' man, adventurer, and free spirit who never seemed to like being in one place for long, McNally attended various colleges and tried his luck at numerous jobs, including working as a casino bouncer, bartender, seaman, farmhand, and newspaper stereotyper. Some of the positions helped pay for his impromptu trips to different cities.

The following story illustrates how McNally became known as the "vagabond halfback." He earned letters in four sports at St. John's in Minnesota, including football, and transferred to Notre Dame. The semester was over, and McNally was working as a clerk-typist at a Studebaker plant in South Bend, when the itch to travel bit him again. Only this time, instead of hopping a train, he purchased a motorcycle. "For the trip, he hooked up with a hot, married blonde he'd met at a dance.... She was 18 years old and had a couple of children."[3]

The cycle trek doubled as an opportunity for him to see off his sisters, who were on the East Coast, sailing for Europe. Their first stops were in Chicago, where he bought a suit, and following a night on a park bench, it was off to Fort Wayne, Indiana, where her parents lived and her kids were staying.

46   Packers Inducted into the Pro Football Hall of Fame, 1960s

Johnny "Blood" McNally was an adventurer who became known as the "Vagabond Halfback." He acquired the nickname "Blood" when he needed to come up with an alias to try out for a semi-pro team and he saw *Blood and Sand* starring Rudolph Valentino on a theater marquee (courtesy Neville Public Museum of Brown County).

From there, McNally experienced "more nights sleeping on park benches, some pawned jewelry, and a few odd jobs"[4]—even sparks flying between his knees caused by static electricity as they drove out of the Cumberland Mountains.

On at least one occasion, McNally and the girl went their separate ways. Always tight on funds, it seemed, he stashed the Ace bike and went back to what he knew best: hopping trains.

Through family connections, he worked for roughly a month in New York as a stereotyper. Then he picked up his abandoned bike in Virginia but was without without his blonde companion, to whom he had sent money so she could make it home on her own. "All told, it was a defining adventure for John—his first foray as a full-fledged vagabond. He was just twenty years old and he'd gone on a free-wheeling, cross-country tear. He'd figured it out as he went, using his cleverness and skills along the way."[5]

The story of how the future star halfback acquired his famous nickname is also worth mentioning. McNally and Ralph Hanson were working full-time as stereotypers at the *Minneapolis Tribune* when McNally noticed an item in the paper—an invitation to try out for a semi-pro football team, the East 26th Street Liberties. Other teams were also looking for players to form a citywide league.

They both had a year of college eligibility remaining and returning to Notre Dame was something McNally was considering. But players couldn't retain their amateur status and get paid at the same time. McNally knew they'd have to use aliases but picking a name like "Smith" or "Jones" was too ordinary for someone who never did things by the book.

After work, the pair hopped on McNally's motorcycle and headed down Hennepin Avenue in Minneapolis. They were still unsure what fake names they would give the Liberties' coach when they arrived for the tryouts. Then a light bulb went on in his head. As they passed the Garrick Theater on his bike, McNally "looked up at the marquee. It read, 'Rudolph Valentino Star of *Blood and Sand* in *Monsieur Beaucaire*.'" "That's it!" McNally yelled back to Ralph. "I'll be Blood and you be Sand"[6] (Johnny Blood and Ralph Sand).

That was the start of Johnny Blood's professional career, where Blood played well and the Liberties won the city championship. "I then moved on to a team that was being formed at Ironwood, Mich. From there I jumped to Milwaukee [joining the Badgers in 1925], and then I got an offer to join Ernie Nevers in Duluth [in 1926]. Then, I went to Pottsville, Pa. [in 1928] and finally was signed by the Packers [in 1929]."[7]

A brief note about the Pottsville Maroons is in order. Although no one at Minersville Park knew it at the time, the Maroons' 26–0 shutout of Green Bay would prove to be their swan song. A McNally touchdown would be the last Pottsville score in the NFL. The Maroons folded, and he moved on to the Packers, where he would have the best years of his career.

"Green Bay was definitely the place for me," Johnny Blood stated. "My destiny, maybe. I loved the place and I have to say, the place, the people loved me. If you play for the Packers, the people in Green Bay know you better than they know their own brothers."[8]

Johnny Blood joined a talented Packers roster for the 1929 season that included center Bernard "Boob" Darling, end Laverne "Lavvie" Dilweg, back Joseph "Red" Dunn, back/punter Verne Lewellen, and fellow newcomers Cal Hubbard and guard August "Mike" Michalske.

Dilweg and Lewellen were talented backs, with the latter doubling as a great punter, which was a vital skill in an era when scoring was often low and thus field position was important. (Many believe Dilweg and Lewellen are deserving of busts in Canton as well.)

But you can never have too many good players, and Lambeau had his eye on Johnny Blood for some time. He was particularly aware of skilled players on other teams in the Midwest, and Johnny Blood had played in Milwaukee and Duluth. Lambeau was certainly paying close attention the year before when Blood, then with the Maroons, scored three touchdowns when they blanked the Packers.

Professional football was slowly evolving into more of a passing game, and versatile backs like the ones the Packers had, who could run, catch, and throw, kept defenses on their toes, not knowing what to expect next. (The "quarterback" was not the focus of the offense in those days.) Backs in the single-wing formation, which the Packers ran a variation of, handled the ball on nearly every play, and having a number of these versatile players on the roster meant Lambeau could rotate them in and out of the lineup to keep them fresh. This was an important consideration in an era when players played both offense and defense.

Little did anyone know at the time that the Packers were about to embark on one of the most successful runs in the team's long, storied history.

The Packers won their first five games in 1929, including a 23–0 shutout of their archrival Bears, in which Blood threw a touchdown pass. But a long road trip, part of it in Chicago against the Bears and Cardinals, loomed next. As was common at the time, more than 2,000 enthusiastic Packers fans took a train from Green Bay to Chicago to watch the rematch against the Bears. Filling in for the injured Lewellen, Blood handled the Packers punting and did an excellent job, keeping Chicago out of scoring range. Green Bay blanked the Bears again, this time 14–0.

They remained unbeaten when the 9–0 Packers faced the Giants, who were also undefeated, in New York. Johnny Blood made several huge plays. First, he tackled a speedy New York player from behind on what looked like a sure-fire Giants touchdown. He later scored on a short run, as the Packers beat the New Yorkers, 20–6.

By virtue of their victory over the Giants, the Packers had clinched their first NFL championship. They wound up with a perfect, 12–0–1 record.

The clutch plays Johnny Blood made against New York would become a trademark of his distinguished career. Making important plays wasn't the

6. Johnny "Blood" McNally (1963)

A statue of Johnny "Blood" McNally is on prominent display at the Heritage Trail Plaza in downtown Green Bay. McNally was among the charter class of the Pro Football Hall of Fame in 1963. Some say that not even Don Hutson made more impossible catches than "Johnny Blood," whose last season with the Packers was in 1936 (Shirley Christl).

only characteristic of his play. As stated, versatility was vital in that era, but catching passes was his specialty.

"Some observers still argue that not even the brilliant Hutson could make more impossible catches than Johnny."[9] "By 1929, he was one of the premier pass-catching backs in the NFL. And he did it all with a certain flair that seemed to make the men drool and the ladies swoon."[10]

His handsome looks, football abilities, and natural charisma made Johnny Blood and the Packers a strong draw at the gate. With so many teams coming and going in those days, gate receipts were crucial.

It should be noted that Johnny Blood's extracurricular activities continued to contribute to his legend. He once climbed down the face of a hotel in downtown Chicago—there's that daring love of climbing again!—to avoid curfew and recite poetry to the swooning women below.

His playful nature did surface on the gridiron from time to time. Blood once ran 50 yards for a touchdown on a lateral from quarterback Red Dunn. When Dunn called the same play later in the game, Blood simply grinned and lateraled the ball back to him as if to say, "Your turn, this time." These stories hardly put a dent in his lengthy resume, but they give you some more ideas about his frolicking personality.

Many years later, writer Raymond Rivard may have summed up Johnny Blood best. "His life was a remarkable celebration of the joys of hearty drinking, convivial women, and late-night fun. Paul Hornung, Joe Namath, and any other subsequent colorful playboys of note are only pale imitations of the Vagabond Halfback."[11]

Back to football: Many coaches would have pretty much stood pat with a defending championship team in 1930, but that was hardly the personality of the gambling Lambeau. The most noteworthy addition to the 1930 roster was quarterback Arnie Herber, a Green Bay native who played collegiately at Regis College in Colorado. One of the game's first "long ball" throwers, Herber could throw a football a country mile as the saying goes, and he was accurate as well.

The Packers finally had their 22-game winning streak snapped when they suffered a 13–6 loss to the Cardinals. Johnny Blood's former Duluth teammate, Ernie Nevers—himself a future Hall of Famer—paid him back with some late-game heroics.

That wasn't their only setback. The Giants edged the Packers, 13–6, at the Polo Grounds, were shut out by the Bears, 21–0, and had to settle for a 6–6 tie with Portsmouth. The Packers ended the season with a still very respectable 10–3–1 record, and the Giants finished at 13–4–0. But because league championships were decided by percentage and not the number of wins, the Packers earned their second-straight title.

Never one to remain idle, Lambeau added talented rookies Hank

Bruder and Milt Gantenbein to the Packers' loaded roster in 1931. Green Bay blew out the opposition with scores like a 26–0 blanking of Cleveland, a 32–6 rout of Brooklyn, and a 27–7 trouncing of New York.

The 1931 season was probably Johnny Blood's greatest as a pro. He snared 10 touchdown passes and was named to the first All-Pro team along with teammates Michalske, Hubbard, and Dilweg.

As a team, Green Bay wound up 12–2, earning a very rare "three-peat."

But no team can stay on top forever, and another 10–3–1 mark was only good enough for second place in 1932. The Packers then slipped to 5–7–1, 7–6 and 8–4 records—the last of which brought another second-place finish. The runner-up campaign in 1935 marked his return after spending a year with the Pittsburgh Pirates. (With Blood's rule breaking and rambunctious ways, Lambeau and the star halfback always had an uneasy relationship, and when Lambeau had finally had enough, he traded him to the Steel City.) The year of 1935 also marked the rookie season of star-to-be Don Hutson.

Perhaps because he was such a late bloomer, Johnny Blood had also lost little, if any, of his trademark speed. When Hutson arrived, Blood was 32 years old, but the youthful Alabama sensation could only beat him by a foot or so in the 100-yard dash. "Blood in his 20's would have outrun Hutson by yards to spare."[12]

The 1936 season would be Blood's last in Green Bay, and he led the team in pass receptions -25—with Hutson snaring 18. John "Blood" McNally's storied Packers career ended on a high note with another championship when Green Bay beat the Boston Redskins, 21–6.

Actually, there was another bright spot, but it was with another team, as player-coach of the Pirates in 1937. "The season inaugural was with the Philadelphia Eagles and on the opening kickoff Blood galloped 92 yards for a touchdown,"[13] wrote Jack Henry of the PFRA's *Coffin Corner*.

"They called him the Vagabond Halfback and the Magnificent Screwball but actually he was the one and only genuine Peter Pan of pro football," Henry wrote. "He put in 15 years in the NFL ... and even attempted a comeback as a player when he was 42 years of age."[14] After hanging it up for good, McNally returned to St. John's (26 years later) to earn his degree. "In retrospect, few members of the pro Hall of Fame can show better credentials than Blood did when he was honored in 1963."[15]

Former Packers historian Lee Remmel would likely agree with Henry's assessment. "He was probably the most colorful character to ever wear a Packers uniform and one of the most interesting and intelligent people I've ever met. I don't think there will ever be another one quite like him," Remmel stated.[16]

7

Mike Michalske (1964)

A Quarterback Playing Guard
(Packers Years 1929–1935, 1937)

In football, all of the action starts in the trenches. Block well, and a play is likely to succeed. But block poorly, and it's most likely doomed to failure. The guards, the men who play closest inside, are the true "grunts" who simply must move the pile, backpedal quickly to pass block effectively, and do all the dirty work in between. The center, who hikes the ball, is slightly more visible. The tackles, who play more outside of the line of scrimmage than the guards, are particularly important as pass blockers, keeping quarterbacks upright as speedy defensive ends come racing across the edge like heat-seeking missiles as they seek their signal-calling prey.

Since they protect the blindsides of today's multi-million-dollar quarterbacks, tackles also receive lavish contract extensions. But there is nothing glamorous about playing guard, a position where veteran players with mileage on their wheels are more likely to be shown their walking papers than their more valuable brethren at tackle.

But guards are vital, nonetheless. Important, yet overlooked. Of the nearly 350 greats in the Pro Football Hall of Fame, fewer than 20 played exclusively, or nearly exclusively, at guard in the NFL. They include Tom Mack, Larry Little, Mike Munchak, Will Shields, Gene Upshaw, and Jerry Kramer—and among early league standouts, Danny Fortmann and Walt Kiesling. But the first guard inducted into the HOF was August "Mike" Michalske in 1964. That likely came as no surprise to Benny Friedman, a contemporary of Michalske and one of the league's first great passers. He joined the Packers great in Canton in 2005.

"I would put him down in my book as the best guard—bar none—I ever saw. Mike weighed about 215 and was one of the fastest and most agile of linemen," stated Friedman. "He was smart, alert, aggressive and, in general, a severe pain in the neck to the opposition."[1]

7. Mike Michalske (1964)

In football, all the action starts in the trenches. Block well, and a play is likely to succeed, and one of the best linemen of his era was Mike Michalske, who played for the Packers in the 1920s and 1930s, shown here in a three-point stance (courtesy Neville Public Museum of Brown County).

"Mike" Michalske Highlights

3× NFL champion (1929, 1930, 1931)
7× First-team All-Pro (1927–1931, 1934, 1935)
NFL 1920s All-Decade Team
Pro Football Hall of Fame (1964)
Charter member Green Bay Packers HOF (1970)
Wisconsin Athletic Hall of Fame (1971)

Professional playing career:
New York Yankees (1926–1928)
Green Bay Packers (1929–1935, 1937)

Coaching career:
Ashland College (1928–1929)
Green Bay Packers (1935–1937)
Lafayette College (1936)
Chicago Cardinals (1939)
St. Norbert College (1940)
*Iowa State (1942–1946)

Baltimore Colts (1949)
Baylor (1950–1952)
*Head coach

The son of German immigrants, August "Mike" Michalske was born in Cleveland, Ohio, in 1903. He was the youngest of six children. He had three older brothers, Arthur, Charles, and George, and two older sisters, Elizabeth and Laura. Michalske's father provided for his family by working as a teamster and later as a "draying" contractor. (A dray is a cart used for hauling heavy loads, especially a low one without sides.)

August Michalske was named after his father but went by "Mike." He starred in three sports at Cleveland's West High School, and in college, he played three positions for coach Hugo Bezdek's Penn State Nittany Lions from 1923–1925. He started out at guard and halfback and was moved from guard to fullback halfway through the 1925 season. Bezdek switched Michalske to the backfield, "where his great speed and weight will serve to add driving power to the speed of the pony backs."[2]

He scored both Penn State touchdowns in a 13–6 win over Michigan State, and by the end of the year he was hailed as one of the greatest fullbacks that season.

Michalske began his professional football career in 1926 as a guard for the New York Yankees of the first American Football League. The Yankees, a short-lived professional team, played their home games at Yankee Stadium. The football Yankees came about as a result of a dispute between Red Grange and his former team, the NFL's Chicago Bears. Grange's agent, C.C. Pyle, claimed that the star halfback's contract was with him, and not Halas. Since Grange was a huge draw in the days when football often did not attract large crowds like today, it was no surprise that Halas and Pyle would fight over him. The controversy ended with a new franchise (the Yankees) and a new league (the AFL). After the AFL folded, New York joined the NFL the following year (1927) and posted mediocre records (at best), although in the process Michalske established himself as a top lineman, earning All-Pro honors in 1927 and 1928.

Michalske was part of a talented threesome who joined the Packers in 1929, along with Cal Hubbard and Johnny "Blood" McNally. Michalske, the former Yankee, appeared in all 13 games for a 12-0-1 team that won the Packers' first NFL championship.

Hubbard and Michalske were the stalwarts on the line, and while the ex-Yankee was smaller, he was also faster and more agile than his larger teammate. He was also just as tough. Michalske was nicknamed "Iron Mike" for his stamina and willingness to play all 60 minutes in a given contest.

7. Mike Michalske (1964)

"The players used to kid me by claiming that I must get paid by the minute," Michalske said.[3]

Michalske again earned First-team All-Pro honors, no small accomplishment in an era where guard may have been football's toughest position. First, he was required to block the biggest opposing linemen head-on. Second, he had to "pull" from the line of scrimmage and lead the blocking for the running back.[4]

Also, unlike today, guards were also important on *defense*. When the opposition had the ball, the guard had a key role in stopping the other team's running attack, which was vital in an era when teams ran the ball much more than they passed. Michalske was known as a deadly tackler, able to run plays down before they developed.

That wasn't all. He also had to be "capable of storming into the backfield to disrupt a passing play."[5]

It was yet another trait he excelled at. "Michalske may have been the first of the greats at rushing the passer among defensive linemen," wrote David Zimmerman.[6]

Iron Mike Michalske discussed his role: "We called it blitzing in those days, too. Our target was the man with the ball, especially the passer. It may not have been exactly ethical, but it was legal in those days to rough the passer, even after he got rid of the ball. We worked him over pretty good. Hubbard and I used to do some stunting in the line to find an opening for a blitz break-through. We figured the best time to stop them was before they got started."[7]

It was little wonder that no less than Ernie Nevers, an early NFL star and later a charter member of the Pro Football Hall of Fame, called Michalske the "greatest star of [the] professional game" in 1929. Not surprisingly, the hometown *Green Bay Press-Gazette* picked up on the story.

In 1930, Michalske returned to the Packers and helped lead the team to its second consecutive NFL title, although it was much harder this time. The Packers posted a 10–3–1 record while the Giants wound up 13–4–0. Championships were decided by percentage at the time, so Green Bay eked out its second straight crown.

It was also in 1930 that Lambeau added Green Bay native Arnie Herber to its talented roster. Herber, who played collegiately at Regis College in Colorado, had a cannon of an arm he would later put to good use on many a long touchdown pass to mercurial wideout Don Hutson. But in 1930, it was an ability Iron Mike Michalske and Johnny "Blood" McNally decided to use to teach a lesson to the inexperienced Packer.

"Rookie," Michalske said, "I'll bet you can't throw a football 100 yards." "You're right Mike," he said. "I guess 80 is about my limit." "Mike means you can't throw the ball 100 yards, including the roll," Blood said. Herber was interested now. "You mean you'll give me the distance the ball bounces after it lands?" he asked. "That's right, kid," Michalske said. "We'll give you the roll, Johnny and I bet $25 each that you can't throw the ball from one goal line to the other."[8]

"The bet was made. Herber threw the ball and it landed between the 20- and 15-yard lines on the other end of the field, bounced backward and came to rest on the 25. Michalske and Blood collected $25 apiece after practice. A long pass, properly thrown, lands nose forward and down, causing it to bounce back toward the thrower. Blood and Michalske, of course, knew this going in."[9]

It proved to be an expensive bet for Herber.

Every lineman dreams of scoring a touchdown, but few ever do. Michalske's thoughts of gridiron glory came true in 1931 when the Packers' standout guard returned an interception 80 yards for a touchdown. The score accounted for every point in a 6–2 triumph over the archrival Chicago Bears. The *Green Bay Press-Gazette* provided an excellent recap of the November 1 contest, played in the Windy City.

> [Carl] Brumbaugh slipped back to pass. Big, broad Cal Hubbard came charging in at him like a locomotive. ... Cal smashed into him, so he [Brumbaugh] threw wildly to the left side of the field. Michalske came bounding out from behind the line. He grabbed the ball on his own 20-yard line and started to gallop. [Dick] Stahlman cut down one Bear man who nearly caught Mike. Cal Hubbard picked himself up after mussing up Brumbaugh and blocked out another Bear man, as Mike continued to tear down the west side of the field.[10]
>
> [Milt] Gantenbein followed Mike, both galloping at top speed as Link Lyman cut across the gridiron to try and head them off. Down they went with Lyman closing in as they got to the 15-yard line. Gantenbein slackened his pace momentarily and threw himself at Lyman and the Bear tackler went down hard. He was the only man with a possible chance to get Mike and when he was blocked out, Mike finished the run. [Red] Dunn missed the try for extra point by a kick, but it didn't matter, as the six points were enough to win.[11]

In 1931, Michalske, Hubbard, and McNally were all named First-Team All-Pro, as the Packers cruised to a third straight title with a 12–2 mark. One could make a case these Packers squads were every bit as dominant as the legendary 1960s teams under Vince Lombardi.

Another interesting story about Iron Mike Michalske stems from a newspaper article in which he was referred to as "a quarterback playing guard." In it, Benny Friedman, a Giants standout and contemporary of Michalske, described both his physical and mental toughness and acuity. On the former, Friedman had this to say about what transpired after throwing a short pass to teammate Red Cagle, who was making his pro debut with the Giants: "I can still see Red gathering in the ball, taking about six steps

7. *Mike Michalske (1964)* 57

Every lineman dreams of scoring a touchdown, but few ever do. Mike Michalske's thoughts of gridiron glory came true in 1931 when the Packers' standout guard returned an interception 80 yards for a touchdown. He is one of a number of Packers greats who enjoyed Green Bay enough to remain there following retirement. The modest Michalske didn't tend to talk about football when he was about town, according to an Iola, Wisconsin, resident who grew up in DePere (courtesy Neville Public Museum of Brown County).

and—wham! Through the air sailed Michalske in a typical, old-fashioned tackle. He hit Red … from the side. All I can recall is a vivid picture of the bandage around Red's head."[12]

Friedman's recap in the same article illustrates how Michalske made such a successful transition into coaching, a career he started part-time while he was still playing for the Packers during the 1935 and 1936 seasons. "Mike was … never out of position. He was always in the right place at the right time," Friedman stated in the *Press-Gazette* article. "Just as Red [Badgro] was" a quarterback who happened to play end, "so was Michalske a quarterback playing guard. I nominate Mike for my line coach."[13] (Michalske was serving as line coach for the Baltimore Colts when the *Press-Gazette* story was written.)

By that time, Michalske had a solid enough track record in coaching; prior to his stint with the Colts, he served as head coach at Iowa State from 1942–1946. He started as line coach with the Cyclones but replaced Ray Donels when he stepped down as head coach. "Michalske, who had held the line coaching spot less than six weeks, was announced as the new head coach at a meeting of the squad and coaches," according to a *Chicago Tribune* article.[14] Donels had asked Athletic Director George Veeter to be released from his job following the team's subpar performance. "Donels declared he was dissatisfied with the showing of this year's team, a team which downed Denver in the opener, and then took drubbings from Nebraska and Marquette," reported the *Lawrence Journal-World*.[15]

Michalske had a mediocre record at Iowa State. The Cyclones wound up 2-4 in his first season, with a career-best 6-1-1, second-place mark in 1944. Overall, his teams finished 18-18-3. Michalske did not comment to the press on his resignation in February 1947, other than to say he had no future plans.[16]

Michalske returned to serving as a line coach for four additional teams through the mid-1950s. In his later years, he lived in De Pere, Wisconsin, and it was there that Ted Willems, a De Pere native, knew the former Packers star when he was growing up in the 1970s and early 1980s. He said that wasn't an unusual occurrence in an era when Packers and ex-Packers were more like "everyday people" and did not charge for their autographs. Willems' family ran a greenhouse in the Green Bay suburb.[17]

Willems noted how approachable Michalske was and how little he knew about Michalske's gridiron success since the Hall of Famer, now in his 70s, talked so little about football.

"He would often stop in our family business," Willems said. "He never flashed his notoriety [as a former Packer]. In fact, he didn't really talk much about the Packers. He was just a gentle person."[18] That doesn't mean he was soft, either, as Willems recalled Michalske's no-nonsense demeanor.

7. Mike Michalske (1964)

"He wasn't harsh, but he was very direct when he talked to you. He wanted you to succeed, to excel at whatever it was you wanted to do in life," which left a big impression on Willems as a middle and high school student at the time.

"He was big on education," Willems added.[19] Not surprisingly, Michalske's two daughters, Lee Ann and Melinda, became teachers in Wisconsin. In fact, the state PTA named Lee Ann Michalske Greenwood its State Teacher of the Year in 1988. "You can turn them [children] on to books by being excited about them yourself," the De Pere Dickinson School librarian told the *Press-Gazette*.[20]

"He was easy to talk to," Willems added about the Packers great. "He was a true gentleman."[21]

Michalske died at age 80 in 1983.

The "Iron Mike" moniker was particularly fitting, as he missed only nine of 104 games during his tenure with the Packers, five of them following a back injury against the Detroit Lions in his final season in 1937. He was hospitalized in Detroit for several days following the game, and he confirmed his retirement as a player the following year.

Michalske received numerous honors and awards for his accomplishments as a football player. In 1964, he was part of the second class of inductees into the Pro Football Hall of Fame. In 1969, he was selected by the HOF as a guard on the NFL 1920s All-Decade Team. He was also in the first group of inductees named to the Green Bay Packers Hall of Fame in 1970.

Packers Inducted into the Pro Football Hall of Fame in the 1970s

8

Tony Canadeo (1974)

The 50-Year Packer
(Packers Years 1941–1944, 1946–1952)

Most players who pass through the smallest city in professional sports recognize that they were part of something special. One might say that anyone who has ever played for an iconic franchise like the Green Bay Packers is a "Packer for life," but the term clearly describes certain players more than others. Some of the prominent Packers in terms of longevity include quarterback Brett Favre, Green Bay's signal caller for 16 years; Aaron Rodgers, also for 16 (and counting); Ray Nitschke, 15; and Donald Driver, 14 years.

Bart Starr and Forrest Gregg not only carved out HOF careers in Green Bay for 16 and 14 years, respectively—but also returned to coach (albeit not very successfully) the team for nine, and four years. Like Driver, Dave "Hawg" Hanner is not in Canton, but it's important to mention him. A defensive tackle in the 1950s–1960s, Hanner not only suited up as a player for 13 years, but he also worked as an assistant coach and then scout for the Packers for decades after that—for a grand total of 43 years, certainly an impressive total.

But topping them all is Packers and Pro Football HOF running back Tony Canadeo, a Chicago native who played for Green Bay for 11 years before retiring after the 1952 season, then served on the Packers' board of directors from 1955–1993, and on the team's executive committee from 1958–1993. He also worked as a broadcaster with Ray Scott, doing color commentary on Packers games. "In fact, his 59 years of service were longer than any person in team history."[1] "Of all the players, coaches, and executives who left an imprint on the Packers organization, none did it longer than the affable Canadeo," wrote Tom Silverstein of the *Milwaukee Journal Sentinel*.[2]

"I would say he would be classified as an icon among all those who were part of the Packers," said Robert Parins, team president from 1982–1989. "I think his contribution to the Packers really was with people away from Green Bay. He had great name recognition wherever he went."[3]

Tony Canadeo Highlights

9th round draft pick (1941, Gonzaga University)
Known as "Gray Ghost of Gonzaga"
NFL champion (1944)
2× First-team All-Pro (1943, 1949)
Second-team All-Pro (1948)
NFL 1940s All-Decade Team
Third player in NFL history to rush for 1,000 yards (1949)
Number "3" retired by Packers (1952)
Green Bay Packers Hall of Fame (1973)
Pro Football HOF (1974)
Playing career (1941–1944, 1946–1952)
Packers Board of Directors (1955–1993)
Packers Executive Committee (1958–1993)

Canadeo was the type of person who, after hanging up his cleats, didn't look back. As a result, when he retired after the 1952 season, he made a relatively smooth transition into not only a sales career for a Chicago-based steel company, but also as a Packers executive. Everything he did in life, he did full steam ahead, giving it his all.

While Canadeo loved the organization, serving in an administrative capacity was a tall task at the time. The team had fallen on hard times after Curly Lambeau left following the 1949 season, and Green Bay had yet to post a winning season in the 1950s. That put a lot of pressure on Packers administration, including Canadeo, to get it right the next time when head coach Ray "Scooter" McLean was dismissed following a 1–10–1 debacle in 1958.

Vince Lombardi was a highly regarded assistant coach with the New York Giants but had yet to serve as a head coach in college or the professional ranks. But Canadeo and other Packers officials, including team business manager Jack Vainisi, kept hearing that he was ready. Canadeo and the president of the Packers' board, Dominic Olejniczak, met with the 45-year-old Lombardi at a hotel in Philadelphia in January. (NFL and college draft meetings were being held there at the time.)

Lombardi was later flown to Green Bay for another interview, this time with Canadeo and fellow executive Dick Bourguignon. While he was not the only candidate during the hiring process, Canadeo sensed that the Packers had their man.

8. Tony Canadeo (1974)

"We met him, and he came to Green Bay and the board liked him right away. You had to like him because he knew where the hell he was going. Yes, I thought he was the guy."[4]

Lombardi was quite selective about whom he would associate with socially, but he and Canadeo soon became close friends. This almost certainly was due to not only their shared heritage as Italian Catholics, but also their common bond as "big city boys" (Lombardi was from New York) before later moving to small-town Green Bay.

As a result of their friendship, Canadeo and his wife, Ruth, saw a side of the gruff Lombardi that many did not. "He wanted the tough image for football. He would chew a guy out but always made up with him," Canadeo stated. "Vince was in our house all the time. He loved the kids; he was a softie and tender with those kids."[5]

The Packers' Executive Committee had a more hands-on role in running the team prior to Lombardi's arrival, but the new coach insisted on total control as not only coach but also general manager. Canadeo and the other board members honored Lombardi's request for non-interference, as none of them reportedly ever attended a team meeting.

Canadeo said he was very impressed with Lombardi when he held his first directors' meeting. "He was a domineering person, as you would say, but he had his program well organized, like any executive would have in a big company. He told us what he intended to do."[6]

The clear delineation in their roles with the Packers no doubt not only helped their working relationship but further cemented their friendship. Post-game cocktail celebrations, known as the Five O' Clock Club, were

Tony Canadeo not only retired as the Packers' all-time leading rusher in 1952, but he also later worked as a broadcaster for Packers games in the 1960s and served on the team's board of directors from the 1950s through 1993. He played a key role in hiring Vince Lombardi as coach in 1959. All told, he was affiliated with the Packers for nearly 60 years (Mark Forseth Collection).

common in the Lombardi home, gatherings that were often attended by, among others, Canadeo, Bourguignon, and their wives. "They were very, very close friends," Parins said about Canadeo and Lombardi. "Even after Vince left, their families remained close. Tony spent a lot of time with him after games."[7]

The 1960s were a great time to be affiliated with the champion Packers, something Canadeo not only enjoyed as an executive and broadcaster for the team, but was especially rewarding given the sorry state of the Packers for much of his playing career.

In 1941, Canadeo was a 9th-round draft pick out of Gonzaga, a small Jesuit college in Spokane, Washington, where he was a triple-threat halfback who could run, pass, and kick. According to one of his press clippings, he did everything but sell programs. He burst on the scene with a 105-yard kickoff return against Washington State when he was a sophomore, a feat the humble Canadeo would barely talk about. As a junior, Canadeo led the Bulldogs in rushing, passing, and punting. Although he earned numerous accolades for his gridiron accomplishments during his four years at Gonzaga, at 5'11", 190 and with prematurely gray hair, he hardly looked like a football star.

His hair was only part of the reason Canadeo was referred to as the "Gray Ghost of Gonzaga." A sportswriter called him the "Spokane Spook" for his "ghostly gallop" and ghost-like appearance. "Later on, 'Spook' became 'Ghost' and 'Gray' was added."[8]

In a day and age in which athletes weren't paid extravagant salaries like today, playing pro football was far from a given for collegiate stars. But when several pro teams, including the Washington Redskins, came calling to express their interest, Canadeo decided the NFL might be a good idea after all.

No doubt he was glad he did. The Packers, who beat the Redskins to the punch and selected Canadeo, were a solid team at the time under their longtime coach, Curly Lambeau. Established stars included Cecil Isbell, Don Hutson, Ted Fritsch, Clarke Hinkle, and Charley Brock.

"I was in awe. Actually, I was a little frightened. You read about players like Hutson and Hinkle and then there you are, standing next to them."[9]

Ironically, years later Canadeo would pass Hinkle to become the team's all-time leading rusher. Canadeo was hardy and unswerving, more quick than fast. Tom Miller, a teammate and one of Canadeo's best friends, recalled him being a great guy—until he stepped onto the football field. "Then he was pretty mean. When he put that uniform on, he changed. He was tough and ready to go all the time."[10]

The Packers lost a Western Conference playoff to the archrival Bears, 33–14 in 1941, Canadeo's rookie year, even though Hutson was named the game's MVP. It was the only time the teams met in the post-season until Green Bay beat Chicago, 21–14, to advance to Super Bowl XLV in 2011.

While Lambeau typically fielded winning teams, the Bears of the early 1940s were even better, as Green Bay finished second behind Chicago in both 1942 and 1943. (The 1941 playoff would, sadly, be the only post-season contest Canadeo would suit up for in his Packers career.)

After seeing little action as a rookie, in 1942 the jack-of-all-trades Canadeo completed 24-of-59 passes, ran back 13 kick returns, caught 10 passes, and ran for 272 yards. The following season (1943) marked a breakout campaign. He completed 56-of-129 passes for a team-high 875 yards, returned 18 kicks, and rushed for 489 yards on a solid 5.2 average, a total he would exceed in only two other seasons as a Packer.

The next year, 1944, was bittersweet for Canadeo on numerous accounts. Like many NFL players at the time, he was called into military service during World War II. It was not unusual for a team to lose a handful of players to the war effort, which watered down play in the NFL during the wartime years. Even Bears star quarterback Sid Luckman was not spared from serving his country.

Of course, the bigger issue was not knowing whether they would return alive, a possibility that always weighed on the mind of their wives and families, particularly so with Canadeo, as Ruth was pregnant. He spent 1944 and 1945 in the U.S. Army but managed to play three games for the Packers in 1944 while home on leave for the birth of their first child.

Since he saw at least some action in 1944, Canadeo could say he contributed to a championship team, as Green Bay beat the New York Giants, 14–7, for the league title that season. Little did he know the campaign would mark the beginning of the end for the powerful Packers.

As opposed to his triple-threat beginnings, Canadeo primarily served as a running back when he returned for the 1946 season. With star split end Don Hutson now retired, 1946 was a difficult season in many respects for the Packers. Canadeo picked up where he left off in 1944, again leading the team in rushing with 476 yards on an average of 3.9 per carry. As a team, Green Bay posted a 6–5, third-place record. It was as high as the Packers would finish during his remaining years as a Packer.

In 1947, Canadeo ran for 464 yards and upped his average to 4.5 an attempt. The Packers came in third again with a 6–5–1 mark. In 1948, the Gray Ghost fared even better, piling up 589 yards on 4.8 a carry. He doubled the number of rushing touchdowns from two to four, but it wasn't enough to keep the Packers from slipping to a dismal 3–9 record.

But if 1946–1948 were solid campaigns, 1949 would prove to be, far and away, Canadeo's best year—one that would eventually land him in Canton. After averaging slightly over 100 carries in the previous three seasons,

Canadeo saw his number of rushing attempts balloon to 208 in 1049—remember, there were only 12 games at the time. Much like running back John Brockington decades later, the star rusher had little help from anyone else on offense. "The poor guy, they only won two games that year," said former *Green Bay Press-Gazette* editor Art Daley about the Packers' awful 2–10 season in 1949. "It was Canadeo right and Canadeo left. He was the first real Hall of Famer for the Packers, and he did it during a losing period."[11]

Despite the heavy workload, Canadeo averaged a career-high 5.1 yards per attempt and, more importantly, amassed 1,052 yards. Canadeo was just the third NFL rusher (and first Packer) to top 1,000 yards rushing. (The others were Beattie Feathers in 1934 and Philadelphia Eagles great Steve Van Buren in 1947.)

The Gray Ghost accomplished his feats by making the most of his abilities. "He wasn't fast. He wasn't big. He wasn't elusive like a lot of players," said an unidentified teammate. "He wasn't really powerful. But when Tony put that ball under his arm, he was a wild man. Tony was all desire. He was fired up."[12]

Following back-to-back losing seasons, Packers brass had about enough with Lambeau, who wasn't the easiest man to get along with even in the best of times. After a falling-out with the team's Board of Directors, he left the Packers after 30 years to coach the Chicago Cardinals. The move proved disastrous for Canadeo when Gene Ronzani was hired as the Packers' head coach. Ronzani played for the archrival Bears in the 1930s–1940s and served as Chicago's backfield coach from 1947–1949.

Certainly, Ronzani was coming into a very tough situation following the legendary Lambeau. Still, the new coach shocked everyone by switching Canadeo from halfback to fullback. His rationale was that he wanted younger, faster halfbacks, and the Gray Ghost had allegedly "lost a step."

Whether he had or not, what was more apparent was that the 5'11", 190, Canadeo was not big enough to play fullback. Yet despite moving to a position that called for more blocking assignments than running plays, Canadeo, always a team player, did not complain, throw a tantrum, or threaten to quit, instead accepting the change with grace and dignity.

The move did make *some* sense. Fleet-footed halfback Billy Grimes, picked up from the Los Angeles Dons of the now defunct All-American Football Conference, moved into Canadeo's former halfback spot and quickly proved his worth, earning Pro Bowl invites after both the 1950 and 1951 seasons. He rushed for 167 yards in a 1950 contest against the New York Yankees. (The 1950 season was the first in which the Packers played in green-and-gold uniforms. They wore blue and gold before then.)

No longer the featured ball carrier, the Gray Ghost saw his rushing totals plummet to 247 and 131 yards over that same span. He did assume a larger role in the passing game, catching 10 passes in 1950 and 22 in 1951. As a team, the Packers were still miserable, posting identical 3–9 marks in 1950 and 1951.

Citing the mounting toll on his body, he decided 1952 would be his last year. November 23, 1952, was "Tony Canadeo Day," and the Packers drubbed the Dallas Texans, 42–14. It would have been a bigger deal today than in those more unassuming days, according to his wife. "Back then, they didn't make a big deal out of his retiring. They gave him some gifts. There was no such thing when Tony was playing where fans idolized ballplayers like they do now,"[13] said Ruth, who died in 2015 at age 94. She didn't recall a ceremony involving retiring Tony's number "3."

Ironically, the Packers' fourth all-time leading rusher is still referred to today by his famous nickname, even though Gonzaga hasn't fielded a football team for decades.

That's no small accomplishment for a football player to remain identified with a school that no longer plays football, said columnist John Blanchette when the Packers' star died in 2003, "and truly Canadeo's legend was made in Green Bay as professional football grew into something worth caring about."[14]

Former Packers president Bob Harlan said: "I admired him for what he did as a player, of course. But I also admired him for his loyalty to the organization and his willingness to fight for the Green Bay Packers."[15]

9

Forrest Gregg (1977)

*Flawless Execution
(Packers Years 1956, 1958–1970)*

Did Vince Lombardi call Forrest Gregg "the finest player I ever coached"? Some aren't sure, while others believe, *yes*. Or was Paul Hornung the "greatest player" Lombardi was talking about, as others attest? Whatever the truth is, maybe it really doesn't matter. Let's just say both were tremendous players, and Gregg was one of the true iron men of his era, playing in a then-record 188 consecutive games in 16 seasons from 1956–1971.

Gregg had plenty of other accolades. Don Hutson and Gregg are the only Packers on offense named to both the NFL 75th Anniversary *and* 100th Anniversary All-Time Teams. An offensive tackle, Gregg was a seven-time First-team All-Pro and was named to nine Pro Bowls during his storied career. Notably, after All-Pro guard Jerry Kramer was injured early in the 1964 season, Gregg slid over to guard and made the 1964 Pro Bowl at *that* position. (Gregg played guard several other times in his Packers career when injuries dictated it, but most notably in 1964.)

In 1999, Gregg was ranked 28th on *The Sporting News* list of the 100 Greatest Football Players, placing him second behind Ray Nitschke among players coached by Lombardi, second behind Anthony Muñoz (whom he coached in Cincinnati) among offensive tackles, and fourth behind Munoz, John Hannah, and Jim Parker among all offensive linemen. NFL Films released its Top 100 Greatest Players in 2010, and Gregg came in at #54. He was also an Iron Man, holding the Packers record for consecutive games played (188) until Brett Favre broke it.

It should be mentioned that unlike the rules in today's NFL that favor the offense, blockers in Gregg's day weren't allowed to grab or otherwise use their hands even though defensive linemen *could*. As Gregg said, "if you passed 30 times a game, you got 30 head slaps." Once, [Carl] Eller knocked his helmet completely off.[1]

9. Forrest Gregg (1977)

It's debatable whether Vince Lombardi actually called Forrest Gregg "the finest player I ever coached." But there is no debate that he would have been worthy of the honor. A nine-time Pro Bowler and All-Pro in the 1960s, he was ranked 28th on a *Sporting News* list of the 100 Greatest Football Players of all time. Gregg also came in fifth in the book *A Century of Excellence: 100 Greatest Packers of All Time* (Photofest).

Forrest Gregg Highlights

2nd round draft pick (1956, SMU)
3× Super Bowl champion (I, II, VI)
5× NFL champion (1961, 1962, 1965–1967)
9× Pro Bowl (1959–1964, 1966–1968)

7× First-team All-Pro (1960, 1962–1967)
2× Second-team All-Pro (1959, 1961)
NFL 75th Anniversary All-Time Team
NFL 100th Anniversary All-Time Team
Green Bay Packers HOF (1977)
Pro Football HOF (1977)

Playing career:
Green Bay Packers (1956, 1958–1970)
Dallas Cowboys (1971)

NFL head coaching career:
Cleveland Browns (1975–1977)
Cincinnati Bengals (1980–1983)
Green Bay Packers (1984–1987)

Such rough tactics didn't stop Gregg from stonewalling some of the best defensive ends the game has ever seen, including David "Deacon" Jones. Jones, another member of the 75th and 100th Anniversary teams, repeatedly lauded Gregg's play in the NFL Films video about the Packers' Hall of Fame tackle. He explained that his flawless technique made Gregg an extremely tough player to go up against. He cited the coordination of his feet and handwork, and his stellar drive blocking.

With some offensive linemen, Deacon Jones said, he could give the player his trademark head slap or two (legal at the time) and he quickly knew he would be able to dominate the tackle the entire game. Not so with Gregg, whose textbook blocking meant you were in for a fight for 60 minutes.

If Jones remembered Gregg well, the Packers' tackle surely never forgot the Rams' great either. "He was so quick he could give you that double head slap on a pass rush, Boom! Boom! You better not flinch or that's what you'd get all day long," Gregg recalled.[2]

On the famous Packers sweep, their bread-and-butter play, Jones noted that Gregg was responsible for executing the difficult seal-off block, which Gregg was great at.

In addition to Deacon Jones, Baltimore Colts standout Gino Marchetti, another future Hall of Famer, presented another tough matchup. "The day after we played the Colts and Marchetti, every muscle in my body would be sore," Gregg stated. "It took everything I had to keep on an even keel with Gino. Sometimes I'd win, and sometimes he'd win, but I know I earned my pay when we played Baltimore."[3]

Elliot Harrison of NFL.com was more effusive in his praise of the Green Bay tackle. "Try finding film of Starr getting sacked off the right edge. You won't be successful," he said.[4]

9. Forrest Gregg (1977)

No doubt going up against All-Pro defensive end Willie Davis in practice helped Gregg perfect his craft. The Packers' defensive star thought much the same thing. "There is no other player who helped me become a Hall of Famer more than Forrest. We lined up in front of each other, squaring off in one-on-one battles against each other for 10 years, and we pushed each other to new limits," Davis explained. "We respected each other so much that we never went easy on each other, even if we noticed the other was tired."[5]

While Gregg got into coaching after retiring as a player, it is not as well known that he almost got into the profession too soon, which might well have derailed his eventual HOF enshrinement. The Packers were coming off a disappointing 1963 season in which star running back Paul Hornung was suspended for gambling, and Green Bay had finished second behind the archival Chicago Bears, who won the NFL title. Gregg was still only 30, but the difficult year was enough to make him think about hanging it up

Forrest Gregg (left) leads fullback Jim Taylor on one of the Packers' signature power sweeps in the 1960s. No less than star defensive end Deacon Jones, another Hall of Famer, noted that Gregg was responsible for executing the difficult seal-off block, a technique Jones said that Gregg excelled at (Mark Forseth Collection).

when University of Tennessee coach Doug Dickey, a friend of his, phoned and said he wanted the Packers' star tackle to join his staff as offensive line coach.

The monetary difference reportedly wasn't that great, but Gregg wondered if the opportunity to coach, something he wanted to do after his playing career, would still be there later on. Lombardi knew about the offer and told Gregg he couldn't do him anything but wish him the best if that was what he wanted to do. A torn Gregg, who also had a wife and two young children to consider, pondered what to do but eventually decided he wasn't ready to call it quits.

"Though I got a pretty good raise, my 'retirement' was not a ploy to wrangle more money from the Packers," Gregg stressed. "I was glad to be back. The coaching career I aspired to would still be there when I retired. Besides, I reasoned, the longer I played the better coach I would become."[6]

Marie Lombardi, Vince's widow, was Gregg's presenter at his HOF induction years later, and she shared the story how the coach found out Gregg was coming back from an assistant who had phoned. Marie said Vince excitedly yelled so loud through the phone that the room shook. "He wanted Forrest back so bad."[7]

It was a good thing for Lombardi that his star tackle returned in 1964 because it was a tough year for injuries on the Packers' line. Both starting guards, Jerry Kramer and Fuzzy Thurston, were injured, meaning there were two new starters—Gregg and Dan Grimm—at the position. Bob Skoronski and Norm Masters manned the tackle slots; it was still a solid starting quartet given the Packers' impressive depth.

Gregg said in his book, *Winning in the Trenches*, that pass protection was easier at guard because the number of bodies inside limited the maneuvering room of defensive linemen. Tackles, on the other hand, just like today, are more or less on an island and must maintain a good set or a quick defensive tackle can get around him and apply a devastating hit to the quarterback.

With an 8–5–1 record, the Packers finished second again after the 1964 campaign, and this time *lost* the so-called Playoff Bowl to the St. Louis Cardinals, 24–17. (After the Bears beat the Giants to claim the 1963 crown, Green Bay had pummeled Cleveland, 40–23, in January 1964.) Known officially as the Bert Bell Benefit Bowl, it was a post-season contest for third place in the NFL in the 1960s. However, it's doubtful anyone wanted to participate in it. Lombardi called it a "hinky-dink game," while others referred to it as the Losers' Bowl or the Toilet Bowl.

The contest, played in Miami, meant an extra playoff match-up and thus additional revenue for the league, important in an era with fewer teams and post-season games. (The meaningless playoff was discontinued

9. Forrest Gregg (1977)

after the 1969 season, when the NFL and AFL officially merged for the 1970 campaign.)

One good thing that came out of losing to the Cardinals in the 1964 Playoff Bowl was that the Packers desperately did not want to play in the contest again, serving as a great source of inspiration for the 1965 season, which would eventually mark the first step toward Green Bay's much-celebrated "three-peat" (referring to titles following the 1965, 1966, and 1967 seasons).

But 1965 was anything but a cakewalk. After getting off to a strong 6–0 start, the Packers split their next two contests before falling to the last-place Rams, 21–10. A disgusted Lombardi famously told his team he was the only one who wanted to win. Gregg jumped in and exclaimed that he did, too. "It tears my guts out to lose," he said to Lombardi and his teammates.[8]

Before long, everyone in the room was yelling "Hell, yeah!" that they wanted to win.

It was just the spark Lombardi was looking for as the Packers ended the regular season tied with Baltimore at 10–3–1, beat the Colts in the playoffs, and defeated the defending champion Cleveland Browns, 23–12, at Lambeau Field to capture their first league title in three years. Hornung, Gregg, Taylor, and others were famously captured on film in their muddy uniforms, showing how they overcame the sloshy, early January elements with relative ease to reclaim their customary spot on top of the NFL.

Two years later, after Green Bay won the Ice Bowl over Dallas and routed the Oakland Raiders in Miami to win Super Bowl II in January 1968, Lombardi retired as coach. Gregg played for the Packers for three more seasons (1968–1970). Under Phil Bengston, they posted losing records in two of them. Gregg was still playing at a reasonably high level and made the Pro Bowl again in 1968.

But Father Time catches up to every player, no matter how good they are, and that's where Gregg figured he stood in summer 1971 when he retired from the Packers. Who phoned but Dallas Cowboys coach Tom Landry—the Packers' nemesis in the 1966 and 1967 championship. He told Gregg his team was suffering injuries on the offensive line and wondered if he would be interested in helping them out.

After both sides discussed contract terms, Gregg agreed that he would make a solid reserve for the Cowboys. He wasn't alone in that role with Dallas. Landry liked veterans, and ex-Packers teammate Herb Adderley, former Bear Mike Ditka, and ex-Chargers great Lance Alworth were also on Dallas's 1971 roster. Joining the Cowboys was likely exhilarating in some ways. While the Packers' best years were long gone, Dallas remained a talented Super Bowl contender. In fact, they lost the first NFC-AFC Super Bowl by a narrow margins (16–13) to the Baltimore Colts the previous season.

But after 14 years with the Packers, and Adderley nearly that long, the former Green Bay greats found the Dallas locker room quite different. Some uneasiness was to be expected. Those two championship games weren't all that long ago, and a lot of the Cowboys who played in those games were now sitting in the same locker room.

There was more to it than that. Unlike Green Bay, where the only colors that mattered were the green and gold on their helmets and uniforms, racial tensions ran high among Cowboys players. Dallas had a reputation for intolerance, which was not unusual in the racially divided 1960s and early 1970s, particularly in the Deep South. (Remember, Lombardi was ahead of his time in his total acceptance of players of different color.)

As an African American, Adderley had his work cut out for him fitting in even more than Gregg, but eventually he did. But race wasn't the Cowboys' only problem. Like their coach, the stoic Landry, Dallas had a more business-like approach to the game and didn't socialize after games. Gregg and Adderley commented how the strong bond the Packers had was missing from their new team, an atmosphere of greater togetherness they were credited as helping change in Dallas.

With Adderley and Gregg on the roster, Dallas finally won it all, beating Miami, 24–3, to win Super Bowl VI. Coincidence? "Cowboys players tell me, 'Having you guys on that team made a difference. Because we decided we wanted to win now instead of wait 'til next year,'" Gregg stated. "The play of Bob Lilly, Mel Renfro, Roger Staubach and Duane Thomas was good, but we made a difference, I think."[9] Another championship ring was a fitting ending to Gregg's (and Adderley's) storied careers. It was time to move on.

Gregg finally turned to coaching. After serving as an assistant with the Chargers and Browns, he was named head coach in Cleveland in 1975. Gregg helped the Browns reverse a downward trend and led the team to a 9–5 record in 1976. He posted an 18–23 mark in Cleveland before he and the Browns parted ways in 1977.

After coaching in Canada, Gregg became head coach in Cincinnati in 1980. In just his second year at the helm, he led the Bengals to their first Super Bowl appearance in franchise history. They narrowly lost Super Bowl XVI to the 49ers, 26–21. It marked an amazing turnaround. The Bengals went from 6–10 to a 12–4 record in 1981 and defeated the San Diego Chargers, 27–7, to claim the AFC title in a bitterly cold home contest known as the "Freezer Bowl."

Cincinnati lost to the Jets in the playoffs in the strike-shortened 1982 season and dipped to 7–9 in 1983. It was a disappointing year, but Gregg was still surprised when Green Bay phoned the Bengals, asking to speak to the ex-Packer about their head coaching vacancy. He wasn't sold on the idea of returning to his former team, but when the Packers offered a longer contract (five years) and complete control of player personnel, Gregg was in.

It looked like a good fit at the time. Despite Bart Starr's popularity, the Packers posted only two winning seasons and a single playoff appearance in nine years under his direction. Gregg, meanwhile, notched an overall winning mark (32–25) in Cincinnati and could boast a Super Bowl appearance on his resume, something the Packers hadn't come close to since the Lombardi days.

But it was not to be. The Packers were not without talent, especially on offense with quarterback Lynn Dickey and wide receiver James Lofton. They finished 8–8 in 1984 and 1985 but slid to 4–12 and 5–9–1 records the next two seasons. Some players loved Gregg; others hated him—*everyone* knew who was in charge. Dickey, in particular, was not a fan. "If you lost a game, he wouldn't let you forget it until Thursday of the next week," Dickey said. "But if you won, you had to forget it the next day. So, I'm thinking, 'Where is the good part?' Everything was negative, negative, negative."[10]

Safety George "Tiger" Greene saw the matter differently. "He's going to call you out in front of everybody," Greene said. "And that didn't sit well with a lot of players. That's just how he was. He didn't pull any punches. If you played like crap, he told you right there in front of everybody."[11]

Recognizing the handwriting was on the wall in Green Bay, Gregg jumped at the opportunity to return to his alma mater and resuscitate the SMU program, which had undergone the NCAA "death penalty" for major rules violations. "I always thought that if the opportunity presented itself I'd like to come back to my school," Gregg told the media at the time.[12]

It was a short honeymoon. The Mustangs went 2–9 in 1989 and 1–10 in 1990, when Gregg resigned to concentrate on his duties as athletic director, a position he held through 1994. SMU was grateful for Gregg's many accomplishments and retired his #73 in 2000. "He was a man of integrity, a seasoned leader and a legendary athlete," said SMU President R. Gerald Turner when Gregg died in 2019.[13]

A fitting epitaph for the HOF tackle.

10

Vince Lombardi (1971)

Much More Than a Stern Taskmaster
(Packers Years 1959–1967)

More than 50 years since his untimely death from cancer, the name *Vince Lombardi* remains synonymous with gridiron success. But while much has been written about the legendary Green Bay Packers coach, not all aspects of his character are as well-known as others. Anyone who knew him would say he was demanding, gruff, and had a volatile temper. But Lombardi was much more than a stern taskmaster. A complex man who died at the age of 57 in 1970, Lombardi was also loving, gregarious, religious, and racially and culturally tolerant in an age when many people were not.

For every story or quote you've ever heard or read about the man who name is emblazoned on the NFL's championship trophy, it's quite possible there's another one—maybe even two or three—that you haven't. Defensive tackle Henry Jordan was famously quoted as saying that Lombardi treated them all the same, "like dogs."

While Jordan was just kidding, it can also lead to Lombardi's quotes being taken out of context. Lombardi certainly treated all of his players both fairly and sternly. In the hot summer months of July and August, many a Packer was tempted to quit during the team's harsh training camp regimens, but they didn't, knowing it was the price they had to pay for success, a fact Lombardi was happy to point out. "Fatigue makes cowards of us all," he said.

That meant each and every Green Bay Packer performed countless, physically draining exercises, wind sprints, drills, etc., recognizing that their superior conditioning would pay off in the long run. And it did. With a coach expecting absolute dedication and effort from his players, the Packers improved from a dismal 1–10–1 campaign in 1958 to a 7–5 mark in Lombardi's first season as head coach in 1959. It was the Packers' only winning season in the 1950s, and Lombardi was named Coach of the Year.

10. Vince Lombardi (1971)

Vince Lombardi Highlights

2× NFL Coach of the Year (1959, 1961)
2× Super Bowl champion (I, II)
5× NFL champion (1961, 1962, 1965–1967; the Packers' "three-peat" has never been equaled)
Super Bowl Trophy renamed the Vince Lombardi Trophy (1970)
Posthumously elected to Pro Football HOF (1971)

Coaching Career:
St. Cecilia HS (1939–1946)
Fordham assistant (1947–1948)
Army assistant (1949–1953)
New York Giants offensive coordinator (1954–1958)
Green Bay Packers head coach and general manager (1959–1967*)
  *General Manager only in 1968; not considered part of HOF qualifications
Washington Redskins head coach (1969)
Career coaching record (105–35–6)
Highland Avenue in Green Bay renamed Lombardi Avenue (1968)
As part of Lambeau Field renovation, a 14-foot statue of Lombardi (along with one of Curly Lambeau) was erected in a plaza outside the stadium (2003)

But were the Packers all treated "the same," as Jordan famously quipped? Not exactly. Packers HOF guard Jerry Kramer stated that Lombardi would ride some players more than others—instinctively knowing who could handle more chewing out and who couldn't. Lombardi knew not only how to yell and berate to get his players to perform better—he could also sense when it was time to let up. The following story is a perfect example.

Kramer recalled Lombardi laying into him during a practice for his lack of attention, which he alluded to as being worse than a kindergartener. Greatly discouraged, Kramer said he was nearly ready to give up and find a different occupation.

Shortly afterward, Lombardi caught Kramer by surprise, good-naturedly ruffled up his hair, and told him how one of these days he was going to be the best guard in football. Receiving the confidence he badly needed from his demanding mentor, Kramer remembered it as a turning point in his career.

In short, everyone knows that Lombardi was a stern, demanding taskmaster. Not as well-known is that he was also a master psychologist and motivator, knowing exactly what buttons to push and when.

Bart Starr offered this explanation. "If you couldn't take it, sometimes he'd get to you through somebody else. We had a couple of linemen that he could just chew their fannies out and another couple who couldn't take it. They'd go crawl into a hole if he chewed them out like that."[1]

Perhaps Lombardi's most famous quote was, "Winning isn't everything, it's the only thing," which only added to his reputation in some circles as a cruel, win-at-all-costs martinet. But he was also quoted as stating, "The will to win is the only thing." There is evidence that the latter is more what he meant. Consider this: When the Packers would *lose* a hard-fought game, rather than admonish his team, he would say something about how the Packers simply ran out of time. On the flip side, if the Packers *won* a game but played sloppily in victory, they were subject to a good tongue-lashing for not performing up to their ability. One Packer quipped that sometimes you couldn't tell if you had won the game or lost!

Vince Lombardi was much more than a stern taskmaster. The Packers' head coach was also a master psychologist who taught life lessons to his players that extended far past the gridiron. Lombardi, a deeply religious man who once considered becoming a Catholic priest, also did not tolerate racism (Photofest).

But his relentless driving of the team reaped major dividends. In 1960, the Packers won the Western Conference title and met the Philadelphia Eagles for the NFL championship. They lost, 17–13, and Lombardi vowed that the Packers would never again lose a championship contest. They didn't.

Neither did the Packers have to worry about a championship nail-biter in 1961 as Green Bay coasted to a 37–0 rout over Lombardi's former team, the New York Giants. Paul Hornung said the Packers played so well that day they could have scored 70 points if they had wanted to. Tight end Ron Kramer scored two touchdowns, and Boyd Dowler and Hornung scored one TD each in the contest, which was unbelievably the first championship the Packers ever won in Green Bay. The versatile Hornung also kicked three field goals in the game—Green Bay's first championship since 1944.

The score might have been closer had Lombardi not successfully

10. Vince Lombardi (1971)

lobbied to get permission from President John Kennedy so Hornung, Dowler, and Ray Nitschke could play in the 1961 championship. To set the scene: Due to the Berlin Crisis, a number of NFL players were called into active military service that fall. Lombardi and Kennedy were friends, and he asked the commander-in-chief if he could pull some strings so his star players could be excused on leave to play in the 1961 title game.

"Paul Hornung wasn't going to win the war on Sunday, but football fans of this country deserve the two best teams on the field that day," Kennedy said.[2]

Ironically, Lombardi could have had the New York coaching job he had once longed for. As the story goes, Lombardi met with Giants owner Wellington Mara following the 1960 championship game and turned down the Giants' coaching job. It was probably not an easy decision for Lombardi as his wife Marie did not like small-town Green Bay and longed to return to the big city lights of their native New York. But Lombardi was reportedly grateful to Green Bay for giving him the opportunity as head coach (and GM), was thus loyal to them, and personally declined the chance to coach in New York.

The Packers had captured the team's first title under Lombardi (and the team's seventh overall), but there were some who felt that the late Jack Vainisi, Packers scout and personnel director from 1950 to 1960, had as much, maybe even more to do with building the Packers into a championship team than Lombardi. During his time in charge of player personnel, the Packers drafted or acquired eight future Pro Football Hall of Famers, including the famed 1958 rookie class of Dan Currie, Jim Taylor, Nitschke, and Kramer. Vainisi, Italian like Lombardi, was instrumental in attracting him to the vacant head coaching job in Green Bay in 1959. Unfortunately, he did not live to see the success of the teams he helped assemble, as he died from a heart attack in 1960 at the age of 33.

There is certainly truth to that statement, but it overlooks the role Lombardi played as a *motivator* in getting the most out of every player. (Remember, a talented but very unmotivated team only won one game in 1958.) It would also be a mistake to underestimate Lombardi's own skills at recognizing and developing talent. In 1959, he traded for reserve defensive tackle Henry Jordan from the Cleveland Browns. One year later, he acquired defensive end Willie Davis from the Browns, and that same season he was the only NFL coach who responded to little-known Willie Wood's plea for a tryout. Wood, converted from quarterback to free safety, became an eight-time All-Pro, and along with Davis and Jordan, future Canton inductees.

Another notable transaction was drafting All-American halfback Herb Adderley from Michigan State in 1961, although converting him to

When you win five championships in seven years, like Vince Lombardi did in the 1960s, numerous accolades, such as the many pictures drawn of him and books written about him, are bound to follow (Mark Forseth Collection).

cornerback was more good fortune than a planned decision. In any case, that was four future Hall of Famers in a three-year span, with all but Adderley being castoffs!

The 1962 Packers bulldozed through the regular season like a hot knife through butter. The 1962 Packers, often considered Lombardi's best team,

10. Vince Lombardi (1971)

scored 415 points and allowed only a stingy 148 points. One-sided scores were common, as Green Bay pitched three shutouts, including identical 49–0 thrashings of Chicago and Philadelphia. The only stumbling block in an eventual 13–1 season was a 26–14, Thanksgiving Day loss at Detroit. Bart Starr was under constant duress from the Lions' ferocious pass rush, which led to the well-known "lookout block" in which a Packers offensive lineman would supposedly yell for Starr to "look out" because the Lions pass rushers were coming again!

The 1962 championship game, held at Yankee Stadium in New York, was a hard-fought contest played in bitter cold conditions, but the Packers prevailed, 16–7, as Jim Taylor scored the Packers' lone touchdown and Jerry Kramer kicked three field goals in harsh, swirling winds.

The Packers did not win the championship in either 1963 or 1964, but the 1963 squad deserves mention. One wonders if the Lombardi Packers wouldn't have posted a "three-peat" earlier than they did if Hornung, the 1961 league MVP who was suspended in 1963 for gambling, had played that season. Green Bay still managed to finish a sterling 11–2–1 in the Western Conference, just behind Chicago's 11–1–2 mark. Both Packers losses came at the hands of the hated Bears, 10–3 and 26–7. But only two teams—the Eastern and Western Conference winners—made the playoffs in those days, so Green Bay, despite its excellent record, stayed home for the post-season. (Chicago won the 1963 title over the Giants.) Would Hornung have made the difference? We'll never know.

The year of 1963 was doubly ironic because four years later, it was the Baltimore Colts' turn to find out what it felt like to have an excellent regular season only to miss out on the playoffs. The year of 1967 was the first year with a four-division, expanded playoff lineup, and the Packers won the first Central Division title at 9–4–1. At 11–1–2, the Rams and Colts tied for the Coastal Division crown, but only the Rams advanced to the postseason as the result of their better point differential in head-to-head games against Baltimore. Tied for the best record in the NFL, but no playoffs! Long story short, while it was the 1967 Packers who finally attained Lombardi's goal of a third straight title with their famous 21–17 Ice Bowl win over Dallas, you could make a good case that the 1963 Packers actually had the better team.

Lombardi's eye for talent deserves another mention. In 1963, he reached into the college ranks for another future standout in linebacker Dave Robinson of Penn State. In 1964, he shrewdly traded a talented, though aging center, Jim Ringo, to the Eagles for linebacker LeRoy Caffey. The following year, recognizing the need for another standout receiver, Lombardi smartly traded Currie to the Rams for the fleet Carroll Dale, who would prove to be an integral pass catcher on three Packers title teams.

By this time, it was well-known that the Packers' head coach was loyal, dedicated, and driven. He was a gifted motivator and shrewd developer of talent. He was demanding, yet fair. Perhaps not so widely recognized was Lombardi's deeply held religious beliefs. Dating back to his childhood, Sunday church attendance was mandatory in the Lombardi household while growing up in the Sheepshead Bay neighborhood of Brooklyn, New York. Lombardi served as an altar boy in his youth, and at one point he was interested in becoming a Catholic priest. Even later on, as Packers coach, he went to Mass each day, just like his father before him.

Lombardi himself admitted how much Mass meant to him: "I derive my strength from daily Mass and Communion."[3] He also regularly attended Sunday Mass at Resurrection Church in the Allouez neighborhood of Green Bay's southeast side, always sitting with his wife in the middle of the ninth pew.[4] It's no wonder that Lombardi felt religion and football could intersect. St. Paul's epistle, which Lombardi paraphrased to his players, refers to how in a race, all the runners run, but only one gets the prize.

Taking charge of the Packers before the 1960s Civil Rights movement, Lombardi was also ahead of his time in his handling of race relations and willingness to use African American players. When he accepted the Packers' job in 1959, Green Bay, a predominantly white community, had *one*

Vince Lombardi, shown here in 1969 leading the Washington Redskins during a drill on the blocking sled, led his 1969 squad to a 7–5–2 record, Washington's first winning season in 14 years. It was his only season as Redskins coach before his untimely death from cancer in 1970 (Photofest).

African American player: Nate Borden. By 1967, they had 13 African American players, including All-Pros Willie Davis, Willie Wood, Dave Robinson, Herb Adderley, and Bob Jeter.[5]

Undoubtedly Lombardi's racial views were a result of his religious faith and the ethnic prejudice he had experienced as an Italian American. He had felt that his Italian heritage was a main reason it took him so long to become a head coach. Understanding the sting of discrimination, Lombardi backed up what he said. He let it be known to all Green Bay establishments that if they did not accommodate his black and white players equally well, that business would be off-limits to the entire team.[6] In addition, before the start of the 1960 regular season, he instituted a policy that the Packers would only lodge in places that accepted all his players.[7]

This policy was put to the test on at least one occasion, and in the turbulent 1960s, there were probably other instances as well. As one story goes, with a pre-season game being played in a Southern city, the Packers were set to check into the hotel when Lombardi was informed that their "Negro" players needed to enter the hotel through the kitchen, in the back. Lombardi subsequently informed hotel management that either all of the players would be allowed through the front door, or the Packers would take their business elsewhere. The hotel backed down on their policy, and the Packers entered the hotel through the front.

Later, as head coach of the Redskins, Lombardi was even further ahead of his time in his acceptance of homosexual players. In Washington, Lombardi's assistant general manager, David Slatterly, was gay, as was PR director Joe Blair, who was described as Lombardi's "right-hand man."[8] According to his son, Vince Lombardi, Jr., "He saw everyone as equals, and I think having a gay brother [Hal] was a big factor in his approach.... I think my father would've felt, 'I hope I've created an atmosphere in the locker room where this would not be an issue at all. And if you do have an issue, the problem will be yours because my locker room will tolerate nothing but acceptance.'"[9]

Redskins tight end Jerry Smith was gay, as was teammate Dave Kopay, who ironically later played for the Packers. Lombardi made it clear to Smith that he would be judged solely on his on-the-field performance. This might not seem a big deal in today's society but remember that homosexual individuals remained predominantly "in the closet" in that era.

It should also be noted that Lombardi's insistence on traits like hard work, dedication, and perseverance translated from gridiron glory to post–NFL business success for many of his former players. He spurred Davis to get an MBA degree during the off-season, while Robinson worked for Schlitz Brewery before starting his own beer distributorship. In describing the indelible mark the late coach had on his life, Adderley once famously said that while he did not think about his father all the time, he thought of Lombardi and the life lessons he taught each and every day.

Read further, dig deeper, and one discovers that Vince Lombardi was more than just a demanding, highly successful football coach—a *lot* more.

11

Ray Nitschke (1978)

Meaner Than a Junkyard Dog ... but Only on the Gridiron (Packers Years 1958–1972)

A hit tune from the 1970s described a fictitious character who hailed from the south side of Chicago, stood six-foot-four, and was "meaner than a junkyard dog." What does this have to do with Ray Nitschke? Like the mean man in the song, Nitschke was from suburban Chicago. And *any* offensive player who lined up against Nitschke in the 1960s and early 1970s would agree that he was *mean*. In fact, in an NFL Films video, Jerry Kramer, a longtime teammate and fellow 1958 Packers draftee, described the linebacker as being like a "junkyard dog," always snarling and with a mean stare that was particularly menacing with his missing front teeth.

Kramer points out that there was good reason for Nitschke's disposition. He was born in Elmwood Park, Illinois, the youngest of three sons. His father, Robert, was killed in a car accident when Ray was four, and his mother died of a blood clot when he was a teenager. That left his older brothers, Robert and Richard, to raise young Raymond, and the lack of parental discipline was not a good thing for him. The loss of both parents at such a young age caused a great deal of rage, which led to plenty of fights with other youth—in essence, a surly, "junkyard dog" type attitude that would take *years* for him to learn to control.

As well as issues with anger, the troubled teen did not fare any better academically at Proviso East High School in Maywood. Nitschke played fullback as a freshman, but the poor student was declared academically ineligible to play as a sophomore. He was able to raise his grades sufficiently to be reinstated as a junior. A stellar athlete, he played quarterback on offense and safety on defense, and he also played varsity basketball and baseball. His skills as a pitcher and leftfielder were good enough to be noticed by the professional St. Louis Browns, who offered Nitschke a $3,000 signing bonus.[1] But he yearned to play football in the prestigious Big Ten and accepted a football scholarship from the University of Illinois in 1954.

Never a good student in high school, Nitschke continued his rebellious behavior at Illinois, where he drank, smoked, and fought. As an Illini player, he was shifted from quarterback to fullback, which wrecked his dream of quarterbacking a team to a Rose Bowl victory.[2] Fortunately for Nitschke, college football had reverted to mainly single-platoon football, meaning players on offense had to switch to defense, and vice versa, when ball possession changed. On defense, Nitschke played linebacker, where he proved to be a skilled player and punishing tackler.

Ray Nitschke Highlights

3rd round draft choice (1958, Illinois)
2× Super Bowl champion (I, II)
5× NFL champion (1961, 1962, 1965–1967)
NFL Championship Game MVP (1962)
Pro Bowl (1964)
2× First-team All-Pro (1964, 1966)
5× Second-team All-Pro (1962, 1963, 1965, 1967, 1969)
Number "66" retired by Packers (1983)
Pro Football HOF (1978)
Green Bay Packers HOF (1978)
NFL 50th Anniversary All-Time Team
NFL 75th Anniversary Team
*Team record for most interceptions by linebacker (25)
    (* Tied with John Anderson)
"Ray Nitschke Field" added to Packers practice facilities (2009)
Ray Nitschke Memorial Bridge dedicated (1998)

Nitschke's legendary, menacing, teeth-missing persona traces its roots to his junior year in 1956. In a contest against Ohio State, Nitschke, who never wore a face mask, lost his four front teeth on the opening kickoff when one of the Buckeyes's helmets hit him in the mouth.[3]

Later, the Illinois native naturally wanted to play professionally for the Chicago Bears, but it was the Green Bay Packers who selected the talented linebacker as part of a draft that would later be called the team's best collection of rookie talent in its long and storied history. In those days, the first four rounds of the NFL draft were actually held the previous December (1957), with the remaining 26 rounds—yes, 26!—occurring in late January (1958).

Michigan State linebacker Dan Currie was the Packers' first-round

11. Ray Nitschke (1978)

Ray Nitschke was part of Green Bay's fabled draft class of 1958, widely considered the best haul of collegiate talent in the Packers' long and storied history, and one of the NFL's best-ever drafts. Not so well known is that Nitschke was frequently in and out of Lombardi's doghouse, and he did not become a full-time starter until 1961. But by the following season, he was voted the game's MVP in the 1962 championship win over New York (Photofest).

selection and the third player picked overall, followed by LSU fullback Jim Taylor in round two. Dick Christy, a North Carolina State back picked at #27 overall, proved to be the team's lone poor selection. Green Bay hit pay dirt again with the selections of Nitschke toward the end of the third round and guard Jerry Kramer of Idaho in the fourth (39th). Taylor, Nitschke, and Kramer, of course, all ended up in Canton. And Currie was a pretty fair player himself until being traded to the Los Angeles Rams in 1965 for wide receiver Carroll Dale.

With four future Pro Football Hall of Famers, only the Pittsburgh Steelers' 1974 draft exceeded the Packers' haul in 1958. That stellar draft, which helped produce four Steelers Super Bowl titles in the 1970s, yielded wide receiver Lynn Swann (round #1) of USC, linebacker Jack Lambert (#2) from Kent State, wide receiver John Stallworth (#4) from Alabama A&M and center Mike Webster of Wisconsin in the fifth round.

While he was a high (third round) draft pick, it took a while for Nitschke to break into the starting lineup full-time. He was erratic, displaying all-out aggressive play, but also self-destructive behavior. Inconsistency and his reputation as a troublemaker were not things Lombardi would stand for.

"In the early days, he was a drinker, a pain in the ass and a loudmouth," Kramer told writer Bob Fox about his tenacious teammate. "He was vulgar, rude and was just a real jerk."[4] Paul Hornung offered a similar comment. "Nitschke could be a complete asshole. But it was usually when he drank too much. I remember how he'd get in fights with bartenders," Hornung said. "There was a time in Milwaukee when he grabbed one and pulled him over the bar. It's a wonder he didn't get killed in Milwaukee."[5]

The fact that he wasn't a starter at first no doubt agitated Nitschke as well—in fact Kramer said as much in a later interview for NFL Films, when Kramer recalled how teammates called him "the judge" because of the amount of time Nitschke spent on the bench during his early years.

But defensive coach Phil Bengston believed in Nitschke and often protected him from Lombardi's wrath. Late in the 1960 season, Bengston talked Lombardi into installing Nitschke as the starting middle linebacker. "Taller, heavier, and faster than Bettis," it was the turning point he needed "to prove he should be the starter."[6]

But Nitschke nearly blew it. Lombardi caught him breaking a team rule by drinking at a bar in Los Angeles prior to the last regular season game against the Rams. "Lombardi said he wouldn't put Nitschke back on the team himself—but would put the matter to a team vote. It was 39–0 to keep Ray."[7]

He helped his cause by playing a great game against the Rams and then the Eagles in the NFL title game. Next, Nitschke finally quit drinking. Then he met the love of his life in Jackie Forchette. Even Lombardi, no slouch at motivating himself, gave partial credit for Nitschke's success to Jackie, whose calming influence helped him concentrate on his career. Unable to have children of their own, they would go on to adopt two boys and a girl. Kramer noted later that Nitschke became a "beautiful" human being.

11. Ray Nitschke (1978)

Settled down with the family he never had growing up, and focused on football, Nitschke overcame his troubled beginning to become the heart and soul of the Packers' formidable defenses of the 1960s. While now caring and loving off the field, he was still as mean as ever on the gridiron. His fierce glare, which was further accentuated by his missing teeth, and hard-hitting abandon set the tone for the Packers' stingy defenses. It was a demeanor he maintained 24/7. Practice or no practice, players recalled they had better keep their helmet and chin strap on, because if Nitschke was anywhere nearby, there was no doubt they were going to get hit, according to Kramer and all-pro offensive tackle Forrest Gregg.

Nitschke's tenacity even extended to the sidelines when the Packers' offense was on the field. His helmet off, he could regularly be seen pacing back and forth, imploring the offense to move the ball. He'd yell to the offense about how they shouldn't "let me down!" No doubt the offensive players heard!

Unbeknownst to some, Nitschke was an athletic, agile linebacker who intercepted 25 passes in his storied career. But his name was much more synonymous with fierce tackling, a point well made in the 1971 movie *Brian's Song*. The flick starred Billy Dee Williams as the late, great Chicago Bears halfback Gale Sayers, and James Caan as Brian Piccolo, a fellow Bears running back stricken with terminal cancer. In one noteworthy scene, the Bears are playing the Packers and Piccolo starts sneezing. Asked if he's allergic to anything, Piccolo (Caan) replies that the only thing he is allergic to is Nitschke.

A famous story that highlighted Nitschke's strength and toughness occurred during a Packers practice in 1960 when a large coaching tower was blown over by a strong gust of wind and fell on top of Nitschke. Wearing his helmet saved his life. "A bolt holding the steel tubing together went completely through Nitschke's helmet and stopped just short of his skull."[8] If you thought Lombardi was worried about the incident, you would be wrong. As the story goes, the Packers coach ran over to see what had happened, but when told it had fallen on Nitschke, Lombardi told the team he'd be all right, and to get back to practice!

Never was Nitschke's ability on better display than in the 1962 NFL Championship Game against the New York Giants. The 1962 game was a rematch of the 1961 title contest, won by the Packers, 37–0. It was the Packers' third straight appearance in the championship game, and the Giants' fourth in five seasons. The weather during the game, played at Yankee Stadium in New York, was so cold that television crews used bonfires to thaw out their cameras, and one cameraman suffered frostbite. The windy conditions also made throwing the ball difficult.[9]

In a contest that featured fierce hitting by both teams, Nitschke recovered two fumbles and deflected a pass (that was picked off by Currie). That turnover and the second fumble recovery were among the biggest plays in the game. In the one miscue, New York was driving and at the Packers' 15-yard-line, when a timely blitz by linebacker Bill Forester and Nitschke enabled him to a get a hand on Giants QB Y.A. Tittle's pass, which Currie intercepted. Later, in the third quarter, Sam Horner fumbled on a punt return at the Giants' 42-yard line, and Nitschke recovered. Five plays later, Kramer kicked a field goal to make the score 13–7. (Kramer was filling in for an injured Hornung, the Packers' regular kicker.) Nitschke garnered MVP honors as the Packers went on to defend their title with a 16–7 triumph. Kramer, who also deserved MVP consideration, had to settle for the game ball.

It's worth repeating that the one-time junkyard dog's on-and-*off*-the-field rage had morphed. He still displayed the same fury on the gridiron, but once off the field the happy family man turned into a mild-mannered gentleman with horn-rimmed glasses who would have passed in many places as a professional businessman. This transformation was clear when Nitschke appeared on CBS TV's *What's My Line*, wearing his thick eyeglasses and a conservative suit to help him hide his size.[10] Panelists, however, guessed his occupation.

Two surprising omissions turn up on Nitschke's otherwise stellar NFL resume. One was his not being named to the NFL's 100th Anniversary squad, the other only being selected to one Pro Bowl in his eventual Hall of Fame career. Regardless of whether the reader agrees with these decisions by NFL writers of both eras, there are plausible explanations for both. First, consider the other linebacking greats who played in his era:

- Joe Schmidt of the Detroit Lions. Schmidt, a 10-time Pro Bowler and eight-time First-team All-Pro at middle linebacker, had his #56 jersey retired by the Lions.
- Sam Huff of the New York Giants and later the Washington Redskins was a five-time Pro Bowl selection at middle linebacker and was twice named a First-team All-Pro. He is on both the Redskins' Ring of Fame and the Giants' Ring of Honor.
- Tommy Nobis, the first player selected by the expansion Atlanta Falcons, was the NFL Rookie of the Year in 1966. He was a five-time Pro Bowl pick at middle linebacker who had his number #60 retired by the Falcons.
- Dick Butkus, a first-round pick of the Chicago Bears in 1965, was an eight-time Pro Bowler and six-time First-team All-Pro. Mean and tough, he is often considered the gold standard at middle linebacker.

11. Ray Nitschke (1978)   91

While Ray Nitschke was amazingly only named to one Pro Bowl squad in his career, there is no question that he was the heart and soul of the Packers' formidable defenses in the 1960s. His #66 was retired by the Packers in 1983, and he was named to the NFL's 50th and 75th Anniversary Teams (Mark Forseth Collection).

Nitschke vied against the talented Huff and Schmidt for post-season honors in the early part of his career, with Huff retiring in 1963 and Schmidt in 1965. After they hung up their cleats, along came Butkus and Nobis.

While Nitschke had tough competition at linebacker throughout the 1960s and early 1970s, his omission from the NFL's 100th Anniversary All-Time Team was surprising to many, since he had already been named to the 50th and 75th anniversary squads. For the record, the inside linebackers selected to the 100th Anniversary team were Butkus, Schmidt, Jack Lambert, Willie Lanier, Ray Lewis, and Junior Seau.

Accolades aside, the name of the game is still championships, and no doubt some of these greats would have gladly traded their awards for a few Super Bowl rings like Nitschke's. (Butkus, for instance, never even played in a postseason contest!)

While perhaps underrated in some circles, Ray Nitschke has also had his fair share of accolades, both in and outside of Wisconsin. His No. 66 was retired by the Packers in 1983, the fourth of six numbers retired by the team. The only other Lombardi-era player to have his number retired is quarterback Bart Starr, whose #15 was retired in 1973. Also, the team named one of its two outdoor practice fields "Ray Nitschke Field" in 2009.

Non-gridiron accomplishments are always worth noting as well. The Pro Football Hall of Fame has a luncheon the day before its induction ceremony, attended by most of the living members who honor the new inductees. Nitschke always spoke at this luncheon, telling the new inductees what a great honor they were receiving. Following his death in 1998, the Hall named the luncheon after him.

In 1969, he was honored as the NFL's all-time top Linebacker by the NFL in honor of the NFL's 50th Anniversary. Nitschke is the only linebacker named to the NFL's 50th and 75th Anniversary Teams.

In 1999, he was ranked number 18 on *The Sporting News* list of the 100 Greatest Football Players, making him the highest-ranked player coached by Vince Lombardi, second among Packers behind only Don Hutson, and third among linebackers behind Lawrence Taylor and Dick Butkus.

Plenty of former players, teammates, and coaches would concur with the accolade. "I can say playing against Ray Nitschke shortened my career dramatically," stated Chicago Bears center Mike Pyle. "I had great respect for Nitschke. I thought he was one of the greatest linebackers to play the game. Raymond hit awfully hard, but he wasn't a dirty player."[11] Pyle pointed out how exasperating it was to block him. "Ray was terribly frustrating to block because he used his linemen so well," he added. "You couldn't get to him."[12]

"Pound for pound, there's never been a linebacker that's come close to Ray Nitschke," said Packers linebacker Dave Robinson, himself a Hall of Famer.[13]

Hall of Fame coach George Allen, an assistant with the Bears from 1958–1965, pointed out that Nitschke was much more than mean and tough, he was also a smart, well-prepared player. "Nitschke was one of those special players who did things others didn't do," Allen stated. "When I was with the Bears, we named one of our defenses '47 Nitschke' because it was copied from the way Ray played a certain situation. Naming a defense after a player is a pretty high compliment in my book."[14]

High praise perhaps, but such statements have been commonplace over the years for #66.

12

Bart Starr (1977)

*Role Model for the Ages
(Packers Years 1956–1971)*

Famous athletes pass away nearly every day. Some are fortunate enough to leave legacies. Others cast such a long shadow it is unlikely to ever be filled. Such was the case with Bart Starr. The vast majority of Packers greats in this book are deceased—Jim Taylor, Forrest Gregg, Willie Davis, and Willie Wood, to name but a few. And each left their own unique imprints. But perhaps because he was the team's quarterback, or maybe due to his humility and integrity—possibly both—and the stellar role model he set, there was something about Starr's passing that seemed like the end of an era—the fabulous Lombardi years of the 1960s.

It was not a big shock when iconic Green Bay Packers quarterback Bart Starr passed away on May 26, 2019. Starr had been in poor health for some time, which made each visit back to Lambeau Field more difficult than the one before. When he died, condolences came *pouring* in to pay tribute to the quarterback who directed the Packers to five world championships. Yet many of the remarks had little, if anything to do with football. They included the following:

> "Bart Starr was one of the kindest men I've ever met. He was a man of faith and lived it. We all will miss this great person."—Don Beebe[1]

> "Bart Starr was the most kind, thoughtful, and classiest person you could ever know."—Brett Favre[2]

"Perhaps no player during pro football's modern era has held the honor of outstanding character better than Bart Starr," said Joe Zagorski, author of *The Year the Packers Came Back: Green Bay's 1972 Resurgence*. "He was a man who lived the Christian ideals of treating other people better than he treated himself. Starr realized that talk was cheap. His actions

12. Bart Starr (1977)

Bart Starr, a stickler for detail like his famous coach, practices a pitchout in this 1950s photograph. While not possessing a great arm like peers Johnny Unitas and Sonny Jurgensen, Starr excelled at other quarterbacking traits, including passing efficiency, play calling, and leadership. Perhaps even more important, he was an outstanding role model both on and off the field (Photofest).

spoke volumes to anyone who was ever fortunate enough to come in contact with him in some way."[3]

Bart Starr Highlights

17th round draft pick (1956, Alabama)
2× Super Bowl MVP (I, II)
5× NFL champion (1961, 1962, 1965–1967)

4× Pro Bowl (1960–1962, 1966)
First-team All-Pro (1966)
NFL Most Valuable Player (1966)
5x NFL passer rating leader (1962, 1964, 1966, 1968, 1969)
Led Packers to 74-20-4 regular season record (1961–1967)
Number "15" retired by Packers (1973)
Green Bay Packers HOF (1977)
Pro Football HOF (1977)
Playing career (1956–1971)
Coaching career (1972, 1975–1983)
Assistant coach, Packers (1972)
Head coach, Packers (1975–1983*)
  * Also, Packers general manager for first five seasons

Packers standout center Larry McCarren, a lowly regarded, 12th-round draft pick out of Illinois, recalled how Starr's confidence gave him an NFL career he believes he would not have had otherwise. McCarren ended up being a two-time Pro Bowl selection and is in the Packers Hall of Fame.

While Starr readily admitted he "just didn't get it done"[4] as coach, he was still held in high enough esteem that not even his 52-76-3 record as the Packers head coach from 1975–1983 tarnished what former players thought about his character or as a person.

"I really thought Bart had no shot when he took over because he didn't have all those draft picks,"[5] said defensive tackle Mike McCoy about the five high draft picks his predecessor, Dan Devine, dealt to the Rams for over-the-hill quarterback John Hadl.

"He gave us hope, he made us believe in ourselves, made us believe in our team and what we were trying to do," said standout tight end Paul Coffman about playing for Starr. "We didn't win as many games as we hoped, we didn't win any Super Bowls, but Bart gave us hope each and every day."[6]

Hope was in short supply when Vince Lombardi was hired as the Packers' head coach and general manager in 1959. Starr, a 17th-round draft choice out of Alabama in 1956 who mostly rode the bench in those early years, and the rest of the Packers had known nothing but losing. And 1958 was the worst of all at 1–10–1. It was enough to make numerous Packers wonder if they should forget football and pursue a different occupation.

The Packers weren't just a losing team, they were a virtual laughingstock in the National Football League, a rudderless organization that hadn't posted a winning record since 1947. Green Bay was known as the "Siberia of the NFL" (supposedly so-named by Cleveland Browns coach Paul Brown), where you were sent if you didn't perform for your current team. The demanding, no-nonsense Lombardi represented a striking difference

12. Bart Starr (1977)

from the easygoing McLean. Lombardi let his players know in no uncertain terms that there were planes and trains coming into and leaving from Green Bay each day, and if they didn't perform, they would be on one of them.

Starr recalled the tough times.

> No disrespect to the coaches at Green Bay prior to Lombardi, but the team was not well organized. When Lombardi came in there, you immediately recognized that what we were lacking was leadership. Scooter McLean, who was the coach before Lombardi, would sit down and play cards with some of the players the night before a game. It was that kind of atmosphere that was very unproductive for everybody.
>
> The first time I met with Lombardi, I was just blown away. It was so powerful how he opened and what he had to say. After about 40 minutes, we took a break, and I ran downstairs and got on the phone and called Cherry back in Alabama. All I said to her was, "Honey, we're going to begin to win." We knew it immediately.[7]

But if Starr had ultimate confidence in his new coach, it took a while for Lombardi to have the same faith in him, as he wasn't convinced that the soft-spoken Starr was the right quarterback to lead his team. "At the time Lombardi arrived, I was just trying to hang on, and it didn't look good for me when he traded for Lamar McHan. I think he felt Lamar was going to be his leader. At first, he did all the talking in our quarterbacks' meetings. We had to earn his trust, and that took some time. We had to learn to do things exactly as he wanted before he would lean on us for comments and so forth. He believed that you don't ever give trust away; it has to be earned."[8]

A turning point in their relationship occurred during a practice, when the coach laid into his young quarterback but good, and Starr talked to Lombardi about it afterward. As the story goes, Starr told the coach if he had a good chewing out coming, fine, but have the courtesy to call him into his office. Starr's explanation was that he couldn't lead the team if the coach was yelling at him in front of his teammates, which meant he didn't have their respect.

Like others during Starr's long career, Lombardi made the mistake of thinking you can't be soft-spoken and tough at the same time. Starr's father, Ben, was a non-commissioned officer in the U.S. Air Force, and he instilled in his son the lifelong habit of discipline. According to one article, Bart was an introverted child who rarely showed his emotions, and his father wanted him to develop meaner tendencies. Undoubtedly Starr's military background helped him develop the grit and determination necessary to succeed under the demanding Lombardi.

Chicago Bears great Bill George evidently also needed some convincing that Starr was in fact tough. Packers guard Jerry Kramer enjoyed

NFL quarterbacks have to be tough, able to take a hit and not flinch when facing heavy pressure from menacing defensive linemen. Starr, who played for the Packers from 1956 to 1971, is shown here able to get off a pass over the outstretched arms of Minnesota Vikings defenders (Photofest).

telling the story of how George, a future HOF linebacker, split Starr's lip during a tackle in a 1961 contest against the Packers' bitter rivals. George taunted Starr about being soft, to which he pointed to George and said, "Bill George, we're coming after you!"[9]

Kramer said, "Bart took us down the field, and we scored. Then he gets stitched up, never misses a play, we win the ballgame and Bart Starr was proven to me."[10]

Toughness aside, it is rather befuddling to many that when NFL pundits list the all-time greats at the quarterback position, Starr seldom cracks the top 10. One online list ranked Starr 12th, while another placed him at #13. Starr *did* come in 10th in a top-ten list that *Sports Illustrated* experts compiled in 2017.[11] The reasons for these omissions include:

The Lombardi mystique. "Whether unfairly or not, some of Starr's successes are extended to legendary Packers head coach Vince Lombardi," Zagorski noted.[12] Keith Dunnavant, author of probably *the* definitive book on the Packers' signal caller, echoed that sentiment. "Four decades after he ended a remarkable career, Starr remains a largely misunderstood figure, discounted by many football historians as a robotic extension of the iconic Vince Lombardi."[13]

Today's game differs from Starr's era. "More recent and current quarterbacks in today's pass-happy NFL since Starr's final snap from center have dwarfed his statistics," Zagorski stated.[14] In 1966, a league MVP season for Starr, he threw for 2,257 yards, 14 touchdowns, and just three interceptions. Today's quarterbacks might have 14 TDs halfway through an NFL regular season, which is also two games longer than it was at that time. While it is true that some QBs threw for more than Starr's total in 1966, his 14 TDs was still *more than* some signal callers. For instance, Rams great Roman Gabriel threw 10 TDs for the season, and the Giants' Earl Morrall tossed just seven.

Starr retired *fifty* years ago. An increasing number of broadcasters and sportswriters barely remember a former star like Joe Montana or John Elway, let alone a quarterback who played in the 1960s and early 1970s like Starr. Since they never saw Starr play, the more years that go by, the easier it starts becoming for them to overlook standout players from that era. That may or may not make it right, but it does help explain it.

It bears repeating: The game has changed. Zagorski noted that the NFL today is a passing league, whereas in Starr's era, it was primarily a running league. Here is but one example. Led by the Browns' Frank Ryan (29), a total of *four* NFL QBs threw for more than 20 touchdowns in 1966, Starr's MVP season. (Sonny Jurgensen, Don Meredith, and Johnny Unitas were the others.) Compare that to 2019, when a total of *19* NFL signal callers reached that mark. Even a middle-of-the-road starter like the Jaguars' Gardner Minshew threw 21 TDs.

Some of Starr's big games get overlooked. This isn't to say that Starr never had impressive passing statistics. As Hornung and Taylor aged, Starr assumed a larger role in the passing game, and in the 1966 championship game against Dallas, he threw four, count 'em *four* touchdowns. Starr spread the wealth around, with Elijah Pitts, Carroll Dale, Boyd Dowler, and Max McGee each getting in on the scoring. For the record, he was 19-of-28 for 304 yards. An impressive game even by today's standards, and the Packers needed every one of the TDs as the high-scoring Cowboys put up 27 points themselves. (Green Bay won its second-straight title, 34–27.) With the famous Ice Bowl sneak the following season, this contest—and thus Starr's huge game—tends to get overlooked.

It's easy to overlook the intangibles that Starr possessed. Play calling and occasional risk-taking, passing efficiency, and leadership are all important characteristics for a pro quarterback to be successful, but traits like these can be overlooked compared to a signal caller with great speed or a cannon arm. "Lombardi gave Starr the reins to call the plays that he

In addition to being tough, pro quarterbacks also have to be accurate, as Bart Starr depicts here, whistling a pass between a pair of Minnesota Vikings (Photofest).

[Starr] wanted to call," Zagorski noted.[15] Lombardi quickly realized that Starr was more than capable, and the results (five championships in seven years) speak for themselves. "Starr was businesslike in his approach to quarterbacking," Zagorski added. "You never saw him try to emulate the style of his contemporary signal callers, such as Joe Namath, Unitas, Jurgensen, etc. Yet Starr was daring enough to take risks on the field, and in his own calculating way, by playing the percentages, Starr often threw for many a completion and many a touchdown pass."[16] The following are some examples.

Play calling and risk-taking. As Zagorski alluded, the supposedly ultra-conservative Starr was not beyond taking a gamble when he was confident it would pay off. If he sensed that Dale or Dowler, for instance, would be wide open on a third-and-one, it was not past him to cross up the defense, fake a handoff to Hornung or Taylor, and throw deep to one of his fleet receivers, often for a score. Steve Sabol, the late NFL Films president, called Starr the master of the calculated risk.

Pulling that off involved knowing how to audible to fool the defense.

"We had a very simple system, terminology-wise, but the complexity of it was to kill the opponents because [of] our audibles, I think," Starr recalled. "They never knew when we were audibilizing because we never changed the tone or inflection of our voice. Hell, we could audibilize against our defense in practice and they didn't know it."[17]

As also noted, Starr called his own plays, which was common for a quarterback in those days. The efficient, intelligent Starr knew how to do so well enough to cut even a good defense to ribbons. The most notable example was in the famed Ice Bowl, when Starr called his own number with just scant seconds remaining to sneak in for the winning score. There was nothing wrong with the wedge play they had been running, Starr said, but the icy field kept the slipping and sliding running backs (Chuck Mercein and Donny Anderson) from getting their footing. Starr, on the other hand, was already upright and merely needed a few good blocks (from Kramer and center Ken Bowman) to lunge in to pay dirt and a third straight title. Cowboys coach Tom Landry remarked later that the play was very risky since it left no time for a possible fourth-down play or attempt at a tying field goal. It was said that Landry would have called a rollout, with an option to run or pass.

None of these traits was an accident. "Tremendous preparation," said Zeke Bratkowski, Starr's longtime backup. "[Starr] didn't have the strongest arm, but it was plenty strong for what he had to do. Sunday was easy for him because he was prepared."[18]

Passing efficiency. Starr's passer rating in 1966, when he was First-Team All-Pro, was 105.0, impressive even by today's lofty standards. The consistent Starr also led the NFL in passing efficiency in 1962 (90.7), 1964 (97.1), 1968 (104.3), and 1969 (89.9). Remarkably, he never attempted 300 passes in a season, a given in today's game. Yet Starr's career completion percentage of 57.4 was once an NFL record. With efficiency also came a propensity for throwing few interceptions, and in 1964–1965 he attempted 294 passes without an interception, a record that lasted until 1991. Moreover, while Colts legend Johnny Unitas, a contemporary Hall of Famer Starr was sometimes compared to, threw 2,000 more passes and more than 15,000 additional yards, Starr biographer Keith Dunnavant points out that they both averaged 7.8 yards per pass attempt—a testament to his efficiency compared with other top-shelf quarterbacks.

Leadership. It's likely true that Starr lacked confidence in his early playing years under Lombardi, but he became one of the game's greatest field generals, an on-the-field extension of his coach. It was said that while the Packers were Lombardi's team during the week, they were Starr's team on Sunday. Today, the Bart Starr Award is given to an NFL player for outstanding character and leadership on and off the field.

The bigger the game, the better Starr performed. NFL historians point out that the Packers were 9–1 in playoff games under his direction, with Starr completing 61 percent of his passes in those games, with 15 touchdowns, three interceptions, and *five* NFL championships. Only the Patriots' Tom Brady has won more titles, and it took him a *lot* longer to do it.

Impressive number of championships aside, Paul Malcore may have summed up Starr's life and legacy the best. "Bart was a fearless leader in an era when football was rough and still trying to attract a stable national audience. But off the field, Bart Starr shines even more. …a quiet supporter of numerous charities, a strong supporter of the local community, and a one-of-a-kind, All-American icon."[19]

13

Jim Taylor (1976)

*Fierce Fullback Fueled Packers Ground Game
(Packers Years 1958–1966)*

When you think of *tough* football players, those who earn their living on the defensive side of the ball usually come to mind more readily. Linebackers Dick Butkus and Ray Nitschke would roll quickly off the tongue for most fans. In more modern times, one might think of safety Ronnie Lott or linebacker Ray Lewis.

On offense, Brett Favre's legendary streak for consecutive starts certainly qualifies him as a pillar of toughness. Jim Taylor, the Green Bay Packers' fierce fullback who fueled Green Bay's vaunted ground game during the 1960s, is another example of a rugged, *tough* football player.

Toughness is a trait one doesn't always associate with running backs. Many, though certainly not all, rushers try to avoid contact whenever possible. They will go out of bounds when given the opportunity, and when you consider the size, speed, and strength of defensive players, you can't blame them.

But that wasn't the way the Packers' fullback toted a pigskin. "Most people ran away from a tackler. Not Taylor," stated 49ers defensive back Abe Woodson. "Even if he had a clear path to the goal line, he'd look for a defensive back to run over on the way."[1]

Jim Taylor Highlights

First-team All-American (1957)
2nd-round draft choice (1958, LSU)
Super Bowl champion (I)
Scored first rushing touchdown in Super Bowl history
4× NFL champion (1961, 1962, 1965–1966)
5× Pro Bowl (1960–1964)
3× First-team All-Pro (1960–1962)
3× Second-team All-Pro (1963, 1964, 1966)

NFL Most Valuable Player (1962)
NFL rushing leader (1962)
NFL leader in rushing touchdowns (1961, 1962)
Green Bay Packers HOF (1975)
Pro Football HOF (1976)

Playing career:
Green Bay (1958–1966)
New Orleans (1967)
Number "31" retired by New Orleans Saints

Post-NFL career:
Commissioner of United States Rugby League
Play-by-play (with Paul Hornung) for LSU pay-per-view broadcasts
Participated in ABC's *Superstars* competition (finishing 4th in 1979)

His tenacious running style, preference or more like *passion* for contact, and ability to both withstand and deliver blows earned Jim Taylor a reputation as one of the league's toughest players. That's saying something in an era when forms of hitting that would be a personal foul today, such as horse collar tackling, were legal.

The future Hall of Famer explained his running style. "You've got to punish 'em," Taylor said. "This is a game of physical contact, and you've got to make them respect you. You've got to deal out more misery than the opponent deals out to you."[2]

Former quarterback Bobby Layne, a pretty hard-nosed SOB himself, named Taylor one of "Pro Football's 11 Meanest Men" in an article for *Sport* magazine in 1964. Even Nitschke agreed in a later interview. "In 15 years with the pros, he's one of the toughest men I ever played against—and we were on the same team. He'd hurt you when you tackled him."[3]

Packers fullback Jim Taylor was the personification of toughness. "You've got to punish 'em," Taylor said about his physical style. He was even named one of "Pro Football's 11 Meanest Men" in a magazine article in 1964 (Photofest).

13. Jim Taylor (1976)

Taylor's toughness was on display in the 1962 Championship Game against the New York Giants. The Giants were hungry for revenge after being embarrassed by Green Bay in the 1961 title matchup, 37–0. In the 1962 rematch, Taylor carried 31 times for 85 yards and scored the Packers' only touchdown against a tough defense. The contest, played in frigid temperatures at Yankee Stadium, was so cold and windy it made passing nearly impossible.

Football fans who have seen any of the *Rocky* movies would gain an appreciation for the amount of punishment the Giants, All-Pro linebacker Sam Huff in particular, inflicted on the Packers' star fullback. Taylor suffered a cut tongue and an elbow gash that took seven stitches to close. "The Giants and Huff went after him like sharks, piling on and kneeing him in the groin on the icy turf, and telling Taylor that he stunk," wrote sportswriter Bud Lea.[4]

But like the mythical Rocky Balboa rising off the canvas after a vicious blow from champion Apollo Creed, the all-too-real Taylor, to the Giants' dismay, would get up after a brutal tackle time and time again. "Taylor isn't human," a dejected Huff said at the time. "No human being could take the punishment he got today."[5] Taylor agreed. "I never took a worse beating on a football field. The Giants hit me hard, and I hit the ground hard."[6] He added that he also got in his share of licks. When the fiercely fought contest was over, the Packers had defended their title with a 16–7 win over New York.

The 1962 championship capped an MVP season for Taylor, who led the NFL in rushing with 1,474 yards and 19 touchdowns, an amazing total in an era when there were two fewer regular season games than there are today. The 1962 campaign marked the only season between 1957 and 1965 that Cleveland Browns legend Jim Brown did not lead the league in rushing. (More on the Taylor-Brown rivalry later in this chapter.)

If Taylor was tough with a capital T, it likely had something to do with his upbringing. His father suffered from rheumatoid arthritis and died when he was a child, leaving his mother, Alice, to raise three boys—ages 12, 10, and 8—on her own. (Jim was the middle child.) She worked as a seamstress and at a dry-cleaning establishment to make ends meet and would even stay late and clean up to make a few extra bucks. "As young as my siblings and I were, we never refused a job that would help support my mother and help to put food on the table. It was a difficult time for all of us, as nothing came easy," Taylor stated.[7]

Although he did not play football until his junior year, Taylor was a star athlete in four sports at Baton Rouge High School. In fact, early on basketball was his first preference, but LSU offered Taylor a full football scholarship, and going there meant he could stay in Baton Rouge and help his mother. Taylor and future Heisman Trophy winner Billy Cannon were rivals on different high school teams before both went on to star at LSU, although in different years. LSU Coach Paul Dietzel called Taylor the best running back he ever coached, and he earned All-American honors as a senior in 1957. (Cannon won the coveted Heisman Trophy in 1959.) Cannon starred for Houston and then Oakland in the early years of the American Football League (AFL). Both remained good friends long after their LSU days.

Little did Taylor know that he would go on to form a more famous tandem in Green Bay with halfback Paul Hornung that came to be known as "Thunder and Lightning." Taylor was "Thunder," an appropriate moniker for a rusher who ran as hard as a bull elephant, while the more nimble-footed Hornung earned the nickname "Lightning."

Under the ill-fated Ray "Scooter" McLean regime in 1958, Hornung was the starting fullback until Taylor took over late in an atrocious 1–10–1 season. But it provided enough tape for new coach Vince Lombardi to see that Hornung was a more natural halfback when he arrived in 1959. It should be noted that unlike today's NFL, in which the fullback is seldom used for anything but blocking, halfbacks and fullbacks alike were both workhorses when running the football was more important than throwing it.

The bread and butter of Lombardi's offense was the sweep. Like most Lombardi plays, the sweep relied on effort much more than deception. The pulling guards formed an escort around end, with one guard taking out the cornerback and the other blocking a linebacker. The center performed a cutoff block on the defensive tackle, and the offensive tackle exploded on the defensive end and then shut off the middle linebacker.

Meanwhile, the blocking back focused on the defensive end as he led the ball carrier into the hole, and the tight end drove the outside linebacker in the direction he wanted him to go. If the linebacker made an inside move, the tight end moved him in that direction, and the runner went outside. If the linebacker went outside, the tight end rode with him that way, and the runner cut inside.

Lombardi called it "running to daylight," and when the sweep was executed properly, there was precious little a defense could do to stop it. "It's my number one play because it requires all eleven to play as one to make it succeed, and that's what 'team' means," Lombardi said.[8]

Taylor agreed. "Hornung and I were big, mobile backs who were perfectly suited to run Lombardi's sweep. Though neither of us were particularly fast, both of us excelled at running under control—that is, reading the blocks of the pulling guards in front of us and then hitting the right hole."[9] It should also be noted that because both were good blockers, the sweep could work equally well on either side.

13. Jim Taylor (1976)

The Packers finished 7–5 in Lombardi's first season, with Hornung leading the team in rushing with 681 yards and Taylor picking up 452. In 1960, the Packers posted an 8–4 record, good enough to win the Western Conference before losing in the NFL Championship Game to the Philadelphia Eagles, 17–13. Hornung racked up 671 yards in the regular season, just ten fewer than the year before, but in 1960 Lombardi's run-to-daylight offense was now in high gear, and "Thunder" rumbled for 1,101 yards, and an impressive 4.8 yards per carry. He was the Packers' first 1,000-yard rusher since Tony Canadeo picked up 1,052 yards in 1949. It was Taylor's first of five straight 1,000-yard campaigns.

It was no accident that he could both dish out and receive that much punishment year in and year out. In the 1960s, football players did not receive anywhere near the extravagant salaries they do today. As a result, nearly everyone worked another job in the off-season and needed training camp to get ready for football. Taylor was different. He was one of the first to religiously lift weights and stay in shape year-around. Even at 215 pounds, slim for a fullback, Taylor remained relatively injury-free compared to other power running backs.

Center Bill Curry recalled his teammate's exceptional conditioning when Lombardi led the team in the dreaded "grass drills." Also known as up-downs, the player runs in place until the coach blows a whistle, at which time he hits the ground, onto his stomach. On the next whistle, he jumps up, starts running in place again, and so on. The drill is a real test of manhood in which some lose their breakfast while many others take breaks or at least slow up.

But not Taylor, who Curry remembered doing the drill perfectly, head held high, shoulders erect, thighs pumping like pistons, leaping to his feet after each dive to the turf. Naturally, Lombardi loved the example his star fullback set for the rest of the team. "Jimmy Taylor! Way to go Jimmy! Watch Taylor work! Atta boy, Jimmy! By God, Jimmy Taylor knows how to get in shape!" he exclaimed.[10]

Second-place finishes in 1963 and 1964—11–2–1 and 10–3–1 respectively—would be considered successful seasons for many teams, but not for Lombardi's Packers, who were used to winning championships. The team made it a mission to reclaim the title in 1965, but it did not come easily. A victory over the Baltimore Colts late in the season was crucial. Like a phoenix rising from the ashes, Hornung, who hadn't been the same player since his 1963 suspension for gambling, scored five touchdowns in leading the Packers to a 42–27 win over the host Colts. A 24–24 tie with the 49ers a week later left the two teams tied for the Western Conference lead, forcing a rare playoff a week later, in which the Packers beat the Colts again, this time 13–10 in overtime.

The 1965 championship game against the defending champion Cleveland Browns featured powerful ground games—the Packers with Taylor and Hornung—and the Browns, with star running back Jim Brown. First snow, then rain, and then light snow left Lambeau Field a muddy mess. The Packers clung to a 13–12 lead at intermission, but it was all Green Bay in the second half, as their punishing, ball-control attack churned out 204 yards rushing. Hornung ran for 105 yards and a touchdown, while Taylor just missed the century mark with 96. The Packers held Jim Brown to a meager 50 yards in what would be his final game in the NFL before he retired to seek an acting career.

It also marked the last matchup between Brown and Taylor, the two best running backs in the league. Brown was faster, more of a threat to break off a long run. Taylor, on the other hand, ran close to the ground and fought for every inch, pitting his strength against larger men who tried, often in vain, to bring him down.

In four meetings between the pair, Taylor amassed 361 yards on 83 carries and seven touchdowns. Brown had 252 yards on 59 attempts and a single TD. Taylor pointed out that Cleveland was blown out in three of the four games, limiting Brown's chances, although one might add that Taylor shared the load with another rusher (Hornung), while Brown did not. "Taylor also rarely fumbled, averaging only one fumble every 64 carries, better than Walter Payton (51), Jim Brown (47) and Eric Dickerson (34)."[11]

For his career, Taylor fumbled 34 times, 33 with the Packers and 1 with the Saints.

Brown retired as the NFL's all-time leading rusher, while Taylor ranked third when he hung up his cleats. In comparing the two, Lombardi may have put it best. "Jim Brown will give you that leg [to tackle] and then take it away from you," Lombardi said. "Jim Taylor will give it to you and then ram it through your chest."[12]

Unlike many of his teammates, Taylor did not finish out his career with the Packers. At the end of the 1966 season, he played out his option to become a free agent. The Packers had signed Donny Anderson from Texas Tech and Jim Grabowski out of Illinois for a *lot* more money than any of the Packers were earning. (They earned the tag "Gold Dust Twins" for signing with Green Bay for a combined $1 million-plus prior to the 1966 season.)

Lombardi insisted that it was a move Green Bay had to make to keep the rival AFL from acquiring all of the good players coming out of college, but that wasn't the only reason. Lombardi also had to look out for the good of the team, and the fact was that Father Time was catching up with Thunder, as it already had for Lightning. After rushing for 1,169 yards and a solid 5.0 per rush in 1964, Taylor slipped to 734 yards and then 705 in 1966, and only 3.5 a carry in both years.

13. Jim Taylor (1976)

Regardless of the reason, the rookies' contracts didn't sit right with the Packers' star. "There was no way those two guys should have been getting more than the established veteran stars. At the end of the '65 season I had insisted to Lombardi that he give me a three-year contract for $75,000. Throughout the 1966 season, he tried to convince me to sign, but I remained adamant in my stance."[13]

Taylor signed with the expansion New Orleans Saints for the 1967 season, but the move was more ceremonial than anything else. "It was the franchise's inaugural year with the NFL, and I became one of its biggest draws. Being from Louisiana, it was not only a natural move but a smart one as well."[14]

(Hornung also signed with the Saints, but never played for them as a lingering neck injury forced him to retire. Taylor hung it up after 1967.)

The Packers would go on to claim one last championship under Lombardi in 1967, but for Thunder and Lightning it was already the end of an era.

Taylor piled up 8,207 yards in his nine-year Packers career, a mark that led club annals for more than 40 years until bested by Ahman Green. His 91 touchdowns are second-most in Green Bay history, behind only the legendary Don Hutson, who had 105. Jim Taylor was also the first Packer from the Lombardi era to be enshrined in Canton.

Packers Inducted into the Pro Football Hall of Fame in the 1980s–1990s

14

Herb Adderley (1980)

*Shutdown Corner and Kick Returner
(Packers Years 1961–1969)*

Racial segregation was widespread in America in the 1940s and 1950s. Jim Crow laws that denied equal opportunity for blacks were on the books, and it would not be until 1955 that Rosa Parks would famously refuse to give up her seat in the "colored section" of a bus to a white passenger. It's said that sports are a microcosm of society, and the NFL was nearly all-white during this era. While there were some black players earlier, one of the most prominent of the post-war era was Kenny Washington of the Los Angeles Rams in 1946. No team followed the Rams in re-integrating the NFL until the Detroit Lions signed Mel Groomes and Bob Mann in 1948, and the New York Giants inked Emlen Tunnell that same year. (More on Tunnell later.)

The Green Bay Packers followed suit when they acquired Mann in 1950, and within several years nearly every team had signed a black player. (The author uses "black" throughout this chapter as that word and "Negro" were the vernacular of the time, not African Americans.)

It's with that backdrop in mind that future Packers star Herb Adderley was growing up in a predominantly black part of Philadelphia. In terms of discrimination, he was more fortunate than some, but that does not mean he had it easy. Adderley was raised by his mother, Reva, and his maternal grandmother, Elizabeth. Materially speaking, they did not have a lot, but he was raised with solid Christian principles, and prayer and Bible study were commonplace.

But being taught strong values doesn't guarantee someone won't get into trouble, something Adderley knew all too well. Unlike the future Packers star, Herb's older brother, Charles, did not listen to spiritual guidance.

He dropped out of school, bought drugs, stole, and broke into cars and homes.

Herb Adderley Highlights

1st round draft choice (1961, Michigan State)
3× Super Bowl champion (I, II, VI)
6× NFL champion (1961, 1962, 1965–1967, Super Bowl VI)
5× Pro Bowl (1963–1967)
4× First-team All-Pro (1962, 1963, 1965, 1966)
3× Second-team All-Pro (1964, 1967, 1969)
NFL 1960s All-Decade Team
Pro Football HOF (1980)
Green Bay Packers Hall of Fame (1981)
Playing career:
Green Bay Packers (1961–1969)
Dallas Cowboys (1970–1972)
Career interceptions: 48
One of only four players to play on six NFL championship teams

Post-football career:
Broadcaster, Temple University, Philadelphia Eagles
Assistant coach, Temple, Philadelphia Bell (World Football League)

The younger Adderley understood the importance of making good choices and could usually be found in school, church, or the boys club. Solid decision-making includes picking the right friends, and Adderley's included Al Chandler; Nelson, Adderley's cousin; and Leonard "Bunky" Rhodes, an older pal who served as an influential role model—vital for boys from broken homes like them.

Adderley was an outstanding athlete growing up in Philly, starring in football, baseball, and basketball. At the end of his high school career, Adderley was voted the best athlete in Philadelphia, no small feat in a city where basketball legend Wilt Chamberlain captured the same award the previous year. As honors and awards were heaped on Adderley, his high school coach, Charles Martin, reminded his star player to remain humble. "Coach Martin said it may be best to 'stand up and be seen, sit down and be appreciated.' I never forgot that and did it as often as possible," Adderley said.[1]

It was Martin who helped direct Adderley to Michigan State. Florida A&M was also interested, but Martin knew Duffy Daugherty, the Spartans' head coach, and told him about his blue-chip running back. A visit to the MSU campus, and its 70,000-plus Big Ten stadium, sealed the deal for the budding star.

14. Herb Adderley (1980)

College is a difficult enough transition for anyone, and Adderley's first obstacle away from home was the devastating news that older brother Charles, always in and out of trouble with the law, had received a life sentence for murder. (He had hit a woman in the head, grabbed her purse, and ran off. She died a week later.) In spite of the distraction, there was no doubt in Adderley's mind that he was staying in school.

As in high school, good friends were important to staying on the straight and narrow in college, and John Young was one of Adderley's first at MSU. Like other black students, they were more aware of racial issues than their white counterparts. As explained in *Lombardi's Left Side*, Adderley, Young, and others understood that the world was not fair but also recognized it was crucial not to make excuses, to compete, persevere, and not get caught up in self-pity. The quality of the person, not his athletic abilities, was key to entering into Adderley's circle of friends. In fact, his sound decision-making was a trait that Young continued to admire years later. "As a high school principal, there were many youngsters I tried to get to have the same mentality that Herb had, to make good sound decisions," Young stated. "Think things through and see the whole picture before you start acting or reacting."[2]

Herb Adderley was an outstanding athlete growing up in Philadelphia in the 1940s and 1950s, but his coach, Charles Martin, reminded his star player to remain humble, a lesson Adderley took to heart. While important, athletics never defined Adderley's entire life (Photofest).

Athletics, while important, never defined Adderley's entire life. He was one of the founders of the Omega Psi Phi fraternity at MSU, which was quite an accomplishment since it was an uphill battle to gain permission to add another black fraternity. On the gridiron, however, is where Adderley shined most. Playing mostly halfback, he led the Spartans in rushing as a junior in 1959 and in receiving in both 1959 and 1960. He was a co-captain as a senior and made the All–Big Ten Conference team.

It's unlikely anyone would have predicted Adderley's next stop: Green Bay, Wisconsin. Packers talent scout Jack Vainisi convinced Vince Lombardi to draft the best athlete available in the NFL draft, and that was the Spartans' number 26. Green Bay had never drafted a black player in the first round, a common practice for *any* team in that era.

The Packers had previously signed free agent safety Willie Wood and traded for defensive end Willie Davis in 1960, so bringing in talented black athletes was nothing new to Lombardi, who was ahead of the curve compared to most NFL teams. Being slow to respond to the growing Civil Rights movement enabled the upstart American Football League to sign black stars such as Abner Haynes, Cookie Gilchrist, Paul Lowe, and Clem Daniels.

Another smart move Lombardi made was in acquiring Tunnell, a veteran safety from their previous team, the Giants, where he was an exceptional defensive back and Lombardi was an assistant coach. Tunnell, who had been part of a championship team in New York, was a perfect selection to help Lombardi change the losing culture in Green Bay. By 1959, Tunnell was on the downward side of an outstanding career, but he was a natural leader who knew how to carry himself and could show the young Packers how to do the same. The addition of Tunnell, a nine-time Pro Bowler who became the first African American player inducted in Canton, served notice: only high-quality people of *any* color would be part of the team's future.

Of course, Adderley was in Green Bay primarily to do one thing—play football—and with Paul Hornung and Jim Taylor at running back, it was not clear where that would be. The Golden Boy was noted for saying that Adderley was the one backup running back he worried about taking his job—the Michigan State standout was *that* athletic and *that* talented.

Adderley began 1961 as a backup halfback; in fact Lombardi was toying with the idea of switching to a three-back set so he could get his intriguing rookie onto the field. Later that season, out of desperation, Adderley was moved to cornerback to replace injured teammate Hank Gremminger in a Thanksgiving Day game against the Lions. Told by his coach to simply do his best, he did much more than that, even making an important interception at his new position.

In 1962, the move became permanent, and Adderley went on to become a five-time Pro Bowler in the 1960s. While Lombardi made a number of shrewd personnel moves over the years, he didn't count the Adderley decision among them. "I was too stubborn to switch him to defense until I had to," he remarked. "Now when I think of what Adderley means to our defense, it scares me to think of how I almost mishandled him."

Adderley took to the position like a duck to water and was named

14. Herb Adderley (1980)

First-team All-Pro in his first year as a starter. "The things Herb could do out there were just incredible," said safety Tom Brown. "He had gifts and talents that most cornerbacks simply didn't have."[3] "God didn't make a lot of Herb Adderleys," added fellow safety Willie Wood. "Guys like Herb weren't growing on trees."[4]

Gifted players like Adderley are often also good at making big plays when they are needed the most. The Packers were on the verge of a 7–6 loss to the Lions in 1962 when he picked Detroit quarterback Milt Plum deep in the Lions' end of the field. Paul Hornung booted a 26-yard field goal, and Green Bay escaped with a 9–7 win.

That same season, Adderley was a one-man wrecking crew in a 17–13 victory over the Colts. "He scored on a 103-yard kickoff return, intercepted a Johnny Unitas pass to set up a field goal and saved the game by deflecting a fourth-down Unitas pass in the final minute with the Colts at the Packers' 2-yard line."[5]

In Super Bowl II, Adderley's 60-yard interception return for a TD against the Raiders sealed the Packers' win and was the first pick-six in Super Bowl history.

While any cornerback can be beat on occasion, the key is to have a short memory about the play and move on. With that in mind, perhaps what opponents feared about Adderley even more than his penchant for timely picks was his smothering man-to-man coverage and physical tackling.

"Herb Adderley simply wouldn't let me get to the outside," said Pro Football Hall of Fame receiver Tommy McDonald. "He'd just beat me up, force me to turn underneath routes all the time.... Other guys tried the same tactic, but he was the only one tough enough and fast enough to get it done."[6]

(Note: Adderley's tactics were completely legal until a rule change in 1978 limited contact to within five yards of the line of scrimmage.)

He was a shutdown corner before the term was ever coined and did not allow a touchdown pass in 14 regular season games in 1965.

He intercepted 48 passes in his career (39 as a Packer), and returned seven of those picks for touchdowns, which stood as a Packers record until broken by Charles Woodson in 2009. Adderley led the NFL in interception-return yardage in 1965 (175) and 1969 (169). In a mainly pre-specialist NFL, he was also a dynamic return man. His 3,080 career return yards still ranks third in club annals. "In my opinion, Herb Adderley was the most complete NFL cornerback I ever saw," said Pro Football Hall of Fame writer Ray Didinger. "Herb could cover, hit, run and return kicks. There wasn't anything he couldn't do."[7]

Others agreed with the assessment. "The greatest cornerback to ever play the game," stated Bart Starr. "He was more athletic than anybody we had. A lot of killer instinct in him," Willie Wood added.[8]

Tired with the losing that occurred after Lombardi left, the final straw came when Packers coach Phil Bengston left Adderley off the 1969 Pro Bowl squad in favor of teammate Bob Jeter. "I don't want to come back," he said. "This year, without a doubt, has been my best year. However, playing my heart out didn't get me any acknowledgment from my own coaching staff."[9]

While the Packers had only notched one winning season since Lombardi's departure (8–6 in 1969), Dallas was still fielding playoff teams, and so one would have thought a trade to a winning organization like the Cowboys would have been met with wide-eyed delight. That was only true on the record.

"I'm very grateful to Coach Bengston for giving me the opportunity to play in another Super Bowl game," Adderley told the Associated Press after the deal. "The way things were going, I figured I'd wind up with a second division club. But with the Cowboys, I feel we have just as good a chance to go all the way as anybody."[10]

Off the record was a much different story. More so than white players, the blacks in the NFL during the 1960s and 1970s talked to each other about various franchises and living conditions in different NFL cities, and Dallas had a bad reputation according to the book *Lombardi's Left Side*.

"I hated like hell to report to the Cowboys because of the terrible racial rumors that all of the black players in the league were aware of," Adderley said. "I had two strikes against me before I reported to the team because,

Herb Adderley intercepted 48 passes in his career—including 39 as a Packer. The five-time Pro Bowl selection, considered one of the best cornerbacks in NFL history, went on to play three seasons for the Dallas Cowboys, helping his one-time nemesis to a victory in Super Bowl VI in 1971. He remains one of only a handful of players to suit up for six championship teams (Mark Forseth Collection).

one, I was a Packer who helped kick the Cowboys' asses and, two, the color of my skin."[11]

Cowboys defensive back Mark Washington agreed that Dallas was an intolerant place. "In the early '70s when I got to Dallas, it's not like we hung out with each other," Washington stated. "To me there was an apparent chasm between some of the white players and the black players. We didn't go over to each other's houses for dinner; we didn't socialize after the games and all that sort of stuff. It wasn't there. We just came together and played football is what it amounted to."[12]

Cowboys players at the time agreed that Adderley energized their locker room. "The first day Herb was in our meeting, Tom Landry introduced him, and Herb stood up," said running back Calvin Hill. "He was like a movie star; he was wearing a Super Bowl ring. I was saying, 'Wow, I'm on the same team as Herb Adderley.' That was the first time I'd seen a Super Bowl ring and that was kind of cool. He was the first World Champion I knew."[13]

Pat Toomay, who is white, said Adderley's soothing presence defused racial tensions that had plagued the team for years. Undoubtedly part of the reason was the fact that he was not accustomed to racism and discrimination in Green Bay, something Lombardi didn't tolerate. As an Italian American, the Packers' coach was familiar with the bite of prejudice himself. He met the tough issues head-on, something not every coach did.

Adderley's influence went beyond improving racial relations. Up to that point, the Cowboys always had a "wait 'til next year" mindset, something Adderley (and later, another ex-Packer, Forrest Gregg), helped change. In the 1970 season, Dallas was humiliated by the St. Louis Cardinals, 38–0, and the Cowboys were hanging their heads in defeat. Accustomed to a more emotional locker room under Lombardi, Adderley had enough and lit into the team, something the stoic Landry did not do.

"Our guys were sitting around with their heads down and Herb just exploded," said teammate Mel Renfro. He said, "'What in the hell is wrong with you guys? You act like a miserable bunch of losers.' The whole locker room got a wakeup call. Nobody had ever taken that approach before because Landry was so laid back as far as his emotions were concerned. Herb just tore into us and it got our attention. He brought that Lombardi ambiance of 'no crap,' 'let's get it done.' He was very tough minded."[14]

Adderley said, "Landry, in my opinion, didn't know what to say to motivate the team; if he did, he didn't do it during my three years there."[15]

The devastating home defeat to the Cardinals was the last time Dallas would lose that season, that is, until Baltimore beat them, 16–13, in Super Bowl V on a last-second field goal by Jim O'Brien. Dallas eventually ended the bridesmaid hex by trouncing Miami, 24–3 the following year in Super Bowl VI.

Not that the huge Dallas victory meant a lot to Adderley. He famously said that he was the only person with a Cowboys Super Bowl ring who didn't wear it because he was "a Green Bay Packer." What Lombardi said to him years earlier meant a *lot* more. "He [Lombardi] said I was the best cornerback he'd ever seen. In front of the whole team he said I was the best athlete," Adderley remembered. "I'll always remember that."[16]

15

Willie Davis (1981)

Stalwart on Outstanding Defenses (Packers Years 1960–1969)

A starting defensive unit in football consists of 11 players. Six of those 11 starters from Green Bay's championship teams in the 1960s are enshrined in Canton. From that side of the ball, that's more players in the HOF than the Pittsburgh Steelers' famous "Steel Curtain" from the 1970s. More than the Dallas Cowboys' famed "Doomsday Defense." More than the Chicago Bears' vaunted 1985 defense. Rarefied air indeed, and one that speaks volumes about the Packers' defensive talent during that era, which was key to them winning five championships in the 1960s.

While the Packers' offense was certainly very good during those years, statistics show that the defense was even better. Packers team historian Cliff Christl explains that from 1965–1967, "Offensively, they finished 12th, eighth and ninth in total yards; whereas, defensively, they ranked third, third and first in fewest yards allowed."[1]

Even those stats are likely skewed because the Packers' pass defense was *so good* (first in four consecutive seasons, 1964–1967) during those years that Green Bay opponents had little choice but to run the ball.[2]

While any great defense needs to play together as a unit, it also needs individual talent to excel, and Willie Davis, a five-time First-team All-Pro and five-time Pro Bowler, was an absolute stalwart on those stingy Packers units.

One should also keep in mind that the Packers didn't possess the only formidable "D" in the NFL in the 1960s. For instance, the Detroit Lions featured Roger Brown, Alex Karras, and Joe Schmidt, while the archrival Chicago Bears had talented defensive players like Bill George, Richie Petitbon, and Doug Atkins.

Willie Davis Highlights

15th round draft pick (Cleveland, 1956)
2× Super Bowl champion (I, II)

5× First-team All-Pro (1962, 1964–1967)
Second-team All-Pro (1963)
5× Pro Bowl (1963–1967)
Packers all-time leader in fumble recoveries (22)
Unofficial all-time leader in quarterback sacks
Green Bay Packers Hall of Fame (1975)
Pro Football HOF (1981)
Black College Football HOF (2011)

Playing career:
Cleveland Browns (1956, 1958–1959)
Green Bay Packers (1960–1969)

The Los Angeles Rams, meanwhile, had a "Fearsome Foursome" defensive line consisting of future Hall of Famers David "Deacon" Jones and Merlin Olsen, in addition to the talented Lamar Lundy and Rosey Grier. The Baltimore Colts lined up defensive stalwarts such as Gino Marchetti, Lenny Lyles, Don Shinnick, and Billy Ray Smith. All told, this makes the Packers' team rankings from that period all the more impressive.

Probably no one could have predicted that Davis would become a stalwart on these outstanding defenses, as well as a future All-Pro and Hall of Famer. He was born in Lisbon, Louisiana, but grew up in Texarkana, a blue-collar city that sits on the Texas-Arkansas border. Ironically, his mother, Nodie, initially did not want Willie to play football for fear of his getting hurt.

Nodie was a no-nonsense woman of strong words, and so was his first football coach at Booker T. Washington High School, Nathan "Tricky" Jones. Jones, one of the premiere black high school coaches in the state, went about 6'5" and 250-plus pounds. *Long* before Willie Davis met Vince Lombardi, Jones was an intimidating man who taught the importance of work and discipline.[3] Davis's athletic abilities earned him a scholarship to historically black Grambling State in his native Louisiana, where he was a two-year team captain and NAIA All-American.

During a period in college football history when segregation ruled the day, especially among Southern universities, Grambling was far off the NFL's radar. It would take some stellar individual play, and a bit of luck, for Davis to be noticed by the pros. Fortunately for the future star, that occurred when the cat-quick Davis made 19 tackles and assisted on 16 others as Grambling upset Florida A&M, 28–21, at the end of his senior season.[4] (Pro scouts were actually on hand to view some of Florida A&M's more celebrated players.)

It should be noted that Grambling was an emerging small college football powerhouse led by (now legendary) coach Eddie Robinson. When

Willie Davis, a 15th-round draft pick in 1956 and reserve tackle for the Cleveland Browns, was traded to Green Bay in 1960, where he turned into a five-time Pro Bowl selection with the Packers. Statistics weren't kept at the time, but it's estimated that he recorded over 100 sacks in his career (Photofest).

Robinson finally retired in 1997, his resume featured an impressive record of 408–165–15, making him arguably the most successful coach in college football history. In addition to Davis, other ex-Grambling Tigers in the Pro Football HOF include Junious "Buck" Buchanan, Willie Brown, and Charlie Joiner.

Davis, an offensive tackle and defensive end at Grambling, was selected in the 15th round of the 1956 NFL Draft by the Cleveland Browns. (Interestingly, Bart Starr was a 17th-round pick of the Packers that same year.) However, Davis's professional career was put on hold when the Army drafted him into military service, which was not an unusual practice at the time. Remember, even Elvis served in the Army around this same time! Davis was able to stay in shape playing service football.

Upon returning to the Browns in 1958, Davis was shifted from position to position on both offense and defense for two years. Finally, Coach Paul Brown slated him for a regular offensive tackle job in 1960, but then he decided to trade him to the Packers for offensive end A. D. Williams. Since Green Bay was considered the Siberia of pro sports at the time, Brown had often used the threat of a trade to Green Bay to motivate his players.

As a result, Davis not only was upset, but he briefly thought about quitting football rather than reporting to the Packers.[5] The Packers only won one game in 1958, and while they improved to 7–5 under first-year coach Lombardi in 1959, it was their first winning season since 1947, so Green Bay's future was still quite uncertain at the time. The Browns, meanwhile, were an NFL powerhouse in the 1950s, winning league titles in 1950, 1954, 1955, and losing in the championship game on four other occasions (1951, 1952, 1953 and 1957).

When the disgruntled Davis arrived in Green Bay, Lombardi quickly assured him that he had engineered the trade because he needed a top-flight defensive end and thought Davis could fill the bill. "Willie, we have seen some films of you where your reactions are just incredible," Lombardi explained. "We feel with your quickness you can be a great pass rusher."[6]

Lombardi offered reasons for his confidence. He told the former Cleveland Brown he had the three main traits necessary to be a successful lineman—speed, size, and agility. "Give me a man who has any two of those dimensions and he'll do OK," Lombardi said. "But give him all three and he'll be great. We think you have all three."[7]

Lombardi asked Davis how much the Browns paid him, and when the embarrassed defensive end replied, Lombardi said he'd pay him $1,000 more to start for the Packers. That nailed it. Lombardi had an anchor for his young and improving defense. Lombardi's confidence was crucial since Davis had felt that Cleveland gave up on him.

The decision soon reaped big dividends for Davis and the Packers. Green Bay lost the NFL championship to the Philadelphia Eagles in 1960, 17–13. It was a bitter pill for Lombardi and the Packers, but one that motivated them for years to come, including 1961, when the host Packers demolished the visiting New York Giants, 37–0.

Lombardi had told the team they would not lose another championship game while he was coaching, and it was a lesson the Packers certainly took to heart when they pummeled the Giants—a high level of performance Davis said was clearly one of their best performances. Again, statistics back up the claim.

"The Packers' defense, led by Davis and Ray Nitschke, held the Giants to six first downs, and 240 total yards, including just 31 rushing. The Packers also forced five turnovers, four interceptions and a fumble, and the defense chalked up the first NFL title game shutout in 12 years."[8] As noted earlier, it was just the beginning of dominant defensive performances by the Packers in the decade.

Individually, Davis also shined, and by 1962 he was a First-team All-Pro. "Willie is the quickest defensive end in the business," Chicago Bears quarterback Bill Wade stressed. "He's not the strongest or the biggest but he's always in there, always managing to get at least his arm in the way." New York Giants great Y.A. Tittle concurred: "Davis is a great pass rusher," said the standout signal caller. "He's strong and aggressive. He's always towering over you, coming, coming, all the time!"[9]

Jerry Kramer, another Hall of Fame teammate and a roommate of Davis's in 1968, also had high praise for the stellar defensive end. "Willie had the respect of the players," Kramer said. "Not just the players of color, but *all* the players."[10]

In an NFL Films tribute to Davis, former Packers center Bill Curry lauded his combination of ability and leadership. In that same tribute, Forrest Gregg said he couldn't recall a game where Davis didn't play his absolute best.

Speaking of being absolutely the best, is Davis the Packers' GOAT defensive end? Or would that be 1990s star Reggie White? That very question was asked on a Packers Facebook page some months back, and the results were evenly split, with a third fan saying it was too difficult to decide between the two all-time greats. "Hard for me to rank players from different eras," posted the fan.

Davis and White could play the run equally well, but both are better remembered for their skills in getting after the quarterback. In a 2016 online article, Packers team historian Cliff Christl said deciding between the two was "no easy call." He pointed out Davis's greatness but also noted White's rare combination of size, strength, and explosiveness. (White was 6'5" and weighed in at 290, while Davis was 6'3", 243, not large, but not necessarily undersized for that era either.)

Davis had the misfortune of playing at a time before sacks became an official statistic, but that did not stop Bob Fox, another authority on Packers history, from naming him GOAT defensive end. "Reggie was great, don't get me wrong, but Willie was a captain on a team that won five NFL titles in seven years, including the first two Super Bowls," Fox said. "Everyone remembers that Reggie had three sacks in Super Bowl XXXI, but Willie had two in Super Bowl I and three in Super Bowl II."[11]

While those sack totals aren't official, Fox noted that, "John Turney, a member of the Professional Football Researchers Association reported that Davis had over 100 sacks in his 10-year career with the Packers."[12]

"I would think I would have to be the team's all-time leader in sacks," Davis stated. "I played 10 years and I averaged in the 'teens' in sacks for those 10 years. I had 25 one season. Paul Hornung just reminded me of that the other day."[13]

Davis was also a humanitarian and a successful businessman. Being born to poor sharecroppers in the Deep South, perhaps Davis feared what the future held after football. He understood that even the greatest pro careers only last 10 or so years. He also recalled how he thought he had a budding career with the Cleveland Browns, only to be traded to the Packers. Yes, NFL football could change, or be over, in a hurry. And then what?

"We all knew football wasn't going to last forever. The longevity of the average football player was less than ten years, and that meant there were many men who were jobless with little financial security by the time they were in their early 30s," Davis said. "That was a scary prospect. I wanted to make sure I didn't fall into that category."[14] Recognizing that reality, Davis attended the University of Chicago in the off-season, earning a master's degree in business administration.

Around this same period, he served as a color commentator for NFL broadcasts for the National Broadcasting Company (NBC). He was also highly successful in business. In 1976, he became president and CEO of All Pro Broadcasting, Inc., a Los Angeles company that owned several radio stations in southern California and the Midwest. He was also a finalist for the NFL commissioner's job in 1989, a job that went to Paul Tagliabue.[15]

Davis's post–NFL success was certainly no accident. In addition to earning an MBA, the traits he and other Packers learned from Lombardi translated well into the business world; Lombardi had pointed out that both football and life extoll the virtues of work, sacrifice, perseverance, competitive drive, and selflessness. "The emphasis on good habits is something that I learned from Coach Lombardi and have preached to myself over my years as a business leader," Davis stated. "We can deceive ourselves by thinking that having a clear goal in mind is enough to keep us on track, but it's not. … We must develop good habits to keep on the path."[16]

"When I got into business, my focus was on the customer," Davis added. "I did whatever I could to make sure they stayed happy.… But customer service goes even further than keeping the happy ones happy. The real challenge is in turning the ones that are a little unsure in your favor."[17]

In the business world, Davis served on many corporate and nonprofit

15. Willie Davis (1981)

The life lessons the Packers learned from Vince Lombardi led to continued success for many players once they left the game. Willie Davis earned an MBA degree and did extremely well in the business world following his retirement from football in 1969. He was on the board of directors for numerous companies, even the Packers (Mark Forseth Collection).

boards, including those of the National Association of Broadcasters, Metro-Goldwyn-Mayer, Schlitz Brewing Company, the Kauffman Foundation, Dow Chemical, Sara Lee, MGM Mirage, and even the Green Bay Packers Board of Directors.

People certainly took notice. Jim Robinson, former CEO and president of American Express stated, "[Davis] quickly became a contributing, thoughtful director who listened, did his homework, and worked as hard as he could."[18]

The football and business worlds intersected to celebrate Davis's 80th birthday in Las Vegas, recalled Kramer. "We had 400 to 500 of his closest friends there," he stated. "That included a number of Packers, the Chairman of Dow Chemical, the Chairman of Johnson Controls, the Chairman of MGM Grand and several other businesspeople of that ilk. Willie sat on 17 boards at one time while he was in the business community."[19]

Davis thought it was vital to lessen the importance of sports in the country. "We've narrowed to a point where almost all the glamour in some parts of society is with athletics," he explained. "We need to know about more examples outside athletics, more businesspeople and technical and professional people, so that we can say, 'Aha, there's an African-American making a difference.' I try to emphasize to people that I am an exception. A lot of folks who are doing what I'm doing didn't play football."[20]

In a day and age in which professional athletes earn extravagant salaries, it might surprise some to learn that Willie Davis made a lot more money off the football field than he ever did on it. Perhaps more important, he left a legacy of public service and as a positive role model for future generations that went well beyond fame and fortune.

"Even though Willie has had significant financial success over the years, he is the same guy," Kramer said about his longtime friend and teammate. "He is a thoughtful, caring, polite, and decent human being."[21]

"And to think, Lombardi acquired him for end A.D. Williams. In Williams' one season with the Browns, he started one game and caught one pass."[22]

16

Paul Hornung (1986)

Mr. Versatility
(Packers Years 1957–1962, 1964–1966)

Paul Hornung used to say that he went through life on scholarship, and it's not hard to see why. On the gridiron, he won the prestigious Heisman Trophy and earned NFL MVP honors as a star halfback on Green Bay Packers championship teams in the 1960s. Off the field, he dined and drank at the nation's finest nightclubs and restaurants. He pitched products like Marlboro cigarettes and hobnobbed with celebrities like Frank Sinatra, John Wayne, jockey Eddie Arcaro, New York Yankees slugger Mickey Mantle, and New York restaurateur Toots Shor. He dated beautiful women, gambled at Las Vegas casinos, attended the Kentucky Derby (he was born and raised in nearby Louisville), and hung out at the Whisky a Go-Go, a hotspot on the Sunset Strip in Los Angeles. Oh, and he repeatedly broke the team curfew to party with fellow Packer Max McGee.

College freshmen weren't allowed to play varsity football in those days, but even as a first-year quarterback at the University of Notre Dame, Hornung began turning heads when he threw three touchdown passes for the varsity in the annual spring practice game that pitted the varsity against a squad of graduating seniors and past Fighting Irish standouts. Afterward, Tommy Fitzgerald, a writer with the *Louisville Courier-Journal*, Hornung's hometown newspaper, christened him "The Golden Boy."[1] It was a nickname that stuck.

After being groomed as a sophomore to replace All-American quarterback Ralph Guglielmi, Hornung had a terrific spring practice as a junior in 1955. Former Notre Dame coach Frank Leahy, who retired after Hornung's freshman year, declared, "Paul Hornung will be the greatest quarterback Notre Dame ever had. He runs like a mower going through grass. Tacklers just bounce off of him. His passing is tops and his kicking is, too."[2] Players had to play both ways in that era, and the 6'3", 195-pound Hornung had learned to play defensive back.

Kicking, however, was a skill that dated back to eighth grade, a skill he developed largely because no one else on the team was interested. "I basically taught myself, kicking ball after ball at the playground near our house at the Marine Hospital in Portland. And once I started doing it, I liked it."[3] He also kept getting better at it, which was important in the pre-specialist football era in which versatility was much more highly valued than it is today.

Paul Hornung Highlights

Heisman Trophy winner (1956)
1st round draft choice (1957, Notre Dame)
Super Bowl champion (I)
4× NFL champion (1961, 1962, 1965, 1966)
2× First-team All-Pro (1960, 1961)
2× Pro Bowl (1959, 1960)
NFL Most Valuable Player (1961)
Green Bay Packers Hall of Fame (1975)
College Football HOF (1985)
Pro Football HOF (1986)
Scored record 176 points in 12-game season *(1960)
Scored record 19 points in NFL championship game **(1961)

*Broken by Chargers LaDainian Tomlinson (2006)
**Broken by Patriots James White (20 points in Super Bowl LI)

Notre Dame posted a sterling 8–2 record in 1955, and as Leahy had predicted, Hornung had a breakout season, finishing fourth in the nation in total offense (1,215 yards passing and rushing). His top game was in a loss to Southern California when he threw and ran for a combined 354 yards. As a blossoming star at a high-profile university, his name began appearing in gossip columns as well as the sports pages. Hornung met Abe Samuels, a millionaire bachelor, and through Samuels, the Notre Dame signal caller was introduced to show-biz celebrities such as Tony Bennett, Sammy Davis, Jr., and Dean Martin. It was high living indeed for a poor kid from Louisville.[4]

The following year was a disastrous one in many respects. As a team, Notre Dame fell to a lowly 2–8 record. The one bright spot in 1956 was Hornung, who finished second nationally in total offense and led the Irish in passing, rushing, scoring, even kickoff and punt returns, and punting. He was the first player on a losing team to win the Heisman Trophy.

After graduating from Notre Dame with a degree in business, Hornung was the first selection overall in the 1957 NFL Draft by the Green Bay Packers. Green Bay hadn't had a winning season in ten years, and to

16. Paul Hornung (1986)

make matters worse, the small town couldn't match the big city lights of Chicago, which would have been a much-preferred destination for the carefree bachelor, regardless of whether it was the Bears or the Cardinals.

The handsome Hornung also had a movie offer from Twentieth Century, but the catch was that he couldn't play football, and so it was off to Green Bay. Packers coach Lisle Blackbourn tried Hornung at quarterback, halfback, and fullback, but didn't deem him good enough to start at any one position, and so the future star mostly rode the bench his rookie season. (Although when he did play, he averaged 5.3 yards a carry.) One good thing that came out of his rookie season with the Packers was meeting wide receiver Max McGee, who soon became Hornung's roommate and lifelong friend. (Blackbourn was dismissed at season's end.)

As if a 3–9 mark in 1957 wasn't bad enough, the following year under new head coach Ray "Scooter" McLean was even worse as Green Bay limped to a 1–10–1 record, the most dismal season in the Packers' long history. Hornung's fortunes appeared to improve under McLean when he claimed the starting fullback job, but before the end of the season, rookie Jimmy Taylor had taken over, leaving Hornung's football future as up in the air as it had ever been.

Fame wasn't anything new for Paul Hornung when the Packers became steady winners in the early 1960s. He won the coveted Heisman Trophy in 1957 even though Notre Dame sported a losing season. As a Packer, Hornung set a scoring record in 1960 that lasted for 46 years, and he captured league MVP honors in 1961 (Photofest).

While Hornung and McGee played cards and hit the local nightspots, the losing and uncertainty that often goes with it can get old very quickly for a professional athlete. "That season had gone so badly I was seriously thinking of quitting football, and I was only 23 years old," Hornung stated. "But it was no fun at that point."[5]

Everything changed when Vince Lombardi was hired as head coach and general manager in 1959. To help instill a winning attitude, Lombardi traded for cagey veterans like safety Emlen Tunnell from the New York Giants, a future Hall of Famer, and defensive end Bill Quinlan from the Cleveland Browns.

Discipline also improved under the new coach. Being in bed at 11 p.m. meant exactly that. Taylor was fined $25 for sitting on his bed with his socks and shorts on but not actually in bed. And while Hornung, McGee, and a few others would sometimes risk going out on the town after curfew, they knew they were risking hefty fines. On one occasion, McGee was fined $125, and Lombardi told him the next violation would run $250, which wasn't chump change considering the meager salaries players earned in those days.

But there was more to Lombardi's strictness and Hornung's penchant for breaking rules than met the eye, and over time, Hornung and Lombardi developed a father-son relationship. "We constantly tested each other, just as a father and son would. I tried to see how far I could push him and what I could get away with, and he tried to see how much of his discipline I could take. He told me once, 'I'm going to get on your ass because you need it but also because you can take it and some of the others can't.'"[6]

Lombardi implemented a simpler offensive scheme, which the players appreciated as the systems of both Blackbourn and McLean were difficult to learn. The sophisticated offense was supposedly a reason Taylor had a hard time earning playing time as a rookie in 1958. Lombardi's more simplistic system consisted of fewer than 20 offensive plays.

Noticing Hornung's similarities to another versatile halfback, Frank Gifford, whom Lombardi coached in New York, the new coach quickly installed Hornung as his starting left halfback. As such, he had the key role in the "Green Bay sweep" or "power sweep." Hornung would get the hand-off from the quarterback and take off around end at roughly three-quarters speed in order to give guards Fuzzy Thurston and Jerry Kramer time to get ahead of him to block. While the play could be run on the weak side, it was more successful when running it to the strong side (the side with the tight end), especially since tight end Ron Kramer was an excellent blocker. Taylor would block the defensive end, and Hornung would find the hole and run to daylight.

Hornung was an ideal back for the crucial play with his power, speed, and instincts, which required him to stay behind the blockers and see how the play was developing before making his cut. "When Elijah Pitts joined the Packers as my backup in 1961, it took him a while to learn about cutting or 'setting up blockers,' as Kramer put it. When Elijah was running the pitch, he wouldn't wait for his blocks. He'd overrun them and not get nearly as many yards as he should have."[7]

16. Paul Hornung (1986)

Kramer would tell Pitts he had to slow down so he could get out in front of him and block. Hornung said that everybody had to do their job to make the sweep work, but when they did, the play looked easy.

As a former college quarterback, Hornung was always a threat to pull up and pass on a halfback option. "Although Hornung threw only 48 option passes from 1959 to 1966, Lombardi said the perpetual threat of the pass was what made his power sweep work even when defenses sensed it was coming," wrote Cliff Christl on Packers.com.[8]

With *one* position (halfback) to focus on, a simpler offensive scheme, and a renewed commitment to football, Hornung's career took off. In his first season under Lombardi in 1959, the halfback basically doubled his offensive output from his first *two* seasons, rushing for 681 yards on a nifty 4.5 average.

The following season, 1960, was a banner year that showcased Hornung's versatility. He rushed for 671 yards and 13 touchdowns and caught two more for a total of 15 TDs. As the Packers' placekicker for five of his nine seasons in Green Bay, Hornung also booted 15 field goals and 41 PATs that season. That added up to 176 points—or roughly 14 points each game. (Interestingly, MVP honors did not go to Hornung, but to Philadelphia quarterback Norm Van Brocklin, who threw for a career-high 24 touchdowns and led the Eagles to a 10–2 record and a 17–13 victory over the Packers for the 1960 championship.)

Despite setting the scoring record in a 12-game season, Hornung's mark stood for 46 years, even though the NFL had twice expanded its schedule to 14, and then 16 games. (The San Diego Chargers' LaDainian Tomlinson finally broke the record when he scored 30 touchdowns for 180 points in 2006.) It took the Chargers' star running back two more games (14) to break the long-standing mark.

Hornung and the Packers fared even better in 1961. In the first NFL championship game played in Green Bay, the Packers steamrolled the New York Giants, 37–0, to capture the franchise's first NFL title since 1944 and its first under Lombardi. The Golden Boy scored a championship game-record 19 points (a touchdown, three field goals, and four PATs). Hornung has commented that the Packers played so well that day they could have scored 70 points if they had wanted to.

Hornung also captured the 1961 NFL MVP award that had eluded him the season before with 146 points, which included 10 touchdowns (eight rushing and two receiving) and 15 field goals.

Those years proved to be the apex of his career. The nagging injuries he sustained throughout his career caused him to miss three games and limited his effectiveness in 1962. But the Packers of that period had so much depth that they were generally able to overcome injuries, and that year's squad, often considered Lombardi's best team, posted a near-perfect 13–1 record and edged the New York Giants, 16–7, to claim their second straight championship.

Then the Packers' and Hornung's fortunes took a turn for the worse in 1963. His penchant for high living caught up with him when he and Detroit Lions defensive tackle Alex Karras were suspended indefinitely for gambling. "Hornung's bets were made during a period from 1959 through 1961 and ranged as high as $500, although most were in the $50 to $100 range. Karras also made bets during several seasons."[9]

"It was always just for fun because I was making pretty good money with the Packers and had a bunch of endorsement contracts, too," Hornung said. "It was never about the money for me. I just enjoyed it."[10]

Hornung said he knew other players who gambled regularly, but he had a hunch NFL Commissioner Pete Rozelle was going to make an example of him. Rozelle, of course, saw the matter differently. He indicated that the "severity of the penalties was based on the fact that NFL player contracts specifically prohibit betting and that players repeatedly have been warned against betting."[11]

As a team, the Packers were unable to defend their title in 1963 when the archrival Chicago Bears edged them for the Western Division crown

Paul Hornung is one of the Packers on prominent display at the Heritage Trail Plaza in Green Bay. The versatile Hornung could do everything—run, throw and catch passes, and kick field goals and extra points. With 760 points, he is still the fifth-leading scorer in Green Bay Packers history (Shirley Christl).

16. Paul Hornung (1986)

with a record of 11–1–2 to the Packers' 11–2–1. (Chicago won the 1963 title over the Giants.)

Hornung was forthright about his mistake, and with Lombardi's constant lobbying of Rozelle, both he and Karras were reinstated for the 1964 season. Hornung agreed not to have anything to do with gambling, to stay out of Las Vegas, and even to forgo attending the Kentucky Derby. Karras, meanwhile, sold his share of a Detroit tavern that was known to be frequented by hoodlums.

There was talk of Lombardi trading Hornung after he was reinstated in 1964, but it was just a rumor. The one caveat was that Lombardi ordered his halfback to come to training camp early to get in shape. But neither the Golden Boy nor the Packers shined in 1964. He rushed for 415 yards and scored five TDs but missed an amazing 26 of 38 field goal attempts. "Those missed field goals and extra points came back to haunt us in several games, including our Week 2 loss to the Colts. Paul muffed an extra point, and we lost the game 21–20," said Willie Davis.[12] The Packers posted an 8–5–1 record and failed to advance to the championship game for the second straight year.

Even in the decline of his career, the Golden Boy still rose to the occasion in big games. Lombardi used to say that Hornung could smell the goal line, and never was that more apparent than in a crucial contest against Baltimore in 1965. Returning from a groin injury, Hornung scored five touchdowns (three rushing and two receiving) in leading the Packers to a 42–27 win over the host Colts. As a result of the key victory, the Packers ended the regular season tied with Baltimore in the Western Conference standings. This forced an extra playoff game that the Packers also won against the Colts (in overtime) to advance to the NFL Championship Game in Green Bay against the defending-champion Cleveland Browns.

On a muddy and snowy field, Hornung shined again, rushing for 105 yards and a touchdown as the Packers beat the Browns, 23–12, for the 1965 title, their third under Lombardi. It proved to be Hornung's swan song, as he missed five games and rushed for only 200 yards in 1966, his last year in Green Bay. Lombardi left Hornung exposed to the newly formed New Orleans Saints in the 1967 expansion draft, but a nagging neck injury caused him to retire.

While Hornung's versatility does not translate well to today's highly specialized NFL, his firm imprint on the Lombardi era remains. "Vince called him our money player and he was just that. He should have been the first player from our team in the Hall of Fame," said cornerback Herb Adderley. Guard Jerry Kramer added, "He was always the star of our team, even after he stopped being the best player."[13]

17

Henry Jordan (1995)

*Tenacious ... and Quick-Witted
(Packers Years 1959–1969)*

Football isn't always as complex as it might seem. Block and tackle better than the other team, and—if you're a defensive lineman—disengage *off* blocks, and the odds of victory are very good. Outstanding defensive tackles in the Pro Football Hall of Fame include greats like Bob Lilly, Merlin Olsen, Joe Greene, and Alan Page. Surrounded by other Hall of Fame talent on dominant Green Bay Packers defenses of the 1960s, the name "Henry Jordan" might not come to mind as readily as these players. But he belongs on any list of all-time defensive tackles. Jordan played a total of 13 years, was an All-NFL selection six times, and was named to four Pro Bowls, according to his page on the Pro Football HOF website.

Jordan was the fifth player selected for Canton from the exceptional Green Bay defensive squad that helped the Packers terrorize NFL offenses in the 1960s. Linebacker Ray Nitschke, cornerback Herb Adderley, fellow defensive lineman Willie Davis, and safety Willie Wood were the defensive stars who preceded the 6'2", 248-pound tackle into the Hall.

A Virginia native, Jordan was a three-sport star at the University of Virginia, where he captained the football team as a senior and was a runner-up in the heavyweight class of the 1957 NCAA wrestling championships. He would later use the wrestling skills he learned, like his understanding of leverage, to great success as an undersized lineman in the pro ranks.

He began his NFL career as a fifth-round pick of the Cleveland Browns in 1957. Jordan earned himself a spot on the roster as a reserve defensive tackle for a Browns squad that captured the 1957 NFL Eastern Conference title before being demolished by the Detroit Lions, 59–14, for the 1957 crown. A year later, they tied the New York Giants for the Eastern title but lost, 10–0, in a playoff game. But before the 1959 season, Cleveland sent him to the Packers for a fourth-round draft choice.

17. Henry Jordan (1995)

Henry Jordan Highlights

5th round draft choice (1957, Virginia)
2× Super Bowl champion (I, II)
5× NFL champion (1961, 1962, 1965–1967)
4× Pro Bowl (1960, 1961, 1963, 1966)
7× All-Pro (1960–1964, 1966–1967)
Virginia Sports Hall of Fame (1974)
Green Bay Packers Hall of Fame (1975)
Pro Football HOF (1995)

Playing career:
Cleveland Browns (1957–1958)
Green Bay Packers (1959–1969)

Since the Browns were perennial contenders, and Green Bay was coming off a 1-10-1 disaster, one might have thought Jordan was dismayed by the trade. Not so. While Cleveland boasted a solid team, Jordan had little to do with its success. As with teammate Willie Davis, the Browns couldn't decide on his best position, so he played every spot on the line, offense and defense.

As a result, Jordan was thrilled that someone would trade for him after spending two uneventful seasons as a backup in Cleveland. "He was ecstatic," said his wife, Olive, when he learned about the trade. "Everything was falling into place. They really wanted him."[1]

It should be noted that one positive that came out from his time with the Browns was meeting the former Olive Sargent. "We were married on New Year's Day, 1958," she stated.[2]

Jordan didn't know where Wisconsin was, so he got out a map and drove all night to get to Green Bay. The Packers were devising a solid defense, and he was seen as playing an important role in the rebuilding effort. The plan was to come up with the players for a scheme that wouldn't allow any weak points for an offense to exploit. "Every player didn't necessarily have to play every position, but they had to be prepared to cover all portions of the field."[3]

One solid lineman already in place was veteran defensive tackle Dave "Hawg" Hanner, who was named to two Pro Bowls in the 1950s. In addition to Jordan, defensive end Bill Quinlan was also acquired in 1959 in Vince Lombardi's first major trade, in which star wide receiver Billy Howton was shipped to the Browns for Quinlan and halfback Lew Carpenter. Although limited as a pass rusher, Quinlan, physical and tough to move, was the Packers' designated run stopper. Jordan, conversely, although undersized for a tackle, had a reputation for being cat-quick, a trait that had caught the attention of Lombardi and defensive coach Phil Bengston. With Quinlan

Decades before Ron Wolf fleeced the Atlanta Falcons in trading for Brett Favre, Vince Lombardi was a pretty shrewd judge of talent, too, picking up reserve lineman Henry Jordan from the Cleveland Browns in 1959. Although undersized for a tackle, Jordan had a reputation for being cat-quick, a trait that had caught the attention of Lombardi and defensive coach Phil Bengston. The future All-Pro was also well known for his quick wit and one-liners (Mark Forseth Collection).

and Hanner as line mates, Jordan was able to focus more on rushing the quarterback than playing the run, although he could also do the latter.

The final piece of the puzzle came a season later, in 1960, when Lombardi dipped into the Browns roster yet again, this time acquiring defensive end Willie Davis for offensive end A. D. Williams. Turning the clock ahead three decades, if you can imagine Ron Wolf picking up not only Brett Favre, but *another* future All-Pro from the Falcons, you have an idea how badly Lombardi fleeced the Browns' normally shrewd Paul Brown in the deals. The keys were that Lombardi saw both Davis's and Jordan's potential, and both were hungry to get on the field and prove their new coach right.

"I know Henry was like me and just wanted to play," said Davis, about the irony in the Packers picking up not one, but two future all-pro linemen from the same team. "I'd say it worked out pretty well for both of us."[4]

Like Jordan, Davis was an outstanding pass rusher. Sack totals were not kept at the time, but if they had been, no doubt the totals would have been substantial, as the Packers were not a big blitzing team and relied on their defensive linemen to put the bulk of the pressure on the opposition's quarterback.

Going up against larger players, Davis noted that Jordan relied on his speed to put him in the right spot to make plays. "Once he got there, he was able to hit just as hard as men twice his size," Davis explained. "Henry was also an intelligent player, which became a staple of Phil's defenses. He was a player who could quickly find a weakness in an opponent and exploit it over the course of a game."[5]

Teammate Jerry Kramer also praised his teammate. "If you would start guessing with Henry, you would get in trouble," Kramer said.[6] "He was small for a defensive tackle, but he had great quickness and he survived on his quickness," Kramer added. "He was also pretty strong, but his quickness was outstanding."[7]

Jordan explained that there was more to his position than brute strength. "Football has developed into a game of playing 'keys,' which means watching what a certain man does and reacting a certain way.... If I have an idea of what the guard is going to do, it will be harder for the tackle or center.... You expect to be blocked ... the secret is to escape the block as quickly as possible and to be in good position to tackle the ball carrier."[8]

As businesslike as he was on the field, Jordan was just as fun-loving and good-natured off it. He was also a friend and neighbor of Kramer. "Henry was just a really good pal. Because we lived so close to each other, we did a lot of things together," Kramer explained. "We went to dinner together. His wife Olive ... always had a sandwich, a bowl of soup or an extra plate for dinner for whoever would drop by."[9]

But Jordan was probably best known for his quick wit. Anyone who has worked in a stressful environment knows what a morale booster a well-timed one-liner can be. It isn't a gift everyone has, but Jordan did. As Hornung and Taylor aged, he would tell them, "You used to be 'Thunder and Lightning.' You're more like 'Cloud and Drizzle' now."[10]

Since quarterback is such a pressure-packed position, Bart Starr, who roomed with Jordan on the road, particularly appreciated his levity. "But rooming with Henry was a real pleasure. He really helped me relax."[11]

While Jordan actually thought very highly of Lombardi, that didn't stop the good-natured tackle from making him the favorite target of his jokes. He once quipped that the coach was a fair man who treated the Packers all the same, "like dogs." "When he says sit, I don't look for a chair," was another well-known remark.

He once famously said, "I play for the love of the game, the love of money and the fear of Lombardi."

Not surprisingly, his vibrant and jovial wit made Jordan a desirable after-dinner speaker. "He could always create a funny situation with just a wise crack," said Starr, who traveled with him on the banquet circuit. "Even if you were the last one to speak, he somehow had the last word. And heaven help you if he had the microphone last."[12]

Prematurely bald, and with a Southern drawl, Jordan wasn't beyond coming up with jokes at his own expense. "I lost my hair because all the girls were constantly stroking their hands through it," he remarked. "But what if y'all had my problem? I have to pay a barber to find my hair."[13]

Jordan also knew how to break the tension before a big game. Asked how the Packers would stop Jim Brown before the 1965 championship game against Cleveland, he deadpanned, "I've got a perfect game plan. I'll just step aside and let Willie Wood get him."[14]

More seriously, the contest had special meaning for the Packers who had played in Cleveland years earlier. "I was determined to win this game," Davis stated. "I wasn't alone. The other three former Browns—Bill Quinlan, Henry Jordan, and Lew Carpenter—also wanted to make a statement. We needed to win this game to show them they had underestimated not only the Green Bay Packers and Coach Lombardi but also what we could accomplish as individuals on a team with a common goal."[15]

Green Bay came up big in the title contest. In what would be his last NFL game, Brown could gain only 50 yards on 12 carries. As a team, Cleveland mustered only 161 yards total offense. Hornung and Taylor picked up 204 yards by themselves as Green Bay won, 23–12, for its first championship in three years.

It should be noted that while tackling the quarterback is a defensive lineman's ultimate goal, pressures are sometimes just as good as they cause incompletions and force turnovers. One example was in the 1966 season opener against the Baltimore Colts. Jordan and his teammates harassed Colts great Johnny Unitas into three interceptions, two of which were returned for Packers touchdowns in a 24–3 romp.

When a team plays as many important games as the Packers did in the 1960s, some of them get overlooked. Most fans fondly remember the famous Ice Bowl 1967 championship game that saw Green Bay slip past Dallas in the waning seconds, 21–17, for its third straight title. But the Packers, and Jordan in particular, actually played much better the previous week in dominating the Los Angeles Rams for the Western Conference title.

To set the stage, the NFL realigned into four divisions for the 1967 season. Green Bay won the first-ever Central Division title at 9–4–1, while Los Angeles and Baltimore both logged 11–1–2 campaigns to tie for the Coastal Division crown. (Yes, the Colts and Rams were in the same division!) The Rams won the division based on better point differential in head-to-head games against the Colts. There were no wild-card teams back then. As a result, Baltimore did not make the playoffs even though they had a better record than either division winner in the Eastern Conference (Dallas and Cleveland, both 9–5).

Under second-year head coach George Allen, the Rams were the leading contender to unseat the champion Packers. They led the league in both offense and defense, and they defeated Green Bay in the regular season, 27–24, at the LA Coliseum. But in that era's system of rotating home field advantage, the teams would square off for the Western Conference crown at Milwaukee County Stadium.

The Rams grabbed a 7–0 lead on a 29-yard pass from Roman Gabriel to Bernie Casey, but it was all Green Bay after that. The Packers knotted the score when Travis Williams, a lightning-fast rookie halfback known as "the Roadrunner," dashed to paydirt from 46 yards out. A 17-yard toss from Starr to Carroll Dale gave the Packers a 14–7 lead at intermission.

A third-quarter interception of Starr deep in the Packers' end of the field gave the visitors the ball at Green Bay's 10-yard-line with an excellent chance to tie the game. "In the huddle, we all talked about keeping them to a field goal and Henry Jordan, normally more reserved in the game spoke up. 'I'll get him,'" Davis recalled his teammate saying.[16] Seconds later, there was Jordan "in the backfield sacking Roman [Gabriel] and setting up yet another field goal attempt, which Herb Adderley promptly blocked."[17]

No question the story of the game was the Packers' smothering defense, which sacked Gabriel five times—3.5 from Jordan alone in one of the finest games in his career. (Sacks weren't official statistics at that time.) "It appeared like Jordan had quarterback Roman Gabriel of the Rams as a dance partner, as he had his arms around Gabriel so much," wrote Bob Fox.[18]

The high-powered Rams, who scored 398 points in the regular season, came up with just 12 first downs and 217 yards total offense. The normally prolific Gabriel was held to just 11 completions in 31 attempts. Los Angeles may have had a talented team, but no squad had the playoff experience, toughness, and discipline of the Packers, who overwhelmed their West Coast visitors, 28–7.

After 11 virtually injury-free seasons in the NFL, Jordan's back gave him problems in 1968, even though he managed to play the entire year. Many suggested he should retire, but he decided to come back.

It was not to be. Jordan played only five games in 1969 and was dropped from the active roster in mid-season. "This year, the pain was more acute than ever."[19]

After retiring, Jordan and his family moved to Oconomowoc in southeastern Wisconsin, where he was an active member of the community. It was also in 1970 that Jordan put his business acumen to work as executive director of Milwaukee World Festival Inc., formed in 1965. Willard Masterson was the first executive director and held that title as head of the Summerfest music festival until 1970, when Jordan took over.[20]

Jordan was credited with putting the fledgling operation on solid financial footing. "They didn't have a lot of sponsors at the time," said his friend, Kramer. "Maybe 25 or 30 sponsors. They were losing money as well. Two years later after Henry took over, they had between 400 to 500 sponsors and the event was doing very well. That was due to Henry Jordan."[21]

In 1977, Jordan died of an apparent heart attack at age 42 at the Milwaukee Athletic Club, where he had been jogging. He was the first of the Lombardi greats to pass away, which came as "a real shock" to Davis. "It's just ironic that it would be Henry," he said. "Physical conditioning was so important to him."[22]

Jordan was recognized for what he had accomplished in the NFL in 1995, when he was inducted into the Pro Football Hall of Fame as a senior candidate. He had previously been a finalist in 1976 and 1984.

18

Jim Ringo (1981)

*Undersized, but Perfect for Packers Offense
(Packers Years 1953–1963)*

The position of center might be the most underrated one in all of football. He is the linchpin of the offensive line, responsible for delivering the ball quickly, cleanly, and efficiently to the quarterback each and every snap. It's a highly unsung job, but fumble or snap the ball early, and all of a sudden everyone knows who the center is, if they didn't before.

As a general of sorts, the center is responsible for making the necessary pre-snap line calls and blocking adjustments. Not only are they asked to adjust the scheme accordingly, but centers must also take on the opposing team's nose tackle in a 3–4 look, double-team or tandem block alongside the guards or get to the second level to cut off a linebacker. All this in the blink of an eye while maintaining his concentration to hike the ball—seamlessly and accurately even if the team is in a shotgun formation. It's no wonder that, next to the quarterback, the center is often considered the smartest player on the field. They have to be assertive and confident in their calls, able to adapt quickly and make decisions under fire. Even if they make the wrong call, a play still has a chance to succeed if the other linemen are aligned correctly.

As if the mental demands of the position aren't hard enough, playing center also requires a unique blend of athletic skills. They aren't physical freaks like their brethren at tackle. Few (even today) exceed 300 pounds. The ideal middleman is athletic, with the speed to pull outside, the strength to grapple with enormous defenders, and the niftiness afoot to throw as many as three blocks on a single play.

Michigan State offensive line coach Mark Staten calls it a "strange position," and indeed it is. There is no doubt that starting a play by placing a ball between one's legs is an odd way of initiating action. "You've got to be precise with that and also be precise with the directions you've given everybody else as that play's about to happen," said Staten. "And a split second before that play happens, [the opponent has] shifted or moved, and you've got to trust your line mates to adjust accordingly."[1]

Jim Ringo Highlights

7th round draft pick (1953, Syracuse University)
2× NFL champion (1961, 1962)
7× First-team All-Pro (1957–1963)
2× Second-team All-Pro (1964, 1966)
10× Pro Bowl (1957–1965, 1967)
NFL 1960s All-Decade Team
Green Bay Packers Hall of Fame (1974)
Philadelphia Eagles Hall of Fame (1987)
Pro Football HOF (1981)

Playing career:
Green Bay Packers (1953–1963)
Philadelphia Eagles (1964–1967)
Coaching career (*Head coach)
Chicago Bears (1969–1971)
Buffalo Bills (1972–1976)
*Buffalo Bills (1976–1977)
New England Patriots (1978–1981)
Los Angeles Rams (1982)
New York Jets (1983–1984)
Buffalo Bills (1985–1988)
Longtime NFL assistant coach, noted for the Bills' vaunted "Electric Company" offensive line in 1970s; served as Bills head coach following resignation of Lou Saban in 1976

The mechanics of the job make center different from any other line position. "While the other four linemen position themselves for power or agility or leverage, the center is, by rule, off balance." Snapping and then getting one's hand back up for blocking is critical. "Your arms move backward, but your feet move forward."[2]

The position might require an unusual skill set, but that hasn't stopped Green Bay from producing some outstanding centers over the years. Ken Bowman, Larry McCarren, Mike Flanagan, Frank Winters, Scott Wells, and Corey Linsley come to mind. But Jim Ringo is the only one enshrined in Canton, and for good reason with 10 Pro Bowl selections in his illustrious career.

Jim Ringo grew up in the town of Phillipsburg in the western part of New Jersey. Easton, Pennsylvania, just across the Delaware River border,

18. Jim Ringo (1981)

was a huge high school rival. When Ringo made the varsity football team at Phillipsburg, he had dreams of touching the ball a lot. While almost no one envisions that involving playing on the line, Ringo got his wish—sort of—when he became the starting center.

Ringo emerged as a star for the Stateliners, and a college scholarship seemed likely. About that same time, the Syracuse Orangemen, a one-time college football power, were mired in losing and needed a new coach. They decided on Ben Schwartzwalder, a friend of the Ringo family who had been running the football program at a small Pennsylvania college. That changed Ringo's plans about where he'd continue his career as he accepted a scholarship from Syracuse in 1949.

By 1951, the Orangemen had a winning season (5–4), but that merely served as a prelude to Ringo's senior year in 1952, when Syracuse improved to 7–2 and made the Top 20. The season did not end well, however, as Alabama spanked them in the Orange Bowl, 61–6.

In the NFL draft the following spring, Ringo was selected in the seventh round by the Packers. In a 12-team league, a seventh-rounder back then was about equal to a third-round selection today. This meant he had a decent chance of making the team. However, at 211 pounds, the undersized Ringo didn't think he did when he saw other Packers linemen who were in the 230–250 range. Discouraged, Ringo decided to move back home. Probably to his surprise, he quickly found out he wasn't welcome.

"Besides, asked his father, where else could he earn $5,250 for four months work?"[3] His parents and wife informed him that he needed to go back to the Packers camp and do his best to make the team.

Ringo earned a roster spot as a backup center in 1953 and played in five contests. He battled injuries that year for one of the few times in his career. Gene Ronzani was dismissed as coach, and Marquette football legend Lisle Blackbourn was hired to lead the Packers the following season. One of his first moves was installing Ringo as starting center, a decision that would reap major dividends over the years.

While Ringo's career would remain on an upward trajectory, the Packers themselves were up-and-down, mostly the latter. The team could only manage a miserable, 2–9–1 record his rookie year, and a 4–8 mark in 1954, before improving to a surprising 6–6 record in 1955.

With a respectable quarterback in Tobin Rote, star receiver Billy Howton, running back Howie Ferguson, and stellar defensive back Bobby Dillon, the Packers were not bereft of talent, and in 1956, Ringo was joined on the line by talented first-year tackles Forrest Gregg and Bob Skoronski.

It mattered little, as the Packers kept losing—plummeting to a 4–8 record in 1956, and then 3–9 in 1957, before bottoming out at a pathetic 1–10–1 mark in 1958. Ringo, meanwhile, was invited to the Pro Bowl for the first time in 1957 and again in 1958. While that wasn't a lot of consolation with all of the losing, it didn't stop coaches from noticing his skills. "He was a great player," said Nick Skorich, the Packers' offensive line coach in 1958 and later the head man in Philadelphia and Cleveland. "He was so quick off the ball. He could make the holes, pass block and a great snapper."[4]

Although there was plenty of talent on the Packers' roster, Ringo was the only established All-Pro when Vince Lombardi took over in 1959. NFL defenses were changing from five- to four-man lines, and the transition to one fewer defensive lineman was huge for the Packers' undersized center.

"The four-man line kept me in pro football,"[5] said Ringo, who was listed at 232 pounds, but usually weighed closer to 220.

In a 4–3 alignment, defenses were usually lining up both tackles directly on the offensive guards, which meant the center (in this case, Ringo) "could still reach or cut block the left defensive tackle. That was a key block in creating the inside alley for Lombardi's famed power sweep."[6]

Jim Ringo was undersized. While listed at 230 pounds, his playing weight was supposedly more around 220. But his speed and other skills made him a natural fit as a blocker in the Packers' signature play—their vaunted power sweep. Ringo made the Pro Bowl 10 times, seven as a Packer and three with the Philadelphia Eagles, where he was traded in 1964 (Mark Forseth Collection).

Indeed, Ringo's skills were well-suited to Lombardi's style. "He was quick on his feet, good with his hands, and had tremendous balance, whether popping open a hole or spearheading Green Bay's pocket protection."[7]

Lombardi was particularly impressed with Ringo's speed. "A bigger man might not be able to make the cut-off blocks on our sweeps the way Jim does. The reason Ringo's the best in the league is because he's quick and he's smart. He runs the offensive line, calls the blocks and he knows what every lineman does on every play."[8]

What's more, Ringo's slashing cross blocks on defensive tackles freed up Packers guards Jerry Kramer and Fuzzy Thurston to lead running backs Paul Hornung and Jim Taylor.[9]

The Packers' signature Lombardi play—the power sweep—was a perfect example of a sum working better than any of the individual parts, even when one of the pieces was an All-Pro center. Consider the lack of consistency in any Packers offense, even with Ringo, prior to Lombardi's arrival.

The 1959 season marked the first of five straight years in which the starting unit of Ringo (center), Skoronski and Gregg (tackles) and Kramer and Thurston (guards) lined up as a starting quintet. It should also be pointed out that since Ringo played before teams used deep snappers, even as the starting center, he was also responsible for snapping punts and place-kicks.

Ringo was among the Packers who sensed things were about to change with Lombardi's work ethic and absolute dedication to his game plan. He was right, as Green Bay posted a 7–5 record in Lombardi's first year as coach, the Packers' only winning season in the decade.

It was only the beginning. Green Bay improved to 8–4 in 1960—this time good enough to win the Western Conference championship. The Packers' now-potent offense, led by the punishing ground game of Hornung and Taylor, tallied 332 points (27.7 per game), an impressive total in a 12-game season. Green Bay also fared well defensively, allowing 209 points (17.4 per game).

But as is often the case in football, it was the Packers' offense, and the sweep in particular, that was the talk of the league. Defenses knew what was coming, but with the unit blocking and running so effectively, teams had little success stopping the vaunted ground game.

In 1960, Green Bay rushed for 2,150 yards (compared to 1,875 passing), with Taylor rumbling for 1,101 yards, the first of five straight campaigns in which he'd post 1,000-plus yards rushing. The versatile Hornung had an even more spectacular year, registering 671 yards, and even more impressively, scoring 15 touchdowns (13 rushing, two receiving) as well as booting 15 field goals and 41 PATs for a walloping 176 points. It was a league record for points in a single season that stood for 46 years.

In just two years, the Packers had gone from league doormat to the brink of a championship when they met the 10–2 Eagles at Franklin Field in Philadelphia for the NFL title. But the inexperienced Packers made too many mistakes to beat a veteran team like the Eagles, and the hosts captured the crown with a 17–13 win. It was a bitter pill for Lombardi and the Packers, but one that motivated them for years to come, including 1961, when they demolished the visiting New York Giants, 37–0. It was Green Bay's first championship since 1944. The Packers repeated as champs against the Giants in 1962.

There were several seasons in the early 1960s when Hornung was either limited by injuries or could not play all together. The fact that the Packers' attack rarely missed a beat was a tribute to both Taylor and their outstanding offensive line. No center was better than Ringo at picking off the middle linebacker on plays up the middle or pancaking the defensive tackle on sweeps—both skills that required exceptional quickness.

But not even a terrific team like the Packers stays together forever, and 1963 was Ringo's last year in Green Bay. Supposedly, the veteran center showed up in Lombardi's office with an agent, looking for a raise. The Packers coach and general manager excused himself, then returned a short while later, informing Ringo that he had been traded to the Eagles. That was the story at least.

While Ringo was indeed traded, Lombardi's move wasn't made in haste. He had determined that Ringo was nearing the end of his career and had been working on a deal with the Eagles for months. When Lombardi decided Ringo's demands were too high, he completed a trade that brought linebacker Lee Roy Caffey and a first-round draft choice (which eventually became fullback Donny Anderson) to Green Bay for Ringo and fullback Earl Gros.[10]

As the tale grew over the years, it only added to the Lombardi mystique. Bring in an agent, deal with the consequences. Just ask Jim Ringo. The last person to squash such a tale was Lombardi himself, who relished the tough-guy role. However, as Ringo pointed out, "There's a lot of stories how the trade existed, but I never had an agent that day."[11]

In fact, the trade was more of a gamble than was generally known. A Pittsburgh paper reported: "The Packers raised an important question last night when they announced the trade of veteran center Jim Ringo and Earl Gros, a promising fullback.... Who is going to play center for the Packers?"[12] The story pointed out that the only candidates to replace the All-Pro appeared to be Skoronski, who had played the position before, and Ken Bowman, an eighth-round draft pick out of Wisconsin in 1964. On the other hand, while he was 32, Ringo hadn't missed a game in ten years and was considered the best center in the NFL.

18. Jim Ringo (1981)

Another newspaper account had a more optimistic tone, largely due to the player the Packers were getting. Caffey, the article noted, was only 23 and had become a starting linebacker for the Eagles the previous season. What's more, Caffey weighed 240, could run the 100-yard dash in 10.1 seconds, "and last year returned an intercepted pass 74 yards against the New York Giants."[13]

While it meant Ringo leaving a team that was always knocking on the doorstep of another title, the trade worked out well for both teams. Caffey was a talented linebacker and Bowman, it turned out, was ready to play. In fact, it's said that he never got enough credit for assisting Jerry Kramer on the famous Ice Bowl block on the Cowboys' Jethro Pugh.

Ringo, meanwhile, "welcomed a chance to play for a team closer to home. He could drive the 70 miles from his house in Easton to practice each day."[14]

Still, it had to have been a letdown for a player used to so much winning. The Eagles registered a 6–8 record in 1964 and went 5–9 in 1965, but reversed their fortunes with a 9–5, second-place finish the following season.

The 1967 campaign would be Ringo's last as a player. The NFL realigned from two conferences (East and West) into four divisions and placed the Eagles in the new Capitol Division with the Cowboys, Washington Redskins, and expansion New Orleans Saints. Philadelphia was wildly inconsistent all year. They would beat the Cowboys one week, 21–14 and then lose to the Saints the following Sunday, 31–24. They finished the year 6–7–1, which marked three losing seasons in Ringo's four years with the Eagles, although the stellar center continued to make the Pro Bowl and still earned Second-team All-Pro honors the only year he wasn't named to the squad (1966).

Since he had been in charge of the offensive line as a player, it stood to reason that Ringo would make a successful transition into coaching, which he did for five teams in 20 years. His most memorable stop was in Buffalo, where he molded the offensive line, led by Reggie McKenzie and Joe DeLamielleure, into the famed "Electric Company," so named because they turned on "the Juice" (O. J. Simpson). Led by his stellar line, Simpson became the first back to crack 2,000 yards in 1973.[15]

Writer Bob Carroll summed up his career by noting that Ringo "used quickness, desire, and savvy to make up for anything he may have lacked in bulk."[16]

19

Willie Wood (1989)

*Overcoming Long Odds
(Packers Years 1960–1971)*

An estimated 25,000 players have suited up in the National Football League. Of that total, only 301 had resumes that were worthy of enshrinement in the Pro Football Hall of Fame. And of *that* number, a scant 18 began their NFL careers as free agents. This means probably no one has overcome longer odds in getting to Canton than Green Bay Packers safety Willie Wood. "Willie's success story, rising from an undrafted rookie free agent to the Pro Football Hall of Fame, is an inspiration to generations of football fans," said Packers president and CEO Mark Murphy when Wood died in 2020.[1]

Even if Wood hadn't become an NFL player, getting even as far as he did could be considered a success story. Raised in Washington, D.C., his parents divorced when he was a youth, and he spent his formative years with his grandparents and at a local Boys Club. Wood excelled in football and baseball at Armstrong High School in Washington, well enough to attract numerous collegiate suitors. But he wanted to play in California, and "his Boys Club coach, Bill Butler, convinced USC coach Don Clark that Willie was a legitimate prospect."[2]

After a year of honing his studies and earning JC All-American honors at Coalinga Junior College in California, Wood transferred to the University of Southern California (USC). Wood was the first black quarterback in the history of the Pacific Coast Conference (now the Pac-12), and he also played safety. Interestingly, his position coach at USC was Al Davis, future owner of the Oakland Raiders.

But the odds remained stacked against Wood playing in the NFL. First, he stood only 5-foot-10 and weighed 190 pounds (if that), not very big, even for that era. Second, he suffered injuries to his shoulders in both his junior and senior years in college, never a good sign for anyone wanting

Willie Wood, signed as a free agent by the Packers in 1960, overcame long odds to be named to the Pro Football Hall of Fame in 1989. Known as a fierce tackler, Wood intercepted 48 passes in his career, second in Packers record books (Photofest).

to embark on a career in the NFL. Further hurting his chances was the fact there were no black signal callers in the NFL at the time—although his height, weight, and injured right shoulder were probably enough reasons why no one selected him in the 1960 NFL Draft.

Willie Wood Highlights

Undrafted free agent (Green Bay, 1960)
College: USC
2× Super Bowl champion (I, II)
5× First-team All-Pro (1964–1967, 1969)
4× Second-team All-Pro (1962, 1963, 1968, 1970)
8× Pro Bowl (1962, 1964–1970)
Green Bay Packers Hall of Fame (1977)
Pro Football HOF (1989)
NFL 1960s All-Decade Team
NFL interceptions leader (1962)
Career interceptions: 48 (second in Packers history)

Playing career:
Green Bay Packers (1960–1971)

Coaching career:
San Diego Chargers assistant (1972–1973)
Philadelphia Bell (1975)
Toronto Argonauts assistant (1979)
Toronto Argonauts (1980–1981)

Determined to get a shot at playing pro football, Wood wrote to teams, asking for at least a tryout. It was easier either to not answer at all or give him a polite brush-off. Vince Lombardi wanted a defensive back, and he responded.

"The Packers saw his heart while the others saw his size," Jim Hill, who played safety for the Packers from 1972–1974, later told the Associated Press. "Vince had an eye like [baseball managers] Joe Torre or Tom Lasorda. He could see talent where other people couldn't."[3] Lombardi didn't "buy into debates or arguments about drafting, trading or [in the case of Willie Wood] letting black players walk on," said Willie Davis, who also joined the Packers in 1960. "Right from the start, he treated us as equals, just players competing for a spot on the team. He chose not to see color in an era where most coaches chose to look the other way in terms of blacks."[4]

It didn't take Wood long to make an impression. He laid out fullback Jim Taylor with a solid tackle. Lombardi ordered the play to be run again, and Wood dropped the larger Taylor a second time. Lombardi and the team were impressed with his toughness.

"It took Willie about ten minutes to realize we had somebody special," recalled Bart Starr. "He could jump higher than anyone else, he outhustled everyone on special teams, covered receivers like a blanket, and returned punts better than anyone else we had on the team."[5]

19. Willie Wood (1989)

Norb Hecker, Wood's secondary coach, was impressed with his tremendous leaping ability. "We have a drill where the defensive backs jump up and try to touch the crossbar on the goal posts," Hecker said back when Wood was still playing. "Willie is only 5-10 and he can touch the crossbar with his elbow."[6]

But Wood didn't think his chances of making the Packers were very good, and he wasn't about to let the stellar play get to his head. "I kept my mouth shut. Lombardi was tough and I thought he yelled a lot. I tried to play as hard as I could and stay out of his way," Wood said. "Lombardi knew I was small, but I had large shoulders and a seventeen-inch neck. Lombardi liked that."[7]

The one thing Lombardi couldn't do anything about was the lack of black people in Green Bay, and in the NFL in general. Bob Mann was the Packers' first black player in 1950. In 1961, one year after Wood made the team, there were still only around 30 black players in the NFL, and the Packers had two black starters (Wood and Davis). "By 1967, one-quarter of the players in the NFL were black ... or more than 150." Green Bay, meanwhile, had 13 black players on their 40-man roster—or nearly 33 percent of the team.[8]

According to books such as Willie Davis's *Closing the Gap*, while there were few overtly racial incidents in Green Bay, the lack of diversity still posed problems, many related to housing.

Simply put, landlords were reluctant to rent to the team's players in that era. There were two basic reasons for this hesitancy: (1) They had little, if any experience, renting to black persons. (2) Some of the Packers' white players had a reputation for being a rowdy bunch, and no one wants to rent to someone who might be less than kind to the premises.

When Lombardi was hired as Packers coach in 1959, one of his first moves was acquiring veteran safety Emlen Tunnell from the New York Giants. Tunnell, who would become the first black player in the Pro Football HOF, stayed at the Hotel Northland in Green Bay, where Lombardi paid for his room.

Tunnell would serve as a role model for his teammates in several ways. Coming from an organization that won the 1956 title, Tunnell could show the young Packers what winning looked like. Second, he could demonstrate how a black professional should conduct himself, on and off the field. Wood, who lived at a local YMCA for $1.50 a night, said he had never lived in a city where there weren't any black people. Davis and running back Elijah Pitts later shared a small one-bedroom place in 1961. They would flip a coin at night to see who would sleep on the cot.

Lombardi viewed all his players as professionals who deserved better places to stay, and he saw to it personally to improve those conditions.

By 1962, Davis rented an apartment on Lori Lane on the west side of town, and in 1963 and 1964, Davis and Wood had a nice, two-bedroom house four blocks from City Stadium (later Lambeau Field). "We had a large yard and a garage. It was a very nice house, thanks to Lombardi," Davis said.[9]

Assimilation and acceptance of black Packers players doesn't happen overnight. "I remember some of the first times I was in downtown Green Bay; people would come up and ask… 'Are you Willie?' which hedged their bets with two Packers by that name," stated teammate Herb Adderley.[10]

If it took the players a while to acclimate to a nearly all-white community, their wives had it worse. Elaine Robinson and Ruth Pitts, two of the first black wives to move to Green Bay, naturally bonded. Several years before, Willie Wood had brought his wife to Green Bay, but she didn't like it there and moved back.

Many white people allegedly weren't malicious; they were largely curious. Elaine and Ruth were still offended, but Green Bay residents had never dealt with black people, so they had no clue what it was like. Such was the life of a black player and his family in Green Bay in the early 1960s.

But the only colors that mattered to Lombardi were green and gold, and Willie Wood's job was to focus on football. He started his Packers career as a skilled punt returner and reserve, backing up Tunnell. Wood finally saw game action, but it was against the best of the best—Johnny Unitas and All-Pro receiver Raymond Berry of the Colts. Jesse Whittenton got hurt, and Wood was installed at left cornerback against Berry. Wood was repeatedly beaten by the crafty veteran and eventually was benched. He was understandably concerned about his career in Green Bay, but Lombardi told him to shrug it off—he had nothing to worry about as far as a job.

Wood won the starting free safety position in 1961, replacing the aging Tunnell. He picked off five passes and led the league in punt returns with a 16.1 average—bringing back two of the punts for touchdowns. It was also the year the Packers won their first championship under Lombardi, demolishing the Giants, 37–0.

If 1961 was a very good year for Wood, the following season was even better. He led the NFL with nine interceptions and averaged 11.9 yards per punt return. He was a ballhawk throughout his stellar Packers career and picked off five, three, six, three, and four passes over his next five seasons in Green Bay. In a largely pre-specialist era, Wood remained a solid punt returner as well.

The most memorable play of his career occurred five years later in Super Bowl I against the Kansas City Chiefs. In a surprisingly close game up to that point, the heavily favored Packers led only 14–10 at intermission. Early in the second half, Wood returned an errant Len Dawson pass 50 yards to the Chiefs' 5-yard line. Halfback Elijah Pitts scored on

19. Willie Wood (1989)

Willie Wood really came into his own in 1961. He replaced the aging Emlen Tunnell as a starting safety, intercepted five passes, and led the league in punt returns. The following season, he led the NFL in interceptions with nine thefts of enemy passes (Mark Forseth Collection).

the next play, and the Packers extended their lead to 21–10. Kansas City coach Hank Stram called Wood's pick the turning point of the contest. "We played well in the first half and at the start of the second half," Stram said after the game. "But that interception by Wood changed the complexion of the game."[11]

"His pass just floated out there with nothing on it," Wood told the *Los Angeles Times* 30 years later. "It was an easy interception."[12]

The Packers scored two insurance touchdowns on a 13-yard pass from Bart Starr to Max McGee and another short run by Pitts that made the final score 35–10. The Chiefs were shut out in the second half.

Because the Super Bowl I interception was so important, Wood's play in Super Bowl II gets overlooked. In the 33–14 rout over the Oakland Raiders in the Orange Bowl, Wood returned five punts, including a 31-yarder that stood as the record for longest punt return until Super Bowl XVIII.

But Wood was more than a ballhawk and punt returner, as he was also known for his fierce tackling. "Pound for pound, Willie was the best tackler in the game," Lombardi once said. Dave Hanner, who spent 44 years in the NFL as a player, coach and scout, concurred. "I think Willie Wood was as good a tackler as I've ever seen."[13]

Not only that, but even Ray Nitschke recognized his toughness. "'I hate to miss a tackle,' Nitschke would say, 'cause if I do, I know I'm gonna get a dirty look from Willie. He'll kill you with that look.'"[14]

Wood later proved to be a pioneer in the coaching ranks. After retiring from the Packers, he joined the San Diego Chargers as a defensive backfield assistant but had a premonition of sorts that the job could lead to something more down the road. "Eventually, I would like to move into a head coaching position," said Wood when the Chargers hired him. "I think the time will come when the NFL will have a black coach. The job will help prepare me to take advantage of the opportunity."[15]

While it wasn't the NFL, he became the first black head coach in the sport's modern era with the World Football League's Philadelphia Bell in 1975. "My original decision was to play that down," Wood told the Associated Press about being the first black coach when he was hired to succeed Ron Waller. "But obviously, the mere fact that I'm black means I feel I have to do a good job."[16]

The job would only last for 11 games when the league folded that October, but it wouldn't be the final time Wood served as a trailblazer. He served as an assistant with the Toronto Argonauts of the Canadian Football League in 1979—ironically under former Packers teammate Forrest Gregg. When Gregg left the following year to take over the Cincinnati Bengals, Wood became the first black head coach in the CFL. Like the Bell position, it was a short-lived job, as he was fired after an 0–10 start in 1981.

Wood was reportedly disappointed that he was never offered another coaching job in the NFL, but with a family to support, he founded a Washington-based mechanical contracting business, which he ran until 2001.[17]

Many felt that Wood's induction into the Pro Football Hall of Fame

19. Willie Wood (1989)

in 1989 was long overdue. In addition to being the Packers' second-leading career interceptor (48), he also ranks first in punt return yardage (1,391). Interestingly, Art Shell, a standout offensive tackle with the Raiders and a HOF inductee with Wood, became the first black head coach in the NFL with the Los Angeles Raiders that same year.

Wood, unfortunately, also left a legacy of what playing a dozen years in the National Football League can do to one's body. Before chronic traumatic encephalopathy (CTE) brought to light the problem of head injuries in the NFL and spurred debate over player safety, Wood was having physical issues that he figured were the result of playing football—although he said it was a decision he did not regret. "The game takes a toll. But I would never wish any harm to the sport or begrudge it. I love the sport, and I had a wonderful career."[18]

In 2007, Wood was already having dementia problems and was about to undergo replacement surgery on his left knee to go with his previously replaced right knee and right hip.[19]

Fast forward nine years, and Wood's dementia had progressed to where he did not have any recollection of his Super Bowl interception. In fact, he didn't even recall being on an NFL roster.

Dee Daniels, an assisted living coordinator at the center where Wood lived, enjoyed telling him he was a great player, even if he didn't remember it. "You were the best of the best," she said.[20]

Packers Inducted Into the Pro Football Hall of Fame in the 21st Century

20

Bobby Dillon (2020)

One-Eyed Ballhawking Safety
(Packers Years 1952–1959)

Who is the Green Bay Packers' all-time leader in interceptions? Herb Adderley? Nope. Willie Wood? No. LeRoy Butler? Wrong again. Charles Woodson? For a final time, the answer is "no." The correct answer is standout safety Bobby Dillon, also known in football circles as Bobby Dan Dillon. If you've never heard of him, the reason is that he had the unfortunate timing of playing for mostly lousy Packers teams in the 1950s.

In fact, Dillon might be the most unlikely Packer in the Pro Football Hall of Fame, even though he had certainly been worthy of Hall selection for decades. Dillon, enshrined in Canton in 2020, hung up his cleats in 1959, which means it took a full decade *longer* for Dillon to be posthumously inducted into the Hall than even Packers great Jerry Kramer famously waited for his HOF bust. (Kramer retired in 1968 and was inducted in the HOF in 2018.)

Those in the know were well aware of Dillon's slight. As a result of his consistently being overlooked for the ultimate honor of induction into the Pro Football Hall of Fame, in 2011 the Professional Football Researchers Association (PFRA) named Dillon to the "Hall of Very Good Class of 2011," which was an informal honor awarded by the PFRA to the best NFL players not yet in the Hall of Fame.[1] (Cowboy Cliff Harris, another member of this PFRA squad, was also finally inducted in 2020.)

On the heels of its 100th anniversary season in 2019, the Pro Football Hall of Fame decided to adjust the by-laws for a special one-time induction of senior players. The 20-member Centennial Class of 2020 (20 in '20) was scheduled for enshrinement during *two separate events*: five modern-era players, two coaches, and three contributors during the annual

Enshrinement Week in August and 10 seniors during the Centennial Celebration in September. (At least, that was the initial plan before the coronavirus pandemic.) Dillon, who passed away at age 89 on August 22, 2019, was one of the 10 seniors scheduled to receive a Hall bust during the fall event (before the coronavirus). The other seniors selected were Harris, Harold Carmichael, Jimbo Covert, Winston Hill, Alex Karras, Donnie Shell, Duke Slater, Mac Speedie, and Ed Sprinkle.

As pointed out by noted Packers writer and HOF enthusiast Bob Fox, a storied franchise like Green Bay meant there were other Packers greats worthy of Hall selection in 2020: guard Gale Gillingham, wide receivers Sterling Sharpe and Boyd Dowler, tight end Ron Kramer, Lambeau-era standouts Verne Lewellen and Lavvie Dilweg, and scout and personnel director Jack Vainisi.

Bobby Dillon Highlights

3rd round draft choice (Texas, 1952)
4× All-Pro (1954, 1955, 1957, 1958)
4× Pro Bowl (1955–1958)
Packers all-time interception leader (52 … achieved in just 94 games)
University of Texas Sports Hall of Fame (1966)
Green Bay Packers Hall of Fame (1974)
Posthumously elected to Pro Football HOF (2020)
Third Temple, Texas, native to be named to Pro Football HOF, along with Sammy Baugh and Joe Greene
Played with just one working eye (the result of a childhood accident)

Undoubtedly the fact that Dillon starred on some mostly lousy Packers teams in the 1950s had a lot to do with the long wait for Canton. Like it or not, stars on elite teams are more in the public's consciousness, and when it comes time to submit HOF ballots, players on lesser teams can be easily overlooked. Consider that the Packers had one winning season in the 1950s. One! Year by year, it was a forgettable decade that read like this:

1950	3–9
1951	3–9
1952 (Dillon's rookie season)	6–6
1953	2–9–1
1954	4–8
1955	6–6
1956	4–8

20. Bobby Dillon (2020)

1957	3–9
1958	1–10–1
1959	7–5

What's amazing about these losing seasons is that, due to Vainisi's shrewd eye for gridiron talent, the Packers weren't exactly bereft of good players. Dillon, for instance, was a third-round draft pick out of the University of Texas in 1952, where he had a fabulous college career.

Dillon was a co-captain on the 1951 Southwest Conference (SWC) champion Longhorns team, which reached a ranking of #3 in the country before losing the 1951 Cotton Bowl to the Tennessee Volunteers.

In addition to playing safety in college, Dillon also played several games at halfback and returned kicks. In his college debut against Texas Tech, Dillon returned a punt 55 yards for a touchdown and scored a 20-yard rushing touchdown. In his career at Texas, Dillon had 47 returns for 830 yards. In the 1950 season alone, Dillon had 15 punt returns for 334 yards, including a game-winning 84-yard touchdown against Baylor University.

What's more, the All-American safety had 13 interceptions for the Longhorns and amassed 190 interception return yards on those thefts, a yardage total that was a school record until 1995.[2] Dillon was also a sprinter on the track team at Texas and was a member of two SWC-champion teams.

Also joining the Packers in 1952 were fellow draft picks quarterback Babe Parilli, receiver Billy Howton, and defensive tackle Dave "Hawg" Hanner. Other eventual stars drafted during that period included Max McGee (1954), Forrest Gregg and Bart Starr (1956), and Paul Hornung (1957).

However, having solid players alone does not necessarily translate into a winning team, and neither head coaches Gene Ronzani, Lisle Blackbourn, and Ray "Scooter" McLean, nor the Packers' often inept Executive Committee proved capable of leading the storied franchise in the 1950s.

That definitely diminished accolades for a star player like Dillon. As a result of the Packers' misfortunes, safeties on much more successful teams of that era—Jack Christiansen (Lions), Yale Lary (Lions), and Emlen Tunnell (Giants)—were named to the 1950s All-Decade Team, but not Dillon. What's more, the Packers' standout had more career interceptions (52) than either Lary (50) or Christiansen (46).[3]

That certainly isn't to say that these players weren't worthy selections; the point is, so was Bobby Dillon, who still managed to shine during one of the most downtrodden periods in Packers history. The stellar safety was an All-Pro in 1954, 1955, 1957, and 1958. He was also a four-time Pro Bowl selection from 1955–1958. Interceptions were a specialty, and he led the NFL in interception return yardage (244) in 1956. In fact, it was due

Bobby Dillon intercepted more passes than any Packer in team history, more than Herb Adderley or Willie Wood. He is also the only Packer to record nine interceptions in multiple seasons. And yet, it took 60 years for Dillon to be enshrined in Canton—no doubt largely due to his being overlooked while playing on so many poor Green Bay teams in the 1950s just prior to Vince Lombardi's arrival (Pro Football Hall of Fame).

to his ballhawking skills that Dillon was nicknamed "The Hawk" by his teammates.[4]

It was a fitting moniker. Of the nine Packers who have recorded nine interceptions in a single season, "The Hawk" is the only one to accomplish this rare feat more than once—in 1953, 1955, and 1957 to be exact. (For the record, the other Packers who have recorded nine picks are Bob Forte, 1947, 12 games; John Symank, 1957, 12 games; Willie Wood, 1962, 14 games; Willie Buchanon, 1978, 16 games; Tom Flynn, 1984, 16 games; Mark Lee, 1986, 16 games; Darren Sharper, 2000, 16 games; and Charles Woodson, 2009, 16 games.) Irv Comp intercepted 10 passes in only 10 games in 1943.

There's more to say about Dillon's legendary thievery. Not surprisingly, he also shares the team record for interceptions in a game with four, which he recorded in a loss against the eventual NFL champion Detroit Lions in a 1953 Thanksgiving contest.[5] With less than two minutes left in his record-setting game, Dillon injured his knee and missed the last two games of the season.Dillon still finished 1953 with nine picks. When he retired six years later, Dillon had the second-most interceptions in NFL history, behind only Tunnell, a Packers teammate at the time.

Dillon's career total of 52 picks is even more impressive when you remember that the NFL played a 12-game schedule back then, and teams ran the ball more than they passed. Dillon also accomplished these feats with only *one* working eye as a result of a series of injuries that occurred during his childhood.

Dillon's partial blindness was a favorite story of many longtime Packers fans. It went something like this: At the age of five or six, Dillon got a small piece of metal in his left eye, which caused a cataract to grow. He had surgery to have it removed. Several years later, he was hit in the face with a board, his eye deteriorated further, and he eventually had it replaced with a glass eye. If having a glass eye affected his vision, Dillon didn't think it was a big deal since he was once quoted as saying it was the only way of seeing he ever knew.

Others thought the affliction a bigger deal than Dillon did. Upon extending a college scholarship, the University of Texas had required that Dillon's father sign a waiver, indicating that if he suffered another eye injury while playing football, the family would not hold Texas responsible; Dillon's father signed the waiver.[6]

While not easy, Dillon was proof positive it was possible not only to play, but play well, with one working eye. Not that it is easy. Someone who loses sight in one eye will lose part of their side vision and, initially, may have problems with depth perception. "Usually, people find that with time their good eye 'takes over' and that tasks that were previously difficult become easier. It's very difficult to say how long this adjustment will take as this is very individual."[7]

Writer JW Nix put the one-eye issue in perspective. "Since it is more than obvious this did not detract from his play, Dillon's exploits on the field are his real mark on the game. He averaged over 6 interceptions a year for his career. His amazing nose for the ball is not matched by many to have ever played the game."[8]

As well as shrugging off his accomplishments, the one-eyed Dillon evidently also had a good sense of humor about his affliction. As the story goes, Dillon's glass eye popped out during a Packers game. After retrieving his eye and putting it back in, the official supposedly said something to Dillon like, "What would you do if you lost your other eye?" Dillon allegedly quipped, "Then I guess I'd become an official."

Longtime Packers fans aren't the only ones who enjoyed talking about Dillon. Another HOFer, former Packers GM Ron Wolf, lauded the safety's skills in an interview with Rick Gosselin, a Pro Football HOF voter and member of the Seniors Selection Committee.

> He was a 9.7 sprinter coming out of the University of Texas and would be a corner in today's game. But back then the best athletes were put inside. In order to qualify for the Pro Football Hall of Fame, I believe you are talking about the best of the best. Bobby Dillon is one of those from his era. Witness the fact that [safeties] Jack Christiansen, Yale Lary and Emlen Tunnell are in the Hall. Dillon accomplished more than those particular players did in the same era. He was a rare football player, the best defensive back of his time.[9]

Dillon's sprinter-like speed was not lost on the Packers at the time. "Although a free safety by trade, Dillon was often used in Green Bay like a shutdown corner, consistently covering the opponent's best receiver. He was, perhaps, the first and only 'shutdown safety' in NFL history," Wolf added.[10]

Dillon and Green Bay Packers great Jerry Kramer were teammates on the 1959 squad under Vince Lombardi, and Fox had the opportunity to interview Kramer about his HOF teammate. "Bobby was exceptionally fast and cat-quick," Kramer said. "He had fantastic instincts as well. He could bait a quarterback into throwing his way because of the way he played off a receiver. But then just like that, Bobby would get to the football and either intercept it or bat it away."[11]

It's worth saying more about 1959, Dillon's last season as a player in the NFL. Coming off a 1–10–1 debacle in 1958, it was probably no huge surprise that The Hawk was ready to hang up his cleats. In addition to being tired of all the losing, one must remember that players did not make big money in those days. Accustomed to already having to work in the off-season to supplement their meager pro salaries, even standout players like Dillon simply didn't have the financial incentive to play longer, as they so often do today.

Dillon's standout play was clearly recalled by longtime Packers fan Dennis Yaeger. "Bobby [was] tailing a wideout with his arms outstretched. He looked totally over his back 180 degrees, caught it as he slid forward, like a father gently cradling his son from a burning building!" Jaeger said in an email.[12]

Vince Lombardi was well aware of Dillon's talents and was not about to give up on him that easily. The Packers' new coach instructed Vainisi to convince the standout safety to return in 1959. Dillon joined a talented Green Bay defensive backfield that now included Emlen Tunnell. "The two pass-defense experts have intercepted the fantastic total of 125 enemy aerials," wrote Art Daley of the *Green Bay Press-Gazette*. "Tunnell bagged 74 in his 11 years; Dillon 51 in his 7."[13]

Unfortunately, Dillon suffered an injury midway through the season, lost his starting job, and retired.

With a record of 7–5, the 1959 squad was the only winning team Dillon played on with the Packers. Had he played longer, and at a level even close to what he had displayed previously, Dillon's skills would have stood out more to the press as the Packers quickly rose to become a league power and eventual champion. Put another way, Dillon flew under the radar for decades because he wasn't on Lombardi's championship teams. The 1950s standout said as much himself. "Willie Wood and Herb Adderley have made it and, if you go by the numbers, I have them both beat. That was a bad deal," Dillon once said.[14]

As noted earlier, Dillon's 52 career interceptions is more than either Wood (48) or Adderley (48, 39 as a Packer).

What's more, Dillon ranked 33rd on a Packers News list of the top 100 all-time Packers players.[15] He finished even higher, 27th, in the book, *A Century of Excellence: 100 Greatest Packers of All Time*.

Wolf and Kramer weren't the only Packers to praise Dillon. Dave "Hawg" Hanner, another teammate of Dillon's, talked to sportswriter Cliff Christl about Dillon in 2004: "He and Willie Wood were the two best safeties we ever had [in Green Bay]. Old Bobby was smart, and he was tough. He'd get knocked out a couple times a game, but he'd come right back. When [Vince] Lombardi came here, he talked about Bobby being the best defensive back in the league at the time."[16]

For readers keeping score, that's both Ron Wolf *and* Vince Lombardi calling Bobby Dillon "the best defensive back of his time."

After retiring from the NFL, Dillon returned to Texas, earned a bachelor's degree in accounting, and went on to work for WilsonArt International, a furnishings manufacturer. He remained with the firm for 36 years, retiring from Wilsonart in 1995.

Bobby Dillon, gone but not forgotten, is in the Pro Football Hall of Fame at long last, one working eye and all.

21

Brett Favre (2016)

*Unpredictable, but Always Entertaining
(Packers Years 1992–2007)*

Brett Favre was tough, resourceful, unpredictable, fun-loving, and controversial. These traits add up to one highly entertaining quarterback who thrilled, delighted, and yes, frustrated fans and coaches alike for 20 years in the National Football League.

At the time of his retirement, the 11-time Pro Bowler held virtually every major NFL passing record. Favre is the only player to win the Most Valuable Player Award three straight years, from 1995–1997. (He shared the honor with Lions running back Barry Sanders in 1997.) Favre was known affectionately as "the gunslinger," and with good reason since the dictionary defines a gunslinger as "a person who acts in an aggressive and decisive manner." This meant Favre could be either very good or very bad, and sometimes in the same game! Let's take a look at those adjectives one at a time.

Tough. A number of Favre's NFL records (such as career touchdown passes and career passing yardage) have already been broken. However, one of those marks—most consecutive starts by a player—is likely to stand the test of time. Favre became the Packers' starting quarterback in the fourth game of the 1992 NFL season and started every game through the 2007 season. He played for the Packers for 16 years before being traded to the New York Jets for the 2008 season and then spending his final two seasons with the Minnesota Vikings.

In that time, he made an NFL-record 297 consecutive starts, which mushrooms into a staggering 321 starts if you include playoffs. Even based on regular season starts alone, that breaks out into an incredible 18.5 seasons of starting EVERY SINGLE GAME of a 16-game NFL season. All the more remarkable was achieving this Iron Man feat when the quarterback is the number-one bullseye of the opposing team's defense every week.

21. Brett Favre (2016)

Brett Favre Highlights

2nd round draft choice (Atlanta, 1991)
Super Bowl champion (XXXI)
3× NFL Most Valuable Player (1995, 1996, 1997)
11× Pro Bowl
6× First—or Second-team All-Pro selection
4× Led NFL in touchdown passes (1995–1997, 2003)
Sports Illustrated Sportsman of the Year (2007)
Most career pass attempts (10,169)
Most career interceptions (336)
Held many other major NFL passing records at time of retirement
Number "4" retired by Packers (2015)
Green Bay Packers Hall of Fame (2015)
Pro Football HOF (2016)

Professional playing career:
Atlanta Falcons (1991)
Green Bay Packers (1992–2007)
New York Jets (2008)
Minnesota Vikings (2009–2010)

Of course, there were many weeks in which the Iron Man streak appeared in jeopardy. One of the most memorable occurred in December 1995, when he had a badly swollen sprained ankle, but still managed to move around well enough to not only play but throw for five touchdown passes in a much-needed, 35–28, late-season home win against the Chicago Bears. Not coincidentally, it ended up being the first of his MVP campaigns.

Sometimes a little luck was involved when Favre got hurt during the game—but somehow managed to suit up the following week. In a 2002 contest against the Washington Redskins, Favre suffered a sprained knee. and backup QB Doug Pederson took most of the snaps in the second half, going 9-for-15 for 78 yards to help win the game, 30–9.

In a 2004, week 4 game against the New York Giants, Favre sustained a concussion in the third quarter, and Pederson again replaced him. Pederson went 7-of-17 for 86 yards and an interception in the loss before he suffered a hit to his side in the third quarter that resulted in a broken rib, among other injuries.

During his consecutive-starts streak, a total of 238 other quarterbacks started in the NFL! Run the math, and that's roughly more than seven quarterbacks for each team in the league. The streak finally ended in Favre's last season, when he was unable to start the Vikings' December 13, 2010, contest against the New York Giants due to a shoulder injury.

Some of the many injuries he sustained during the streak included

While a number of quarterbacks have since broken some of Brett Favre's NFL passing records, his regular-season record of 297 consecutive starts may never be broken (Mark Forseth Collection).

first-degree shoulder separation,* deep thigh bruise, severely bruised left hip, severely sprained left ankle, wind knocked out coupled with coughing up blood, sprained right thumb, right elbow tendinitis, left mid-foot sprain, broken left thumb, softball-sized bruise of left hamstring, mild concussion,

21. Brett Favre (2016)

sprained right hand, injured ulnar nerve of right elbow, and bone spurs in left ankle.[1] (*It was said that Favre's injury, sustained in a 1992 win over the visiting Philadelphia Eagles, convinced Reggie White of Favre's toughness prior to signing with Green Bay the following year.)

In addition to the physical aspects of playing quarterback, the position also requires *mental sharpness*. Could *you* go to the office right after your dad died—let alone get ready to go up against 300-pound linemen who want to hit you as hard as they can? That's what Brett Favre faced on December 22, 2003. His father Irvin had died the day before, and rumor winds swirled about whether Favre would play that Monday night against the Oakland Raiders. Few would have blamed him if he didn't, but play he did, and spectacularly, throwing for four touchdowns and 399 yards, as the Packers routed the host Raiders, 41–7. Even the normally hostile Raider Nation was impressed and gave him resounding applause. On an emotionally draining night, the Gunslinger completed 73 percent of his passes and posted a near-perfect 154.9 quarterback rating. (A perfect rating is 158.3.) It was one of the best performances of his career on a night when few would have expected it.

The death of his father was the first in a series of unfortunate family events. In October 2004, ten months after the death of Favre's father, his brother-in-law, Casey Tynes, was killed in an all-terrain accident on Favre's Mississippi property. Soon after in 2004, Favre's wife, Deanna, was diagnosed with breast cancer. Following aggressive treatment, she recovered.

Resourceful and unpredictable. Other characteristics that made the Gunslinger unique were his resourcefulness and unpredictability, traits that often went hand in hand. Turn the clock back to 1996 in a road contest against the Seattle Seahawks at the Kingdome. Favre scrambles and flips the ball more or less underhanded to Antonio Freeman in the end zone for a Packers touchdown. But much more than fun and games, unique plays were more about Favre's resourcefulness—his boundless determination to do what it took to lead the Packers to victory.

Case in point: January 1997, NFC Championship against the Carolina Panthers at Lambeau Field. The stakes were never higher: win and the Packers were in their first Super Bowl in 29 years. As he so often did, the Gunslinger overcame the *bad*—two early turnovers, a fumble and an interception—that set up 10 Panthers points, he settled down, played well from then on, and the Packers won going away, 30–13. On one particularly memorable play, Favre, falling to the ground after being hit by a number of Panthers, somehow managed to pitch the ball forward to running back Dorsey Levens for a Packers first down.

Another example: the 1994 regular season finale against the Atlanta Falcons in the Packers' last game at Milwaukee County Stadium. With Favre under strict orders from Coach Mike Holmgren to *not run* or risk not getting off another play before the clock expired, the Gunslinger took off anyway, outran several Atlanta defenders, and dove into the end zone for a Packers victory, one that clinched another playoff berth. Ecstatic Packers players. Delirious fans. Resourceful. Unpredictable. That was Brett Favre. With #4 under center, it seemed like almost no lead was out of reach—that he could snatch victory out of certain defeat.

Former teammate Tim Couch said much the same. "He's a gunslinger. He may throw three picks in the first half, but he's still going to come out giving it all he's got in the next half and he may throw three touchdowns and pull the game out in the end."[2]

Fun-loving. Out of all of Favre's traits, it might have been his love of the game that endeared him to fans the most. In the serious, win-at-all-costs NFL, Favre was one of the few who seemed to *get it*: that NFL players are blessed with playing a *game* that most of us have to give up when we become adults. The Gunslinger would pump his fists after a touchdown pass, rip off his helmet, and run around the field rejoicing after firing a 54-yard TD pass to Andre Rison early in Super Bowl XXXI. He would jubilantly hoist receiver Donald Driver onto his shoulders after another Packers score. He'd joke with officials before the game. He'd pass wind in the huddle. Such enthusiasm is contagious, and it was what made Favre seem more like one of the guys than a superstar. "He'll throw water on you after you've put on your coat and tie, he'll take your clothes and throw 'em in the shower or stuff 'em in an ice bag," remarked Packers center Mike Flanagan. "He's big on stink bombs every once in a while, too. You would never know he's a $100 million guy. He just likes to have fun."[3]

Of course, all the winning the Packers did with Favre as quarterback made the game fun, too. Along with Ron Wolf, Mike Holmgren, and Reggie White, Favre was instrumental in leading the Packers to a winning era that hadn't been seen in Green Bay since the glory days of the 1960s.

Controversial. Controversy followed Favre throughout his career. First there was an admitted addiction to Vicodin painkillers and subsequent 46-day rehab prior to the start of the 1996 season. The "will-he-or-won't-he retire?" saga that went on for years was well known. There were also the messy "divorce" from the Packers in 2008; an alleged sexting scandal while he was quarterback of the New York Jets in 2008; and infuriating legions of Packers fans by signing with the archrival Minnesota Vikings in 2009. Sometimes it seemed the Gunslinger was more of an actor in a daytime soap opera than a star quarterback in the NFL.

Favre's addiction to Vicodin became public knowledge when he suffered a seizure following routine ankle surgery in February.[4] The story had a happy ending as the Gunslinger used the setback as motivation for the 1996 season. He paced the league in touchdown passes (39) and garnered a second

21. Brett Favre (2016)

Favre was nicknamed "Gunslinger," a nod to both his tremendous throwing arm and his reputation for risk-taking (Mark Forseth Collection).

straight MVP Award, as the Packers went on to win Super Bowl XXXI over New England, 35–21. It was Green Bay's first championship in 29 years.

The ongoing "will-he-or-won't-he retire" saga likely began in September 2002, when Favre told sportswriter Peter King that he missed his home in Mississippi and was thinking more and more about retirement. When head coach Mike Sherman told his players they could have Saturday and Sunday off, Favre said he wished he could be back home.

Not surprisingly, retirement talk surfaced again after the Packers suffered a rare 4–12 losing season in 2005, one in which Favre led the league in interceptions (29). But not long after that, Favre confirmed that he would in fact be back for the 2006 season—perhaps not wanting to make the difficult job of first-year coach Mike McCarthy any harder by not returning as quarterback. The Packers stumbled to a 4–8 start but rebounded to finish 8–8 with a resounding 26–7 win over the playoff-bound Chicago Bears in the season finale. Was it Favre's swan song? Following the game, Favre choked up in an interview with sideline reporter Andrea Kremer when she asked him if he was going to retire.

But Favre not only came back to play in 2007, it proved to be one of his best campaigns. In his *17th* season in the NFL, the Gunslinger threw for 4,155 yards, 28 touchdowns, and a passer rating of 95.7, his best mark since his MVP years in 1995–1996. And that wasn't all. In a September 30 contest against the Vikings, Favre connected with receiver Greg Jennings on a 16-yard strike for his 421st career touchdown, breaking Dan Marino's record of 420.[5] The Packers finished 13–3 and defeated Seattle in the divisional playoffs, 42–20, before losing a heartbreaking NFC championship game against the Giants at Lambeau Field (23–20) when Favre threw a costly pick in overtime that led to New York's winning field goal.

Coming so close to a Super Bowl berth, surely Favre would return in 2008? Surprisingly to some, it was the lofty expectations coming off such a great season that led the unpredictable Favre to do the unthinkable and announce his retirement in a teary-eyed March press conference. Sports pundits lamented the news in special sports editions. "There is plenty left in Favre's rocket right arm, but the expectations of the sport's most passionate fan base exhausted him, and he was weary of the preparation required to summon his best," stated *Sports Illustrated* writer Alan Shipnuck.[6]

The news certainly didn't surprise King, who had covered the Gunslinger since 1995, the first of Favre's MVP seasons. "He grew to really hate two things about his job: the never-ending demands on his time, which only worsened as the NFL got bigger and his stature increased, and the pressure on a quarterback to deliver Super Bowls [plural] to his team."[7]

The rumor mill kicked into high gear by summer when ESPN aired a bombshell that Favre wanted to un-retire, but the Packers were reluctant to welcome him back.[8] There was more. In a now-famous interview with FOX's Greta Van Sustern, Favre criticized Packers general manager Ted Thompson for forcing him to make a decision on returning to the team too quickly.

Next came perhaps the biggest stunner of all: Favre getting off a charter plane in Green Bay in early August, ready for training camp. Did Favre really expect to remain the starter when the Packers had already announced that Aaron Rodgers would be the number-one quarterback in 2008? Would the two of them battle it out for the starting job? If Favre lost, would he be willing to be Rodgers's caddy? None of these scenarios seemed likely, and when Favre rejected a multi-million-dollar marketing deal from the Packers to remain retired, the team traded him to the New York Jets. The Gunslinger was now "Brett the Jet" or "Broadway Brett."

Difficult as it was to see Favre traded to another team, this was small potatoes compared to a year later, when he would retire again, this time from the Jets; only to *un-retire* and sign with the Vikings, the Packers' chief NFC North nemesis. Those two years with Minnesota were so painful, it would take *years* for the two sides to mend fences. They finally did, and the Packers retired Favre's #4 in a memorable 2015 ceremony at Lambeau Field.

Entertaining. These adjectives all add up to one key trait: *entertaining*. The Joe Montana–Steve Young quarterback battle sparked plenty of unrest in San Francisco, but to approach the Favre saga, Montana would have needed to purposely sign with a rival like the Rams, not play for a team in the AFC like the Chiefs. Imagine if Favre had played two or three years in New York instead. Still unsettling, but nothing like playing for an *archrival* like Minnesota. Yet controversy is also entertainment, isn't it?

To sum up the other characteristics, Favre was tough, like a linebacker who played quarterback—but what linebacker ever had a howitzer for a right arm like Brett? In the serious business of the NFL, Favre was also fun, a breath of fresh air.

There have probably been other quarterbacks as resourceful, but when it came to unpredictability, Favre seemed to be in a category all his own. His ongoing retirement saga was unpredictable enough, but Favre's sometimes inconsistent play was even harder to believe at times.

Case in point: on October 14, 2001, the Packers faced the defending Super Bowl champion Baltimore Ravens, who had just turned in one of the greatest seasons ever by a team defense. Fans were likely afraid of a hard day at the office for the Packers, but Favre completely picked apart the talented Ravens with masterful precision, throwing for 337 yards and three touchdowns as the Packers beat the champs, 31–23.

Roughly a year later, in a January 20, 2002, divisional playoff in St. Louis, Favre turned in perhaps the ugliest game in his long career. The Rams picked off the Gunslinger *six* times, with Aeneas Williams bringing back not one, but two pick-sixes as St. Louis routed the Packers, 45–17.

It might be tempting to try to forget games like that but being unpredictably good also means that being unpredictably *bad* is also possible in any given contest. It's what made him the Gunslinger. Ever the aggressor—always a risk taker. Sometimes great, other times awful, but *always* highly entertaining.

22

Jerry Kramer (2018)

Overcoming Adversity; "You Can If You Will"
(Packers Years 1958–1968)

The success stories of many NFL players boggle the mind. Bart Starr was a 17th-round draft choice. Willie Wood was a free agent. Name the player, and each has his own special tale to tell in overcoming adversity to attain gridiron acclaim. While many Hall of Famers buck the odds to wind up in Canton, plenty of additional players, including first-round draft picks, never measure up to the tremendous potential general managers saw in them when they were drafted. What makes the difference? That's hard to say, but it undoubtedly has something to do with the inner make-up of a person ... how some persevere, while others give up.

The story of how Packers standout guard Jerry Kramer, the only member of the NFL 50th Anniversary All-Time Team not in Canton, waited, ... pushed on, and then persevered some more, before he was finally enshrined in the Pro Football Hall of Fame in 2018, is perhaps his best-known tale. Reasons why it took so long for induction have never been clear, but the imperfect, subjective process in which football beat writers nominate players for Canton has been cited as a contributing factor.

When it finally came in 2018, the ceremony featured the induction saying, "you can, if you will." As the story goes, Dusty Klein, Kramer's high school line coach, told him, "Son, you've got big hands, big feet—one of these days you'll grow into them. You're going to be a helluva player one day." Then Klein said to Kramer, "You can if you will."[1]

Of course, there's also the famous block he made on the Cowboys' Jethro Pugh to spring Bart Starr's one-yard sneak in the Ice Bowl. "People want to always talk about that play. But what personifies the character and make-up of that football team was the drive," he said, referring to the 12-play, 68-yard march to win the title. "That was a perfect example of what those teams were all about."[2]

22. Jerry Kramer (2018)

But battling subzero temperatures and a lengthy Hall wait weren't the only times Kramer overcame adversity in his football career. Not by a long shot. But some background is in order first.

Jerry Kramer Highlights

4th round draft pick (Green Bay, 1958)
5× NFL champion (1961, 1962, 1965–1967)
2× Super Bowl champion (I, II)
5× First-team All-Pro (1960, 1962, 1963, 1966, 1967)
2× Second-team All-Pro (1961, 1968)
3× Pro Bowl (1962, 1963, 1967)
NFL 1960s All-Decade Team
NFL 50th Anniversary All-Time Team
Green Bay Packers Hall of Fame (1975)
Pro Football HOF (2018)
Noted for throwing crucial block in 1967 championship win over Dallas

Prolific author:
Instant Replay (with Dick Schaap, 1968)
Farewell to Football (1969)
Winning is the Only Thing (1970)
Distant Replay (1985)
Locker Room (CD set, 2005)
Re-released *Instant Replay* (2006)
You Can If You Will: The Jerry Kramer Story (documentary and CD, 2021)

Born in Jordan, Montana, Jerry Kramer moved with his parents and five siblings to Utah and then to Sandpoint, in northern Idaho, when he was in the fourth grade. After graduating from Sandpoint High School in 1954, he accepted a football scholarship to the University of Idaho to play for new head coach Skip Stanley.

Kramer was a standout two-way player for the Vandals, along with teammate Wayne Walker of Boise, a future All-Pro linebacker with the Detroit Lions. Kramer also lettered in track and field, throwing the shot and discus. Following the 1957 season, the Idaho teammates played on the winning side in the East-West Shrine Game in San Francisco, as the underdog West team upset the East, 27–13.

Kramer, besides kicking three conversions, played a steady game in the offensive line, "helping open holes through the heavier East line for the West's running backs, [Gerald] Nesbitt and Jimmy Shofner."[3] The same *Lewiston Morning Tribune* article lauded the play of, among others, Walker, who blocked a Lou Michaels conversion attempt.

At the College All-Star game in Chicago, the collegiate standouts defeated the defending NFL champion Detroit Lions, 35–19. Kramer and Walker again played key roles. The *Tribune* noted that the collegians' defensive line did a surprising job in bottling up the pro attack, "but Kramer drew the most notice for the holes he opened up for the speedy all-star backs."[4]

In helping the college all-stars upset the champion Lions in 1958, Kramer was clearly ready for the pros. The Packers selected him in the fourth round (39th pick overall). He was part of the most heralded draft class in the Packers' history, a haul that also included Michigan State linebacker Dan Currie in the first round, LSU fullback Jim Taylor in round two, and Ray Nitschke of Illinois in the third round. Taylor, Nitschke, and Kramer, of course, all ended up in Canton. And Currie was a pretty fair player himself who was traded to the Los Angeles Rams in 1965 for wide receiver Carroll Dale.

In spite of a roster that Packers scout and personnel director Jack Vainisi was loading with talent, the Packers finished a miserable 1–10–1 in Kramer's rookie season. Even to this day, the atrocious season befuddles Kramer. "Bart, Forrest, Paul, we had some players," said Kramer.[5]

Following the horrid campaign, the Packers fired easygoing coach Ray "Scooter" McLean and hired strict, volatile New York Giants assistant Vince Lombardi. He let it be known that there were planes and trains leaving from Green Bay each day, and if players didn't perform, they would be on one of them.

In fact, that was exactly what Kramer thought would happen after one fateful practice, when Lombardi laid into him for his lack of attention. He remembers Lombardi yelling, "Mister, the concentration period of a college student is five minutes, high school is three minutes, a kindergartner is 30 seconds. You don't have that? Where does that put you?"[6]

Practice didn't last much longer, and a dejected Kramer headed into the locker room, arriving roughly 30 minutes before the receivers were done for the day.

> I'm sitting there by myself, wondering if my football career is over. What am I going to do with the rest of my life? You couldn't feel any lower than I did.
>
> I'm sitting there for what seemed like forever, and Coach walks over to where I'm sitting at the end of the locker room. He comes up behind me, messes up my hair and says, "Son, one of these days you're going to be the best guard in football."[7]

It was just the vote of confidence he needed from his demanding mentor. "That statement gave me a new feeling about myself," Kramer told writer Bob Fox. "From that point on, I really became a player. That positive reinforcement by him at that moment changed my whole career."[8] It was a turning point for Jerry Kramer in overcoming adversity.

22. Jerry Kramer (2018)

Encouragement from Vince Lombardi following a tongue-lashing from the coach proved to be the spark and turning point in his career that Jerry Kramer needed. A perennial All-Pro, Kramer was named to the NFL 50th Anniversary All-Time Team in 1969, a year after his retirement from the Packers (Mark Forseth Collection).

The guards played a crucial role in the Packers' bread-and-butter play, the "Green Bay sweep" or power sweep. Paul Hornung or Jim Taylor would get the handoff from quarterback Bart Starr and take off around end at roughly three-quarters speed in order to give Kramer and left guard Fuzzy Thurston time to get ahead of the back to block. Speed, timing, and the running back's instincts for knowing when to cut upfield (especially Hornung) were keys in making the play work.

The 1961 season was the first in which the Packers wore their trademark "G" logo on their helmets. They posted an 11–3 regular season record to win the Western Conference title for the second straight year, earning the right to face Lombardi's former team, the Giants, for the championship. Playing in Green Bay in a championship game for the first time, the ecstatic Packer faithful witnessed a 37–0 drubbing of the New Yorkers.

The contest was also noteworthy for Lombardi phoning President Kennedy to pardon Hornung, Nitschke, and Boyd Dowler from their military service to play in the championship tilt. Kramer wasn't as fortunate. He badly injured an ankle in late October and was sidelined for the remainder of the season. Forrest Gregg took over at right guard, and Norm Masters started at right tackle in place of Gregg.

It didn't seem possible that the Packers could top their 1961 championship season, yet they did. Green Bay outscored its first three opponents, 100–7, and was challenged just twice in streaming to a 10–0 start. The only blemish on the terrific campaign came in a 26–14 setback at Detroit on Thanksgiving, an annual tilt between the two teams that the Packers usually lost. "I think we'll be a better football team for having lost this one," Lombardi said after the game. "That business about an undefeated season was a lot of bunk. Nobody in his right mind could have expected it."[9]

The Packers outscored their foes, 415–148, a scoring margin of nearly 3-to-1. Everyone, it seemed, had career years in 1962. Taylor led the league with 1,474 yards rushing and 19 touchdowns, Starr completed 62.5 percent of his passes and finished with a 90.7 passer rating. Max McGee and Boyd Dowler combined for 98 receptions, an impressive total in a largely running era. The offensive line was unequaled. The defense allowed a miserly 10.6 points per contest and forced an unbelievable 59 turnovers, more than four a game.

While starting at right guard, Kramer was also the team's placekicker in 1962, 1963, and part of 1968. It was a role that proved pivotal as the Packers traveled to New York to face the Giants, winners of the Eastern Conference, for the 1962 title. (In those days, the championship game alternated between conference winners, meaning the 13–1 Packers had to travel to the Big Apple since they had hosted the contest the year before.) The contest was played in brutal conditions at Yankee Stadium, with winds gusting up to 40 miles per hour and a game-time temperature of 13 degrees.

Embarrassed the year before, the New Yorkers were out for blood, and the game was especially physical on both sides. Green Bay led, 3–0, on a 26-yard first quarter field goal by Kramer. The Packers extended their lead to 10–0 in the second stanza on a seven-yard run by Taylor.

22. Jerry Kramer (2018)   177

In the third quarter, the Giants pulled to within 10–7 on a blocked punt they recovered in the end zone. Kramer later booted a second field goal, a 29-yarder, but the Packers still only led, 13–7, heading into the fourth frame. Yet another three-point kick by the Packers guard, this time

The Green Bay Packers were riding high in the early 1960s, capturing back-to-back NFL titles in 1961 and 1962. Then misfortune struck both the team and Jerry Kramer. Green Bay finished second in 1963 and 1964, and the Packers' star right guard became seriously ill in 1964, missing nearly the entire season. It turned out that pieces from a splintered board stemming from a boyhood accident had remained lodged in his body for 11 years (Mark Forseth Collection).

from 30 yards out, extended the lead to 16–7. "That was huge. That gave us a two-score lead," Kramer said.[10] It not only was an important field goal, it was also a difficult one for Kramer under the windy conditions. "I had to aim 10 yards outside the right goal post in order for the ball to [come back and] go through the uprights."[11]

After the Packers secured a second straight championship, the players voted him the game ball. Ray Nitschke took the MVP Award and won a Corvette. "I got a ball. He got a car. I guess that's the life of a lineman," Kramer quipped.[12]

A newspaper account noted that two costly Giants fumbles, "both recovered by Green Bay linebacker Ray Nitschke, set up the Taylor touchdown and one of Kramer's field goals."[13]

If 1961 and 1962 were Camelot for the Packers, the following two years would prove to be nightmares in many respects. As a team, Green Bay had to settle for second-place finishes in 1963 and 1964. Hornung was suspended for gambling and missed the entire 1963 campaign.

Kramer, meanwhile, overcame a series of accidents and health issues prior to and during his NFL career, the most serious of which occurred in 1964. He played the first two games, complained of abdominal pains, and missed the remainder of the season. He was diagnosed at the Mayo Clinic with actinomycosis, a rare affliction characterized by the formation of painful abscesses that can occur in various areas, including the abdominal tract.

How he got the disease remained a mystery for months. Eventually, during surgery, doctors discovered wood splinters that he had amazingly been carrying around in his body for 11 years. When it happened, Kramer was living on the family ranch in Sandpoint, Idaho. "I really wanted to go swimming, but a calf had gotten away. I was trying to catch it so I could go [swimming]," he recalled. "I was reaching for its tail when the calf jumped on a board and it splintered."[14]

Pieces of the splintered board lodged in his body. Several days after surgery to remove them, the doctor went back to the Kramer house and, when trying to fit the board back together, discovered a big piece missing. Surgeons went back in and removed more splinters. They thought they had them all, only to be proven wrong a decade later, when Kramer's abdominal pains indicated something was amiss.

In May 1965, surgeons extracted three splinters, two of which were four inches long and one-half inch around that were still stuck in his intestine.[15] Kramer recalled how fortunate he had been all those years. "One [of the splinters] came within a half-inch of coming out my back," he said about how close he came to having a major medical issue, if not dying, years earlier.[16]

Recovering from a serious operation takes time for anyone, but a professional football player like Kramer faced a lengthy ordeal getting back to full health and his customary spot at right guard. All told, the multiple surgeries led to removal of a tumor in his intestine, weight loss (he was below 200 pounds at one point), and a colostomy before the last of the pieces were taken out. "'Playing football again was the next step.' Lombardi said, 'We'll take care of your [medical] bills, but can we count on you [to play]?' I said, 'Coach, I'm ready to go,' but he wasn't going to let me practice at first."[17]

And so Kramer trotted out *on defense* so he could at least get on the field. That was step one. The second involved doing the necessary running and drills. Kramer's new teammate, Don Chandler, a placekicker the Packers had acquired from the Giants, helped him complete the exercises that Kramer could not yet do. "I'd run a few laps; he'd run the rest. Finally, I was able to do all of the calisthenics after 37 days, and I was back on offense. Although I didn't start right away."[18]

Kramer estimates that Chandler's willingness to help him until he was more physically ready saved his career. Another example of overcoming adversity.

The wait for both the Packers, and Kramer, proved worth it, as the Packers were set to embark on history, capturing three straight championships, defeating the Cleveland Browns for the 1965 title. Following the "three-peat," something no NFL team has done since, Kramer roomed with star defensive end Willie Davis for the 1968 season, Kramer's last with the Packers. At the time, a white player rooming with a black one was rare in the NFL, but it was a non-issue on the color blind Packers.

"Willie was a bright guy, and he was funny. He went to college six years to earn his MBA degree," said Kramer, noting that no topic was off-limits, including racial issues. "He asked me one time, 'J, do you believe in white power?' Surprised, I said, 'No, Willie, I don't. Do *you* believe in black power?' 'No, J, I don't. I tell you what I do believe, I believe in GREEN power.'"[19]

The pair remained close friends until Davis's death in 2020. Davis, Wood, Starr, Taylor, Nitschke, Gregg, and others—all gone. And it never gets any easier, Kramer said. "The closeness, respect, love, and appreciation we had for each other; we were like brothers. It's painful to lose any of them. It's like losing a family member"[20]

The losses continue with each passing year. "It makes you check on your standing with the man upstairs. That is for sure," Kramer said. Is Lombardi rebuilding a powerful team "upstairs"? "I'll bet we could beat the Bears," he laughed.[21]

23

James Lofton (2003)

Shining Light in Dim Era
(Packers Years 1978–1986)

If you're roughly 40 or younger, you probably take very good Green Bay Packers football for granted. In the 1990s, the Packers had only two losing seasons, one .500 season (8–8 in 1999), and a Super Bowl championship (1996). Subsequent decades brought similar results. The 2000s likewise fielded just two losing teams and one .500 campaign (8–8 in 2006). More of the same occurred in the most recent decade: two losing years (7–9 in 2017 and 6–9–1 in 2018), and one championship season (2010). And in only ten of those *30* years did the Packers *fail* to make the playoffs. It is true that painful losses are tough, but fans can take solace that at least the Packers are usually post-season participants.

But it wasn't always like that. The two decades following the Lombardi years in the 1960s marked a dramatic fall from grace for the once-powerful Packers, who captured five championships in that Camelot-like decade. Green Bay recorded just two *winning* seasons in the 1970s and *one* playoff appearance (1972). Losing continued in the 1980s, which also saw the Packers post just two *winning* teams (10–6 in 1989 and 5–3–1 in a strike-shortened 1982), and a *single* playoff appearance (1982). The Packers were maddeningly mediocre in the 1980s with four break-even, 8–8 campaigns in the decade.

It was that type of atmosphere that James Lofton found himself in when the California native was drafted by Green Bay in the first round with the sixth overall pick in the 1978 draft. Lofton's gridiron success could trace its roots to his talents as an accomplished track and field standout. At Stanford, he won the long jump at the 1978 NCAA Track and Field Championships with a leap of 26 feet, 11¾ inches. A sprinter of note, Lofton timed a personal best 20.5 seconds in 200 meters. "Impressed by his speed and fluid motion as a track-and-field athlete," it wasn't long before Stanford coach

23. James Lofton (2003)

Bill Walsh soon made Lofton "the centerpiece of his Cardinal [sic] passing attack."[1]

JAMES LOFTON HIGHLIGHTS

1st round draft pick (Green Bay, 1978)
8× Pro Bowl (1978, 1980–1985, 1991)
First-team All-Pro (1981)
3× Second-team All-Pro (1980, 1982, 1983)
First player to eclipse 14,000 yards receiving
NFL 1980s All-Decade Team
Green Bay Packers Hall of Fame (1999)
Pro Football HOF (2003)

Playing career:
Green Bay Packers (1978–1986)
Los Angeles Raiders (1987–1988)
Buffalo Bills (1989–1992)
Los Angeles Rams (1993)
Philadelphia Eagles (1993)

Broadcasting:
NFL analyst for Westwood One
Co-host, Sirius XM NFL Radio
CBS, Packers TV Network

At 6-foot-3, 194 pounds and with exceptional speed, Lofton caught 53 passes for 931 yards and 12 touchdowns his senior year at Stanford. He was a second-team All-American, a member of Theta Delta Chi fraternity, and earned a bachelor's degree in industrial engineering in 1978. In fact, had it not been for Bill Walsh recognizing Lofton's potential, he may well have pursued a career in that field.

It would seem that Lofton would not have minded. "What would have been really great," he mused in a *Sport* interview, "is if I had met the guys from Apple [Computer], maybe my sophomore year [at Stanford], and hooked up with them. That would have been more fun than playing football."[2]

While Green Bay had not posted a winning season in six years, Lofton was clearly not disappointed by the pick. "I'm really kind of happy about the Packers taking me," said Lofton at the time. "I thought it would be either Buffalo or Green Bay, and my initial preference was Green Bay. I thought I would like the lifestyle there a little better."[3]

The first-round selection marked a meteoric rise up draft boards for Lofton, who thought he might have gone undrafted the previous season, until an All-American year at Stanford and MVP honors in the Senior Bowl cemented his status as a top pick.

Blessed with blazing speed and plenty of size (6'3", 194), the gazelle-like James Lofton was a nightmare for opposing defenses. Here, the Packers' star receiver heads upfield, ready to elude a trio of Tampa Bay Buccaneers. Lofton was also very intelligent, earning a degree in engineering from Stanford (Pro Football Hall of Fame).

Despite the losing records at the time, hope sprang eternal for Packers fans, especially when coach and general manager Bart Starr brought in talent like Lofton and Michigan linebacker John Anderson, a Waukesha, Wisconsin, native, selected later in the first round in 1978. Linebacker Mike Douglass of San Diego State proved to be a steal in round five. (Both would eventually be named to the Packers Hall of Fame.)

Walsh, hired by the San Francisco 49ers in 1979, was effusive in his praise of Lofton. "James will be one of the major factors in the NFL next year," he stated, referring to 1978. "I predict a great rookie year for him. He'll be outstanding almost immediately."[4]

He was just that. Lofton caught 46 balls for 818 yards (a blistering 17.8 average), six scores, and a spot on the All-Rookie team. The scorching per-catch average was an indicator of the deep threat the gazelle-like Lofton would remain throughout his storied career. The rest of his rookie numbers would not be outstanding first-year stats now, but 1978 was the first year in which defensive players couldn't bump receivers beyond five yards of the line of scrimmage. This meant 1978 was the initial step in the direction toward today's pass-crazy league.

(It should be pointed out that David Whitehurst, not Lynn Dickey, was the Packers' quarterback that season. Green Bay also fared well running the football, with Terdell Middleton rushing for 1,116 yards, sixth-best in the league.)

Lofton's rookie year was also a respectable one for the Packers, who registered an 8–7–1 record, their first winning season since 1972. Green Bay got off to a torrid 6–1 start but stumbled down the stretch and lost out to the Minnesota Vikings on a tiebreaker for the division crown.

The next season brought incremental increases as Lofton snared 54 passes for 968 yards, although his touchdowns dipped from six to four. As a team, the Packers slipped to a disappointing 5–11. The losses took their toll on Lofton, who was used to winning. First, he had words with Starr after the Packers lost to the Vikings in overtime. Then, booed after fumbling a fourth-quarter pass, he gave Green Bay fans a middle-fingered salute during a loss to the New York Jets. "It was a bad time," he stated. "I was rebelling against losing. I came back that second year [1979] expecting things to get better, and when they didn't, I became frustrated."[5]

When Lofton discovered that anger didn't make him play better, he knew he had to change, which he did after meeting Beverly Fanning later that season. With someone to talk to and be himself with, Lofton mellowed out. "I don't have to be like those guys who go out and smash up bars when they're frustrated," he said.[6]

The following campaign—1980—proved to be Lofton's breakout year. He snatched 71 passes for 1,226 yards (17.3 average). He was named Second team All-Pro and selected to the Pro Bowl for the second time.

All the more impressive was how effortless the graceful Lofton made it all seem. This was largely due to his quick, soft hands and long stride that allowed him to get so far past defensive backs that many of his receptions were uncontested. There were times he actually had to slow down and wait for the ball.

Number 80 also used his size to his advantage. He was frighteningly adept at getting his long frame in front of the defender and then turning upfield.

Slowly but surely, Starr got more help for his sometimes one-man offense. The addition of John Jefferson in a 1981 trade with San Diego meant opposing defenses couldn't focus solely on Lofton. Paul Coffman also emerged as a three-time Pro Bowl tight end during that period. The 1982 season marked a rare return to the playoffs, the Packers' first at Lambeau since the Ice Bowl, and their now-potent offense blasted the St. Louis Cardinals, 41–16. Lofton caught a 20-yard touchdown pass.

Green Bay's post-season came to an end in the second round, when the host Dallas Cowboys notched a 37–26 victory. Lofton shined in defeat with five catches for 109 yards and a touchdown, and a 71-yard TD run on a reverse. (One shudders to think how an offensive coordinator would get Lofton in space in today's ever-expanding offensive repertoire.)

The Packers' offense peaked in 1983 when they scored a team-record (at the time) 429 points. Lofton, Jefferson, and Coffman snared 26 of quarterback Lynn Dickey's league-leading 32 touchdown passes. The highlight was a thrilling, 48–47 win over the defending Super Bowl champion Washington Redskins on a Monday night at Lambeau Field.

But the Packers' defense was usually about as bad as the offense was good, which meant eight wins was as many victories as the Packers would post in that era. Dickey himself later said that one reason he was willing to risk so many interceptions (29 in 1983) was because he did not feel confident that the defense could hold any lead, which meant he felt like the Packers had to score on nearly every possession.

Perhaps Green Bay didn't win as many games as it should have in the 1980s, but with a high-octane offense, they were always a fun team to watch. The centerpiece of the offensive assault, however, was still Lofton, as the deep-ball artist averaged a blistering 22.4 yards per grab in 1983 and 22.0 in 1984.

Amazingly, Lofton never caught more than 71 balls in a single season—almost undoubtedly, he would snare 30 more passes a year in today's game. Still, there is something to be said for the *quality* of a receiver's catches, and not just the *quantity*. The recollection of Lofton streaking wide-open downfield, running like a deer, is etched in the memories of Packers fans. Those same images probably still give now-retired defensive backs nightmares!

The *quantity* of catches might be the name of the game in today's NFL, but it didn't make sense for the Packers to send #80 underneath to catch simple five- and 10-yard hitch routes over the middle when they had a thoroughbred who could attack deep. What's more, Lofton surprisingly never posted more than eight receiving touchdowns in a season. In the NFL of the 21st century, with its more wide-open offenses, he would have found the end zone more often than when he played, but it's mostly a moot point.

Fame and fortune aside, all was not rosy for Lofton during his Packers career. A 1984 incident would begin tarnishing his reputation in Titletown, when he and teammate Eddie Lee Ivery were accused by a white exotic dancer of demanding sex in the dressing room of a Milwaukee night club. Both were fined $500 for trespassing.[7]

Two years later, a white woman in a Green Bay bar claimed that Lofton forced her into a stairwell and demanded sex. The NFL suspended him just prior to the end of the 1986 season after he was charged with second-degree sexual assault.

Forrest Gregg, who was now Lofton's coach, and former coach Starr came to court every day in support of Lofton. Phil McConkey, a Giants receiver and former teammate, also felt the star receiver was innocent. "The guy's not guilty of anything as far as I'm concerned. He is a good person and a good family man."[8]

Although he was found not guilty, Lofton's reputation had been sufficiently smeared that the Packers felt they had little choice but to trade him, and he was dealt to the Los Angeles Raiders for two draft choices. "Obviously, I would have liked to have ended my career here in Green Bay differently, but under the circumstances, I can accept the way that Judge Parins [Robert Parins, Packers president] acted," Lofton told the *Los Angeles Times* in 1987. "I think we all learned lessons and it doesn't have to be because of my behavior."[9]

During Lofton's nine-year Packers career, he passed legendary receiver Don Hutson in total catches (530–488) and yards (9,656–7,848), totals that still rank fourth and second, respectively, in Packers annals.

While the trade meant returning to his native California, his two years

James Lofton, shown here taking a breather on the Packers bench, had the most productive seasons in his career while in a Green Bay uniform (1978–1986). During that time, he passed legendary receiver Don Hutson in number of catches (530–488) and yards (9,656–7,991), totals that still rank high in team annals (Mark Forseth Collection).

with the Raiders were largely forgettable ones. Lofton's catches dropped from 64 with the Packers in 1986 to 41 in 1987 and dipped still further to 28 grabs the following campaign. Following the two nondescript years (for him) the Raiders cut Lofton, and he was picked up as a reserve by the Buffalo Bills, where he made a paltry eight catches in 1989. Lofton's career was clearly at a crossroads.

Buffalo's decision to acquire the aging star for their explosive "K-Gun" offense, led by quarterback Jim Kelly, reaped dividends the following year. In 1990, Lofton latched onto 35 passes for 712 yards, and another remarkable 20.3 average per catch.

The following season was even better. At age 35, he snared 57 passes for 1,072 yards—in the process becoming the oldest player in league history to register 1,000 receiving yards in a season. That same year, he recorded a career-best 220 receiving yards in a game against the Cincinnati Bengals. His often-inspirational play earned him his eighth Pro Bowl bid.[10] "The Bills' elder statesman looked like the Lofton of old with his deep speed and uncanny ability to come down with spectacular over-the-shoulder catches," wrote Ralph Mancini.[11]

Of course, individual statistics aren't everything; star athletes play first and foremost for a chance to win a championship, and Lofton finally got that opportunity with the Bills. He brought a measure of maturity to the youthful Bills "and their locker room bickering. The team warmly accepted him, and it showed."[12]

Buffalo pasted his former team, the Raiders, 51–3, to capture the AFC title and the right to face the New York Giants in Super Bowl XXV. Lofton caught a single pass for 61 yards in the Bills' heartbreaking 20–19 loss when Buffalo kicker Scott Norwood missed a 47-yard field goal in the waning seconds that would have won the game.

Lofton and Buffalo coach Marv Levy "held hands in watchful anticipation. Then they wilted."[13] While it was a crushing loss for Lofton and the rest of the Bills, the truth was that he had known much worse adversity in his decorated career.

While not as prolific the following year, the aging receiver still grabbed 51 passes for 786 yards. However, Lofton did make a bigger impact in Super Bowl XXVI, catching seven balls for 92 yards. But Buffalo could not overcome a 24–0 deficit to Washington and lost, 37–24.

It proved to be Lofton's swan song as the Bills released him the following year. He went to training camp with his former team, the Los Angeles Raiders, in July but was released during the last roster cuts.

Lofton played three games for the Rams in 1993 before hooking on with the Eagles for the last 10 games of the year, "culminating with the final regular-season game against the San Francisco 49ers, winning in overtime.

In fact, I caught a pass, my last reception, to set up the game-winning field goal."[14] "So, over 12 months, I wore four uniforms ... that's when I knew the writing was on the wall to retire."[15]

Of all his statistics, the most amazing was that Lofton averaged 20 yards or more per catch in five seasons, leading the league in 1983 and 1984 with averages of 22.4 and 22 yards, respectively. Extremely durable, Lofton holds the distinction of being the first NFL player to score a touchdown in the 1970s, 1980s, and 1990s.

Lofton's longevity was a reflection of his tireless work ethic and professionalism. Former coach Marv Levy summed up what Lofton meant to his team: "He was a true gentleman and a great leader. There was no showboat in him, no hot dog in him. He did everything with class."[16]

While Lofton ended his career in a different uniform, it should be remembered that nine of his 16 years (more than half)—and his best seasons at that—were spent in Green Bay. He was the first Packer after the Lombardi era to be enshrined in Canton.

In 2018, 15 years after his Hall induction, it was announced Lofton would partner with Kevin Harlan as a color analyst on pre-season games for the Packers Television Network. Maybe Thomas Wolfe was wrong. Maybe you *can* go home again.

24

Dave Robinson (2013)

*Trailblazing Linebacker
(Packers Years 1963–1972)*

As of this writing, there are 31 linebackers in the Pro Football Hall of Fame. They include great outside 'backers such as Lawrence Taylor, Derrick Thomas, Bobby Bell, Jack Ham, and Derrick Brooks. Taylor quickly comes to mind as a trailblazer at the position. Who might be another? Surrounded by other Hall of Fame talent on dominant Green Bay Packers defenses of the 1960s, the name "Dave Robinson" likely would not come up. But it should. In fact, it's been said that he *was* Lawrence Taylor before there was a Lawrence Taylor, just with a different scheme and with *much* less fanfare.

"Robby" was a terrific athlete and physical specimen. In an era when some linebackers went no bigger than 210 pounds, Robinson weighed 245. Not only was he a big linebacker for that time, but he was also fast and tough. Packers teammate Herb Adderley said, "In my opinion, there was no outside linebacker in either the NFL or the AFL who was smarter or better than Dave Robinson. He made very few mistakes and would never make the same mistake twice in a game."[1]

Adderley and Robinson had a lot in common. Both were from the North (Adderley was from Pennsylvania, Robinson from New Jersey), and both played different positions in college than they did in the professional ranks. Adderley was a standout running back at Michigan State, while Robinson played tight end and defensive end at Penn State. Both were first-round draft picks (Adderley in 1961, Robinson in 1963), almost unheard-of at the time for players of their color, but racism was something Lombardi wouldn't tolerate partially because, as an Italian American, he had experienced bigotry himself.

There weren't a lot of black players in the NFL in the 1950s and early 1960s. This meant that—in addition to his size and speed—Robinson was also a trailblazer as one of the first black linebackers in the league.

24. Dave Robinson (2013)

Dave Robinson Highlights

1st round draft choice (1963, Penn State)
2× Super Bowl champion (I, II)
3× NFL champion (1965–1967)
3× Pro Bowl (1966, 1967, 1969)
First-team All-Pro (1967)
2× Second-team All-Pro (1968, 1969)
NFL 1960s All-Decade Team
Green Bay Packers Hall of Fame (1982)
Pro Football HOF (2013)
First-team All-American (1962)

Playing career:
Green Bay Packers (1963–1972)
Washington Redskins (1973–1974)

Post football career:
Engineer, Campbell's Soup, later Schlitz Brewery
Started his own beer distributorship in Akron, Ohio
Served on the Board of Directors for the Pro Football Hall of Fame

To put that year into perspective, Packers biographer Bob Fox points out that the Civil Rights Act wasn't passed until 1964, the year *after* Robinson was drafted by the Packers. He added that the rival American Football League (AFL), which began play in 1960, had a number of black linebackers (Robinson's position).[2]

While late-1940s–1950s Cleveland Browns star (and future Hall of Famer) Marion Motley was better known as a fullback, football historian Ralph Hickok points out that the African American Motley also played linebacker, a position he played exclusively in his last season with Pittsburgh in 1955.[3]

The point is that there weren't many black athletes in predominantly white schools (or sports leagues) at a time when segregation was still the norm, and the sting of discrimination was not unusual, Robinson among the victims. He grew up in a small town in New Jersey, and it was on family trips to Atlantic City that he was rudely introduced to segregation. There were two big piers in the vacation mecca—the Million-Dollar Pier and the Steel Pier—the latter, he quickly learned, was for whites only. He and a friend wandered off to the Claridge Hotel, where they were promptly chased off, as they discovered that blacks weren't allowed there either.

The hotel is a casino today, but the hurt remained fresh in Robinson's mind many years later when he and his wife, Elaine, settled in a nearby community. Elaine wanted to go to the casino, but he replied that he wouldn't "give them a penny."[4]

He wasn't exactly a stranger to segregation at home either. His elementary school was only for blacks, but since Robinson and his friends played

While Dave Robinson's first sport in high school was basketball, he blossomed into an outstanding tight end and defensive end at Penn State, and a first-round draft pick of the Green Bay Packers in 1963. The final step in his playing evolution involved being molded into an All-Pro linebacker with the Packers. He is widely considered a trailblazer at the position (Mark Forseth Collection).

football with some white boys in the neighborhood, he couldn't figure out why they went to different schools.

Desegregation arrived in New Jersey in 1948, but Robinson, a second grader at the time, heard muffled concerns that the black kids might not be able to keep up with the white students academically—although the young Robinson excelled in his studies. (He was one of only 20 blacks in his Moorestown High School class of 400.)

His first sport was basketball, where, as a 6'3" center, he led Moorestown High School to undefeated state championships in 1958 and 1959. His mom did not want him to play football because she didn't want him getting hurt like his older brothers, but eventually she gave in. It was another sport he excelled in, as the Quakers finished 9–0 and won the South Jersey Group 3 championship under coach Pete Monska.

Older brother Frank, a talented offensive guard in his own right who played at Maryland State, encouraged him to further his football career. Dave was bright and more academically than athletically minded, but Frank helped him recognize that he could study *and* continue to compete in sports. In college, he opted for football, where he was a two-way player (tight end and defensive end) at Penn State under fabled coach Rip Engle.

Robinson experienced racism in college. In 1959, he was one of only two black players who suited up for Penn State. In the racially tense South, Robinson became the first black player in a Gator Bowl, in Jacksonville, Florida, on December 30, 1961. He was disappointed to learn he would not start but would enter the game in the second quarter. After the contest, he found out why when coaches gave him the letters they had been withholding. The letters, Robinson learned, threatened violence to black players introduced before the start of the game. "That's why they didn't start me." Robinson said.[5]

While he wasn't without confidence, neither was Robinson sure he was good enough to compete against the very best players. That is, until he fared well against John Mackey of Syracuse and Mike Ditka of Pittsburgh—the iron-tough Ditka in particular. (Both were future HOF tight ends.) "We played on top of each other all day long," Robinson said of his matchups with Mackey, who would go on to star for the Baltimore Colts. "I had to block him, he had to block me."[6]

"My sophomore year, I went one-on-one with Mike Ditka, and we put Mike out of the game," he added. "We had a good day against Mike. He was a dominant defensive end in college."[7] Like Robinson, Ditka played both offense and defense in college.

In 1962, his senior season, Robinson led Penn State to a 9–1 regular-season, snatched 17 passes for 178 yards, and was named a First-team All-America. That same year, when Ditka was selected NFL Rookie of the

Year, Robinson knew for certain he could forge a career as a pro. So it was on to the NFL when Robinson graduated from Penn State with a degree in engineering in 1963.

Robinson was still on the board at the final first-round slot in the 1963 draft, and the Packers happily snapped him up. Joe Paterno, later a legendary head coach at Penn State but an assistant under Engle at the time, knew Lombardi (both hailed from Brooklyn) and advised the Packers coach to draft Robinson.

Even though they were the defending NFL champs, it was no lead-pipe cinch that Robinson would become a Packer. The AFL was just getting off the ground in 1963 and wanted to make a statement by hijacking Green Bay's first-round draft choice. The San Diego Chargers made a huge push for him. But when the bidding got to $38,000, which was big bucks in those days, San Diego was out of money. "Robinson then accepted a two-year, $45,000 deal from Green Bay that included a $15,000 signing bonus. In those days, that was good money."[8]

Lombardi and his prize rookie did not get off to the best start. In those days, the defending NFL champions squared off against a team of College All-Stars in a pre-season contest at Soldier Field in Chicago. It was an opportunity for soon-to-be NFL players to test their mettle against the best. Lombardi's Packers took the game for granted, but when former Wisconsin Badgers stars Ron Vander Kelen and Pat Richter connected on a long touchdown pass, the All-Stars led, 20–10. on their way to a 20–17 upset.

When Packers practice began the following week, Lombardi played game film and went berserk, particularly when it showed All-Star Robinson beating tight end Ron Kramer's block and stoning running back Tom Moore for a loss. "He was just screaming and yelling at Kramer," Robinson stated. "He said, 'How can you let that rookie beat you? He's probably not even going to make the team!' I wasn't sure Lombardi would keep me."[9]

Lombardi may have been steamed about a bunch of collegians beating his mighty Packers, but he was no idiot. Robinson had nothing to worry about.

There was no questioning Robinson's athleticism, but as with Adderley in the beginning, it was unclear what position he would play. The Packers were initially looking for him to replace Kramer, who was nearing the end of a solid career at tight end. "When I played tight end, I hit, too," Robinson pointed out. "When I was at Penn State, we ran more than we passed, and they used to say, 'Dave Robinson out there is like having a third tackle.'"[10]

It's possible Robinson might have revolutionized the tight end position like his collegiate rivals, Mackey and Ditka. He probably could have played defensive end, too, like he did at Penn State. The matter partially sorted itself out when fellow rookies Lionel Aldridge, a 4th-round DE out of Utah State, and Marv Fleming, an 11th-round TE from Utah, appeared very promising and worthy of roster spots. Aldridge, in fact, became the first rookie to start for Lombardi.

But once a need arose for the Packers during training camp, Robinson was moved to linebacker. Veteran Bill Forester, in his last season in 1963, took Robinson under his wing and taught him the ropes, lessons that, as a four-time Pro Bowler, served Robinson well. He became the starting left side linebacker for the Packers in 1964 and remained in that role through 1972.

Great players need to play well not just individually, but also as a unit, and Robinson shined there as well.

> Robinson had a specific job to do for both [Willie] Davis and Adderley. Aldridge said Willie had such small legs he could get an off-season job stomping holes in donuts, so Davis needed Robinson to keep tight ends off his legs. Adderley wanted a clean shot at running backs that were not halted at the line of scrimmage, and Robinson was the man to make it happen. 'I wanted Dave to keep those big guards off me," Adderley said. "I didn't care if it was Jim Brown, Gale Sayers or Leroy Kelly, if I had them one-on-one, they're down."[11]

Robinson delivered. Davis added, "The greatest years I had and the greatest time I had was playing next to Dave Robinson."[12]

While he helped his teammates succeed, Robinson was also a playmaker. There is a big difference between a calculated risk by an intelligent player and the reckless gamble of a gullible one. As he often did, Robinson came up big in a crucial 1965 contest against the archrival Colts at Memorial Stadium in Baltimore. Fog had rolled in, and Colts quarterback Gary Cuozzo had led his team deep in Green Bay territory. He then threw a pass in Robinson's direction. "Robby made a great interception, leaping very high in the air in front of me," Adderley stated, noting that Cuozzo was trying to hit his man, Jimmy Orr, for a crucial first down.[13]

Robinson dashed 87 yards to the Colts' 10-yard line before Lenny Moore tackled him. Bart Starr promptly hit Boyd Dowler with a touchdown pass and took a 21–13 lead into halftime.

Paul Hornung scored a team-record five touchdowns as the Packers posted a 42–27 victory. Playmakers deliver when they are needed most, and one of those leaders was clearly Dave Robinson.

But the most noteworthy play of Robinson's career came the following season in the NFL championship game in Dallas against the Cowboys. The Packers were three-time champs under Lombardi, but success was something new for Dallas and coach Tom Landry, whom Lombardi knew from their days as assistant coaches with the New York Giants. The Cowboys, an expansion team in 1960, posted an abysmal 0–11–1 record their inaugural season. They finally broke through with a 10–3–1 record in 1966 to win the

Eastern Conference and the right to face the defending champion Packers, who were also 10–3–1.

Green Bay scored first on a 17-yard pass from Bart Starr to Elijah Pitts. Mel Renfro fumbled the ensuing kickoff, and rookie Jim Grabowski recovered and rumbled 18 yards for an early 14–0 Packers lead. But the Cowboys came storming back and knotted the score at 14–14 on touchdown runs by Dan Reeves and Don Perkins. A 51-yard bomb from Starr to Carroll Dale and a Dallas field goal gave the Packers a 21–17 lead at intermission.

A 32-yard field goal pulled the hosts within a point, 21–20, but TD tosses from Starr to Boyd Dowler and Max McGee gave Green Bay a two-touchdown lead at 34–20 in the final quarter. The upstart Cowboys refused to go away. Don Meredith and Frank Clarke hooked up on a 68-yard score to make it 34–27. The Packers were unable to run out the clock, and under a heavy rush, Don Chandler's punt traveled just 17 yards, giving Dallas the ball at Green Bay's 47 with just 2:12 remaining.

A costly pass interference penalty against Tom Brown gave the Cowboys a first down at the 2-yard line. Dallas then made a pair of big miscues—an offsides penalty followed by Reeves dropping a second-down pass.

A third-down completion moved the ball back to the 2. Landry, inexplicably, had 185-pound wide receiver Bob Hayes, and not Clarke, lined up against Robinson on fourth down. "Hayes couldn't have blocked me if he'd had a twin with him," Robinson said.[14]

If not for Starr's Ice Bowl sneak the following season, the ensuing play might have been the most memorable in Packers history. After easily brushing off Hayes, Robinson draped himself over Meredith, who somehow got off a wobbly pass, which Brown picked off in the end zone, and the Packers escaped with a 34–27 win.

Lombardi gave Robinson a "minus 2" on the play for being out of position—he wasn't supposed to be blitzing—but later gave him a big hug on the plane ride home. "As a teacher, Vince wanted me to understand how it was designed and what I did wrong. But it was a play that was meant to be, I guess."[15]

In 2004, he was named to the Professional Football Researchers Association's Hall of Very Good in the organization's second HOVG class. "I wanted to make it very badly at one time," Robinson stated. "I served on the Hall of Fame board for many years and had to take my name off the ballot. Then it went back on as an old-timer and people had kind of forgotten about me."[16]

Finally, after the lengthy wait, Robinson was the 11th member of Vince Lombardi's championship Green Bay Packers, including the coach himself, to be enshrined in the Pro Football Hall of Fame in 2013. He was the sixth Nittany Lion to be honored in Canton, joining Pittsburgh greats Jack Ham,

24. Dave Robinson (2013)

Franco Harris, former Packer August "Mike" Michalske, Lenny Moore, and Mike Munchak.

But the good news also marked a very bittersweet time for Robinson. His wife, Elaine, died after complications from a stroke in 2007. (Richard also passed away in 2007, and Robert died in 1967.)

His remaining son, David, asked to be his Hall of Fame presenter. "He wants to represent his mother and his two brothers. So, when I'm on that stage, it'll be me, the bust and my entire family."[17]

25

Reggie White (2006)

Leaving a Legacy On and Off the Field (Packers Years 1993–1998)

Death and taxes are the two constants in life, and sports lovers are often hard hit when a favorite athlete dies. It's usually a cruel reminder that the athletic greats we adored really *had* grown old, and they *did* in fact play a long time ago. Jim Taylor, Forrest Gregg, and then Bart Starr passed away as the author was wrapping up *A Century of Excellence: 100 Greatest Packers of All Time*. While the author wrote this book for McFarland, Packers greats Herb Adderley and Paul Hornung died, and two more Hall of Famers, Willie Wood and Willie Davis, passed away shortly before that. Tragic, and yet, given their ages, not totally surprising. Sad? Yes. Shocking? Not really.

Then there are players who left us much too soon. Packers Hall of Fame defensive tackle Henry Jordan died of a heart attack in 1977 at the young age of 42. Legendary middle linebacker Ray Nitschke was 61 when he passed away in 1998. More recently, Hall of Fame linebacker Kevin Greene, considered one of the fiercest pass rushers of all time—and a one-time Packers coach—died December 21, 2020, at age 58.

Like Greene, tragic *and* surprising was also the case when Reggie White passed away the day after Christmas, December 26, 2004, at age 43. "Dr. Michael Sullivan, of the Mecklenburg County [NC] Medical Examiner's Office, ruled that White died from a cardiac arrhythmia, an irregular heartbeat that was caused by the complications from sarcoidosis."[1] (Sarcoidosis forms inflamed cells in important bodily organs.)

"A 43-year-old is not supposed to die in his sleep," said his pastor, Keith Johnson. "It was not only unexpected, it was a complete surprise. Reggie wasn't a sick man."[2]

Reggie White Highlights

4th pick in supplemental draft (Memphis, 1984)
Super Bowl champion (XXXI)

2× NFL Defensive Player of the Year (1987, 1998)
2× NFL sacks leader (1987, 1998)
13× Pro Bowl (1986–1998)
8× First-team All-Pro (1986–1991, 1995, 1998)
5× Second-team All-Pro (1992–1994, 1996, 1997)
NFL 1990s All-Decade Team
NFL 1980s All-Decade Team
Pro Football Hall of Fame (2006)
Green Bay Packers HOF (2006)
Philadelphia Eagles HOF (2005)
NFL 75th Anniversary All-Time Team
NFL 100th Anniversary All-Time Team
Green Bay Packers #92 retired
Philadelphia Eagles #92 retired
Tennessee Volunteers #92 retired

Playing career:
Memphis Showboats (1984–1985)
Philadelphia Eagles (1985–1992)
Green Bay Packers (1993–1998)
Carolina Panthers (2000)
Career sacks: 198.0 (second all-time behind Bruce Smith)
Reggie White Way in Green Bay named in his honor
Died: December 26, 2004 (Cornelius, North Carolina)

While reports were not definitive, sleep apnea was deemed as likely playing a role in his death: "A study has shown the disorder is unusually common among NFL linemen. Researchers say it could become more common as players' size keeps increasing."[3] According to the *New England Journal of Medicine*, the study of more than 300 NFL players revealed that the overall sleep apnea rate of 14 percent was "five times higher than males of similar ages. Among linemen, the rate was 34%."[4]

Even in death, White's legacy as a humanitarian lived on through his widow, Sara White. In conjunction with the Sleep Wellness Institute, she founded the Reggie White Sleep Disorders Research and Education Foundation. White's death was a wakeup call for many about the dangers of sleep apnea, including the author, who was diagnosed with the condition in 2017.

The defensive star was also well known for his strong faith and evangelization efforts. "During his playing days, he preached at every opportunity. … He even had a habit, after mowing over some opposing offensive lineman, to go back, help him up and say, 'Jesus loves you.'"[5]

White was raised by a deeply religious mother and grandparents who regularly attended a Baptist church. "My grandmother—she never forced

As young as age 12, Reggie White told his mother that he wanted to be a minister and pro football player when he grew up. Undoubtedly, many offensive linemen over the years wished the nearly unblockable star wouldn't have made good on the latter promise. He recorded 198 sacks in his career, second all-time behind Bruce Smith (Mark Wallenfang).

us to go to church or anything, but it was just her commitment of going to church that got me interested," White told *Focus on the Family*.[6]

His mother, Thelma, later told *Sports Illustrated* that when White was 12 years old, he declared that he wanted to do two things in life: be a football player and a minister.[7] White began his football career at Howard High School in Chattanooga, where he registered 140 tackles and was rated the number-one college recruit in Tennessee by the *Knoxville News-Sentinel*.

White remained in-state to play college football at the University of Tennessee from 1980 to 1983, where he became involved in the Fellowship of Christian Athletes. He was selected a pre-season All-American heading into the 1982 season but was bothered by an ankle injury, and his productivity dropped off. He still managed to lead the Volunteers in sacks with seven. Determined to improve upon a discouraging junior year, White exploded in his senior season with 100 tackles, 15 sacks, nine tackles for loss, and an interception, according to the *1984 Tennessee Volunteers Football Guide*. By this time, he had acquired the nickname the "Minister of Defense." What's more, his 32 career sacks remained a school record until broken by Derek Barnett in 2016.

In 1984, White signed with the Memphis Showboats of the fledgling United States Football League (USFL). He joined a number of high-profile college stars in the upstart league that included Jim Kelly, Steve Young, and Herschel Walker. According to the Pro Football Hall of Fame, in two seasons with the Showboats, White tallied 23.5 sacks, one safety, and a fumble recovery returned for a touchdown.

When the USFL folded, he took a cut in salary to sign with the Philadelphia Eagles. But it *was* a chance for the budding defensive star to prove just how good he really was. He did just that, terrorizing quarterbacks for eight seasons in Philadelphia. Incredibly, he recorded more sacks (124) than number of games played (121) with the Eagles. White was particularly dominant in the strike-shortened 1987 campaign, when he tallied an unbelievable 21 sacks in just 12 games. A *rare* blend of power, explosiveness, and speed, he followed that up with 18 sacks in 1988. White also forced 11 fumbles and, in 1991, set a record for most passes defended in a season by a defensive lineman with 13, a mark that has since been broken by the Texans' J.J. Watt.

Philadelphia notched five consecutive double-digit win seasons between 1988–1992, but not even White's stellar play could get his team past the divisional round of the playoffs. Disillusioned in the City of Brotherly Love, he was ready to move on, and a landmark ruling would provide the opportunity to do just that.

In 1992, White and a group of NFL players sued the league for its restricted free agency system, "which courts found disregarded antitrust laws. The players won the case and the NFL finally established complete free agency."[8]

"He had his name on the lawsuit and he didn't get one penny," said Gene Upshaw, executive director of the NFL Players Association. "That's just the type of guy he was. His character, his integrity was everything any NFL player should aspire to be."[9]

It was great news for the players, including White, but it sent shivers down the backs of NFL owners, who were used to calling all the shots. Since he could decide where he would play next, he embarked on a whirlwind tour of NFL cities, where his suitors included Washington, San Francisco, and Cleveland.

Free agency seemed to strongly favor the more desirable markets. The task of putting together a competitive team was about to get more difficult in smaller cities, particularly Green Bay. Or so it seemed.

"Among players, Green Bay was depicted as some Russian place where you go and no one ever hears from you," said former NFL tight end Keith Jackson, a first-round draft pick of the Eagles in 1988 who went on to play for the Dolphins and Packers.[10]

White reportedly visited Green Bay as almost an afterthought after checking out Detroit. Other cities could wine and dine Reggie at the finest restaurants. Green Bay offered a local Red Lobster to visit with the former Eagles star. But what the NFL's smallest city *had* was a tradition like no other. He was told that he could go anywhere and be a great player, but in Green Bay he would become a *legend*. That was a selling point. A community with a small black population did not afford White the opportunity to minister to inner-city youth, like he wanted. But he learned that Milwaukee, the largest city in Wisconsin, was only a two-hour drive from Green Bay.

White also stated that as a Christian, he would ultimately sign where God wanted him to be. Coach Mike Holmgren phoned White and left a message on his answering machine: "Reggie," the coach stated. "This is God. Come to Green Bay." Fortunately for Holmgren and the Packers, White was known for his sense of humor.

Actually, Ray Rhodes, the Packers' black defensive coordinator, did the majority of the coaxing to bring White to Green Bay. "Everybody suspected he'd go to a big city for outside endorsements," said Greg Blache, a defensive line coach. "But Ray Rhodes did a phenomenal job of talking to and recruiting Reggie."[11]

The money the Packers offered, $17 million over four years, *huge* at the time, didn't hurt either. "The Packers, with about $30 million cash reserves, had the money to front-load their offer that basically blew away the opposition," reported longtime Packers writer Bob McGinn.[12]

White's signing sent shock waves throughout the league. "I think it blew everybody's mind that he would come to Green Bay. It set the tone. He was the premier guy, and it turned the tables to where guys didn't just run to the big market," Blache added.[13]

It wasn't a move without risk. At 31, White was on the back end of his career, but even a less than 100 percent Reggie White was still a terrific player. He had an immediate impact. Led by his 13 sacks, two forced fumbles, and two fumble recoveries, the Packers' defense leaped from 23rd to second in the league in 1993. His back-to-back, fourth-quarter sacks

25. Reggie White (2006)

A jubilant Reggie White was never a welcome sight for opposing offenses during his years in a Green Bay uniform in the 1990s. In addition to White's considerable football skills, he was also known for his strong faith and humanitarian efforts. His shocking signing with the Packers put the team on the map with other African American players, who might not otherwise have signed with Green Bay (Mark Wallenfang).

of Denver quarterback John Elway preserved a 30–27 home win over the Broncos. Green Bay returned to the playoffs for the first time in 11 seasons, defeating Detroit, 28–24, in a wild-card thriller, before losing to Dallas in the divisional round, 27–17.

Along with *his* effect on the Packers, White's role in getting *other players* interested in coming to Green Bay is a legacy that's easy to overlook. Not only was Green Bay a nearly all-white city with little racial or cultural diversity, but the Packers hadn't been serious Super Bowl contenders since the Lombardi years. But White saw what others didn't: an up-and-coming team on the verge of something special.

"It was monumental because not only did he sign but he recruited for Green Bay and got guys like [defensive end] Sean Jones to come here," said former Packers president Bob Harlan. "He sent a message to the rest of the NFL that Green Bay was a great place to play."[14]

Jackson, who signed off on a trade from the Dolphins to the Packers in 1995, said White showed that Green Bay was a place "where the people are super fans. And when you lose a game, there's nobody screaming at you saying you're a bum. It was actually an oasis to play football, and you really concentrated on being a football player."[15]

But there were also challenges in day-to-day living in Green Bay for a black in the NFL accustomed to the lifestyle of large metropolitan areas. Defensive end Sean Jones, who played for the Los Angeles Raiders and Houston Oilers before coming to Green Bay in 1994, said it was the city's lack of cultural and racial diversity that posed problems, and not racism. "It's probably the least racist place I've ever been in my life," Jones stated. "Where's the black history museum? Where's Chinatown? They didn't have any of that, but they embraced you and they wanted to win."[16]

White helped teammates adjust by having barbers come to provide haircuts, bringing in catered soul-food dinners, and conducting bible studies. Mark Brunell, a backup quarterback who went on to star in Jacksonville, spoke of White as a great role model, as he remembered him booming: "Why y'all going to the parties? Why y'all doing these things when you won't even open your Bible?"[17]

While Brunell testified to White's faith, offensive lineman Harry Galbreath pointed to his character as he recalled the time he rented a video with a sexually suggestive scene in it, and White told him to turn it off. "I said, 'No, man, I'm watching the movie.' Reggie then got up and turned off the TV, and I didn't say a thing."[18]

White's desire not only to win, but also to alter perspectives of the team and set a positive example proved infectious. Fellowship grew to the point where nearly the entire team could be found at a local bowling alley on a Thursday night where White, a non-drinker, could be found sipping a diet coke. He was a mentor for younger players, and "he even served as a sort of marriage counselor for young couples."[19]

A caring team bond is an underestimated aspect of gridiron success, and in 1994, the Packers finished 9–7 for a third straight year. More important, it marked a second consecutive playoff berth, something not seen in Green Bay since the Lombardi era. White's sack total fell from 13 to eight, but he also forced two fumbles, recovered a fumble, and defended five passes. Green Bay again met division rival Detroit in the playoffs and turned in a defensive effort for the ages in turning back the Lions, 16–12. The Packers held the visitors to nine first downs, just 171 yards total offense, and incredibly limited shifty superstar running back Barry Sanders to minus-one yard on 13 carries. Green Bay's season came to a crashing end when Dallas, Green Bay's postseason nemesis in the 1990s, blasted them the following week, 35–9.

The following campaign, 1995, was marked by highs and lows. The highs included a Christmas Eve gift-wrapped division title, Green Bay's first since 1972, when Steelers receiver Yancey Thigpen dropped a sure-fire touchdown pass, allowing the Packers to escape with a 24–19 victory. White notched 12 sacks, two forced fumbles, and four defended passes on the season, as the Packers improved to 11–5 after being stuck at 9–7 for three years.

After dispatching the Atlanta Falcons in the wild-card round, Green Bay pulled off a major upset in upending the defending Super Bowl champion 49ers at Candlestick Park, 27–17. Craig Newsome returned a fumble for a touchdown, and linebacker Wayne Simmons had a monster game with 10 tackles. Even when White didn't show up much on the stat sheet, his presence freed up one-on-one blocking for his defensive line mates.

The following week, the NFC championship was the low point. Green Bay led the host Cowboys, 27–24, heading into the fourth quarter, but Dallas took charge in the final frame to claim a 38–27 victory and a berth in Super Bowl XXX. It was a long, discouraging flight home in an otherwise great year.

Coming so close, Packers players vowed it was Super Bowl or bust in 1996. White famously sealed the deal with three fourth-quarter sacks of Patriots quarterback Drew Bledsoe, as Green Bay captured Super Bowl XXXI over New England, 35–21. In his 12th NFL season, the Minister of Defense, and the Packers, had their long-awaited title. There is no question that Wisconsin is forever indebted to White for not only bringing Green Bay a championship but also making it a "cool" place to play.[20]

26

Ron Wolf (2015)

*Savior of a Franchise
(Packers Years 1991–2001)*

Who had the largest reclamation project in Green Bay Packers history? Vince Lombardi? Ron Wolf? Lombardi, who of course led the Packers to five NFL championships in the 1960s, would readily come to mind for many. Consider the dire times the six-time world champs had fallen upon when he took over in 1959. It had been 15 years since Green Bay's last title under Curly Lambeau. Under new regimes in the 1950s after Lambeau left, the best the Packers could do were 6–6 records in 1952 and 1955.

Green Bay bottomed out with a 1–10–1 debacle under Ray "Scooter" McLean in 1958. They not only lost but were frequently embarrassed, the worst being a humiliating, 56–0 defeat at the hands of the Baltimore Colts. The Packers had become a league laughingstock. Enter Lombardi, and the Packers posted their first winning season since 1947. One year later, they were playing for the championship, and the year after that (1961), they *won* the NFL title, the first of *five* in *seven* years under the legendary coach.

But a Packers fan shouldn't overlook the wealth of talent that scout and personnel director Jack Vainisi had acquired prior to Lombardi's arrival: Forrest Gregg, Bart Starr, Paul Hornung, Jim Taylor, Jerry Kramer, and Ray Nitschke, among others. No doubt Lombardi faced a difficult task in motivating these underachievers into a winning team. Nor should one underestimate the talented players he also brought in, such as future stars Willie Davis, Henry Jordan, and Willie Wood.

The point is that the roster Ron Wolf inherited when he took over as Packers general manager in 1991 was in much worse shape, and a losing atmosphere was even more entrenched than it was in the 1950s. Consider: From the time Lombardi left following the 1968 season (6–7–1) to when Mike Holmgren took over as coach in 1992, the Packers had five winning seasons! Those were in 1969, 1972, 1978, 1982, 1989, and only 1972 and 1982 marked playoff appearances. That's nearly a *quarter-century* of football in which a losing year was not only routine but likely. To make matters worse, each successive coach posted a worse record than the one before. Green Bay was again an undesirable place to play.

Ron Wolf Highlights

3× Super Bowl champion (*XV, *XVIII, XXXI)
  *With Raiders
2× NFC champion (1996, 1997)
Signed Reggie White as free agent (1993)
6× playoff appearances with Green Bay (1993–1998)
Pro Football Hall of Fame (2015)
Green Bay Packers HOF (2000)

Professional career:
Oakland Raiders (1963–1974)
Scout
Tampa Bay Buccaneers (1976–1978)
Vice President of Football Operations
Oakland/Los Angeles Raiders (1979–1989)
Scout
New York Jets (1990–1991)
Personnel Director
Green Bay Packers (1991–2001)
General Manager and Executive Vice President

Books:
The Packer Way
Nine Stepping Stones to Building a Winning Organization

Many wondered if the Packers would ever be steady winners again, and even the normally optimistic Packers faithful had grown jaded. To keep things interesting come playoff time, it was not unusual for fans to adopt a second team to cheer for because their beloved Packers were usually out of post-season contention by November.

That was the rebuilding effort Ron Wolf faced when Packers president Bob Harlan hired him in November 1991.

Wolf succeeded Tom Braatz, who became the team's first Director of Football Operations in 1987. The move was made after a series of poor drafts by Bart Starr, and then Forrest Gregg, when it became clear that it was too much to ask the head coach to do all of the drafting as general manager. Despite being able to focus more on personnel, Braatz, who had been a front-office executive with the Atlanta Falcons, fared little better. Wide receiver Sterling Sharpe proved to be an excellent number-one pick in 1988 but running back Brent Fullwood (1987) and offensive tackle Tony Mandarich (1989) were colossal busts.

Green Bay appeared to be turning things around in 1989 when the Packers, led by quarterback Don Majkowski, posted a 10–6 record and just missed a playoff berth. The winning season proved to be a fluke, not a trend. Majkowski got hurt in 1990, and Green Bay slid back to a 6–10 mark. The

Many wondered if the Packers would ever become steady winners again when Ron Wolf took the helm in 1991. One could make a good argument that he had an even bigger rebuilding job than Vince Lombardi. Ten years, six straight playoff appearances, two NFC titles, and a Super Bowl championship later, Wolf was roundly cheered whenever he made an appearance before the adoring faithful at Lambeau Field (Mark Wallenfang).

26. Ron Wolf (2015)

Packers had two number-one draft selections that year: linebacker Tony Bennett, a very capable player, and Darrell Thompson from Minnesota, an average back at best. With Green Bay spiraling downward with a 2–9 mark in November 1991, Harlan had seen enough, and Braatz was out.

Harlan recognized that restructuring the football operations was in order. At the time, the Packers coach and GM shared agreements in terms of personnel and the draft, and Harlan knew he needed a no-nonsense, take-charge type to oversee *all* football decisions. Wolf was that sort of man. In fact, it was the lack of control in the previous arrangement that led him to grow disenchanted about the job after learning about it in 1987. "With Judge Parins, there were no clear lines of authority, and you have to have that. The judge was in charge, but he didn't know that much about the game of football. ... No one was in charge," Wolf said.[1]

Harlan, now the Packers president, offered more authority than was possible in 1987, but the Green Bay job was still considered risky, and Wolf's friends advised him to decline. He ran the offer past Al Davis, his mentor and former boss with the Raiders, who offered a different take. He told his star pupil that he thought the job was not unlike an owner like himself in which the buck would start—and end—with him.

It had yet to be determined if Wolf would be the type of winner that Davis was with the Raiders, but Wolf was widely acknowledged as having the type of football know-how the Packers needed. "Ron is a tireless worker," said Bill Parcells. "I don't think there is a better personnel guy. He has a tremendous understanding of the game, and he is smart. He always wants to learn, his mind is always working."[2]

The first steps were to examine the Green Bay roster and determine the future of head coach Lindy Infante. As part of that process, Wolf flew to Atlanta to watch the Packers and Falcons in a December 1 matchup. The first thing the Packers' new head man wanted to know was whether Falcons backup quarterback Brett Favre could still throw the ball as well as he had remembered. A year earlier, when Wolf was personnel director of the New York Jets, he was enamored with Favre, a rifle-armed quarterback from Southern Mississippi who had led the Golden Eagles to major upsets over Auburn and Alabama. But to Wolf's dismay, the Falcons snatched him in the second round, one pick before the Jets.

Wolf told Harlan about his intentions. "Bob, we're going to make a trade for Brett Favre. Are you OK with that?' And I told him, 'I promised you it was your team to run.... I'm fine with it.'"[3]

Atlanta coach Jerry Glanville surely *didn't* want him, so Wolf knew it was mostly a matter of working out the details with Ken Herrock, the Falcons' head of player personnel. Favre was talented but in Glanville's doghouse due to his penchant for drinking and partying. He even showed up late for the Falcons' team picture, claiming he had been delayed by a train wreck. "Mississippi," as Glanville called him, "you *are* a train wreck."

The Packers won the 1991 season finale over the Vikings, 27–7, but with a 4–12 record, it was too little, too late, for Infante. Wolf was originally interested in Parcells, but he had suffered a heart attack and notified the new Packers GM that he was taking the year off from coaching.

Wolf turned his attention to Mike Holmgren, coordinator of the powerful San Francisco 49ers offense, who was highly sought-after by a number of teams. The Niners' esteemed assistant, noted for developing quarterbacks Joe Montana and Steve Young, was in enough demand that Wolf had to ship a second-round draft pick to the 49ers in exchange for allowing Green Bay to break his contract. He was named the Packers' 11th head coach in January 1992.

It was a perfect partnership. Without a meddlesome owner looking over their shoulder, Wolf knew he had an ideal situation to create the team they wanted to build, much like Lombardi did as coach and GM decades earlier.

In February 1992, the Packers got Favre, and the Falcons received the Packers' first-round draft pick, which was the 17th choice overall.

It's easy to look back now and see that Wolf made one of the best trades in NFL history. But the move was harshly criticized at the time. Brett who? No one could pronounce his last name. FAV-ray? FAY-vor? And what, upset Packers fans wanted to know, was the new GM doing trading Green Bay's first-round draft pick for a *third*-string quarterback? Was this the second coming of the John Hadl debacle in 1974? In that massive blunder, then GM Dan Devine shipped five high draft picks off to the Rams in exchange for an aging, washed-up quarterback.

To the skeptical Packers faithful, Wolf couldn't have gotten off to a worse start. But the confident GM didn't care what the fans thought. He was sure Favre was the type of talented quarterback he needed to build a franchise around.

A team that's done a lot of losing needs an upgrade in talent, and Wolf made a good haul in his first draft as Packers GM in 1992, making picks that included cornerback/kick returner Terrell Buckley, wide receiver Robert Brooks, running back Edgar Bennett, and tight end Mark Chmura. All but Buckley would be strong contributors in future years.

In an up-and-down 1992 campaign, Green Bay started out 0–2 before Favre took over for an injured Majkowski and engineered a memorable, come-from-behind 24–23 win over the visiting Cincinnati Bengals. No one knew it at the time, but it was the start of the Brett Favre Era in Green Bay.

Bumps in the road remained. A 27–7 loss to New York at Giants Stadium left the Packers at 4–6, and another losing year appeared likely.

As General Manager and Executive Vice President, Ron Wolf was charged with lifting the Packers' sagging fortunes, and without question his biggest, boldest move was trading a first-round pick to the Atlanta Falcons for third-string quarterback Brett Favre in 1992, a decision that was met with a great deal of skepticism at the time. Luckily for Packers fans, Wolf knew what he was doing (Pro Football Hall of Fame).

But the Pack reeled off six straight wins to improve to 9–6, before a season-ending loss to Minnesota left Green Bay out of the post-season. Still, at 9–7, it was a rare winning campaign, and with a talented young quarterback, there was reason for optimism in Titletown.

The Packers had their coach and their quarterback. The player who would spearhead their defense loomed next in 1993, but landing Reggie White was a real long-shot. White, a Philadelphia Eagle for eight seasons, wrecked countless offensive game plans in recording 124 sacks in 121 games. The star defensive end was courted by Washington, San Francisco, and Cleveland, all of which seemed to have a much better chance at signing White than small-town Green Bay. "The Packers, with about $30 million in cash reserves, had the money to front-load their offer that basically blew away the opposition, including Cleveland, which was fourth in line."[4]

White shocked the football world by agreeing to a $17 million contract to sign with the Packers, which was huge money at the time.

The monumental signing didn't keep Wolf from continuing to upgrade other positions. His calling card was as a scout, and the former Raiders personnel man brought in another treasure trove of collegiate talent in 1993. They included first-round selections Clemson linebacker Wayne Simmons and safety George Teague, offensive tackle Earl Dotson in round three, and cornerback Doug Evans, a sixth-round pick from Louisiana Tech.

Wolf was relentless in his pursuit of talent. During an average week in the regular season, he would be on the road scouting from Tuesday through Saturday. "I look for guys who make plays," he once said. "If I watch a guy, and he isn't making plays at the college level, how can he make them at this level?"[5]

This sounds pretty basic, but many a scout and GM has been enamored by a player's blazing time in the 40 or his hefty number of reps on the bench press, only to see the can't-miss prospect fail miserably in the pros. Athleticism isn't unimportant, but first and foremost Wolf understood he was drafting a *football player*.

Wolf's nonstop search for players was paying off. Green Bay posted a 9–7 record in 1993 and captured its first playoff spot in 11 years. It also marked the first back-to-back winning seasons in Titletown since 1966–1967. In 1994, the Packers notched a 9–7 mark for the third straight year, but a second consecutive campaign of beating Detroit but then losing to Dallas in the playoffs left Packers fans a little restless.

Green Bay turned the corner in 1995. Always a go-getter, Wolf acquired Pro Bowl tight end Keith Jackson from the Dolphins in exchange for a second-round draft pick. The college draft brought cornerback Craig Newsome in the first round and an embarrassment of riches in the third round: defensive tackle Darius Holland, fullback William Henderson, linebacker Brian Williams, and wide receiver Antonio Freeman. Even seventh-rounder Adam Timmerman turned into a solid starter at guard.

A 24–19 Christmas Eve win over the Pittsburgh Steelers gave the Packers an 11–5 record and their first division title since 1972. After disposing of the Falcons in the Wild Card round, Green Bay faced the tall task of taking on the world champion 49ers in San Francisco. While the Packers were a solid team, the 49ers and Cowboys were still the top dogs in the NFC. But in a game more one-sided than the final score would indicate, Green Bay shocked the defending champs, 27–17, to advance to the NFC title game against the Dallas Cowboys for the right to appear in Super Bowl XXX.

In a back-and-forth affair, Green Bay led, 27–24, heading into the fourth quarter, but it was all Dallas in the final stanza, and they came away with a 38–27 victory. Still, the Packers' stupendous season marked a changing of the guard for NFC supremacy. Green Bay knocked on the championship door in 1995; in 1996 they would break it down.

Many GMs would have stood pat with a roster that came within a quarter of playing in a Super Bowl, but Wolf believed you can never have enough playmakers, so he continued to wheel and deal. He hit the jackpot in the off-season, landing WR Don Beebe, safety Eugene Robinson, and defensive tackle Santana Dotson, and snatching WR/kick returner Desmond Howard off the scrap heap from Jacksonville. Howard barely made a loaded team in 1996, securing a roster spot with a punt return TD in the pre-season. Each of these Packers played a vital role in helping Green

Bay to a 13–3 regular season mark and an eventual Super Bowl XXXI championship.

But Wolf would be the first to admit that not every move works out. Top draft pick John Michels, an offensive tackle from USC, and wide receiver Derrick Mayes, a second-round selection in 1996, were among his flops in the draft. Three years later, he erred in drafting defensive backs in the first three rounds, with only third-round pick Mike McKenzie becoming a viable starter.

Still, Wolf hit more than he missed, and landing a future HOF quarterback like Favre is more than enough to offset some bad moves! In addition, his talented personnel staff, which included the late Ted Thompson, Reggie McKenzie, and John Schneider, all learned valuable lessons from their boss and kept the Packers' track record of success intact after Wolf retired in June 2001.

During his tenure, Green Bay did not log a losing record and only missed the playoffs three times. Over his nine-year term as GM, the Packers compiled a 92–52 record, good for a .639 winning percentage.

In the 20-plus years that have passed since Wolf's retirement, the lessons his pupils learned are illustrated by the fact the Packers have posted only three losing marks (2005, 2017 and 2018).

Trading for Brett Favre was clearly Wolf's greatest legacy. How many front office men have made *that* big a gamble on a single player? Great GMs aren't afraid of pulling the trigger. Lesser men never do and miss out. In addition, since it's even harder to remain on top than it is to get there, planting the seeds for future success may well be his second-leading legacy.

Wolf was a Raider, Buccaneer, and Jet, but it was being a Packer that meant the most to him, when "he informed Hall of Fame officials that he wished to be enshrined as a Packer, the 23rd member from Green Bay."[6]

For a man who was the savior of a franchise, that seemed only fitting.

27

Charles Woodson (2021)

Takeaway Machine
(Packers Years 2006–2012)

Given the way turnovers lift one team up and demoralize the other, it's no wonder they often represent a major shift in momentum in football games. Fumble recoveries are big, but interceptions are especially etched in the minds of fans. In Super Bowl I, the Packers led the AFL's Kansas City Chiefs by a slim, 14–10 margin at intermission. Early in the second half, Chiefs quarterback Len Dawson tossed an errant pass that Willie Wood easily picked off, and he raced 50 yards before being tackled deep in Kansas City territory. Elijah Pitts scampered to pay dirt, and suddenly Green Bay had extended its lead to 21–10. "We played well in the first half and at the start of the second half," Kansas City coach Hank Stram said after the game. "But that interception by Wood changed the complexion of the game."[1]

Some turnovers *win* games. The Packers were on the verge of a 7–6 loss to the Lions in 1962 when Herb Adderley picked Detroit quarterback Milt Plum deep in the Lions' end of the field. Paul Hornung booted a 26-yard field goal, and Green Bay escaped with a 9–7 win. In more recent times, Green Bay corner Al Harris jumped a Seattle receiver's route, snared the Matt Hasselbeck pass, and dashed 52 yards for an electrifying game-winning interception in the Packers' 2004 overtime playoff win over the Seahawks.

Still other fumble recoveries and interceptions *preserve* victories. Late in the 1966 NFL championship game in Dallas, the Packers were clinging to a 34–27 lead over the upstart Cowboys, but Dallas was knocking on the door with a chance to tie the contest and send it into overtime. On fourth-and-goal at the 2-yard line, Dave Robinson blitzed and draped himself over Cowboys quarterback Don Meredith, who somehow got off a wobbly pass. Safety Tom Brown picked it off in the end zone, allowing the Packers to earn another hard-fought title. Again, more recently, Packers

27. Charles Woodson (2021)

Charles Woodson bursts up-field on a punt return in a 2006 contest against the St. Louis Rams at Lambeau Field. While he played more years for the Oakland Raiders and returned there in 2013, Woodson's most productive years came as a Green Bay Packer, where he recorded nine of his 11 career pick-sixes and Defensive Player of the Year honors in 2009 (Steve Tate).

nose tackle B.J. Raji inexplicably dropped into coverage, snatched Chicago quarterback Caleb Hanie's pass, and rumbled 18 yards for an unlikely pick-six for the final margin of victory in Green Bay's 21–14 NFC championship win over the archrival Bears in January 2011.

For some, like Harris, Brown, and Raji, these were once-in-a-lifetime plays. Only elite talents like Wood, Adderley, and Packers and Raiders great Charles Woodson can say they were certified takeaway machines who made many highlight reels. In his stellar 18-year career, Woodson, a cornerback and later safety, forced 33 fumbles and intercepted 65 enemy passes, running back 11 of them for touchdowns. Paul Krause, Emlen Tunnell, Rod Woodson (no relation), and Dick "Night Train" Lane are the only players with more career interceptions. And with 12 TDs, only his namesake Woodson tallied more pick-sixes.

Charles Woodson Highlights

4th overall draft pick (Oakland, 1998)
Heisman Trophy winner (Michigan, 1997)
Super Bowl champion (XLV)
9× Pro Bowl (1998–2001, 2008–2011, 2015)

4× First-team All-Pro (1999, 2001, 2009, 2011)
4× Second-team All-Pro (2000, 2008, 2010, 2015)
2× NFL interceptions leader (2009, 2011)
NFL Defensive Player of the Year (2009)
NFL 2000s All-Decade Team
Pro Football Hall of Fame (2021)
Green Bay Packers HOF (2021)
College Football Hall of Fame (2018)

Playing career:
Oakland Raiders (1998–2005)
Green Bay Packers (2006–2012)
Oakland Raiders (2013–2015)
Career interceptions: 65

Post football career:
College football analyst for ABC
NFL analyst for ESPN

Interestingly, nine of Woodson's 11 career pick-sixes came as a Packer, where he resurrected his career.

"Woodson played like a first-ballot Hall of Famer during his seven seasons with the Packers (2006–2012)," wrote Phil Barber. "He was twice an all-pro there. He was the NFL Defensive Player of the Year in 2009. The year after that he helped the Pack win a Super Bowl."[2]

Peter King and Bob Fox also wrote that Woodson's best years were in Titletown and not Oakland. "[He was] very good, mostly, in 1998 through 2005 and good in 2013 through 2015 in Oakland. Better, in my opinion, with the Packers from 2006 through 2012," King stated.[3]

Fox backed his case with statistics: "Woodson played in 154 games with the Raiders and picked off 27 passes for 398 yards and two touchdowns. ... Woodson only played in 100 games with the Packers but picked off 38 passes for 568 yards and nine touchdowns. ... Woodson defended 84 passes in 11 years in Oakland and defended 99 in seven years in Green Bay."[4]

Courtesy of Packers Wire[5] and Pro Football Reference, in reverse chronological order, here is a recap of his nine interception returns with Green Bay:

> October 2, 2011—**Green Bay 49, Denver 23**. With 50 seconds remaining in the first quarter, Woodson picked Denver quarterback Kyle Orton and went 30 yards to the house to extend the Packers' lead to 14–3 in a Green Bay cakewalk.
> October 3, 2010—**Green Bay 28, Detroit 26**. Early in the third quarter, Woodson snared a Shaun Hill pass and dashed 48 yards

with what proved to be the winning points as the Packers went up 28–14 before Detroit rallied with four field goals. Woodson was also in on 13 tackles, 11 of them solo.

January 3, 2010—**Green Bay 33, Arizona 7**. The Packers dominated in the 2009 season finale. Woodson's 45-yard, second-quarter pick-six off Matt Leinart ballooned Green Bay's lead to 26–0. (The Packers returned to Arizona the following week for a wild card playoff and this time lost an overtime thriller, 51–45.)

November 26, 2009—**Green Bay 34, Detroit 12**. Woodson picked off Lions rookie Matthew Stafford twice, returning the second one for a 38-yard score in a Thanksgiving Day romp.

September 20, 2009—**Cincinnati 31, Green Bay 24**. This time, Woodson's efforts weren't enough as the visiting Bengals emerged with the win. His second-quarter, 37-yard pick-six off Carson Palmer gave the Packers a brief, 24–21 advantage, but it was all Cincinnati after that.

September 28, 2008—**Tampa Bay 30, Green Bay 21**. The standout corner brought back a Brian Griese pass 62 yards to put the Packers up, 21–20, early in the fourth quarter. But the host Buccaneers scored 10 unanswered points as Woodson's pick-six again went in vain.

September 14, 2008—**Green Bay 48, Detroit 25**. Woodson and teammate Nick Collins registered back-to-back interception returns in the fourth quarter off Detroit's Jon Kitna, as the Packers pummeled the host Lions.

November 4, 2007—**Green Bay 33, Kansas City 22**. A 45-yard field goal by rookie Mason Crosby gave the visiting Packers a 26–22 lead in the fourth quarter. Woodson's 46-yard pick off Damon Huard sealed the road win.

October 22, 2006—**Green Bay 34, Miami 24**. A 23-yard, third-quarter pick-six off Joey Harrington provided the Packers with their first lead (13–10) over the host Dolphins. It was an advantage Green Bay didn't give up in grabbing a road victory.

The reader might notice that three of Woodson's interception returns came against the Lions, which was likely doubly gratifying for the former Michigan Wolverine.

His penchant for big plays dates back to Fremont, Ohio, where, as a senior at Ross High School, Woodson was a *USA Today* All-America selection and was named Ohio's Mr. Football in 1994, "after he rushed for 2,028 yards and scored 230 points" at a high school "halfway between Columbus and Ann Arbor."[6] His older brother loved the Wolverines, so he went to Michigan, where he played for coach Lloyd Carr from 1995–1997.

In addition to cornerback, Woodson returned punts and occasionally played wide receiver. In 1997, he beat out Tennessee quarterback Peyton Manning to win the prestigious Heisman Trophy. He remains the only primarily defensive player to capture the coveted award. During his Heisman-winning junior season, Woodson made three memorable plays in a Michigan victory over archrival Ohio State: he returned a punt for a touchdown, snared an interception in the end zone, and grabbed a 37-yard reception that led to the Wolverines' only offensive touchdown. The win propelled Michigan to the Rose Bowl, where they defeated Washington State to grab a share of the 1997 national championship.

Woodson declared his eligibility for the NFL Draft following his junior year at Michigan and was selected with the fourth overall pick of the 1998 draft by the Oakland Raiders. He started all 16 games, recorded 64 tackles, forced a fumble, and intercepted five passes, returning one for a touchdown against the Arizona Cardinals. He was named the NFL Defensive Rookie of the Year and was selected to the Pro Bowl.

On November 28, 1999, against the Kansas City Chiefs, he had a 15-yard interception return for a touchdown in a 37–34 loss. Woodson finished the season with 61 total tackles and a fumble recovery to go along with the pick-six. Woodson was selected to his second Pro Bowl and was named All-Pro by the Associated Press.

In the 2000 season, Woodson again started all 16 games but suffered a turf toe injury that kept him from practicing. He finished the year with a career-high 79 tackles, intercepted four passes, forced three fumbles, and recovered one fumble. Woodson was named to the All-Pro team by *Sports Illustrated* and garnered second-team honors from the Associated Press.

The 2001 campaign marked the fourth consecutive season Woodson played in every game. He registered two sacks, one interception, one forced fumble, and blocked a field goal. Woodson also returned punts for the first time in the NFL.

In January 2002, New England defeated Oakland, 16–13, in an AFC divisional playoff better known as the "Tuck Rule Game," a name that originated from a controversial 4th-quarter play. Woodson had tackled quarterback Tom Brady, which seemed to cause a fumble recovered by the Raiders. A recovery would have likely sealed the game for Oakland. However, officials reviewed the play and determined that because Brady was trying to "tuck" the ball back into his body, it was an incomplete pass and not a fumble. As a result, the Patriots kept the ball and drove into field-goal range. The first successful kick sent the game into overtime, and the second won the game for the Patriots. Even more heartbreaking, New England went on to upset St. Louis in Super Bowl XXXVI, 20–17, for its first championship, while Oakland was left to wonder what might have been.

Woodson experienced more despair the following season when the Tampa Bay Buccaneers routed the Raiders, 48–21, in Super Bowl XXXVII. It also marked a rare shoulder injury that forced him to the sidelines for eight games. He returned in time for the playoffs and recorded an interception in the losing effort against the Bucs.

The shoulder mishap was the first in a series of injuries that would eventually lead the Raiders to part ways with their star corner. Woodson played the entire 2003 campaign, although Oakland finished a dismal 4–12. He had a solid 2004 season with 73 tackles, 2½ sacks, and an interception, but a leg injury forced him to miss the final three games. In 2005, he started the first six games but broke his leg and was sidelined for the rest of the year. It was the end of a very good career in Oakland but one that could have been even better.

"Woodson was so absurdly gifted as a football player that he didn't really have to work at it," Barber said. "[He] probably spent less time in the weight room than you did, and maybe even less than that in his playbook. He knew he could show up on Sundays and compete with the best receivers in the league."[7]

What's more, he liked to have a good time and didn't always show the best judgment. He was charged with a DUI in 2000 and arrested in another alcohol-related incident four years later. After paying him $19 million over a two-year span with only 19 games to show for it, the Raiders let him walk in free agency.

In April 2006, Woodson and the Packers reached a seven-year contract agreement that stunned Packers fans and the rest of the NFL. "A big-name free agent with some baggage and the Green Bay Packers seemed to be the unlikeliest pairing. The Packers broke from their norm to pursue the veteran cornerback."[8]

The Raiders star was extremely skeptical about coming to small-town Green Bay, but the Packers were the only team that still saw him as a lockdown corner. Everyone else felt he was now a safety. "Charles Woodson and the Packers turned out to be a perfect match for each other. The Packers offered Woodson a spot to focus on football and get his life together. Woodson offered the Packers the skills of a top cornerback."[9]

Woodson's exceptional play in 2006 proved the rest of the league wrong. He recorded a then-career-high eight interceptions, forced three fumbles, and registered a sack. Compare that to seven interceptions in his previous *five years* in Oakland. His production dipped in 2007, but he scored two touchdowns, one a pick-six and the other a fumble recovery. Big plays like that helped lead Green Bay to a 13–3 season that fell one win short of the Super Bowl.

The following season was one of transition with a new quarterback

Widely considered on the downward slide of a solid career when he signed with Green Bay in 2006, Charles Woodson proved all the naysayers wrong four years later when he helped lead the Packers to a Super Bowl triumph over the Pittsburgh Steelers. Not even an injured shoulder, which sent him to the bench toward the end of the first half, could dampen his spirits in celebrating the championship (Steve Tate).

in Aaron Rodgers, and the Packers finished 6–10. But "instead of getting frustrated and uninterested like he did when the Raiders struggled," a now more mature Woodson earned Pro Bowl and All-Pro recognition for his seven interception and three sack campaign.[10]

He was a certified takeaway and touchdown machine with the Packers, inflicting misery on teams and quarterbacks through his timely blitzes from the slot and his knack for jumping pass patterns by his thorough understanding what opposing offenses were doing. "He's just seen so much and trusts himself to just play what his eyes tell him," quarterback Matthew Stafford stated.[11]

Woodson's play reached an even higher level in 2009, when he earned NFL Defensive Player of the Year honors. Defensive coordinator Dom Capers used Woodson all over the field, deep on pass coverage, in the slot, and as a blitzer. He registered a career-high nine interceptions, forced four fumbles, and recorded two sacks. In an important, 17–7, late-season win over Dallas, Woodson caused two fumbles and picked off a Tony Romo pass on the goal line. All told, Green Bay surged to an 11–5 record and Wild Card playoff spot. "In Green Bay, we saw the Charles Woodson we had always been promised," Barber noted. "He was a leader. He wasn't just strong and fast, he was smart, disciplined, nurturing of younger players."[12]

Never would that be put to the test more than in 2010, when the Packers were decimated by injuries. Woodson's ability to sustain a high level of play while the Packers shuffled players in and out of the lineup demonstrated great leadership. He led the team in tackles (76) and forced fumbles (5).

The Packers sneaked into the post-season with a 10–6 record and then knocked off Philadelphia, Atlanta, and Chicago, all on the road, to advance to Super Bowl XLV. It had taken eight years for Woodson to get back to the Super Bowl, and he was not about to let his teammates forget it in the locker room after defeating the Bears. "For two weeks, think about one. Let's be one mind. Let's be one heartbeat. One purpose. One goal. … Let's get it."[13]

Woodson registered two tackles against Pittsburgh before snapping his collarbone stretching out to break up a deep pass intended for the Steelers' Mike Wallace. Out for the game, the emotional leader told his teammates at halftime how much he wanted it.

Woodson was later shown on the sideline trying to lift his right arm on the sideline, and immediately wincing in pain. But all you need is one arm to hoist a Lombardi Trophy, which he jubilantly did after Green Bay claimed a 31–25 victory. Every NFL player dreams of winning a championship, and Woodson finally had his.

Appendix A

Packers Who Should Be (or Will Be) in the Pro Football Hall of Fame

Aaron Rodgers
(Packers Years 2005–)

Let's get this no-brainer out of the way first. Like his predecessor, Brett Favre, there is no doubt that when Green Bay Packers quarterback Aaron Rodgers retires, he will be a first ballot Hall of Famer in his initial year of eligibility. In his 14 years as a starting quarterback in the NFL, *some* of the incredible passing statistics his name appears next to in league record books include:

- 122.5 highest passer rating, season (2011)
- 0.3 lowest interception percentage, season (2018)
- 402 consecutive passes without an interception
- Fastest NFL QB to 400 career passing touchdowns (193 games)
- Most seasons with 40-plus total touchdowns (5)
- Most seasons with 120-plus passer rating (2)

Career NFL statistics as of 2020:

TD-INT: 412–89 (former is 7th all-time)
First player to have 4:1 touchdown to interception ratio
Passing yards: 51,245 (11th all-time)
Completion percentage: 65.1
Passer rating: 103.9
Rushing yards: 3,271
Rushing touchdowns: 31
3× NFL MVP (2011, 2014, 2020)

Packers records include:

Highest passer rating, career (103.8)
Highest passer rating, season (122.5, 2011)

Most passes completed, season (401, 2016)
Most yards passing, season (4,643, 2011)
Most yards passing, game (480, 2013, tie)
Most games, 300-plus passing yards (60)
Most touchdown passes season (48, 2020, breaking his own record of 45 in 2011)

That doesn't even include his Hail Marys or any other number of additional records he's likely to set by the time you read this. One of the statistics that leaps out the most is his incredible touchdown-to-interception ratio. *Many* quarterbacks are throwing for a lot of yards and touchdowns in today's pass-happy NFL, but it is difficult to throw *that* many passes and still have so few picks, a testament to Rodgers' mental acumen.

The bigger questions aren't about Rodgers' obviously HOF-worthy resume—it's where he ends up all-time in categories like touchdown passes and passing yardage, *and* whether he's the GOAT at his position. That's a loaded question, but many would say that Rodgers' accomplishments merit being included in the conversation.

LeRoy Butler
(*Packers Years 1990–2001*)

It is definitely not a matter of *if* LeRoy Butler will be enshrined in Canton but *when*? Butler has more career interceptions than a number of safeties already in the Hall—including Cliff Harris (29), Kenny Easley (32), and Brian Dawkins (37). According to the Pro Football HOF, here is the career stat line on Butler:

- 953 tackles
- 38 interceptions
- 12 fumble recoveries
- 20 quarterback sacks
- 4× Pro Bowler
- NFL 1990s All-Decade Team
- First defensive back in NFL history to register 20 sacks and 20 interceptions in a career.

Butler, named to the Packers HOF in 2007, stacks up well to John Lynch, a 9× Pro Bowler with the Tampa Bay Buccaneers and another Hall-worthy safety elected to the 2021 class. His key career stats include 1,000-plus tackles, 26 picks (12 fewer than Butler), and 13 sacks (seven fewer). In addition, Lynch played four more seasons than Butler.

A broken shoulder blade sustained while tackling Atlanta Falcons running back Jamal Anderson in 2001 forced Butler into retirement before the following campaign, when it was discovered it had not healed properly.

LeRoy Butler was also a colorful character, quick with a quote for the media and the improvisational originator of the Lambeau Leap in a 28–0 win over the LA Raiders in 1993, when Reggie White picked up a recovered fumble and lateraled it to his quicker teammate, who dashed the distance for a Packers touchdown, jumping into the stands after he crossed the goal line.

Butler is even a real-life Forrest Gump of a sort. Challenged by physical problems as a youth, he was forced to wear a leg brace and even used a wheelchair while undergoing therapy.

On November 21, 2017, Butler was named one of 27 semi-finalists for the 2018 class of the Pro Football Hall of Fame. It marked the first time he was named a semi-finalist for the honor. In January 2022, he was announced as one of the modern-era finalists for the 2022 class of the Hall of Fame. It was his third time being named as a finalist, joining 14 other modern-era finalists. He was selected as a finalist again in 2021. He is the only member of the Hall's All-1990s team who has not yet been welcomed into the Hall.

Sterling Sharpe
(Packers Years 1988–1994)

Sharpe's brilliant seven-year career was cut short by a severe neck injury that forced him to retire just as the Packers were becoming big winners. Thus the big question is whether his injury-shortened stat line is impressive enough for Hall selection. In an era in which 100-catch seasons were a rarity among wide receivers, Sharpe set (then) league records with 108 receptions in 1992 and 112 in 1993.

Despite his abbreviated career, Sharpe still ranks second in team annals in receptions with 595, third in receiving yardage (8,134), and fifth in touchdowns with 66. That breaks out into an average of 85 catches and just over nine scores per season. (Davante Adams tied his team record of 18 TDs in 2020.)

Assume that Sharpe, sans injury, plays seven additional seasons to equal Donald Driver, the Packers' leading receiver all-time who snared 743 passes and amassed 10,137 yards in 14 campaigns. If Sharpe had maintained the pace he was on, he would have grabbed 1,190 balls for 16,268 yards, meaning Driver would have been *looking up* at both top spots in Packers record books by a wide margin. At the clip Sharpe was scoring touchdowns, he would have tallied 129 in 14 years, far eclipsing the legendary Don Hutson's team record of 105.

The yardage total would rank *third* all-time in the NFL, behind only Jerry Rice and Larry Fitzgerald. The number of catches would fare *fifth*, just behind Jason Witten, but passing Marvin Harrison for the #5 spot. Receiving touchdowns? Again, *fifth*, just ahead of Harrison. (Harrison is in the Hall and Witten will be.)

This isn't to say Sharpe *would have* attained these lofty totals in 6–7 more seasons, but the fact that he *could have* illustrates his dominance.

Some might say seven years isn't a large enough body of work to qualify for Canton. Legendary running backs Terrell Davis and Gale Sayers also suited up for the same number of seasons, and they are both in the Hall, so that argument doesn't wash. Longevity is important, but the play of a Hall of Famer should also clearly stand out among his peers. With that in mind, a strong case can be made for Sharpe belonging in Canton.

Gale Gillingham
(*Packers Years 1966–1974, 1976*)

Because he was drafted at the tail end of the Vince Lombardi years, the contributions of guard Gale Gillingham, a first-round draft pick out of Minnesota in 1966, tend to get overlooked. He was a part-time starter in his rookie season, and in 1967, he took Fuzzy Thurston's spot full time, opposite perennial All-Pro Jerry Kramer. "Gilly," as he was known, started in the Ice Bowl and Super Bowl II, coach Lombardi's final games after nine seasons with the team. He was the last member of the Lombardi era active with the franchise.

Noted for his impressive strength, Gillingham was one of the earliest proponents of a weight training program. (His sons later became professional strongmen and power lifters.)

Gillingham was a five-time Pro Bowler and six-time All-Pro. He was also the inaugural winner of the Forrest Gregg Award for the NFL Offensive Linemen of the Year following the 1970 season. Those accolades compare favorably to Packers greats who *are* in the Hall of Fame: Henry Jordan, four Pro Bowls and seven times All-Pro; Willie Davis, five and six; and Jerry Kramer, three and seven.Gillingham's honors also stack up well to a number of guards enshrined in Canton, including Larry Little, six Pro Bowls and six All-Pro selections; Gene Upshaw, seven and seven; and Russ Grimm, four and four.

But unlike these linemen who had the good fortune of playing on outstanding Dolphins, Raiders, and Redskins teams, respectively, Gillingham was one of the few standouts on mediocre to poor Packers squads after Lombardi left. He also had the extreme misfortune of playing for Dan Devine, who inexplicably switched Gillingham to defensive tackle in 1972 even though he was the team's best offensive lineman. As if that wasn't bad enough, he sustained a season-ending knee injury that season.

In 2016, the Pro Football Researchers Association named Gillingham to the PFRA Hall of Very Good Class of 2016. He died at age 67 in Little Falls, Minnesota, in 2011, but his three sons and daughter deserve to see him posthumously selected to the Hall.

Jack Vainisi
(*Packers Years 1950–1960*)

Contributors such as Washington Redskins GM Bobby Beathard and Bills and later Colts GM Bill Polian have been selected for the Pro Football HOF in recent years, and rightly so. Yet the role Jack Vainisi played in acquiring future Packers standouts who would star for Vince Lombardi has been underestimated. Vainisi, hired by Gene Ronzani in 1950, scouted and directed the team's player personnel department for ten years. He did the legwork in acquiring eight future Pro Football Hall of Famers. They were:

Center Jim Ringo, 1953;
Tackle/guard Forrest Gregg and quarterback Bart Starr in 1956;
Halfback Paul Hornung in 1957; and
Fullback Jim Taylor, linebacker Ray Nitschke, and guard Jerry Kramer all in 1958—widely considered the best college draft in the Packers' long history.

He also signed free agent Willie Wood in 1960. When the Packers won their first championship since the Curly Lambeau era, in 1961, 17 of the 22 offensive and defensive starters were acquired in some fashion by Vainisi.

As if acquiring a collection of talent like that isn't enough, Vainisi was also instrumental in hiring Vince Lombardi in 1959, lobbying on Lombardi's behalf to team president Dominic Olejniczak and the team's board of directors.

It should also be pointed out that pro scouting in that era was nowhere near as complex and with the large personnel departments like today. Vainisi was often the only professional scout the Packers had on staff, making his accomplishments all the more impressive. Sadly, Vainisi did not live to see the fruits of his labor, dying of a heart attack at age 33 in 1960. He may not be as well remembered as Lombardi or the team's talented players, but he is deserving of a bust in Canton.

Boyd Dowler
(*Packers Years 1959–1969*)

Including coach Chuck Noll, the vaunted Pittsburgh Steelers teams of the 1970s have 11 franchise standouts in the Pro Football Hall of Fame, while

10 Canton immortals played a vital role in the Cleveland Browns' championship teams in the 1950s. An even dozen Green Bay Packers legends, not including coach Vince Lombardi, were key cogs in the team's 1960s titles.

With 10-to-12 evidently an unofficial maximum of players from any single dynasty, maybe that has something to do with the fact that Boyd Dowler's position (wide receiver) is one of only two from the Lombardi-era Packers not represented in Canton (the other being tight end).

Of course, *many* players who never had the good fortune of wearing a single championship ring were also worthy of immortality—Deacon Jones, Fran Tarkenton, and Dick Butkus, to name but a few. With that in mind, not every great player from a great team is going to make it.

But that doesn't mean that Dowler, and many others, aren't deserving. A third-round draft pick out of Colorado in 1959, he earned two trips to the Pro Bowl and was named to the NFL 1960s All-Decade Team. Entering the 2020 season, *Dowler still ranked seventh in Packers record books* with 448 catches for 6,918 yards—impressive figures considering he played in the largely run-first 1960s. Playing in the mostly pre-specialist era, Dowler was also an accomplished punter, and his pair of 75-yard boots rank third in Packers annals.

Like Rodgers-Nelson and Rodgers-Adams after them, Dowler and Bart Starr likewise possessed great chemistry. Over time, quarterbacks and receivers often develop an uncanny rapport, their experience and savvy alerting them to a play call that proves pivotal in a given contest.

Such was the case with Dowler and Bart Starr on both of Dowler's first-half touchdown catches in the 1967 Ice Bowl championship win over Dallas, when Cowboys cornerback Mel Renfro's position on the field alerted them to the proper passing play.

A week later, Dowler again made a big impact in Super Bowl II with a 62-yard touchdown reception from Starr in Green Bay's 33–14 victory over the Oakland Raiders.

If 10-to-12 are only unofficial cap numbers, and one would tend to think they are, maybe Dowler will one day join his Lombardi-era teammates in Canton. One thing is for sure: Between his size (6'5", 220) and savvy, Boyd Dowler would have been a *solid* wideout in any era.

Bob Harlan
(Packers Years 1971–2008)

If former Packers general manager Ron Wolf has a bust in Canton, doesn't that mean the man *who hired him* deserves to be there, too? Bob Harlan worked his way up the corporate ranks, starting out as assistant general manager in 1971, until he was elected as the ninth team president in 1989, following the resignation of Robert J. Parins.

Two decades of on-the-field ineptitude was proving that the Packers' power-sharing organizational hierarchy, in which no single individual had final say over football decisions, was not working. But giving Wolf that authority was still a bold move when Harlan fired head of football operations Tom Braatz and handpicked Wolf, a noted scout and talent evaluator as general manager and executive vice president, in 1991.

That decision started a chain of events that led to Wolf bringing in Mike Holmgren, Brett Favre, and Reggie White. All told, the moves ended the 24-year free-fall following the departure of Vince Lombardi. While best remembered for the crucial hiring of Wolf, it was hardly the only tough and defining decision Harlan made during his 19 years as head of the organization. Other accomplishments included:

- Moving all home games to Lambeau Field, but appeasing Milwaukee fans with season ticket packages that would allow them to attend games at the much larger, more profitable Lambeau once contests at Milwaukee County Stadium were discontinued with the 1994 season finale.
- Renovating Lambeau Field into a state-of-the-art facility, with increased stadium capacity and year-round atrium housing restaurants, the Packers Hall of Fame, and Pro Shop. The project was completed in 2003 at a cost of $295 million, chump change by today's standards. While a terrific move in retrospect, it was not a given—only becoming a reality as the result of Harlan's *active* campaigning for a taxpayer referendum approved by Brown County voters in 2000.
- Launching the fourth stock sale in team history in 1997, which raised more than $20 million and brought more than 100,000 new shareholders into the organization.
- Hiring Ted Thompson as general manager in 2005. Thompson would select Aaron Rodgers with the Packers' first-round draft pick that same year.

As a result of his franchise-changing moves that cemented success for many years to come, Harlan was named to the Packers HOF in 2004. Could Canton be next?

David Bakhtiari
(Packers Years 2013–)

In today's NFL, in which star quarterbacks are often locked in to lucrative, long-term deals, it makes sense that the left tackles who guard signal callers' blind sides are valuable and usually quite well-paid, too. Prominent tackles in the Pro Football Hall of Fame include Orlando Pace, a seven-time Pro Bowler and member of the 2000s All-Decade Team (class of 2016); Willie Roaf, selected for 11 Pro Bowls (class of 2012); and Walter Jones, nine Pro Bowls (class of 2014).

Assuming that David Bakhtiari fully recovers from a late-season ACL tear in 2020, his career appears to be on a trajectory toward Canton. The eight-year pro, a fourth-round selection out of Colorado in 2013, has already been selected to three Pro Bowls (2016, 2019, 2020) and twice been named a First-team All-Pro (2018, 2020). He was a Second-team All-Pro in 2016, 2017, and 2019.

His outstanding play in keeping superstar quarterback Aaron Rodgers upright earned Bakhtiari a four-year, $105 million contract extension in 2020, making him the highest-paid offensive lineman in NFL history, according to ESPN's Ian Rapoport.

Bakhtiari, a junior who declared himself eligible for the 2013 NFL Draft, still managed to stand out despite a horrid Buffaloes campaign in which the team only won one game. "The way he prepared and practiced, the way he worked, you knew there was something a little bit different about him," Packers GM Brian Gutekunst told Wes Hodkiewicz of Packers.com.

Bakhtiari is just the second Green Bay tackle in team history (HOFer Forrest Gregg being the other) to earn AP All-Pro recognition in four-plus consecutive seasons.

Davante Adams
(Packers Years 2014–)

Just as pro prospects shoot up NFL draft boards after impressive workouts, so has the Packers' Davante Adams climbed the ladder from very good to elite status in 2020 as perhaps the game's best wide receiver.

Adams first turned heads in 2018, when he caught 111 passes for 1,386 yards and 13 touchdowns. But it was the first season in which the second-round draft pick out of Fresno State recorded 100-plus catches and 1,000-plus yards, so he was selected Honorable Mention in the author's 2019 book, *A Century of Excellence: 100 Greatest Packers of All Time*.

Despite missing four games in 2019 due to a turf toe injury, Adams still managed to snare 83 balls for 997 yards. He demonstrated just how good he could be when healthy with a pair of playoff performances for the ages. In the Divisional round, Adams caught eight passes for a post-season franchise-record 160 yards and two scores in Green Bay's 28–23 victory over Seattle. In the NFC Championship against the 49ers, he shined in defeat with nine receptions for 138 yards.

All told, Adams cracked the Packers' top ten receiving list heading into the 2020 season with 431 catches in just six years. The total ranked ninth all-time, jumping ahead of Greg Jennings and tying Antonio Freeman in Packers record books.

In 2020, Adams not only made his fourth straight Pro Bowl but more importantly earned First-team All-Pro honors for the first time after breaking Sterling Sharpe's team record with 115 grabs and 18 touchdowns, tying the mark Sharpe set in 1994.

Following the sensational campaign, Adams's totals stood at 546 catches, bumping James Lofton out of the #4 spot in Packers annals. He'll pass Jordy Nelson for third place with his fifth grab in 2021 and needs fewer than 200 catches to catch Donald Driver as the Packers' leading career receiver, barring injury likely in 2022.

His 6,568 receiving yards and 62 TDs are also rapidly moving up Packers receiver lists. Assuming he can remain healthy, 1,000 career receptions are certainly within reach, a total that would warrant Hall discussion.

Honorable Mention

Lavvie Dilweg Clay Matthews
Mike Holmgren Bob Skoronski
Verne Lewellen

Appendix B

Player Statistics, Biographies and Fast Facts

Packers Inducted into the Hall of Fame in 1960s

Arnie Herber

Name: Arnold Charles Herber
Born: April 2, 1910 (Green Bay, Wisconsin)
Parents: Peter, Sophia
High school: Green Bay West
College: University of Wisconsin (freshman team)
College: Regis College (Denver)
Wife: Lois
Children: Jean
Post-football career: Secretary, treasurer, and sales manager for a Green Bay bottling firm
Died: October 14, 1969 (Green Bay, Wisconsin)

Year	Team	Comp.	Att.	Yds.	TD	Int.
*1930	GNB	0	0	0	3	0
*1931	GNB	0	0	0	0	0
1932	GNB	37	101	639	9	9
1933	GNB	50	124	656	3	12
1934	GNB	42	115	799	8	12
1935	GNB	40	109	729	8	14
1936	GNB	77	173	1239	11	13
1937	GNB	47	104	684	7	10
1938	GNB	22	55	336	3	4
1939	GNB	57	139	1107	8	9

Year	Team	Comp.	Att.	Yds.	TD	Int.
1940	GNB	38	89	560	6	7
1944	NYG	36	86	651	6	8
1945	NYG	35	80	641	9	8
Career		481	1175	8041	81	106

*The NFL did not keep official statistics until 1932.
Unless otherwise indicated, statistics are for regular seasons only.

Clarke Hinkle

Name: William Clarke Hinkle
Born: April 10, 1909 (Toronto, Ohio)
College: Bucknell University
Parents: Charles Hinkle and Lillian Ault Clark
Married: Emillie Cobden (1963, later divorced)
Served in U.S. Coast Guard
Post-football career: Kimberly-Clark (Neenah, Wisconsin), Sales representative (Steubenville, Ohio), Sports anchor for Ohio television station
Died: November 9, 1988 (Steubenville, Ohio)

Year	Team	Rush	Yds	TD	Rec	Yds	TD
1932	GNB	95	331	3	0	0	0
1933	GNB	139	413	4	6	38	0
1934	GNB	144	359	1	11	113	1
1935	GNB	77	273	2	1	-4	0
1936	GNB	100	476	5	0	0	0
1937	GNB	129	552	5	8	116	2
1938	GNB	114	299	3	7	98	4
1939	GNB	135	381	5	4	70	0
1940	GNB	109	383	2	4	28	1
1941	GNB	129	393	5	8	78	1
Career		1171	3860	35	49	537	9

Robert "Cal" Hubbard

Name: Robert Calvin Hubbard
Born: October 31, 1900 (Keytesville, Missouri)
Parents: Robert and Sarah (Ford) Hubbard
Married: Mildred

Children: Dr. Robert Hubbard
High school: Glasgow (Glasgow, Missouri)
College: Centenary (Shreveport, Louisiana)
Geneva (Pittsburgh, Pennsylvania)
Died: October 17, 1977 (St. Petersburg, Florida)

Year	Team	Games	Games Started	TD
1927	NYG	10	10	0
1928	NYG	13	13	0
1929	GNB	12	10	0
1930	GNB	14	13	1 (Receiving)
1931	GNB	12	4	0
1932	GNB	13	11	0
1933	GNB	13	8	0
1935	GNB	11	7	1 (INT)
1936	2 TMS	7	1	0
Career		105	77	2

Fast Fact: Never a fan of big cities, Cal Hubbard moved to Milan, Missouri, in 1944, but moved back in 1948. (Milan is only 50 miles from his native Keytesville.) Later in life, Hubbard developed emphysema, so doctors suggested he move away from cold weather. He relocated to St. Petersburg, Florida, in 1976.

Don Hutson

Name: Donald Montgomery Hutson
Born: January 31, 1913 (Pine Bluff, Arkansas)
Parents: Roy and Mabel (Clark) Hutson
Siblings: Raymond and Robert (twins)
High school: Pine Bluff
College: Alabama
Married: December 14, 1935—Julia Richards
Children: Three daughters (Julia, Missy, Jane)
Post-football career:
Operated successful Cadillac and Chevrolet dealerships in Racine, Wisconsin
Died: June 26, 1997 (Rancho Mirage, California)

Year	Team	Rec.	Ave.	Yards	TDs
1935	GNB	18	23.3	420	6

Year	Team	Rec.	Ave.	Yards	TDs
1936	GNB	34	15.8	536	8
1937	GNB	41	13.5	552	7
1938	GNB	32	17.1	548	9
1939	GNB	34	24.9	846	6
1940	GNB	45	14.8	664	7
1941	GNB	58	12.7	738	10
1942	GNB	74	16.4	1211	17
1943	GNB	47	16.5	776	11
1944	GNB	58	14.9	866	9
1945	GNB	47	17.7	834	9
Career		**488**	**16.4**	**7991**	**99**

Curly Lambeau

Name: Earl Louis Lambeau
Born: April 9, 1898 (Green Bay, Wisconsin)
Parents: Marcelin and Mary (LaTour) Lambeau
Married: Marguerite Van Kessel (1919–1934, divorced; one son)
Susan Johnson (1935–1940)
Grace Garland (1945–1955)
High school: Green Bay East
College: Notre Dame
Died: June 1, 1965 (Sturgeon Bay, Wisconsin)
City Stadium renamed Lambeau Field prior to 1965 season

Team	Year	W	L	T	Finish
*GNB	1921	3	2	1	6th
*GNB	1922	4	3	3	7th
*GNB	1923	7	2	1	3rd
*GNB	1924	7	4	0	6th
*GNB	1925	8	5	0	9th
*GNB	1926	7	3	3	5th
*GNB	1927	7	2	1	2nd
*GNB	1928	6	4	3	4th
GNB	1929	12	0	1	**1st
GNB	1930	10	3	1	**1st

Team	Year	W	L	T	Finish
GNB	1931	12	2	0	**1st
GNB	1932	10	3	1	2nd
GNB	1933	5	7	1	3rd in West
GNB	1934	7	6	0	3rd in West
GNB	1935	8	4	0	2nd in West
GNB	1936	10+	1	1	Def. Boston for NFL title
GNB	1937	7	4	0	2nd in West
GNB	1938	8	3	0	Lost to NYG for NFL title
GNB	1939	9	2	0	Def. NYG for NFL title
GNB	1940	6	4	1	2nd
GNB	1941	10	1	1	T-1st, Lost to Bears in Western playoff
GNB	1942	8	2	1	2nd
GNB	1943	7	2	1	2nd
GNB	1944	8	2	0	Def. NYG for NFL title
GNB	1945	6	4	0	3rd
GNB	1946	6	5	0	3rd
TNB	1947	6	5	1	3rd
GNB	1948	3	9	0	4th
GNB	1949	2	10	0	5th
		209	**104**	**21**	
CHI	1950	5	7	0	5th
CHI	1951	2	8	0	5th
WASH	1952	4	8	0	5th
WASH	1953	6	5	1	3rd
		226	**132**	**22**	

*Player-coach until retired as player in 1929.
**Top regular season finisher was NFL champion. Playoff system with East vs. West winners playing for championship was not started until 1933.

Because the NFL did not keep official statistics until 1932, and Lambeau played before then, this is a synopsis of his coaching—but not playing—career with the Packers.

Johnny "Blood" McNally

Name: John Victor McNally
Born: November 27, 1903 (New Richmond, Wisconsin)

Parents: John McNally Sr., and Mary (Murphy) McNally
Married: Marguerite Streater (1940s)
   Catherine Kopp (1966)
College: River Falls Normal School (WI), St. John's (MN), Notre Dame
U.S. Army Air Corps (1941–1945)
Degree in economics
Ran for St. Croix County Sheriff (1958)
Died: November 28, 1985 (Palm Springs, California)

Year	Team	Rush	Yards	TDs	Rec.	Yards	TDs
1932	GNB	37	130	0	14	168	3
1933	GNB	14	41	0	8	215	3
1934	PIT	3	3	0	1	10	0
1935	GNB	42	115	0	25	404	3
1936	GNB	13	65	0	7	147	2
1937	PIT	9	37	0	10	168	4
1938	PIT	2	-5	0	2	5	0
Totals		120	386	0	67	1117	15

The vast majority of NFL statistics are not considered "official" until 1932 onward, so earlier stats are not included above.

Fast Fact: Johnny "Blood" McNally earned a reputation for extracurricular exploits both on and off the football field. He was famous for perching on hotel ledges and the tops of bar tables as he sang the song "Galway Bay."

Mike Michalske

Name: August Mike Michalske
Born: April 24, 1903 (Cleveland, Ohio)
Parents: August, Anna (Becker) Michalske
Married: Doris Luke (1932)
Children: Lee Ann, Melinda
High school: West High School (Cleveland)
College: Pennsylvania State University (1923–1925)
Died: October 26, 1983 (Green Bay, Wisconsin)

Year	Team	Games	Games Started	TD
1927	NYY	14	12	0

Year	Team	Games	Games Started	TD
1928	NYY	13	13	0
1929	GNB	13	11	0
1930	GNB	14	12	0
1931	GNB	13	8	1
1932	GNB	13	9	0
1933	GNB	13	8	0
1934	GNB	13	12	0
1935	GNB	10	8	0
1937	GNB	6	1	0
Career		**122**	**94**	**1**

Fast Fact: Mike Michalske wore nine uniform numbers over his Packers career, the most by any player in team history: 19 (1932), 24 (1934), 28 (1931), 30 (1932), 31 (1933), 33 (1935), 36 (1929–30, 37), 40 (1935) and 63 (1934).

Packers Inducted in Hall of Fame in 1970s

Tony Canadeo

Name: Anthony Robert Canadeo
Born: May 5, 1919 (Chicago, Illinois)
High school: Steinmetz (Chicago)
College: Gonzaga
Married: Ruth Toonen (October 11, 1943)
Children: Tom, Bob, Tony, Mary Kay, Nancy
Broadcaster for CBS, covering Packers games with Ray Scott.
Died: November 29, 2003 (Green Bay, Wisconsin)

Year	Team	Rush	Yards	TDs	Rec.	Yds	TDs
1941	GNB	43	137	3	0	0	0
1942	GNB	89	272	3	10	66	0
1943	GNB	94	489	3	3	31	2
1944*	GNB	31	149	0	1	12	0
1946	GNB	122	476	0	2	25	0
1947	GNB	103	464	2	0	0	0

Year	Team	Rush	Yards	TDs	Rec.	Yds	TDs
1948	GNB	123	589	4	9	81	0
1949	GNB	208	1052	4	3	-2	0
1950	GNB	93	247	4	10	54	0
1951	GNB	54	131	1	22	226	2
1952	GNB	65	191	2	9	86	1
Career		1025	4197	26	69	579	5

*Shortened season due to World War II service.

Forrest Gregg

Name: Alvis Forrest Gregg
Born: October 18, 1933 (Birthright, Texas)
High school: Sulphur Springs (S. Springs, Texas)
College: Southern Methodist University (SMU)
Married: Barbara Dedek (1960)
Children: Forrest Jr., Karen
Additional coaching career: SMU (1989–1990), Shreveport Pirates (1994–1995)
Died: April 12, 2019 (Colorado Springs, Colorado)

Year	Team	Games	Games Started	Fumble Recoveries
1956	GNB	11	2	
1958	GNB	12	1	1
*1959	GNB	12	12	
*1960	GNB	12	12	
*1961	GNB	14	14	
*1962	GNB	14	14	
*1963	GNB	14	14	2
*1964	GNB	14	13	
1965	GNB	14	14	1
*1966	GNB	14	14	
*1967	GNB	14	14	1
*1968	GNB	14	14	2
1969	GNB	14	14	

Year	Team	Games	Games Started	*Fumble Recoveries*
1970	GNB	14	4	1
1971	DAL	6	0	
Career		193	156	8

*Pro Bowl
Missed 1957 season due to military service.

Fast Fact: Forrest Gregg wore the number 75 for 15 seasons in Green Bay, but that number belonged to Jethro Pugh in Dallas, so Gregg wore number 79 for his final season in 1971.

Vince Lombardi

Name: Vincent Thomas Lombardi
Born: June 11, 1913 (Brooklyn, New York)
Parents: Enrico "Harry" and Matilda (Izzo) Lombardi
Married: Marie Planitz (August 31, 1940)
Children: Vincent Jr., Susan
High school: Brooklyn (NY) St. Francis Prep
College: Fordham
Died: September 3, 1970 (Washington, D.C.)

Head Coaching Record

Year	Team	W	L	T	Finish	Postseason
1959	GNB	7	5	0	2nd, West	—
1960	GNB	8	4	0	1st, West	Lost to Phila. in champ., 17–13
*1961	GNB	11	3	0	1st, West	Def. NYG for champ., 37–0
1962	GNB	13	1	0	1st, West	Def. NYG for champ., 16–7
1963	GNB	11	2	1	2nd, West	Won Playoff Bowl
1964	GNB	8	5	1	2nd, West	Lost Playoff Bowl
1965	GNB	10	3	1	1st, West	Def. Clev. for champ., 23–12
1966	GNB	12	2	0	1st, West	Def. Dal. for champ, 34–27**
1967	GNB	9	4	1	***1st, Central	Def. Dal for champ., 21–17****

Year	Team	W	L	T	Finish	Postseason
1969	WASH	7	5	2	2nd, Capitol	
Career	Reg. season record	96	34	6		
Overall		105	35	6		

*NFL switched to 14-game schedule.
**Then def. KC in Super Bowl I, 35-10.
***Postseason expanded, def. LA Rams for West. Conf. title, 28-7.
****Then def. Oak. In Super Bowl II, 33-14.
Lombardi served as general manager only in 1968. The Packers finished 6-7-1 under first-year coach Phil Bengston.

Fast Fact: Vince Lombardi's funeral was held September 7, 1970, at St. Patrick's Cathedral in Manhattan. Approximately 1,500 people lined Fifth Avenue, which was closed to traffic between 39th and 50th Streets. Terence Cardinal Cooke delivered the eulogy.

Ray Nitschke

Name: Raymond Ernest Nitschke
Born: December 29, 1936 (Elmwood Park, Illinois)
Parents: Robert and Anna
Brothers: Robert Jr., Richard
High school: Proviso East (Maywood, Illinois)
College: University of Illinois
Married: Jackie Forchette (June 26, 1961)
Children: John, Richard, Amy
Died: March 8, 1998 (Venice, Florida)

Year	Team	Games	GS	FR	INT
1958	GNB	12	8	2	1
1959	GNB	12	1	2	—
1960	GNB	12	6	1	3
1961	GNB	12	10	1	2
1962	GNB	14	14	1	4
1963	GNB	12	12	1	2
*1964	GNB	14	14	2	2
1965	GNB	12	12	3	1
1966	GNB	14	14	—	2
1967	GNB	14	14	1	3

Year	Team	Games	GS	FR	INT
1968	GNB	14	14	3	2
1969	GNB	14	14	3	2
1970	GNB	14	14	2	—
1971	GNB	9	2	1	1
1972	GNB	11	1	—	—
Career		190	150	23	25

*Pro Bowl

Fast Fact: At the end of the 1972 season, the 9–4 Packers traveled to New Orleans to take on the 2–10–1 Saints on December 17 at Tulane Stadium, which proved to be Ray Nitschke's last regular season contest. He registered the only pass reception of his career, a 34-yard gain after a blocked Packers field goal attempt.

Bart Starr

Name: Bryan Bartlett Starr
Born: January 9, 1934 (Montgomery, Alabama)
High school: Sidney Lanier (Montgomery)
College: Alabama
Married: Cherry Morton (May 1954)
Children: Bart Jr., Bret (deceased)
Co-founded the Rawhide Boys Ranch for at-risk youth (1965)
Co-founded the Vince Lombardi Cancer Foundation (1971)
Died: May 26, 2019 (Birmingham, Alabama)

Year	Team	Comp.	Att.	Pct.	Yds.	TD	Int.
1956	GNB	24	44	54.5	325	2	3
1957	GNB	117	215	54.4	1489	8	10
1958	GNB	78	157	49.7	875	3	12
1959	GNB	70	134	52.2	972	6	7
*1960	GNB	98	172	57.0	1358	4	8
*1961	GNB	172	295	58.3	2418	16	16
*1962	GNB	178	285	62.5	2438	12	9
1963	GNB	132	244	54.1	1855	15	10
1964	GNB	163	272	59.9	2144	15	4
1965	GNB	140	251	55.8	2055	16	9

Player Statistics, Biographies and Fast Facts

Year	Team	Comp.	Att.	Pct.	Yds.	TD	Int.
**1966	GNB	156	251	62.2	2257	14	3
1967	GNB	115	210	54.8	1823	9	17
1968	GNB	109	171	63.7	1617	15	8
1969	GNB	92	148	62.2	1161	9	6
1970	GNB	140	255	54.9	1645	8	13
1971	GNB	24	45	53.3	286	0	3
Career		1808	3149	57.4	24718	152	138

*Pro Bowl
**NFL MVP (also Pro Bowl)

Post-season

Record	TD	Int	Comp. Pct.
9–1	15	3	61%

Fast Fact: Bart Starr is the NFL record holder with a 104.8 career playoff passer rating, nearly 20 points higher than Brett Favre.

Jim Taylor

Name: James Charles Taylor
Born: September 20, 1935 (Baton Rouge, Louisiana)
Parents: Clark and Alice Taylor
Siblings: Clark, Webb
High school: Baton Rouge
College: Louisiana State University (LSU)
Married: Dixie Grant (later divorced)
Married: Helen Spillman
Children: JoBeth, Chip
Died: October 13, 2018 (Baton Rouge, Louisiana)

Year	Team	Rush	Yards	Average	TD	Rec	TD
1958	GNB	52	247	4.8	1	4	1
1959	GNB	120	452	3.8	6	9	2
*1960	GNB	230	1101	4.8	11	15	0
*1961	GNB	243	1307	5.4	15	25	1
*+1962	GNB	272	1474	5.4	19	22	0
*1963	GNB	248	1018	4.1	9	13	1

Year	Team	Rush	Yards	Average	TD	Rec	TD
*1964	GNB	235	1169	5.0	12	38	3
1965	GNB	207	734	3.5	4	20	0
1966	GNB	204	705	3.5	4	41	2
1967	NO	130	390	3.0	2	38	0
Career		1941	8597	4.4	83	225	10
9 years	GNB	1811	8207	4.5	81	187	10
1 year	NO	130	390	3.0	2	38	0

*Pro Bowl selection
+League MVP

Packers Inducted into the Hall of Fame in 1980s–90s

Herb Adderley

Name: Herbert Anthony Adderley
Born: June 8, 1939 (Philadelphia, Pennsylvania)
Parents: Charles and Reva (White) Adderley
High school: Northeast (Philadelphia)
College: Michigan State University (1961)
Post football career: Owner, president, Tele-Communications
Died: October 30, 2020

Year	Team	Int.	Yards	TD	KR. No.	Yds.	TD–Long
1961	GNB	1	9	0	18	478	0–61
1962	GNB	7	132	1	15	418	1–103
*1963	GNB	5	86	0	20	597	1–98
*1964	GNB	4	56	0	19	508	0–43
*1965	GNB	6	175	3	10	221	0–33
*1966	GNB	4	125	1	14	320	0–65
*1967	GNB	4	16	1	10	207	0–37
1968	GNB	3	27	0	14	331	0–50
1969	GNB	5	169	1	—	—	—
1970	DAL	3	69	0	—	—	—
1971	DAL	6	182	0	—	—	—
1972	DAL	0	0	0	—	—	—

Year	Team	Int.	Yards	TD	KR. No.	Yds.	TD-Long
Career		48	1046	7	120	3080	2–103
9 years	GNB	39	795	7	120	3080	2–103
3 years	DAL	9	251	0	—	—	

*Pro Bowl

Fast Fact: Herb Adderley was a childhood friend of Bill Cosby. Cosby wrote the foreword for the book *Lombardi's Left Side*, which featured profiles of Adderley and teammate Dave Robinson.

Willie Davis

Name: William Delford Davis
Born: July 24, 1934 (Lisbon, Louisiana)
Married: Carol Davis
    Andrea (1990s) … Ann (1960s)
Children: Duane, Lori (while married to Ann)
High school: Booker T. Washington (Texarkana, Arkansas)
College: Grambling State University (1956)
Master of Business Administration—University of Chicago (1968)
President of All-Pro Broadcasting (1976–2020)
Served on many corporate and other boards including:
    Dow Chemical (1988–2006)
    Johnson Controls (1991–2006)
    Green Bay Packers (1994–2005)
Died: April 15, 2020 (Santa Monica, California)

Year	Team	Games	Games Started	FR
1958	CLEV	12	6	—
1959	CLEV	12	2	—
1960	GNB	12	12	1
1961	GNB	14	14	3
1962	GNB	14	14	3
*1963	GNB	14	14	4
*1964	GNB	14	14	2
*1965	GNB	14	14	2
*1966	GNB	14	14	2
*1967	GNB	14	14	—
1968	GNB	14	14	3

Year	Team	Games	Games Started	FR
1969	GNB	14	14	2
Career		162	144	22

No statistics listed for 1956.
In military service in 1957.
*Pro Bowl

Fast Fact: In 1999, Willie Davis was ranked number 69 on *The Sporting News* list of the 100 Greatest Football Players.

Paul Hornung

Name: Paul Vernon Hornung
Born: December 23, 1935 (Louisville, Kentucky)
Parents: Loretta and Paul Hornung, Sr.
Married: Pat Roeder (1967, later divorced)
Married: Angela DiBonaventura Cerelli
High School: Flaget (Louisville, Kentucky)
College: Notre Dame (1957)
Post-football career: CBS Sports analyst (with play-by-play announcer Lindsey Nelson), Hosted the sports program *Paul Hornung's Sports Showcase*.
Died: November 13, 2020

Year	Team	Rush	Yds	TD	Ave.	Rec.	Yds.	TD
1957	GNB	60	319	3	5.3	6	34	0
1958	GNB	69	310	2	4.5	15	137	0
*1959	GNB	152	681	7	4.5	15	113	0
*1960	GNB	160	671	13	4.2	28	257	2
+1961	GNB	127	597	8	4.7	15	145	2
1962	GNB	57	219	5	3.8	9	168	2
1964	GNB	103	415	5	4.0	9	98	0
1965	GNB	89	299	5	3.4	19	336	3
1966	GNB	76	200	2	2.6	14	192	3
Career		893	3711	50	4.2	130	1480	12

*Pro Bowl
+League MVP
Missed 1963 season due to suspension.

Scoring Summary

Year	Team	All TD	XPM	XPA	FGM	FGA	Pts
1957	GNB	3	—	—	—	4	18
1958	GNB	2	22	23	11	21	67
1959	GNB	7	31	32	7	17	94
1960	GNB	15	41	41	15	28	*176
1961	GNB	10	41	41	15	22	146
1962	GNB	7	14	14	6	10	74
1964	GNB	5	41	43	12	38	107
1965	GNB	8	—	—	—	—	48
1966	GNB	5	—	—	—	—	30
Career		62	190	194	66	140	760

*Stood as an NFL record for 46 years until broken by the Chargers' LaDainian Tomlinson in 2006, and it took him two more games to do it. Had Hornung been a more accurate placekicker (though this was not uncommon at that time), it's likely an even greater total might never have been broken.

Henry Jordan

Name: Henry Wendell Jordan
Born: January 26, 1935 (Emporia, Virginia)
Parents: Henry, Catherine (Wendell) Jordan
Married: Olive Sargent (New Year's Day, 1958)
Children: Henry Jr., Theresa, Suzanne
High school: Warwick (Newport News, Virginia)
College: University of Virginia (1957)
Post football career: Executive Director of Summerfest (Milwaukee)
Died: February 21, 1977 (Milwaukee, Wisconsin)
Warwick High School athletic field named in his honor (2000)

Year	Team	Games	Games Started	FR
1957	CLEV	12	0	
1958	CLEV	12	0	1
1959	GNB	12	12	2
*1960	GNB	12	12	5
*1961	GNB	14	9	—
1962	GNB	14	14	1+
*1963	GNB	14	12	4

Year	Team	Games	Games Started	FR
1964	GNB	12	12	3
1965	GNB	14	14	3
*1966	GNB	14	13	—
1967	GNB	14	14	—
1968	GNB	14	14	2
1969	GNB	5	5	—
Career		163	131	21

+Jordan also had an interception in 1962.
*Pro Bowl

Fast Facts: In 2000, the Warwick High School athletics field (Newport News, Virginia) was named in his honor. In May 2009, Henry Jordan was named to the Hampton Roads Sports Hall of Fame, which honors athletes, coaches and administrators who contributed to sports in southeastern Virginia.

Jim Ringo

Name: James Stephen Ringo
Born: November 21, 1931 (Orange, New Jersey)
Parents: James, Elvera
Married: Betty (1951)
Children: Michelle, James Jr., Tony, Kurt
High School: Phillipsburg (NJ)
College: Syracuse University (1953)
Died: November 19, 2007 (Chesapeake, Virginia)

Year	Team	Games	Games Started	Fumble Recoveries
1953	GNB	5	5	
1954	GNB	12	11	
1955	GNB	12	12	1
1956	GNB	12	12	2
*1957	GNB	12	12	
*1958	GNB	12	12	2
*1959	GNB	12	12	1
*1960	GNB	12	12	
*1961	GNB	14	14	

Year	Team	Games	Games Started	Fumble Recoveries
*1962	GNB	14	14	1
*1963	GNB	14	14	
*1964	PHILA	14	14	
*1965	PHILA	14	14	
1966	PHILA	14	14	
*1967	PHILA	14	14	
Career		187	186	7

*Pro Bowl

Fast Facts: When Jim Ringo was traded to Philadelphia, he had not missed a game with Green Bay in the previous 10 years. Because the Packers fielded losing seasons prior to Vince Lombardi's arrival, it gets overlooked that Ringo was already an outstanding player—named to the Pro Bowl in 1957 and 1958.

Willie Wood

Name: William Vernell Wood, Sr.
Born: December 23, 1936 (Washington, D.C.)
Wife: Sheila (died 1988)
Children: Willie Jr., Andre, LaJuane
High school: Armstrong (Washington, D.C.)
College: University of Southern California (1960)
Died: February 3, 2020 (Washington, D.C.)

Year	Team	Int.	Yards	TD	PR. No.	Yds.	TD-Long
1960	GNB	—	—	—	16	106	0–33
1961	GNB	5	52	0	14	225	2–72
*1962	GNB	+9	132	0	23	273	0–65
1963	GNB	5	67	0	19	169	0–41
*1964	GNB	3	73	1	19	252	0–64
*1965	GNB	6	65	0	13	38	0–14
*1966	GNB	3	38	1	22	82	0–13
*1967	GNB	4	60	0	12	3	0–3
*1968	GNB	2	54	0	26	126	0–16
*1969	GNB	3	40	0	8	38	0–13

Year	Team	Int.	Yards	TD	PR. No.	Yds.	TD–Long
*1970	GNB	7	110	0	11	58	0–12
1971	GNB	1	8	0	4	21	0–9
Career		48	699	2	187	1391	2–72

*Pro Bowl
+Led NFL

Fast Facts: Wood made six fumble recoveries—two in 1960, and one each in '62, '64, '68 and '70.

Packers Inducted in Hall of Fame in the 21st Century

Bobby Dillon

Name: Bobby Dillon
Born: February 23, 1930 (Pendleton, Texas)
Parents: Clyde, Ruby Dillon
Married: Ann Morgan (January 27, 1951)
Children: Dan, Karen
High school: Temple, Texas
College: University of Texas
Post-football career: WilsonArt International—president and CEO
Died: August 22, 2019 (Temple, Texas)

Year	Team	Int.	Yards	TD	PR. No.	Yds.	TD–Long
1952	GNB	4	35	0	2	22	0
1953	GNB	9	112	1	—	—	—
1954	GNB	7	111	1	1	7	0
*1955	GNB	9	153	0	—	—	—
*1956	GNB	7	244	1	—	—	—
*1957	GNB	9	180	1	1	8	0
*1958	GNB	6	134	1	—	—	—
1959	GNB	1	7	0	—	—	—
Career		**52	976	5	4	37	0

*Pro Bowl
**Packers all-time interception leader

Fast Fact: Bobby Dillon is the only Packer to record nine interceptions in more than one season.

Brett Favre

Name: Brett Lorenzo Favre
Born: October 10, 1969 (Gulfport, Mississippi)
Parents: Irvin and Bonita (French) Favre, Irvin deceased (December 21, 2003)
Siblings: Scott, Jeff, Brandi
Married: Deanna Tynes (July 14, 1996)
Children: Brittany (1989); Breleigh (1999)
High school: Hancock North Central (Kiln, Mississippi)
College: Southern Mississippi
Started Brett Favre Fourward Foundation (1996)
Served as offensive coordinator at Oak Grove High School in MS (2012–2013)

Year	Team	Comp.	Att.	Pct.	TD	Yds	Int.
1991	ATL	0	4	0	0	0	2
*1992	GNB	302	471	64.1	18	3227	13
*1993	GNB	318	522	60.9	19	3303	24
1994	GNB	363	582	62.4	33	3882	14
+*1995	GNB	359	570	63.0	38	4413	13
+*1996	GNB	325	543	59.9	39	3899	13
+*1997	GNB	304	513	59.3	35	3867	16
1998	GNB	347	551	63.0	31	4212	23
1999	GNB	341	595	57.3	22	4091	23
2000	GNB	338	580	58.3	20	3812	16
*2001	GNB	314	510	61.6	32	3921	15
*2002	GNB	341	551	61.9	27	3658	16
*2003	GNB	308	471	65.4	32	3361	21
2004	GNB	346	540	64.1	30	4088	17
2005	GNB	372	607	61.3	20	3881	29
2006	GNB	343	613	56.0	18	3885	18
*2007	GNB	356	535	66.5	28	4155	15
2008	NYJ	343	522	65.7	22	3472	22
*2009	MINN	363	531	68.4	33	4202	7
2010	MINN	217	358	60.6	11	2509	19
Career		6300	10169	62.0	508	71838	336

+NFL MVP
*Pro Bowl

Postseason

Record	TD	Int	Comp. Pct.
13–11	44	30	60.8

Jerry Kramer

Name: Gerald Lewis Kramer
Born: January 23, 1936—Jordan, Montana
Children: Tony, Diane, Daniel, Alicia, Matthew, Jordan
Matt and Jordan also played football at the University of Idaho
High school: Sandpoint (Sandpoint, Idaho)
College: University of Idaho (1958)
Bought ranch near Parma, Idaho, with second wife, Wink; later moved to Boise.
NFL commentator for CBS, later NBC

Year	Team	Games/GS	FGM	FGA	XPM	XPA
1958	GNB	12–6				
1959	GNB	12–12				
1960	GNB	12–12				
1961	GNB	8–7				
*1962	GNB	14–14	9	11	38	39
*1963	GNB	14–14	16	34	43	46
+1964	GNB	2–1				
1965	GNB	14–13				
1966	GNB	14–14				
*1967	GNB	14–14				
1968	GNB	14–13	4	9	9	10
Career		130–120	29	54	90	95

*Pro Bowl
+Missed nearly all of season due to actinomycosis.

Fast Fact: After turning 80 in 2016, Jerry Kramer auctioned off several items of memorabilia to raise college funds for his grandchildren, including his ring from the first Super Bowl, which sold for $125,000.

James Lofton

Name: James David Lofton
Born: July 5, 1956 (Fort Ord, California)

Parents: Mike, Violet
Wife: Beverly
Children: David, Daniel, Rachael; David played in Canadian Football League
High school: Washington Prep (Los Angeles, California)
College: Stanford University (1978)
Assistant coaching career: San Diego Chargers (2002–2007)
Oakland Raiders (2008)

Year	Team	Rec.	Yards	Ave.	TD
*1978	GNB	46	818	17.8	6
1979	GNB	54	968	17.9	4
*1980	GNB	71	1226	17.3	4
*1981	GNB	71	1294	18.2	8
*1982	GNB	35	696	19.9	4
*1983	GNB	58	1300	22.4	8
*1984	GNB	62	1361	22.0	7
*1985	GNB	69	1153	16.7	4
1986	GNB	64	840	13.1	4
1987	LA Raiders	41	880	21.5	5
1988	LA Raiders	28	549	19.6	0
1989	BUF	8	166	20.8	3
1990	BUF	35	712	20.3	4
*1991	BUF	57	1072	18.8	8
1992	BUF	51	786	15.4	6
1993	PHILA / RAMS	14	183	13.1	0
Career		764	14004	18.3	75

*Pro Bowl

Fast Fact: The majority of James Lofton's stellar statistics occurred during the nine years he played for the Packers, in which he grabbed 530 passes for 9,656 yards, an average of 18.2 yards per catch.

Dave Robinson

Name: Richard David Robinson
Born: May 3, 1941 (Mount Holly, New Jersey)
Parents: Leslie and Mary (Gaines) Robinson

Married: Elaine
Children: Robert, Richard, David (twins)
High school: Moorestown (NJ)
College: Penn State University (1963)

Year	Team	Games	GS	INT	FR
1963	GNB	14	3	—	—
1964	GNB	11	4		—
1965	GNB	14	14	3	2
*1966	GNB	14	14	5	2
*1967	GNB	14	14	4	1
1968	GNB	14	14	2	1
*1969	GNB	14	14	—	1
1970	GNB	4	4	2	—
1971	GNB	14	11	3	1
1972	GNB	14	13	2	1
1973	WASH	14	14	4	2
1974	WASH	14	14	2	1
Career		155	133	27	12

*Pro Bowl

Fast Fact: Dave Robinson was the sixth Nittany Lion to be honored in the Professional Football Hall of Fame in Canton, joining Jack Ham, Franco Harris, August Michalske, Lenny Moore, and Mike Munchak.

Reggie White

Name: Reginald Howard White
Born: December 19, 1961 (Chattanooga, Tennessee)
High school: Howard (Chattanooga)
College: University of Tennessee
Parents: Charles, Thelma
Wife: Sara
Children: Jeremy, Jecolia
Fellowship of Christian Athletes
Christian Athletes United for Spiritual Empowerment
Ordained Baptist minister
Died: December 26, 2004 (Cornelius, North Carolina)

Year	Team	GMs-GS	Forced Fumbles	FR	Sacks
1985	PHILA	13–12	0	2	13.0
*1986	PHILA	16–16	1	0	18.0
+1987	PHILA	12–12	4	1	21.0
*1988	PHILA	16–16	1	2	18.0
*1989	PHILA	16–16	3	1	11.0
*1990	PHILA	16–16	4	1	14.0
*1991	PHILA	16–16	2	3	15.0
*1992	PHILA	16–16	3	1	14.0
*1993	GNB	16–16	3	2	13.0
*1994	GNB	16–15	2	1	8.0
*1995	GNB	15–13	2	0	12
*1996	GNB	16–16	3	3	8.5
*1997	GNB	16–16	0	2	11.0
+1998	GNB	16–16	4	0	16.0
1999	DNP–Retired				
2000	CAR	16–16	1	1	5.5
Career		232–228	33	20	198.0

*Pro Bowl
+In addition to Pro Bowl, NFL Defensive Player of Year
Statistics with Memphis of USFL not included.

Fast Fact: Reggie White also scored two touchdowns in his career off fumble recoveries (1987, 1992) and intercepted three passes (1990, 1991, 1996).

Ron Wolf

Name: Ron Wolf
Born: December 30, 1938 (New Freedom, Pennsylvania)
Married: Edie (1978)
Children: Elliot (1982; NFL scout, executive with Packers 2004–2017)
First wife, Ginny, three children (divorced 1974)
High school: Susquehannock (Glen Rock, Pennsylvania)
College: Maryville (Tennessee)
Served in U.S. Army

Drafts as Packers GM

1992—Terrell Buckley, 1, CB, Florida State; Mark D'Onofrio, 2, LB, Penn State; **Robert Brooks**, 3, WR, South Carolina; **Edgar Bennett**, 4, RB, Florida State; Dexter McNabb, 5, FB, Florida; Orlando McKay, 5, WR, Washington; **Mark Chmura**, 6, TE, Boston College; Christopher Holder, 7,

WR, Tuskegee; **Ty Detmer**, 9, QB, Brigham Young; Shazzon Bradley, 9, DT, Tennessee; Andrew Oberg, 10, T, North Carolina; Gabe Mokwuah, 11, LB, American Int.; Brett Collins, 12, LB, Washington.

1993—**Wayne Simmons**, 1, LB, Clemson; **George Teague**, 1, S, Alabama; **Earl Dotson**, 3, T, Texas A&M-Kingsville; **Mark Brunell**, 5, QB, Washington; James Willis, 5, LB, Auburn; **Doug Evans**, 6, DB, Louisiana Tech; Paul Hutchins, 6, T, West. Michigan; Tim Watson, 6, DB, Howard; Bob Kuberski, 7, DT, Navy.

1994—**Aaron Taylor**, 1, G, Notre Dame; LeShon Johnson, 3, RB, Northern Illinois; Gabe Wilkins, 4, DE, Gardner-Webb; Terry Mickens, 5, WR, Florida A&M; **Dorsey Levens**, 5, RB, Georgia Tech; Jay Kearney, 6, WR, West Virginia; Ruffin Hamilton, 6, LB, Tulane; **Bill Schroeder**, 6, WR, Wisconsin-La Crosse; Paul Duckworth, 6, LB, Connecticut.

1995—**Craig Newsome**, 1, DB, Arizona State; Darius Holland, 3, DT, Colorado; **William Henderson**, 3, FB, North Carolina; **Brian Williams**, 3, LB, USC; **Antonio Freeman**, 3, WR, Virginia Tech; Jeff Miller, 4, T, Mississippi; Jay Barker, 5, QB, Alabama; Travis Jervey, 5, RB, The Citadel; Charlie Simmons, 6, WR, Georgia Tech; **Adam Timmerman**, 7, T, South Dakota St.

1996—John Michels, 1, T, USC; Derrick Mayes, 2, WR, Notre Dame; **Mike Flanagan**, 3, C, UCLA: **Tyrone Williams,** 3, DB, Nebraska; Chris Darkins, 4, DB, Minnesota; **Marco Rivera**, 6, G, Penn State; Kyle Wachholtz, 7, QB, USC; Keith McKenzie, 7, DE, Ball State.

1997—**Ross Verba**, 1, T, Iowa; **Darren Sharper**, 2, DB, William & Mary; Brett Conway, 3, K, Penn State; Jermaine Smith, 4, DT, Georgia; Anthony Hicks, 5, LB, Arkansas; Chris Miller, 7, WR, USC; Jerald Sowell, 7, FB, Tulane; Ron McAda, 7, QB, Army.

1998—**Vonnie Holliday**, 1, DE, North Carolina; Jonathan Brown, 3, DE, Tennessee; Roosevelt Blackmon, 4, DB, Morris Brown; Corey Bradford, 5, WR, Jackson State; Scott McGarrahan, 6, DB, New Mexico; **Matt Hasselbeck**, 6, QB, Boston College; Eddie Watson, 7, RB, Purdue.

1999—Antuan Edwards, 1, DB, Clemson; Fred Vinson, 2, DB, Vanderbilt; **Mike McKenzie**, 3, DB, Memphis; Cletidus Hunt, 3, DT, Kentucky St.; **Aaron Brooks**, 4, QB, Virginia; **Josh Bidwell**, 4, P, Oregon; De'Mond Parker, 5, RB, Oklahoma; Craig Heimburger, 5, G, Missouri; Dee Miller, 6, WR, Ohio State; Scott Curry, 6, T, Montana; Chris Akins, 7, DB, Ark.–Pine Bluff; **Donald Driver**, 7, WR, Alcorn State.

2000—**Bubba Franks**, 1, TE, Miami; **Chad Clifton**, 2, T, Tennessee; Steve Warren, 3, DT, Nebraska; **Na'il Diggs**, 4, LB, Ohio State; Anthony Lucas, 4, WR, Arkansas; Gary berry, 4, DB, Ohio State; **Kabeer Gbaja-Biamila**, 5, DE, San Diego State; Joey Jameson, 5, Texas Southern; **Mark Tauscher**, 7, T, Wisconsin; Ron Moore, 7, DT, NW Oklahoma St.; Charles Lee, 7, WR, Central Florida; Eugene McCaslin, 7, LB, Florida; Rondell Mealey, 7, RB, LSU.

Charles Woodson

Name: Charles Cameron Woodson
Born: October 7, 1976 (Fremont, Ohio)
High school: Fremont Ross
College: University of Michigan
Wife: April
Children: Chase, Charles Jr.
Charles Woodson Wines:
Developed signature wine label, "Twentyfour by Charles Woodson"

Year	Team	Int.	Yards	TD	FF	FR	Sacks
*1998	OAK	5	118	1	2	0	—
*1999	OAK	1	15	1	0	1	—
*2000	OAK	4	36	—	3	1	—
*2001	OAK	1	64	—	1	0	2.0
2002	OAK	1	3	—	4	1	—
2003	OAK	3	67	—	1	1	1.0
2004	OAK	1	25	—	2	1	2.5
2005	OAK	1	0	—	1	0	—
2006	GNB	8	61	1	3	1	1.0
2007	GNB	4	48	1	0	2	—
*2008	GNB	7	169	2	1	1	3.0
+*2009	GNB	**9**	179	3	4	1	2.0
*2010	GNB	2	48	1	5	0	2.0
*2011	GNB	7	63	1	1	1	2.0
2012	GNB	1	0	—	1	0	1.5
2013	OAK	1	13	—	3	2	2.0
2014	OAK	4	35	—	0	1	1.0
*2015	OAK	5	22	—	1	4	—
Career		65	966	11	33	18	20

Bold indicates led NFL in interceptions.
+Defensive Player of the Year
*Pro Bowl

Fast Fact: In addition to the 11 interceptions for touchdowns in his career, Charles Woodson also recorded two TDs off fumble recoveries (2007 and 2013).

Chapter Notes

Introduction

1. "Sept. 17, 1923: Community Roots," *Green Bay Packers Official Yearbook*, 2018, 142.
2. "Aug. 15, 1933: Darkest Day, But Eventually Saved," *Green Bay Packers Official Yearbook*, 2018, 139.
3. "April 11, 1950: Survival Stock," *Green Bay Packers Official Yearbook*, 2018, 131.

Chapter 1

1. "Packer Immortal Arnie Herber, 59, Dies of Cancer," *Green Bay Press-Gazette*, October 15, 1979, 1.
2. John Crist, "Chalk Talk: The Notre Dame Box," June 28, 2007, accessed October 16, 2020, https://247sports.com/nfl/chicago-bears/Article/Chalk-Talk-the-Notre-Dame-Box-104429461/.
3. Cliff Christl, "Arnie Herber," Green Bay Packers website, accessed October 16, 2020, https://www.packers.com/history/hof/arnie-herber.
4. *Ibid.*
5. Rob Reischel, *100 Things Packers Fans Should Know and Do Before They Die* (Chicago: Triumph, 2010), 197.
6. Don Smith, "Arnie Herber," *Coffin Corner* 6, no. 7 (1984), https://www.profootballresearchers.org/archives/Website_Files/Coffin_Corner/06-07-189.pdf.
7. *Ibid.*
8. Reischel, *100 Things Packers Fans Should Know and Do Before They Die*, 197.
9. "The Fourth Face on Green Bay's Quarterback Mount Rushmore: Arnie Herber," *PackersHistory.com*, September 23, 2019, accessed October 19, 2020, https://packershistory.com/2019/09/the-fourth-face-on-green-bays-quarterback-mount-rushmore/
10. Smith, "Arnie Herber."
11. David Zimmerman, *Curly Lambeau: The Man Behind the Mystique* (Hales Corners, WI: Eagle Books, 2003), 89.
12. Christl, "Arnie Herber."
13. Smith, "Arnie Herber."
14. *Ibid.*
15. George Strickler, "Packers Win Pro Title, Whip Giants, 27–0," *Chicago Tribune*, December 11, 1939, 21.
16. "The Fourth Face on Green Bay's Quarterback Mount Rushmore: Arnie Herber," *PackersHistory.com*, September 23, 2019.
17. Oliver E. Kuechle, "Packers Ask Waivers on Herber, Five Others," *Milwaukee Journal*, September 10, 1941.
18. "The Fourth Face on Green Bay's Quarterback Mount Rushmore: Arnie Herber."
19. *Ibid.*
20. Smith, "Arnie Herber."
21. *Ibid.*
22. "The Fourth Face on Green Bay's Quarterback Mount Rushmore: Arnie Herber."

Chapter 2

1. David Zimmerman, *Curly Lambeau: The Man Behind the Mystique* (Hales Corners, WI: Eagle Books, 2003), 101.
2. *Ibid.*
3. *Ibid.*
4. David Zimmerman, *Lambeau Legends: Packer Profiles of Courage* (Hales Corners, WI: Eagle Books, 2008), 40.
5. Rob Reischel, *100 Things Packers Fans Should Know and Do Before They Die* (Chicago: Triumph, 2010), 59.

Notes—Chapters 3 and 4

6. *Ibid.*
7. Richard Whittingham, *What a Game They Played: An Inside Look at the Golden Era of Pro Football* (Lincoln: University of Nebraska Press, 1984), 91.
8. Neil Reynolds, *Pain Gang: Pro Football's Fifty Toughest Players* (Lincoln: University of Nebraska Press, 2006), 68.
9. Reischel, *100 Things Packers Fans Should Know and Do Before They Die*, 59.
10. "Clarke Hinkle Bio," Pro Football Hall of Fame website, October 23, 2017, accessed November 2, 2020, https://www.profootballhof.com/players/clarke-hinkle/biography/.
11. Associated Press, "Hinkle Bucknell Fullback Leads Scoring," *Daily Capital Journal* (Salem, OR), December 2, 1929, 8..
12. "Clarke Hinkle," National Football Foundation, October 23, 2017, accessed November 2, 2020, https://footballfoundation.org/hof_search.aspx?hof=1461.
13. Allanson W. Edwards, "All-Eastern Grid Team Humbles Westerners, 6 to 0," *Nevada State Journal*, January 2, 1932, 7.
14. Zimmerman, *Curly Lambeau*, 100.
15. *Ibid.*, 103.
16. *Ibid.*, 100.
17. "Clarke Hinkle Bio," Pro Football Hall of Fame website.
18. "They Click First Year as Pros," *Racine* (WI) *Journal Times*, November 10, 1932.
19. Zimmerman, *Lambeau Legends*, 39.
20. "Clarke Hinkle Here to Play with Bay Grid Squad Again," *Green Bay Press-Gazette*, September 8, 1933, 13.
21. "Clarke Hinkle," *Pro-Football-Reference.com*, accessed October 23, 2017, www.pro-football-reference.com.
22. Zimmerman, *Curly Lambeau*, 269–270.
23. "Clarke Hinkle Is Champ Field Goal Kicker for 1941," *Green Bay Press-Gazette*, February 5, 1942, 15.
24. Zimmerman, *Curly Lambeau*, 102.
25. Zimmerman, *Lambeau Legends*, 38.
26. "Hinkle Is Lieutenant in U.S. Coast Guard," *Green Bay Press-Gazette*, May 23, 1942, 11.

Chapter 3

1. Cork Gaines, "NFL Linemen Weren't Always So Enormous—See How Much They've Grown Over the Years," *Business Insider*, September 13, 2015, accessed November 27, 2020, https://www.businessinsider.com/nfl-offensive-lineman-are-big-2011-10.
2. *Ibid.*
3. "Robert (Cal) Hubbard," Pro Football Hall of Fame website, accessed November 27, 2020, https://www.profootballhof.com/players/robert-cal-hubbard/.
4. Roger E. Robinson, "Historic Missourians: Robert Calvin Hubbard," State Historical Society of Missouri website, April 5, 2013.
5. *Ibid.*
6. David Zimmerman, *Curly Lambeau: The Man Behind the Mystique* (Hales Corners, WI: Eagle Books, 2003), 74.
7. *Ibid.*, 72.
8. *Ibid.*, 75.
9. *Ibid.*
10. Richard Whittingham, *We Are the Giants! The Oral History of the New York Giants* (Chicago: Triumph, 2014), 183.
11. *Ibid.*
12. Zimmerman, *Curly Lambeau*, 84.
13. Whittingham, *We Are the Giants!*, 183.
14. Zimmerman, *Curly Lambeau*, 84.
15. Robinson, "Historic Missourians: Robert Calvin Hubbard."
16. "Robert (Cal) Hubbard," Pro Football Hall of Fame website.
17. Zimmerman, *Curly Lambeau*, 128.
18. Broeg, "Cal Hubbard, Big Umpire, Was a Man for All Sports,"16.
19. *Ibid.*
20. "Robert (Cal) Hubbard," Pro Football Hall of Fame website.
21. Zimmerman, *Curly Lambeau*, 75.
22. "Cal Hubbard," Missouri Sports Hall of Fame website, accessed March 7, 2021, http://mosportshalloffame.com/inductees/cal-hubbard-3/.
23. Robinson, "Historic Missourians."
24. "Cal Hubbard," Missouri Sports Hall of Fame website.
25. *Ibid.*

Chapter 4

1. Bob Oates, "Don Hutson: After Having Help Invent the Forward Pass, the Former Packer Star Grabbed the Brass Ring of Life as Well," *Los Angeles Times*. April 30, 1989, 3C.

2. David Whitley, "Hutson Was First Modern Receiver," ESPN.com, February 27, 2010, https://www.espn.com/sportscentury/features/00014269.html.
3. Ibid.
4. Ibid.
5. John Garrity, "The Game's Greatest Receiver Don Hutson Remains the Standard by Which All Wideouts Are Measured," *Sports Illustrated Vault*, October 6, 1995, https://vault.si.com/vault/1995/10/06/the-games-greatest-receiver-don-hutson-remains-the-standard-by-which-all-wideouts-are-measured.
6. Bob Oates, "Don Hutson: After Having Help Invent the Forward Pass, the Former Packer Star Grabbed the Brass Ring of Life as Well," *Los Angeles Times*, April 30, 1989, 3C.
7. "The Alabama Antelope: One of Football's Greatest Pioneers," Paul. W. Bryant Museum, August 21, 2016, https://web.archive.org/web/20160821073406/http://bryantmuseum.com/stories.asp?ID=34.
8. Garrity, "The Game's Greatest Receiver Don Hutson Remains the Standard by Which All Wideouts are Measured."
9. "The Alabama Antelope," Paul W. Bryant Museum.
10. Ibid.
11. Whitley, "Hutson Was First Modern Receiver."
12. "The Alabama Antelope," Paul W. Bryant Museum.
13. Ibid.
14. Stoney McGlynn, "Bays Crush Giants in Title Game," *Milwaukee Sentinel*, December 10, 1939, https://archive.jsonline.com/sports/packers/373175711.html/.
15. Associated Press, "Don Hutson Retires, Because of Old Injuries," *Daytona Beach Morning Journal*, January 30, 1943, 2.
16. Oliver E. Kuechle, "Dazzling End Thrills Crowd," *Milwaukee Journal Sentinel*, October 7, 1945, accessed June 15, 2016, http://archive.jsonline.com/sports/packers/206356261.html.
17. Jim Hodges, "Green Bay Great Hutson Dies at 84," *Los Angeles Times*, June 17, 2016, C15.
18. Rick Joslin, "The Best in the Business: Hutson Set Standard for Pass Receivers," *Pine Bluff Commercial*, July 6, 1997.
19. Tom Andrews, "Don Hutson Is, Statistically, the Most Dominant Player in NFL History (and He's the Babe Ruth of Football)," PackersHistory.com, December 18, 2019, accessed July 16, 2020, https://packershistory.com/2019/12/don-hutson-is-statistically-the-most-dominant-player-in-nfl-history-and-hes-the-babe-ruth-of-football/?fbclid=IwAR0wNrFuj6s7OY24Et3zLd3gzJpoj4KGS3yV9Hc3Nk0q2YRnvyLN-1JT3ejQ.

Chapter 5

1. George Whitney Calhoun, "Cal's Comment," *Green Bay Press-Gazette*, September 29, 2017, 8.
2. David Zimmerman, *Lambeau Legends: Packer Profiles of Courage* (Hales Corners, WI: Eagle Books, 2008), 8.
3. Ibid.
4. Ibid.
5. Rob Reischel, *100 Things Packers Fans Should Know & Do Before They Die* (Chicago: Triumph, 2010), 73.
6. David Zimmerman, *Curly Lambeau: The Man Behind the Mystique* (Hales Corners, WI: Eagle Books, 2003), 75.
7. Ibid., 75–76.
8. Richard Whittingham, *Sundays Heroes* (Chicago: Triumph Books, 2003), 14–15.
9. Zimmerman, *Curly Lambeau*, 81.
10. Ibid.
11. Ibid., 164.
12. David Fleming, "How the Green Bay Packers Averted Financial Ruin in a Mysterious Blaze of Glory," *ESPN.com*, September 19, 2013, accessed February 23, 2021, https://www.espn.com/nfl/story/_/id/9669836/mysterious-fire-1950-saved-green-bay-packers-espn-magazine.
13. Zimmerman, *Lambeau Legends*, 8.
14. Associated Press, "Curly Lambeau, Packers' First Coach, Dies at 67," *La Crosse (WI) Tribune*, June 2, 1965, 9.

Chapter 6

1. Denis J. Gullickson, *Vagabond Halfback: The Life and Times of Johnny Blood McNally* (Madison, WI: Trails Books, 2006), 14.
2. Ibid., 10.
3. Ibid., 38.
4. Ibid.
5. Ibid., 40.
6. Ibid., 42.

7. Gerald Holland, "Is That You Up There, Johnny Blood?" *Sports Illustrated Vault*, archived from the Original on July 28, 2020.
8. Denis J. Gullickson, *Vagabond Halfback*, 65–66.
9. Jack Henry, "Johnny Blood: The Vagabond Halfback," *Coffin Corner* 1, no. 7 (1979), Pro Football Researchers Association.
10. Denis J. Gullickson, *Vagabond Halfback*, 64.
11. Raymond Rivard, "Green Bay Packers: 55 Days to Football—remembering Johnny Blood McNally," *Fansided*, 2015.
12. Jack Henry, "Johnny Blood: The Vagabond Halfback," *Coffin Corner*, Vol. 1, No. 7 (1979).
13. Ibid.
14. Ibid.
15. Ibid.
16. Rob Reischel, *100 Things Packers Fans Should Know & Do Before They Die* (Chicago: Triumph, 2010), 105.

Chapter 7

1. Art Daley, "A Quarterback Playing Guard, That Was Iron Mike Michalske," *Green Bay Press-Gazette*, January 6, 1950, 13.
2. "Coach Bedzek Shifts Lineup: Michalske, the Big Guard, Goes to Backfield; Needs Punter," *Harrisburg Telegraph*, October 14, 1925, 14.
3. David Zimmerman, *Curly Lambeau: The Man Behind the Mystique* (Hales Corners, WI: Eagle Books, 2003), 76.
4. Pro Football Hall of Fame, "Mike Michalske (1964)," Hall of Fame Bio, accessed December 14, 2020, https://www.profootballhof.com/players/mike-michalske/.
5. Ibid.
6. David Zimmerman, *Curly Lambeau: The Man Behind the Mystique* (Hales Corners, WI: Eagle Books, 2003), 76.
7. Ibid.
8. Ibid., 89.
9. Ibid.
10. "Packers Win 8th in Row; Beat Bears, 6–2," *Green Bay Press-Gazette*, November 1, 1931. (Article posted online at Packershistory.homstead.com, accessed December 14, 2020, http://packershistory.homstead.com/1931PACKERS/GAME8.html.)
11. Ibid.

12. Art Daley, "A Quarterback Playing Guard, That Was Iron Mike Michalske," *Green Bay Press-Gazette*, January 6, 1950, 13.
13. Ibid.
14. Associated Press, "Donels Steps Down as Coach at Iowa State; Michalske, Ex-Packer, Is Named Head Man," *Chicago Tribune*, October 15, 1942, 29.
15. Art Edson, "New Coach Named for the Cyclones," *Lawrence (KS) Journal-World*, October 15, 1942.
16. United Press, "Michalske Resigns at Iowa State," *Green Bay Press-Gazette*, February 5, 1947, 17.
17. Ted Willems interview with author, December 10, 2020.
18. Ibid.
19. Ibid.
20. Diane Page, "State PTA Chooses Michalske Teacher of the Year," *Green Bay Press-Gazette*, March 21, 1988, 13.
21. Ted Willems interview.

Chapter 8

1. Rob Reischel, *100 Things Packers Fans Should Know and Do Before They Die* (Chicago: Triumph, 2010), 71.
2. Tom Silverstein, "Running Back Stuck with Pack," *Milwaukee Journal Sentinel*, November 30, 2003, 1A.
3. Ibid.
4. David Zimmerman, *In Search of a Hero: Life and Times of Tony Canadeo, Green Bay Packers Gray Ghost* (Hales Corners, WI: Eagle Books, 2003), 198.
5. Ibid., 199.
6. Ibid., 200.
7. Silverstein, "Running Back Stuck with Pack," 1A.
8. Zimmerman, *In Search of a Hero*, 29.
9. Ibid., 49.
10. Rob Reischel, *100 Things Packers Fans Should Know and Do Before They Die* (Chicago: Triumph Books, 2010), 71.
11. Silverstein, "Running Back Stuck with Pack," 1A.
12. David Zimmerman, *Lambeau Legends: Packer Profiles of Courage* (Hales Corners, WI: Eagle Books, 2008), 49.
13. Cliff Christl, "Life Was Different During Tony Canadeo's Day," Green Bay Packers official website, May 15, 2013.
14. John Blanchette, "Canadeo, Veeter

Leave Void in History," *Spokane* (WA) *Spokesman-Review*, December 5, 2003.
15. Rob Reischel, *100 Things*, 72.

Chapter 9

1. Tyler Dunne, "Packers Great Gregg Faces the Battle of His Life," *Milwaukee Journal Sentinel*, July 7, 2012.
2. Forrest Gregg and Andrew O'Toole, *Winning in the Trenches* (Cincinnati: Clerisy, 2009), 102.
3. Ibid., 99.
4. Elliot Harrison, "Forrest Gregg's Legacy? One of the Best Offensive Linemen Ever," NFL.com, April 12, 2019, accessed August 20, 2020, https://www.nfl.com/news/forrest-gregg-s-legacy-one-of-the-best-offensive-linemen-ever-0ap3000001026196.
5. Willie Davis, *Closing the Gap: Lombardi, the Packers Dynasty, and the Pursuit of Excellence* (Chicago: Triumph, 2012), 78.
6. Gregg and O'Toole, *Winning in the Trenches*, 98.
7. Elliot Harrison, "Forrest Gregg's Legacy? One of the Best Offensive Linemen Ever," NFL.com, April 12, 2019, accessed August 20, 2020, https://www.nfl.com/news/forrest-gregg-s-legacy-one-of-the-best-offensive-linemen-ever-0ap3000001026196.
8. Gregg and O'Toole, *Winning in the Trenches*, 105.
9. Herb Adderley, Dave Robinson, and Royce Boyles, *Lombardi's Left Side* (Olathe, KS: Ascend Books, 2012), 205.
10. Tyler Dunne, "Packers Great Gregg Faces the Battle of His Life," *Milwaukee Journal Sentinel*, July 7, 2012.
11. Ibid.
12. "Forrest Gregg Eager to Resurrect Mustangs," *Tuscaloosa News*, January 15, 1988, 15.
13. "SMU Remembers Forrest Gregg, '56," Southern Methodist University website, December 28, 2019, accessed August 21, 2020, https://www.smu.edu/News/2019/SMU-Remembers-Forrest-Gregg.

Chapter 10

1. Paul Hornung with Billy Reed, *Lombardi and Me: Players, Coaches, and Colleagues Talk About the Man and the Myth* (Chicago: Triumph, 2006), 12.
2. Josh Katzowitz, "Remember When: John F. Kennedy, Vince Lombardi Were Friends," CBS Sports, November 22, 2013.
3. Fr. Richard Heilman, "Vince Lombardi—Strive," *Roman Catholic Man*, April 30, 2015, accessed July 19, 2020, https://www.romancatholicman.com/drive-to-strive-2/.
4. "Special Section: Priests' Jubilee," *The Compass*, April 1, 2016.
5. Johnny Smith, "Vince Lombardi Would Be Proud," *Slate*, September 30, 2017.
6. David Maraniss, *When Pride Still Mattered: A Life of Vince Lombardi* (New York: Simon & Schuster, 1999), 241.
7. Ibid., 241–242.
8. Alex Dunlap, "The NFL Beat: Lombardi and Kopay," *Austin Chronicle*, February 3, 2013.
9. Ian O'Connor, "Lombardi: A Champion of Gay Rights," ESPN.com, May 2, 2013.

Chapter 11

1. Edward Gruver, *Nitschke* (Lanham, MD: Taylor Trade, 2002), 37.
2. Ibid., 44.
3. Martin Hendricks, "The Face of a Smashmouth Approach," *Milwaukee Journal Sentinel*, February 24, 2009, accessed February 23, 2021, http://archive.jsonline.com/sports/packers/40250287.html/.
4. Bob Fox, "Jerry Kramer Talks About Ray Nitschke," August 4, 2015, accessed July 31, 2020, https://greenbaybobfox.wordpress.com/2015/08/04/jerry-kramer-talks-about-ray-nitschke/
5. Paul Hornung and Chuck Carlson, *The Paul Hornung Scrapbook* (Chicago: Triumph Books, 2014), 85.
6. David Zimmerman, *Lambeau Legends: Packer Profiles of Courage* (Hales Corners, WI: Eagle Books, 2008), 104–105.
7. Ibid.
8. Associated Press, "Crashing Tower Falls on Player," *Lewiston Morning Tribune*, September 2, 1960, 10.
9. Norman Miller, "Packers Good Bet for a New Pro Dynasty," *Bend* (OR) *Bulletin*, December 31, 1962, 2.
10. Ray Kenney, "Miller All-Stars Get Cash on the Barrelhead," *Milwaukee Journal*, November 18, 1987.

11. Raymond Rivard, "Green Bay Packers: Ray Nitschke Was Nicest Off Field, Meanest on It," LombardiAve (Packers fan site), 2017, accessed July 31, 2020, https://lombardiave.com/2017/01/31/green-bay-packers-ray-nitschke-2/.
12. Rob Reischel, *100 Things Packers Fans Should Know and Do Before They Die* (Chicago: Triumph, 2006), 42.
13. Rivard, "Green Bay Packers: Ray Nitschke Was Nicest Off Field, Meanest on It."
14. *Ibid.*

Chapter 12

1. Richard Ryman, "Bart Starr Tributes Reflect a 'Kind, Humble' Packers Icon Who Exuded Class," *Green Bay Press-Gazette*, May 26, 2019, https://www.greenbaypressgazette.com/story/news/2019/05/26/bart-starr-tributes-reflect-kind-humble-icon-who-exuded-class-packers-icon-quarterback-coach/1244918001/.
2. *Ibid.*
3. Interview with Joe Zagorski, June 3, 2020.
4. Rob Reischel, *Packers Essential: Everything You Need to Know to Be a Real Fan!* (Chicago: Triumph, 2006), 76.
5. *Ibid.*
6. Heather Graves, "Starr Left a Lasting Impression on Many," *Green Bay Press Times*, September 19, 2019, accessed March 7, 2021, https://gopresstimes.com/2019/09/19/bart-starr-left-a-lasting-impression-on-many/.
7. Paul Hornung with Billy Reed, *Lombardi and Me: Players, Coaches and Colleagues Talk About the Man and the Myth* (Chicago: Triumph, 2006), 11.
8. *Ibid.*, 11–12.
9. "Jerry Kramer Knew Bart Starr Was Tough," *Spokane (WA) Spokesman-Review*, updated May 26, 2019, https://www.spokesman.com/stories/2019/may/26/jerry-kramer-knew-bart-starr-was-tough/.
10. *Ibid.*
11. "Football's Greatest: Ranking the Top 10 Quarterbacks in NFL History," *Sports Illustrated*, October 27, 2017, https://www.si.com/nfl/2017/10/27/nfl-top-10-quarterbacks-tom-brady-joe-montana-john-elway.
12. Interview with Joe Zagorski, June 3, 2020."
13. Keith Dunnavant, *Bart Starr: America's Quarterback and the Rise of the National Football League* (New York: St. Martin's, 2011), 2.
14. Interview with Joe Zagorski, June 3, 2020.
15. *Ibid.*
16. *Ibid.*
17. Hornung with Reed, *Lombardi and Me*, 14.
18. Ryman, "Bart Starr Tributes Reflect a 'Kind, Humble' Packers Icon."
19. Paul Malcore, "The Legend of Bart Starr," Rawhide History, Rawhide.org, September 30, 2016, accessed September 22, 2020, https://www.rawhide.org/blog/supporters/legend-bart-starr/.

Chapter 13

1. Genaro C. Armas, "Hall of Famer and Green Bay Packer Legend Jim Taylor Dies at 83," additional reporting from Brett Martel, October 13, 2018, accessed August 3, 2020, https://www.cantonrep.com/sports/20181013/hall-of-famer-and-green-bay-packer-legend-jim-taylor-dies-at-83.
2. Bud Lea, "Jim Taylor's Fearless Game Stands Test of Time," *Milwaukee Journal Sentinel*, November 8, 2000, accessed March 14, 2021, http://archive.jsonline.com/sports/packers/245471751.html/.
3. John Maxymuk, *Packers by the Numbers: Jersey Numbers and the Players Who Wore Them* (Denver: Bower House, 2003), 140.
4. Lea, "Jim Taylor's Fearless Game Stands Test of Time."
5. Bob Berghaus, *The First America's Team: The 1962 Green Bay Packers* (Covington, KY: Clerisy, 2011), 15.
6. *Ibid.*
7. Jim Taylor with Kristine Setting Clark, *The Fire Within* (Chicago: Triumph, 2010), 4.
8. Ed Gruver, "The Lombardi Sweep: The Signature Play of the Green Bay Dynasty; It Symbolized an Era," *Coffin Corner* 19, no. 5 (1997), accessed March 14, 2021, http://www.profootballresearchers.org/archives/Website_Files/Coffin_Corner/19-05-712.pdf.
9. Taylor with Clark, *The Fire Within*, 36.
10. *Ibid.*, 187.
11. *Ibid.*, xii.

12. Armas, "Hall of Famer and Green Bay Packer Legend Jim Taylor Dies at 83."
13. Taylor with Clark, *The Fire Within*, 146.
14. *Ibid.*, 147.

Chapter 14

1. Herb Adderley, Dave Robinson, and Royce Boyles, *Lombardi's Left Side* (Olathe, KS: Ascend Books, 2012), 31.
2. Adderley, Robinson, and Boyles, *Lombardi's Left Side*, 20.
3. Rob Reischel, *100 Things Packers Fans Should Know and Do Before They Die* (Chicago: Triumph, 2010), 68.
4. *Ibid.*, 69.
5. Cliff Christl, "Herb Adderley's Calling Card: Big Picks in Big Moments," *Packers.com*, August 8, 2019, accessed September 8, 2020, https://www.packers.com/news/herb-adderley-s-calling-card-big-picks-in-big-moments.
6. *Ibid.*
7. Adderley, Robinson, and Boyles, *Lombardi's Left Side*, 45.
8. Christl, "Herb Adderley's Calling Card."
9. "Adderley Says He's Fed Up with Packers," *Meriden* (CT) *Morning Record*, December 23, 1969, 11.
10. Ed Schuyler, Jr., "Adderley Traded to Cowboys," *Tuscaloosa* (AL) *News*, September 2, 1970, 11.
11. Adderley, Robinson, and Boyles, *Lombardi's Left Side*, 198.
12. *Ibid.*, 200.
13. *Ibid.*, 201.
14. *Ibid.*, 202.
15. *Ibid.*, 204.
16. Michael David Smith, "Hall of Famer Herb Adderley Dies at 81," *Pro Football Talk*, October 30, 2020, accessed October 30, 2020, https://profootballtalk.nbcsports.com/2020/10/30/hall-of-famer-herb-adderley-dies-at-81/.

Chapter 15

1. Cliff Christl, "The 1960s Packers: A Product of Vince Lombardi's Prejudice-free Culture," Packers.com, February 4, 2021, accessed February 9, 2021, https://www.packers.com/news/the-1960s-packers-a-product-of-vince-lombardi-s-prejudice-free-culture.
2. "1960 NFL Opposition & Defensive Statistics," Pro-Football-Reference.com, accessed July 25, 2020, https://www.pro-football-reference.com/years/1960/opp.htm.
3. Willie Davis with Jim Martyka and Andrea Erickson Davis, *Closing the Gap: Lombardi, the Packers Dynasty, and the Pursuit of Excellence* (Chicago: Triumph, 2012), 15, 17.
4. Don Smith, "Willie Davis: Speed, Agility and Size," *Coffin Corner* 7, no. 1 (1985), https://www.profootballresearchers.org/archives/Website_Files/Coffin_Corner/07-01-216.pdf.
5. *Ibid.*
6. *Ibid.*
7. Bill Huber, "Packers Legend Willie Davis Dies: Hall of Famer Willie Davis Was Acquired in One of the Most Lopsided Trades in NFL History," *Sports Illustrated*, April 15, 2020, accessed January 14, 2021, https://www.si.com/nfl/packers/news/packers-legend-willie-davis-dies.
8. Smith, "Willie Davis: Speed, Agility and Size."
9. *Ibid.*
10. "Bob Fox, "Jerry Kramer Talks About Willie Davis," Green Bay Bob Fox, August 11, 2015, accessed July 25, 2020, https://greenbaybobfox.wordpress.com/2015/08/11/jerry-kramer-talks-about-willie=davis/?fbclid=IwAR1Z6aSQxbQ22Og3VX1XJDVhqf3mvN6h9HZw_FThqQtyHYFm9iPJ8Rwv-f4.
11. Interview with Bob Fox, June 9, 2020.
12. *Ibid.*
13. Ryan Wood, "Hall of Fame Green Bay Packers Defensive End Willie Davis Dies at 85," *USA Today*, April 15, 2020, https://www.usatoday.com/story/sports/nfl/packers/2020/04/15/willie-davis-hall-fame-green-bay-packers-defensive-end-dies/5138702002/.
14. Davis with Martyka and Davis, *Closing the Gap*, 176.
15. Huber, "Packers Legend Willie Davis Dies."
16. *Ibid.*
17. "It's Been All Business for Entrepreneur, Packers Great Willie Davis," *Investor's Business Daily*, January 21, 2017, https://www.investors.com/news/management/leaders-and-success/its-been-all-business-for-packers-great-entrepreneur-willie-davis/.
18. *Ibid.*

19. Fox, "Jerry Kramer Talks About Willie Davis."
20. Huber, "Packers Legend Willie Davis Dies."
21. Fox, "Jerry Kramer Talks About Willie Davis."
22. Huber, "Packers Legend Willie Davis Dies."

Chapter 16

1. Paul Hornung and Chuck Carlson, *The Paul Hornung Scrapbook* (Chicago: Triumph, 2014), 37.
2. Paul Hornung, *Golden Boy: Girls, Games, and Gambling at Green Bay and Notre Dame, too* (New York: Simon & Schuster, 2004), 44.
3. Hornung and Carlson, *Paul Hornung Scrapbook*, 22–23.
4. Hornung, *Golden Boy*, 45.
5. Hornung and Carlson, *Paul Hornung Scrapbook*, 65.
6. Paul Hornung with Billy Reed, *Lombardi and Me: Players, Coaches and Colleagues Talk About the Man and the Myth* (Chicago: Triumph, 2006), xxi.
7. Hornung, *Golden Boy*, 92–93.
8. Cliff Christl, "Paul Hornung," Packers.com, accessed July 20, 2020, https://www.packers.com/history/hof/paul-hornung.
9. Associated Press, "N.F.L. Lifts Suspensions: Hornung, Karras Cleared After Season on Sidelines," *The Spokesman-Review* (Spokane, WA), March 17, 1964, 12.
10. Hornung and Carlson, *Paul Hornung Scrapbook*, 109.
11. Associated Press, "N.F.L. Lifts Suspensions," 12.
12. Willie Davis, *Closing the Gap: Lombardi, the Packers Dynasty, and the Pursuit of Excellence* (Chicago: Triumph, 2012), 184.
13. Christl, "Paul Hornung," Packers.com, accessed July 20, 2020, https://www.packers.com/history/hof/paul-hornung.

Chapter 17

1. Rob Reischel, *100 Things Packers Fans Should Know and Do Before They Die* (Chicago: Triumph, 2010), 90.
2. Don Smith, "Henry Jordan," *Coffin Corner* 17, no. 2 (1995), accessed March 24, 2021, https://www.profootballresearchers.org/archives/Website_Files/Coffin_Corner/17-02-598.pdf.
3. Willie Davis with Jim Martyka and Andrea Erickson Davis, *Closing the Gap: Lombardi, the Packers Dynasty, and the Pursuit of Excellence* (Chicago: Triumph, 2012), 80.
4. Reischel, *100 Things Packers Fans Should Know and Do Before They Die*, 90.
5. Davis with Martyka and Davis, *Closing the Gap*, 81.
6. Bob Fox, "Jerry Kramer Talks About Henry Jordan," Green Bay Bob Fox, September 5, 2015, accessed November 8, 2020, https://greenbaybobfox.wordpress.com/2015/09/05/jerry-kramer-talks-about-henry-jordan/?fbclid=IwAR2RJCTdpW0k_c-brQ_UlC6-Qb_uieibUonzUV-xg4ZqHh8xOAJ-lm-mqNE.
7. Ibid.
8. Smith, "Henry Jordan."
9. Fox, "Jerry Kramer Talks About Henry Jordan."
10. Smith, "Henry Jordan."
11. Associated Press, "Henry Jordan Is Dead of Apparent Heart Attack," *Owosso* (MI) *Argus Press*, February 22, 1977, 16.
12. Ibid.
13. Don Smith, "Henry Jordan."
14. United Press International, "All-Pro Henry Jordan Dies," *Ellensburg* (WA) *Daily Record*, February 22, 1977, 6.
15. Davis with Martyka and Davis, *Closing the Gap*, 123.
16. Ibid., 258.
17. Ibid., 259.
18. Bob Fox, "Jerry Kramer Talks About Henry Jordan."
19. Don Smith, "Henry Jordan."
20. FOX 6 Now Milwaukee, "Leading the Big Gig Is No Simple Feat: You Have to Keep It Fresh," June 26, 2017, accessed November 11, 2020, https://www.fox6now.com/news/leading-the-big-gig-is-no-simple-feat-you-have-to-keep-it-fresh.
21. Bob Fox, "Jerry Kramer Talks About Henry Jordan."
22. United Press International, "All-Pro Henry Jordan Dies," 6.

Chapter 18

1. Adam Rittenberg, "Meet the Smartest Guys on the Field," ESPN, December 28,

2015, accessed November 21, 2020, https://www.espn.com/college-football/story/_/id/14453565/why-centers-smartest-guys-field.

2. *Ibid.*

3. Bob Carroll, "Jim Ringo," *Coffin Corner* 4, no. 4 (1982), accessed March 24, 2021, https://www.profootballresearchers.org/archives/Website_Files/Coffin_Corner/04-04-095.pdf.

4. Cliff Christl, "Jim Ringo Was Perfect Fit for Lombardi's Offense," Packers.com, March 7, 2019, accessed March 24, 2021, https://www.packers.com/news/jim-ringo-was-perfect-fit-for-lombardi-s-offense.

5. *Ibid.*

6. *Ibid.*

7. "Jim Ringo, Trigger Man," Jock Bio Legends, 2008, accessed November 21, 2020, http://www.jockbio.com/Classic/Ringo/Ringo_bio.html.

8. "Jim Ringo," Pro Football Hall of Fame, accessed November 21, 2020, https://www.profootballhof.com/players/jim-ringo/.

9. Matt Schudel, "NFL's Jim Ringo: Hall of Famer with Packers and Eagles," *Washington Post*, November 22, 2007, accessed March 24, 2021, https://www.washingtonpost.com/wp-dyn/content/article/2007/11/21/AR2007112102536.html.

10. Reischel, *100 Things Packers Fans Should Know and Do Before They*, 97.

11. *Ibid.*

12. United Press International, "Packers Pull Trade, Create New Problem," *Pittsburgh Press*, May 6, 1964, 2C.

13. Associated Press, "Packers Trade Ringo, Gros," *St. Petersburg* (FL) *Times*, May 6, 1964, 58.

14. "Jim Ringo, Trigger Man."

15. *Ibid.*

16. Carroll, "Jim Ringo."

Chapter 19

1. Beth Harris, "Willie Wood, Packers Great and Hall of Fame DB, Dies at 83," *Philadelphia Tribune*, February 4, 2020, accessed September 30, 2020, https://www.phillytrib.com/obituaries/willie-wood-packers-great-and-hall-of-fame-db-dies-at-83/article_1a87f321-8494-5a37-8a5a-44831e2cb5bc.html.

2. Don Smith, "Willie Wood," Pro Football Researchers Association. *The Coffin Corner* 11, no. 2 (1989), https://www.profootballresearchers.org/archives/Website_Files/Coffin_Corner/11-02-369.pdf.

3. Harris, "Willie Wood, Packers Great and Hall of Fame DB, Dies at 83."

4. Willie Davis with Jim Martyka and Andrea Erickson Davis, *Closing the Gap: Lombardi, the Packers Dynasty, and the Pursuit of Excellence* (Chicago: Triumph, 2012), 84.

5. David Zimmerman, *Lambeau Legends: Packer Profiles of Courage* (Hales Corners, WI: Eagle Books, 2008), 122.

6. "Former Packers Safety Willie Wood Dies at 83," Packers.com, February 3, 2020, accessed September 27, 2020, https://www.packers.com/news/former-packers-safety-willie-wood-dies-at-83.

7. Zimmerman, *Lambeau Legends*, 122.

8. Cliff Christl, "The 1960s Packers: A Product of Vince Lombardi's Prejudice-Free Culture," Packers.com, February 4, 2021, accessed February 9, 2021, https://www.packers.com/news/the-1960s-packers-a-product-of-vince-lombardi-s-prejudice-free-culture.

9. Davis with Martyka and Davis, *Closing the Gap*, 100.

10. *Ibid.*

11. "Former Packers Safety Willie Wood Dies at 83."

12. Matt Schudel, "Willie Wood, Hall of Fame Defensive Back for Vince Lombardi's Packers, Dies at 83," *Washington Post*, February 4, 2020, accessed October 2, 2020, https://www.washingtonpost.com/local/obituaries/willie-wood-hall-of-fame-defensive-back-for-vince-lombardis-packers-dies-at-83/2020/02/04/be4b0a18-475f-11ea-ab15-b5df3261b710_story.html.

13. "Former Packers safety Willie Wood dies at 83."

14. Schudel, "Willie Wood, Hall of Fame Defensive Back for Vince Lombardi's Packers, Dies at 83."

15. Associated Press, "Packers' Willie Wood Retires, Looks to Head Pro Coaching Job."

16. Associated Press, "Willie Wood Named Coach of the Bell," *Bangor* (ME) *Daily News*, July 30, 1975, 22.

17. Schudel, "Willie Wood, Hall of Fame Defensive Back for Vince Lombardi's Packers, Dies at 83."

18. Rob Reischel: *Packers Essential:*

Everything You Need to Know to Be a Real Fan! (Chicago: Triumph, 2006), 61.

19. Bill Pennington, "Willie Wood Made the Most Memorable Play of Super Bowl I. He Has No Recollection," *New York Times*, February 4, 2016, https://www.nytimes.com/2016/02/05/sports/football/williewood-made-the-most-memorable-play-of-super-bowl-i-he-has-no-recollection.html.

20. Ibid.

Chapter 20

1. "Hall of Very Good," *Coffin Corner* 33, no. 4 (2011), Professional Football Researchers Association, http://www.profootballresearchers.com/hall-of-very-good-2011.html.

2. "Hall of Honor: Bobby Dan Dillon," University of Texas Athletics, accessed April 24, 2021, https://texassports.com/honors/hall-of-honor/bobby-dan-dillon/577.

3. Bob Fox, "Why Bobby Dillon Deserves to Be Considered for the Pro Football Hall of Fame," August 19, 2018, accessed July 25, 2020, https://greenbaybobfox.wordpress.com/2018/08/19/green-bay-packers-why-bobby-dillon-deserves-to-be-considered-for-the-pro-football-hall-of-fame/.

4. Tim Waits, "Column: Dillon Lived with No Regrets," *Temple Daily Telegram*, August 28, 2019, https://www.tdtnews.com/sports/article_e94b207c-ca00-11e9-811a-2bee5116c43b.html.

5. Associated Press. "Packers' Great, Who Had Four INTs vs. Lions on Thanksgiving 1953, Dies at 89," *Detroit News*, September 5, 2019, https://www.detroitnews.com/story/sports/nfl/lions/2019/09/05/packers-great-who-had-four-ints-vs-lions-thanksgiving-1953-dies-89/2217587001/.

6. Bill Huber, "One-Eyed Interception Machine Dillon Picked for Hall of Fame," *Sports Illustrated*, January 16, 2020, https://www.si.com/nfl/packers/news/dillon-picked-for-hall-of-fame.

7. "Monocular Vision (Sight in One Eye)," RNIB, accessed October 27, 2020, https://www.rnib.org.uk/eye-health/eye-conditions/monocular-vision.

8. J. W. Nix, "Crazy Canton Cuts = Bobby Dillon," Bleacher Report, March 15, 2009, accessed October 27, 2020, https://bleacherreport.com/articles/139312-crazy-canton-cuts-bobby-dillon.

9. Bob Fox, "Why Bobby Dillon Deserves to Be Considered for the Pro Football Hall of Fame."

10. Ibid.

11. Ron Borges, "Countdown to Canton: Bobby Dillon Has His Eye on Finally Arriving in Canton," *SI.com*, January 1, 2020, https://www.si.com/nfl/talkoffame/state-your-case/countdown-to-canton-bobby-dillon-has-his-eye-on-finally-arriving-in-canton.

12. Bob Fox, "Why Bobby Dillon Deserves to Be Considered for the Pro Football Hall of Fame."

13. Art Daley, "Dillon, Em Tunnell Boost Packers' Defensive Savvy," *Green Bay Press-Gazette*, September 2, 1959, 19.

14. Huber, "One-Eyed Interception Machine Dillon Picked for Hall of Fame."

15. Richard Ryman, "Dillon, Packers' Interception Leader, Dies," *Green Bay Press-Gazette*, August 30, 2019, B2.

16. Borges, "Countdown to Canton."

Chapter 21

1. Patrick Hruby, "Feeling the Pain of a Brett Favre Injury," ESPN.com, December 17, 2010, http://www.espn.com/espn/page2/story?sportCat=nfl&page=hruby/101216_brett_favre_injuries.

2. "Through the Years," *FAVRE*, F+W Publications, 2008.

3. Ibid.

4. Peter King, "Brett Favre Details How the Pain of Playing in the NFL Led to His Addiction to Painkillers," *Sports Illustrated Vault*, May 27, 1996, accessed July 24, 2020, https://vault.si.com/vault/1996/05/27/nhl-26norc-3d1-26zx-3d1430450275468.

5. Associated Press, "Favre Surpasses Marino with 421st Career TD," ESPN.com, September 30, 2007, https://www.espn.com/nfl/news/story?id=3043571.

6. Alan Shipnuck, "Top of His Game: It Was Never About Me," *Sports Illustrated*, March 17, 2008, https://vault.si.com/vault/2008/03/17/top-of-his-game.

7. Peter King, "Living Day to Day," *Sports Illustrated*, March 17, 2008, https://vault.si.com/vault/2008/03/17/living-day-to-day.

8. J.R. Radcliffe, "Remembering the Strange Moment the Packers Traded Brett Favre, 10 Years Ago Today," *USA Today*,

Notes—Chapters 22 and 23

August 7, 2018, https://www.usatoday.com/story/sports/nfl/packers/2018/08/07/brett-favre-trade-green-bay-packers-new-york-jets/928127002/.

Chapter 22

1. Interview with Bob Fox, October 8, 2020.
2. Rob Reischel, *100 Things Packers Fans Should Know and Do Before They Die* (Chicago: Triumph, 2006), 103.
3. Associated Press, "Idaho Linemen Shine as West Topples Favored East, 27–13," *Lewiston* (ID) *Morning Tribune*, December 29, 1957, 8.
4. Associated Press, "College Star Eleven Upsets Pros, 35–19," *Lewiston* (ID) *Morning Tribune*, August 16, 1958, 8.
5. Jerry Kramer, phone interview with author, October 1, 2020.
6. Pete Dougherty, "Jerry Kramer Hails Vince Lombardi, Former Packers Teammates as Enters Hall of Fame," *Green Bay Press-Gazette*, August 4, 2018, accessed October 6, 2020, https://www.packersnews.com/story/sports/nfl/packers/2018/08/04/jerry-kramer-hails-vince-lombardi-former-teammates-he-enters-hall/902296002/.
7. Jerry Kramer, phone interview.
8. Bob Fox, "Jerry Kramer Talks About Vince Lombardi," Green Bay Bob Fox (blog), July 23, 2015, accessed October 6, 2020, https://greenbaybobfox.wordpress.com/2015/07/23/jerry-kramer-talks-about-vince-lombardi/.
9. Rob Reischel, *Packers Essential: Everything You Need to Know to Be a Real Fan!* (Chicago: Triumph, 2006), 30–31.
10. Jerry Kramer, phone interview.
11. Ibid.
12. Ibid.
13. Associated Press, "Packers Grind Out Grim 16–7 Win," *Spokesman-Review*, December 31, 1961, 8.
14. Jerry Kramer, phone interview.
15. Associated Press, "Splinters from Old Injury Caused Kramer's Illness," *Lewiston* (ID) *Morning Tribune*, May 12, 1965, 15.
16. Jerry Kramer, phone interview.
17. Ibid.
18. Ibid.
19. Ibid.
20. Ibid.
21. Ibid.

Chapter 23

1. Ralph Mancini, "Green Bay Packers 100: Second best receiver in franchise history," Lombardi Ave (fan site), June 11, 2016, accessed October 22, 2020, https://lombardiave.com/2016/06/11/green-bay-packers-100-second-best-receiver-franchise-history/.
2. "Lofton, James 1956–," *Encyclopedia.com*, accessed October 23, 2020, https://www.encyclopedia.com/education/news-wires-white-papers-and-books/lofton-james-1956.
3. Dale Hoffman, "May 2, 1978: Packers Draft Full of Surprises," *Milwaukee Sentinel*, May 3, 1978, https://archive.jsonline.com/sports/packers/249075821.html/.
4. Ibid.
5. Rick Telander, "A Picture-Perfect End: That's Green Bay's James Lofton, a Troubled Young Man Until He Met the Woman Who Gave New Focus to His Life," *Sports Illustrated Vault*, December 6, 1982, https://vault.si.com/vault/1982/12/06/a-picture-perfect-end.
6. Ibid.
7. Richard Carter, "James Lofton Beats the Odds for Pro Football Hall of Fame," *New York Amsterdam News*, July 31–August 6, 2003.
8. Ibid.
9. Mark Heisler, "Lofton Is Acquitted of Sexual Assault by Green Bay Jury," *Los Angeles Times*, May 23, 1987, 84.
10. "James Lofton," Pro Football Researchers Association, *Coffin Corner* 25, no. 4 (2003), https://www.profootballresearchers.org/archives/Website_Files/Coffin_Corner/25-04-990.pdf.
11. Ralph Mancini, "Green Bay Packers 100: Second Best Receiver in Franchise History," Lombardi Ave, June 11, 2016, https://lombardiave.com/2016/06/11/green-bay-packers-100-second-best-receiver-franchise-history/.
12. Carter, "James Lofton Beats the Odds."
13. Ibid.
14. Ross Forman, "James Lofton Reflects on 40 Years in Professional Football," *Sports Collectors Digest*, February 12, 2018, https://

sportscollectorsdigest.com/news/james-lofton-professional-football.
   15. Forman, "James Lofton Reflects on 40 Years in Professional Football."
   16. Mancini, "Green Bay Packers 100."

Chapter 24

   1. Herb Adderley, Dave Robinson and Royce Boyles, *Lombardi's Left Side* (Olathe, KS: Ascend, 2012), 154.
   2. Interview with Bob Fox, September 17, 2020.
   3. Interview with Ralph Hickok, September 17, 2020.
   4. Adderley, Robinson and Boyles, *Lombardi's Left Side*, 52–53.
   5. Steve Doerschuk, "HOF 13: Robinson Toasts His Beloved Wife, Career," Pro Football Hall of Fame, July 31, 2013, accessed September 18, 2020, https://www.cantonrep.com/article/20130731/NEWS/307319885.
   6. Adderley, Robinson and Boyles, *Lombardi's Left Side*, 74.
   7. Ibid., 75.
   8. Rob Reischel, *100 Things Packers Fans Should Know and Do Before They Die* (Chicago: Triumph, 2010), 204.
   9. Ibid.
   10. Adderley, Robinson and Boyles, *Lombardi's Left Side*, 83.
   11. Ibid., 4.
   12. Ibid.
   13. Ibid., 156.
   14. Ibid., 169.
   15. Martin Hendricks, "An Unsung Hero," *Milwaukee Journal Sentinel*, October 14, 2009, accessed September 21, 2020, https://archive.jsonline.com/sports/packers/64174112.html/.
   16. Ibid.
   17. Doerschuk, "HOF 13."

Chapter 25

   1. Len Pasquarelli, "Final Autopsy Complete for Reggie White," ESPN.com, May 19, 2005, https://www.espn.com/nfl/news/story?id=2063708.
   2. Paul Nowell, "NFL Defensive Great Reggie White, 43, Dies," *Miami Herald*, December 26, 2004, 5B-1.
   3. Michael Hiestand and Gary Mihoces, "NFL Linemen Awaken to Sleep Apnea Dangers," *USA Today*, December 29, 2004, http://usatoday30.usatoday.com/sports/football/nfl/2004-12-29-sleep-apnea_x.htm.
   4. Ibid.
   5. "Reggie's Self-Revelation," *Yahoo! News*, February 4, 2006, accessed December 27, 2020, https://sports.yahoo.com/news/reggies-self-revelation-230500053--nfl.html.
   6. Erin Curry, "Reggie White, Who Used Football to Spread Gospel, Dies at 43," *Baptist Press*, December 27, 2004, https://www.baptistpress.com/resource-library/news/reggie-white-who-used-football-to-spread-gospel-dies-at-43/.
   7. Mark Kram and Tom Pendergast, "Reggie White Biography: Loved His Tennessee Home, Jumped from USFL to NFL, Emerged as Team Leader, Joined the Packers," Biography.Jrank.org, retrieved May 17, 2017, accessed December 29, 2020, https://biography.jrank.org/pages/2548/White-Reggie.html.
   8. Josepha DaCosta: "Reggie White's Legacy Is Much Bigger Than Just Football," *Madison* (WI) *Capital Times*, July 13, 2020, https://madison.com/ct/opinion/column/josepha-da-costa-reggie-whites-legacy-is-much-bigger-than-just-football/article_0acc4457-db9a-5efd-874c-c08127526bda.html.
   9. Nowell, "NFL Defensive Great Reggie White, 43, Dies."
   10. Robert Klemko, "How Reggie White Made Green Bay Cool," *Sports Illustrated*, December 6, 2016, https://www.si.com/nfl/2016/12/06/nfl-reggie-white-green-bay-black-players-free-agency-history.
   11. Ibid.
   12. Bob McGinn, "Ron Wolf in His Words: How Fate and Football Came Together," *Milwaukee Journal Sentinel*, August 7, 2015, http://archive.jsonline.com/sports/packers/ron-wolf-in-his-words-how-fate-and-football-came-together-b99552142z1-321055271.html/.
   13. DaCosta, "Reggie White's Legacy."
   14. Nowell, "NFL Defensive Great Reggie White, 43, Dies."
   15. Klemko, "How Reggie White Made Green Bay Cool."
   16. Ibid.
   17. Curry, "Reggie White, Who Used Football."
   18. Ibid.

19. Klemko, "How Reggie White Made Green Bay Cool."
20. DaCosta, "Reggie White's Legacy."

Chapter 26

1. Bob McGinn, "Ron Wolf in His Words: How Fate and Football Came Together," *Milwaukee Journal Sentinel*, August 7, 2015, accessed December 10, 2020, http://archive.jsonline.com/sports/packers/ron-wolf-in-his-words-how-fate-and-football-came-together-b99552142z1-321055271.html/.
2. Rob Reischel, *100 Things Packers Fans Should Know & Do Before They Die* (Chicago: Triumph, 2010), 24.
3. Rob Reischel, *Packers Essential: Everything You Need to Know to Be a Real Fan!* (Chicago: Triumph, 2006), 99–100.
4. Bob McGinn, "April 6, 1993: $17 Million Reasons Convince Reggie White," *Milwaukee Journal*, April 7, 1993, https://www.packersnews.com/story/sports/nfl/packers/2018/04/14/april-6-1993-17-million-reasons-convince-reggie-white-join-packers/509369002/.
5. Reischel, *100 Things Packers Fans Should Know*, 24.
6. Bob McGinn, "Ron Wolf in His Words."

Chapter 27

1. "Former Packers Safety Willie Wood Dies at 83," Packers.com, February 3, 2020, accessed September 30, 2020, https://www.packers.com/news/former-packers-safety-willie-wood-dies-at-83.
2. Phil Barber, "Charles Woodson: Great, but Not the Greatest," *Santa Rosa (CA) Press-Democrat*, December 20, 2015, https://110percent.blogs.pressdemocrat.com/10453/charles-woodson-great-but-not-the-greatest/.
3. Peter King, "Who Is Friggin' Tougher Than Charles Woodson?" *Sports Illustrated*, December 22, 2015, https://www.si.com/nfl/2015/12/22/charles-woodson-retirement-raiders-nfl-power-rankings.
4. Bob Fox, "Green Bay Packers: Charles Woodson Is a Lock to Be in the Class of 2021 for the Pro Football Hall of Fame," Green Bay Bob Fox (blog), December 11, 2020, accessed December 22, 2020, https://greenbaybobfox.wordpress.com/2020/12/11.
5. Zach Kruse, "Take Your Pick: Which Was Your Favorite Charles Woodson Pick-six?" *Packers Wire*, May 26, 2020, accessed December 21, 2020, https://www.msn.com/en-us/sports/nfl/take-your-pick-which-was-your-favorite-charles-woodson-pick-six/ar-BB14DltV.
6. King, "Who Is Friggin' Tougher Than Charles Woodson?"
7. Barber, "Charles Woodson."
8. Michael Dulka, "Remembering Charles Woodson's Rise to Greatness with the Green Bay Packers," *Bleacher Report*, February 17, 2013, accessed December 23, 2020, https://bleacherreport.com/articles/1531202-remembering-charles-woodsons-rise-to-greatness-with-the-green-bay-packers.
9. Ibid.
10. Ibid.
11. John Katzenstein, "Raiders' Woodson Still Excelling at 39," *Detroit News*, November 18, 2015, https://www.detroitnews.com/story/sports/nfl/lions/2015/11/18/raiders-woodson-still-excelling/76032114/.
12. Barber, "Charles Woodson."
13. Jim Polzin, "Packers: In the Locker Room, Woodson Chooses His Words and His Teammates Listen," *Wisconsin State Journal*, January 27, 2011, https://madison.com/sports/football/professional/packers-in-the-locker-room-woodson-chooses-his-words-and-his-teammates-listen/article_02f31a2a-29ce-11e0-add9-001cc4c002e0.html.

Bibliography

Except where otherwise noted, all statistics come from pro-football-reference.com.

Interviews

Bob Fox, June 9 and September 17, 2020.
Ralph Hickok, September 17, 2020.
Jerry Kramer, phone interview, October 1, 2020.
Ted Willems, phone interview, December 10, 2020.
Joe Zagorski, June 3, 2020.

Books

Adderley, Herb, Dave Robinson, and Royce Boyles. *Lombardi's Left Side*. Olathe, KS: Ascend, 2012.
Berghaus, Bob. *The First America's Team: The 1962 Green Bay Packers*. Covington, KY: Clerisy, 2011.
Davis, Willie, with Jim Martyka and Andrea Erickson Davis. *Closing the Gap: Lombardi, the Packers Dynasty, and the Pursuit of Excellence*. Chicago: Triumph, 2012.
Dunnavant, Keith. *Bart Starr: America's Quarterback and the Rise of the National Football League*. New York: St. Martin's, 2011.
Gregg, Forrest, and Andrew O'Toole. *Winning in the Trenches*. Cincinnati: Clerisy, 2009.
Gruver, Edward. *Nitschke*. Lanham, MD: Taylor Trade, 2002.
Gullickson, Denis J. *Vagabond Halfback: The Life and Times of Johnny Blood McNally*. Madison, WI: Trails, 2006.
Hornung, Paul. *Golden Boy: Girls, Games, and Gambling at Green Bay and Notre Dame, Too*. New York: Simon & Schuster, 2004.
Hornung, Paul, and Chuck Carlson. *The Paul Hornung Scrapbook*. Chicago: Triumph, 2014.
Hornung, Paul, with Billy Reed. *Lombardi and Me: Players, Coaches, and Colleagues Talk About the Man and the Myth*. Chicago: Triumph, 2006.
Maraniss, David. *When Pride Still Mattered: A Life of Vince Lombardi*. New York: Simon & Schuster, 1999.
Maxymuk, John, *Packers by the Numbers: Jersey Numbers and the Players Who Wore Them*. Denver: Bower House, 2003.
Reischel, Rob. *100 Things Packers Fans Should Know and Do Before They Die*. Chicago: Triumph, 2010.
_____. *Packers Essential: Everything You Need to Know to Be a Real Fan!* Chicago: Triumph, 2006.
Reynolds, Neil. *Pain Gang: Pro Football's Fifty Toughest Players*. Lincoln: University of Nebraska Press, 2006.
Taylor, Jim, with Kristine Setting Clark. *The Fire Within*. Chicago: Triumph, 2010.
Whittingham, Richard. *Sunday's Heroes*. Chicago: Triumph, 2003.
_____. *We Are the Giants! The Oral History of the New York Giants*. Chicago: Triumph, 2014.
_____. *What a Game They Played: An Inside Look at the Golden Era of Pro Football*. Lincoln: University of Nebraska Press, 1984.
Zimmerman, David. *Curly Lambeau: The Man Behind the Mystique*. Hales Corners, WI: Eagle, 2003.
_____. *In Search of a Hero: Life and Times of Tony Canadeo, Green Bay Packers Gray Ghost*. Hales Corners, WI: Eagle, 2003.

Articles

"The Alabama Antelope: One of Football's Greatest Pioneers." Paul. W. Bryant Museum, August 21, 2016. https://web.archive.org/web/20160821073406/http://bryantmuseum.com/stories.asp?ID=34.

Andrews, Tom. "Don Hutson Is, Statistically, the Most Dominant Player in NFL History (and He's the Babe Ruth of Football)." PackersHistory.com, December 18, 2019. https://packershistory.com/2019/12/don-hutson-is-statistically-the-most-dominant-player-in-nfl-history-and-hes-the-babe-ruth-of-football/?fbclid=IwAR0wNrFuj6s7OY24Et3zLd3gzJpoj4KGS3yV9Hc3Nk0q2YRnvyLN1JT3ejQ.

Armas, Genaro C. "Hall of Famer and Green Bay Packer legend Jim Taylor dies at 83." Associated Press, additional reporting from Brett Martel, October 13, 2018. https://www.cantonrep.com/sports/20181013/Hall-of-Famer-and-green-bay-packer-legend-jim-taylor-dies-at-83.

Associated Press. "Adderley Says He's Fed Up with Packers," *Meriden* (CT) *Morning Record*, December 23, 1969, 11.

———. "College Star Eleven Upsets Pros, 35–19." *Lewiston* (ID) *Morning Tribune*, August 16, 1958, 8.

———. "Crashing Tower Falls on Player." *Lewiston* (ID) *Morning Tribune*, September 2, 1960, 10.

———. "Curly Lambeau, Packers' First Coach, Dies at 67." *Appleton* (WI) *Post Crescent*, June 2, 1965. https://www.newspapers.com/newspage/287532846/.

———. "Don Hutson Retires, Because of Old Injuries." *Daytona Beach* (FL) *Morning Journal*, January 30, 1943, 2.

———. "Donels Steps Down as Coach at Iowa State; Michalske, Ex-Packer, Is Named Head Man." *Chicago Tribune*, October 15, 1942, 29.

———. "Favre Surpasses Marino with 421st Career TD." ESPN.com, September 30, 2007. https://www.espn.com/nfl/news/story?id=3043571.

———. "Henry Jordan Is Dead of Apparent Heart Attack." *Owosso* (MI) *Argus Press*, February 22, 1977, 16.

———. *Lambeau Legends: Packer Profiles of Courage*. Hales Corners, WI: Eagle, 2008.

———. "Hinkle Bucknell Fullback Leads Scoring." *Salem* (OR) *Daily Capital Journal*, December 2, 1929, 8.

———. "Idaho Linemen Shine as West Topples Favored East, 27–13." *Lewiston* (ID) *Morning Tribune*, December 29, 1957, 8.

———. "N.F.L. Lifts Suspensions: Hornung, Karras Cleared After Season on Sidelines." *Spokane* (WA) *Spokesman-Review*, March 17, 1964, 12.

———. "Packers' Great, Who Had Four INTs Vs. Lions on Thanksgiving 1953, Dies at 89." *Detroit News*, September 5, 2019. https://www.detroitnews.com/story/sports/nfl/lions/2019/09/05/packers-great-who-had-four-ints-vs-lions-thanksgiving-1953-dies-89/2217587001/.

———. "Packers Grind Out Grim 16–7 Win." *Spokane* (WA) *Spokesman-Review*, December 31, 1961, 8.

———. "Packers Trade Ringo, Gros." *St. Petersburg* (FL) *Times*, May 6, 1964, 58.

———. "Splinters from Old Injury Caused Kramer's Illness." *Lewiston* (ID) *Morning Tribune*, May 12, 1965, 15.

Barber, Phil. "Charles Woodson: Great, but Not the Greatest." *Santa Rosa* (CA) *Press-Democrat*, December 20, 2015. https://110percent.blogs.pressdemocrat.com/10453/charles-woodson-great-but-not-the-greatest/.

Blanchette, John. "Canadeo, Veeter Leave Void in History." *Spokane* (WA) *Spokesman-Review*, December 5, 2003, C1.

"Bobby Dan Dillon: Hall of Honor." University of Texas Athletics, 1972. https://texassports.com/hof.aspx?hof=577.

Borges, Ron. "Countdown to Canton: Bobby Dillon Has His Eye on Finally Arriving in Canton." SI.com, December 31, 2019. https://www.si.com/nfl/talkoffame/state-your-case/countdown-to-canton-bobby-dillon-has-his-eye-on-finally-arriving-in-canton.

Bower, Bradley C. "NFL Linemen Awaken to Sleep Apnea Dangers." Associated Press, December 29, 2004. https://usatoday30.usatoday.com/sports/football/nfl/2004-12-29-sleep-apnea_x.htm.

Broeg, Bob. "Cal Hubbard, Big Umpire, Was a Man for All Sports." *St. Louis Post-Dispatch*, October 23, 1977, 16.

"Cal Hubbard." *Missouri Sports Hall of Fame*, n.d. http://mosportshalloffame.com/inductees/cal-hubbard-2/.

Bibliography

Calhoun, George Whitney. "Cal's Comment." *Green Bay Press-Gazette,* September 29, 1917, 8.

Carroll, Bob. "Jim Ringo." *The Coffin Corner* 4, no. 4 (1982). Pro Football Researchers Association.

Carter, Richard. "James Lofton Beats the Odds for Pro Football Hall of Fame." *New York Amsterdam News,* July 31–August 6, 2003.

Christl, Cliff. "Arnie Herber." *Packers.com,* n.d. https://www.packers.com/history/hof/arnie-herber.

———. "Herb Adderley's Calling Card: Big Picks in Big Moments." *Packers.com,* August 8, 2019.

———. "Jim Ringo Was Perfect Fit for Lombardi's Offense." *Packers.com,* March 7, 2019. https://www.packers.com/news/jim-ringo-was-perfect-fit-for-lombardi-s-offense#:~:text=Although%20listed%20at%20232%20pounds,perfect%20fit%20for%20Lombardi's%20offense.

———. "Life Was Different During Tony Canadeo's Day." *Packers.com,* May 15, 2013. https://www.packers.com/news/life-was-different-during-tony-canadeos-day-15285504.

———. "The 1960s Packers: A Product of Vince Lombardi's Prejudice-free Culture." *Packers.com,* February 4, 2021. https://www.packers.com/news/the-1960s-packers-a-product-of-vince-lombardi-s-prejudice-free-culture.

"Clark Hinkle." Pro Football Hall of Fame website. Retrieved October 23, 2017.

"Clarke Hinkle." National Football Foundation. Retrieved October 23, 2017. https://footballfoundation.org/hof_search.aspx?hof=1461.

"Clarke Hinkle." *Pro-Football-Reference.com.* Retrieved October 23, 2017. https://www.pro-football-reference.com/players/H/HinkCl20.htm.

"Clarke Hinkle Here to Play with Bay Grid Squad Again." *Green Bay Press-Gazette,* September 8, 1933, 13.

"Clarke Hinkle Is Champ Field Goal Kicker for 1941." *Green Bay Press-Gazette,* February 5, 1942, 15.

"Coach Bedzek Shifts Lineup: 'Michalske, the Big Guard, Goes to Backfield; Needs Punter.'" *Harrisburg Telegraph,* October 14, 1925, 14.

Crist, John. "Chalk Talk: The Notre Dame Box." June 28, 2007. https://247sports.com/nfl/chicago-bears/Article/Chalk-Talk-the-Notre-Dame-Box-104429461/.

Curry, Erin. "Reggie White, Who Used Football to Spread Gospel, Dies at 43." *Baptist Press,* December 27, 2004. https://www.baptistpress.com/resource-library/news/reggie-white-who-used-football-to-spread-gospel-dies-at-43/.

DaCosta, Josepha. "Reggie White's Legacy Is Much Bigger Than Just Football." *Capital Times,* Madison, WI, July 13, 2020. https://madison.com/ct/opinion/column/josepha-da-costa-reggie-whites-legacy-is-much-bigger-than-just-football/article_0acc4457-db9a-5efd-874c-c08127526bda.html.

Daley, Art. "Dillon, Em Tunnell Boost Packers' Defensive Savvy." *Green Bay Press-Gazette,* September 2, 1959, 19.

———. "A Quarterback Playing Guard, That Was Iron Mike Michalske." *Green Bay Press-Gazette,* January 6, 1950, 13.

Doerschuk, Steve. "HOF' 13: Robinson Toasts His Beloved Wife, Career." Pro Football Hall of Fame, July 31, 2013. https://www.timesreporter.com/x997486912/HOF-13-Dave-Robinson-toasts-his-beloved-wife-career.

Dougherty, Pete. "Jerry Kramer Hails Vince Lombardi, Former Packers Teammates as Enters Hall of Fame." *Green Bay Press-Gazette,* August 4, 2018.

Dulka, Michael. "Remembering Charles Woodson's Rise to Greatness with the Green Bay Packers." *Bleacher Report,* February 17, 2013. https://bleacherreport.com/articles/1531202-remembering-charles-woodsons-rise-to-greatness-with-the-green-bay-packers.

Dunlap, Alex. "The NFL Beat: Lombardi and Kopay." *Austin Chronicle,* February 3, 2013. https://www.austinchronicle.com/daily/sports/2013-02-03/the-nfl-beat-lombardi-and-kopay/.

Dunne, Tyler. "Packers Great Gregg Faces the Battle of His Life." *Milwaukee Journal Sentinel,* July 7, 2012. https://archive.jsonline.com/sports/packers/packers-great-gregg-faces-the-battle-of-his-life-jr5hqgs-161696785.html/.

Edson, Art. "New Coach Named for the Cyclones." *Lawrence* (KS) *Journal-World,* October 15, 1942. https://news.google.com/newspapers?nid=2199&dat=19421015&id=dSNdAAAAIBAJ&sjid=uVoNAAAAIBAJ&pg=4512,721745&hl=en.

Edwards, Allanson W. "All-Eastern Grid Team Humbles Westerners, 6 to 0." United Press International. *Nevada State Journal,* January 2, 1932, 7.

"Favre Surpasses Marino with 421st Career TD." Associated Press, ESPN, September 30, 2007. https://www.espn.com/nfl/news/story?id=3043571.

Fleming, David. "How the Green Bay Packers Averted Financial Ruin in a Mysterious Blaze of Glory." *ESPN the Magazine,* September 19, 2013. https://www.espn.com/nfl/story/_/id/9669836/mysterious-fire-1950-saved-green-bay-packers-espn-magazine.

"Football's Greatest: Ranking the Top 10 Quarterbacks in NFL History." *Sports Illustrated,* October 27, 2017. https://www.si.com/nfl/2017/10/27/nfl-top-10-quarterbacks-tom-brady-joe-montana-john-elway.

Forman, Ross. "James Lofton Reflects on 40 Years in Professional Football." *Sports Collectors Digest,* February 12, 2018. https://sportscollectorsdigest.com/news/james-lofton-professional-football#:~:text=James%20Lofton%20celebrated%20his%2040th,coach%2C%20and%20broadcaster%20once%20again.&text=In%202016%20seasons%2C%20Lofton%20caught,14%2C004%20yards%20and%2075%20touchdowns.

"'Former Packers Safety Willie Wood Dies at 83," *Packers.com,* February 3, 2020. https://www.packers.com/news/former-packers-safety-willie-wood-dies-at-83.

"Forrest Gregg Eager to Resurrect Mustangs." *Tuscaloosa News,* Associated Press, January 15, 1988, 15.

"The Fourth Face on Green Bay's Quarterback Mount Rushmore: Arnie Herber." *PackersHistory.com,* September 23, 2019. https://packershistory.com/2019/09/the-fourth-face-on-green-bays-quarterback-mount-rushmore/.

Fox, Bob. "Green Bay Packers: Charles Woodson Is a Lock to Be in the Class of 2021 for the Pro Football Hall of Fame." *Green Bay Bob Fox,* December 11, 2020.

_____. "Jerry Kramer Talks About Henry Jordan." *Green Bay Bob Fox,* September 5, 2015. https://greenbaybobfox.wordpress.com/2015/09/05/jerry-kramer-talks-about-henry-jordan/?fbclid=IwAR2RJCTdpW0k_c-brQ_UlC6-Qb_uieibUonzUV-xg4QHh8xOAJ-lm-mqNE.

_____. "Jerry Kramer Talks About Ray Nitschke." *Green Bay Bob Fox,* August 4, 2015. https://greenbaybobfox.wordpress.com/2015/08/04/jerry-kramer-talks-about-ray-nitschke/.

_____. "Jerry Kramer Talks About Willie Davis.'" *Green Bay Bob Fox,* August 11, 2015. https://greenbaybobfox.wordpress.com/2015/08/11/jerry-kramer-talks-about-willie-davis/?fbclid=IwAR1Z6aSQxbQ22Og3VX1XJDVhqf3mvN6h9HZw_FThqQtyHYFm9iPJ8Rwv-f4.

_____. "Why Bobby Dillon Deserves to Be Considered for the Pro Football Hall of Fame." *Green Bay Bob Fox,* August 19, 2018. https://greenbaybobfox.wordpress.com/2018/08/19/green-bay-packers-why-bobby-dillon-deserves-to-be-considered-for-the-pro-football-hall-of-fame/.

FOX 6 Now Milwaukee. "Leading the Big Gig Is No Simple Feat: You Have to Keep It Fresh." June 26, 2017. https://www.fox6now.com/news/leading-the-big-gig-is-no-simple-feat-you-have-to-keep-it-fresh.

Gaines, Cork. "NFL Linemen Weren't Always So Enormous—see How Much They've Grown Over the Years." *Business Insider,* September 13, 2015. https://www.businessinsider.in/sports/nfl-lineman-werent-always-so-enormous-see-how-much-theyve-grown-over-the-years/slidelist/48948469.cms.

Garrity, John. "The Game's Greatest Receiver Don Hutson Remains the Standard by Which All Wideouts Are Measured." *Sports Illustrated Vault,* October 6, 1995. https://vault.si.com/vault/1995/10/06/the-games-greatest-receiver-don-hutson-remains-the-standard-by-which-all-wideouts-are-measured.

Graves, Heather. "Starr Left a Lasting Impression on Many." *Press Times* (Green Bay, WI), September 19, 2019. https://gopresstimes.com/2019/09/19/bart-starr-left-a-lasting-impression-on-many/.

Gruver, Ed. "The Lombardi Sweep: The Signature Play of the Green Bay Dynasty, It Symbolized an Era." *The Coffin Corner* 19, no. 5 (1997). Pro Football Researchers Association.

"Hall of Very Good." *The Coffin Corner* 33 (2011). Professional Football Researchers Association.

Harris, Beth. "Willie Wood, Packers

Bibliography

Great and Hall of Fame DB, Dies at 83." *Philadelphia Tribune,* February 4, 2020. https://www.phillytrib.com/obituaries/willie-wood-packers-great-and-hall-of-fame-db-dies-at-83/article_1a87f321-8494-5a37-8a5a-44831e2cb5bc.html.

Harrison, Elliot. "Forrest Gregg's Legacy? One of the Best Offensive Linemen Ever." *NFL.com,* April 12, 2019. https://www.nfl.com/news/forrest-gregg-s-legacy-one-of-the-best-offensive-linemen-ever-0ap3000001026196.

Heilman, Fr. Richard. "Vince Lombardi—Strive." *Roman Catholic Man,* April 30, 2015. https://www.romancatholicman.com/drive-to-strive-2/.

Heisler, Mark. "Lofton Is Acquitted of Sexual Assault by Green Bay Jury." *Los Angeles Times,* May 23, 1987. https://www.latimes.com/archives/la-xpm-1987-05-23-sp-1829-story.html.

Hendricks, Martin. "The Face of a Smashmouth Approach." *Milwaukee Journal Sentinel,* February 24, 2009. http://archive.jsonline.com/sports/packers/40250287.html/.

_____. "An Unsung Hero." *Milwaukee Journal Sentinel,* October 14, 2009. https://archive.jsonline.com/sports/packers/64174112.html/.

Henry, Jack. "Johnny Blood: The Vagabond Halfback." *The Coffin Corner* 1, no. 7 (1979). Pro Football Researchers Association.

Hiestand, Michael, and Gary Mihoces. "NFL Linemen Awaken to Sleep Apnea Dangers." *USA Today,* December 29, 2004. https://usatoday30.usatoday.com/sports/football/nfl/2004-12-29-sleep-apnea_x.htm.

"Hinkle Is Lieutenant in U.S. Coast Guard." *Green Bay Press-Gazette,* May 23, 1942, 11.

Hodges, Jim. "Green Bay Great Hutson Dies at 84." *Los Angeles Times,* June 17, 2016. https://www.latimes.com/archives/la-xpm-1997-06-27-sp-7545-story.html.

Hoffman, Dale. "May 2, 1978: Packers Draft Full of Surprises." *Milwaukee Sentinel,* May 3, 1978. https://archive.jsonline.com/sports/packers/249075821.html/.

Holland, Gerald. "Is That You Up There, Johnny Blood?" *Sports Illustrated Vault,* July 28, 2020. https://vault.si.com/vault/1963/09/02/is-that-you-up-there-johnny-blood.

Hruby, Patrick. "Feeling the Pain of a Brett Favre Injury." ESPN, December 17, 2010. http://www.espn.com/espn/page2/story?sportCat=nfl&page=hruby/101216_brett_favre_injuries.

Huber, Bill. "One-Eyed Interception Machine Dillon Picked for Hall of Fame." *Sports Illustrated /Packer Central,* January 16, 2020. https://www.si.com/nfl/packers/news/dillon-picked-for-hall-of-fame#:~:text=One%2DEyed%20Interception%2DMachine%20Dillon%20Picked%20for%20Hall%20of%20Fame&text=In%20his%2058th%20year%20of, Pro%20Football%20Hall%20of%20Fame.

_____. "Packers Legend Willie Davis Dies: Hall of Famer Willie Davis Was Acquired in One of the Most Lopsided Trades in NFL History." *Sports Illustrated,* April 15, 2020. https://www.si.com/nfl/packers/news/packers-legend-willie-davis-dies.

"It's Been All Business for Entrepreneur, Packers Great Willie Davis." *Investor's Business Daily,* January 21, 2017. https://www.investors.com/news/management/leaders-and-success/its-been-all-business-for-packers-great-entrepreneur-willie-davis/.

"James Lofton." *The Coffin Corner* 25, no. 4 (2003). Pro Football Researchers Association.

"Jerry Kramer Knew Bart Starr Was Tough." *Spokesman-Review,* May 26, 2019. https://www.spokesman.com/stories/2019/may/26/jerry-kramer-knew-bart-starr-was-tough.

"Jim Ringo." Pro Football Hall of Fame website. Retrieved November 21, 2020. https://www.profootballhof.com/players/jim-ringo/.

"Jim Ringo, Trigger Man." Jock Bio Legends (website). Published 2008. Accessed November 21, 2020. http://www.jockbio.com/Classic/Ringo/Ringo_bio.html.

Joslin, Rick. "The Best in the Business: Hutson Set Standard for Pass Receivers." *Pine Bluff Commercial,* July 6, 1997.

Katzenstein, John. "Raiders' Woodson Still Excelling at 39." *Detroit News,* November 18, 2015. https://www.detroitnews.com/story/sports/nfl/lions/2015/11/18/raiders-woodson-still-excelling/76032114/.

Katzowitz, Josh. "Remember When: John F. Kennedy, Vince Lombardi Were Friends." CBS Sports, November 22,

2013. https://www.cbssports.com/nfl/news/remember-when-john-f-kennedy-vince-lombardi-were-friends/.

Kenney, Ray. "Miller All-Stars Get Cash on the Barrelhead." *Milwaukee Journal,* November 18, 1987.

King, Peter. "Brett Favre Details How the Pain of Playing in the NFL Led to His Addiction to Painkillers." *SI Vault,* May 27, 1996. https://www.si.com/nfl/2018/05/22/brett-favre-painkillers-alcohol-rehab.

———. "Living Day to Day." *Sports Illustrated,* March 17, 2008. https://vault.si.com/vault/2008/03/17/living-day-to-day.

———. "Who Is Friggin' Tougher Than Charles Woodson?" *Sports Illustrated,* December 22, 2015. https://www.si.com/nfl/2015/12/22/charles-woodson-retirement-raiders-nfl-power-rankings.

Klemko, Robert. "How Reggie White Made Green Bay Cool." *Sports Illustrated,* December 6, 2016. https://www.si.com/nfl/2016/12/06/nfl-reggie-white-green-bay-black-players-free-agency-history.

Kruse, Zach. "Take Your Pick: Which Was Your Favorite Charles Woodson Pick-six?" *Packers Wire,* May 26, 2020. https://packerswire.usatoday.com/2020/05/26/take-your-pick-which-was-your-favorite-charles-woodson-pick-six/.

Kuechle, Oliver E. "Dazzling End Thrills Crowd." *Milwaukee Journal Sentinel,* October 7, 1945. https://archive.jsonline.com/sports/packers/206356261.html/.

——— "Packers Ask Waivers on Herber, Five Others." *Milwaukee Journal,* September 10, 1941, 3, part 2.

Lea, Bud. "Jim Taylor's Fearless Game Stands Test of Time." *Milwaukee Journal Sentinel,* November 8, 2000. http://archive.jsonline.com/sports/packers/245471751.html.

"Lofton, James 1956-." *Encyclopedia.com.* https://www.encyclopedia.com/education/news-wires-white-papers-and-books/lofton-james-1956-.

Malcore, Paul. "The Legend of Bart Starr." *Rawhide History, Rawhide.org,* September 30, 2016. https://www.rawhide.org/blog/supporters/legend-bart-starr/.

Mancini, Ralph. "Green Bay Packers 100: Second Best Receiver in Franchise History." *Fansided,* June 11, 2016. https://lombardiave.com/2016/06/11/green-bay-packers-100-second-best-receiver-franchise-history/.

McGinn, Bob. "April 6, 1993: $17 Million Reasons Convince Reggie White." *Milwaukee Journal,* April 7, 1993. http://archive.jsonline.com/sports/packers/191927631.html/.

———. "Ron Wolf in His Words: How Fate and Football Came Together." *Milwaukee Journal Sentinel,* August 7, 2015. http://archive.jsonline.com/sports/packers/ron-wolf-in-his-words-how-fate-and-football-came-together-b99552142z1-321055271.html/.

McGlynn, Stoney. "Bays Crush Giants in Title Game." *Milwaukee Sentinel,* December 10, 1939, 15.

"Mike Michalske." Pro Football Hall of Fame website. Retrieved December 14, 2020. https://www.profootballhof.com/players/mike-michalske/.

Miller, Norman. "Packers Good Bet for a New Pro Dynasty." *The Bulletin* (Bend, OR), December 31, 1962.

Nix, JW. "Crazy Canton Cuts = Bobby Dillon." *Bleacher Report,* March 15, 2009. https://bleacherreport.com/articles/139312-crazy-canton-cuts-bobby-dillon.

Nowell, Paul. "NFL Defensive Great Reggie White, 43, Dies." *Miami Herald,* December 26, 2004, 5B-1.

Oates, Bob. "Don Hutson: After Having Help Invent the Forward Pass, the Former Packer Star Grabbed the Brass Ring of Life as Well." *Los Angeles Times.* April 30, 1989. https://www.latimes.com/archives/la-xpm-1989-04-30-sp-3081-story.html.

O'Connor, Ian. "Lombardi: A Champion of Gay Rights." ESPN, May 2, 2013. https://www.espn.com/new-york/nfl/story/_/id/9237535/vince-lombardi-proud-jason-collins.

"Packer Immortal Arnie Herber, 59, Dies of Cancer." *Newspapers.com.* Accessed October 16, 2020, p. 1. https://www.newspapers.com/clip/17560028/arnie-herber-dies/.

"Packers Pull Trade, Create New Problem." *Pittsburgh Press,* May 6, 1964, 2C.

"Packers Win 8th in Row; Beat Bears, 6–2." *Green Bay Press-Gazette,* November 1, 1931, 29.

Page, Diane. "State PTA Chooses

Bibliography

Michalske Teacher of the Year." *Green Bay Press-Gazette*, March 21, 1988, 13.

Pasquarelli, Len. "Final Autopsy Complete for Reggie White." ESPN, May 19, 2005. https://www.espn.com/nfl/news/story?id=1953876.

"Paul Hornung." Green Bay Packers website. Retrieved July 20, 2020. https://www.packers.com/history/hof/paul-hornung.

Pennington, Bill. "Willie Wood Made the Most Memorable Play of Super Bowl I. He Has No Recollection." *New York Times*, February 4, 2016. https://www.nytimes.com/2016/02/05/sports/football/willie-wood-made-the-most-memorable-play-of-super-bowl-i-he-has-no-recollection.html.

Polzin, Jim. "Packers: In the Locker Room, Woodson Chooses His Words and His Teammates Listen." *Wisconsin State Journal*, January 27, 2011. https://madison.com/sports/football/professional/packers-in-the-locker-room-woodson-chooses-his-words-and-his-teammates-listen/article_02f31a2a-29ce-11e0-add9-001cc4c002e0.html.

Radcliffe, JR. "Remembering the Strange Moment the Packers Traded Brett Favre, 10 Years Ago Today." *USA Today*, August 7, 2018. https://www.jsonline.com/story/sports/nfl/packers/2018/08/07/look-back-brett-favre-trade-jets-10-years-later/924042002/.

"Reggie's Self-revelation." *Yahoo! News*, February 4, 2006.

Rittenberg, Adam. "Meet the Smartest Guys on the Field." ESPN, December 28, 2015. https://www.espn.com/college-football/story/_/id/14453565/why-centers-smartest-guys-field.

Rivard, Raymond. "Green Bay Packers: Ray Nitschke Was Nicest Off Field, Meanest on It." *Fansided*, 2017. Retrieved July 31, 2020. https://lombardiave.com/2017/01/31/green-bay-packers-ray-nitschke-2/.

"Robert (Cal) Hubbard." Pro Football Hall of Fame website. Retrieved November 27, 2020.

Robinson, Roger E. "Historic Missourians: Robert Calvin Hubbard." State Historical Society of Missouri, April 5, 2013. https://historicmissourians.shsmo.org/historicmissourians/name/h/hubbard/#:~:text=Cal%20Hubbard%20is%20the%20only,1900%2C%20in%20Keytesville%2C%20Missouri.

Ryman, Richard. "Bobby Dillon, Green Bay Packers' Interception Leader, Dead at 89." *Green Bay Press-Gazette*, September 3, 2019. https://www.greenbaypressgazette.com/story/news/2019/08/29/bobby-dillon-green-bay-packers-leading-interceptor-dead-89/2153732001/.

_____. "Tributes Reflect Icon's Class." *Green Bay Press-Gazette*, May 27, 2019, 10.

Schudel, Matt. "Willie Wood, Hall of Fame Defensive Back for Vince Lombardi's Packers, Dies at 83." *Washington Post*, February 4, 2020. https://www.washingtonpost.com/local/obituaries/willie-wood-hall-of-fame-defensive-back-for-vince-lombardis-packers-dies-at-83/2020/02/04/be4b0a18-475f-11ea-ab15-b5df3261b710_story.html.

Schuyler, Ed, Jr. "Adderley Traded to Cowboys." *Tuscaloosa News*, AL, September 2, 1970, 11.

Shipnuck, Alan. "Top of His Game: It Was Never About Me." *Sports Illustrated*, March 17, 2008. https://www.si.com/nfl/2008/03/11/favre.

Silverstein, Tom. "Running Back Stuck with Pack." *Milwaukee Journal Sentinel*, November 30, 2003, 1A.

Smith, Don. "Arnie Herber." *The Coffin Corner* 6, no. 7 (1984). Pro Football Researchers Association.

_____. "Henry Jordan." *The Coffin Corne* 17, no. 2 (1995). Pro Football Researchers Association.

_____. "Willie Davis: Speed, Agility and Size." *The Coffin Corner* 7, no. 1 (1985). Pro Football Researchers Association.

_____. "Willie Wood." *The Coffin Corner* 11, no. 2 (1989). Pro Football Researchers Association.

Smith, Johnny. "Vince Lombardi Would Be Proud." September 30, 2017. https://slate.com/culture/2017/09/vince-lombardi-hated-protests-but-he-fought-for-racial-justice.html.

Smith, Michael David. "Hall of Famer Herb Adderley Dies at 81,' *Pro Football Talk*, NBC Sports, October 30, 2020. Retrieved October 30, 2020. https://profootballtalk.nbcsports.com/2020/10/30/Hall of Famer-herb-adderley-dies-at-81/.

"SMU Remembers Forrest Gregg, '56." Southern Methodist University, December 28,

2019. https://www.smu.edu/News/2019/SMU-Remembers-Forrest-Gregg.

"Special Section: Priests' Jubilee." *The Compass,* April 1, 2016. https://www.thecompassnews.org/compass/2000-07-14/00cn0714pj2.htm.

Strickler, George. "Packers Win Pro Title, Whip Giants, 27–0." *Chicago Tribune,* December 11, 1939, 21.

Telander, Rick. "A Picture-Perfect End: That's Green Bay's James Lofton, a Troubled Young Man Until He Met the Woman Who Gave New Focus to His Life." *Sports Illustrated Vault,* December 6, 1982. https://vault.si.com/vault/1982/12/06/a-picture-perfect-end.

"'They Click First Year as Pros.'" *Racine* (WI) *Journal Times,* November 10, 1932, 15.

"Through the Years." *FAVRE.* F+W Publications, 2008.

United Press. "Michalske Resigns at Iowa State.'" *Green Bay Press-Gazette,* February 5, 1947, 17.

United Press International. "All-pro Henry Jordan Dies.'" *Ellensburg* (WA) *Daily Record,* February 22, 1977, 6.

_____. "Packers Pull Trade, Create New Problem." *Pittsburgh Press,* May 6, 1964, 2C.

Waits, Tim. "Column: Dillon Lived with No Regrets." *Temple Daily Telegram,* August 28, 2019. https://www.tdtnews.com/sports/article_e94b207c-ca00-11e9-811a-2bee5116c43b.html.

Whitley, David. "Hutson Was First Modern Receiver." ESPN.com, Packerville USA, February 27, 2010. https://www.espn.com/sportscentury/features/00014269.html.

Wood, Ryan. "Hall of Fame Green Bay Packers Defensive End Willie Davis Dies at 85." *USA Today,* April 15, 2020. https://www.usatoday.com/story/sports/nfl/packers/2020/04/15/willie-davis-hall-fame-green-bay-packers-defensive-end-dies/5138702002/.

Yearbook

Green Bay Packers Official Yearbook, 2018.

Index

Adams, Davante 223, 226, 228–229
Adderley, Herb 3, 5, 73–74, 79, 83–84, 111–118, 133–134, 139, 152, 157, 160, 163, 188, 193, 196, 212–213; awards-highlights 112, 116; biography 242; career statistics 242–243; family 111, 113
Akron, Ohio 38, 189
Alabama A&M University 88
Alabama Antelope 31
Aldridge, Lionel 192
All-America Football Conference 43, 66
All-Pro Broadcasting 124
Allen, George 29, 92–93, 139
Alworth, Lance 73
American Electric Power 2
American Express 125
American Football League 108, 114, 188, 192, 212
American Football League (first league) 54
American League (baseball) 27
American Professional Football Association 38
Anderson, Donny 101, 108, 146
Anderson, Jamal 222
Anderson, John 182
Andrews, Tom 35
Arcaro, Eddie 127
Arizona Cardinals 215–216
Armstrong High School 148
Ashland College 53
Associated Press 116, 150, 154, 216
Atkins, Doug 119
Atlanta Falcons 90, 136, 167, 203, 205, 207, 222
Atlantic City, New Jersey 189
Auburn University 207

Badgro, Red 58
Bakhtiari, David 227–228
Balboa, Rocky 105
Baltimore Colts 58, 70, 73, 81, 107, 120, 133, 138–139, 152, 191, 193, 204
Baltimore Ravens 171
Barber, Phil 214, 217–219

Barnett, Derek 199
Barnum, P.T. 38
Bart Starr Award 101
Baseball Hall of Fame 27
Baton Rouge High School 105
Baugh, Sammy 13
Baylor University 54, 159
Beathard, Bobby 225
Beaver Falls, Pennsylvania 23
Beebe, Don 94, 210
Belichick, Bill 43
Bell, Bobby 188
Bengston, Phil 73, 88, 116, 135, 136–137
Bennett, Edgar 208
Bennett, Tony (Packer) 207
Bennett, Tony (singer) 128
Berlin Crisis 79
Berry, Raymond 152
Bert Bell Benefit Bowl 72
Bettis, Tom 88
Bezdek, Hugo 54
Big Ten (conference) 86, 112–113
Big Umpire 27
Blache, Greg 200
Blackbourn, Lisle 129–130, 143, 159
Blair, Joe 83
Blanchette, John 65
Bledsoe, Drew 203
Blood and Sand 46
Booker T. Washington High School 120
Borden, Nate 83
Boston Redskins 12, 19, 32, 42, 51
Bourguignon, Dick 62
Bowman, Ken 101, 142, 146
Boyles, Royce 5
Boys Club 148
Braatz, Tom 205, 207, 227
Brady, Tom 102, 216
Bratkowski, Zeke 101
Brian's Song 88
Brock, Charley 64
Brockington, John 66
Brooklyn, New York 82
Brooklyn Dodgers (football team) 32, 51

279

Index

Brooks, Derrick 188
Brooks, Robert 208
Brown, Gilbert "Gravedigger" 21
Brown, Jim 6, 105, 108, 138, 193
Brown, Paul 96, 122, 137
Brown, Roger 119
Brown, Tom 115, 195, 212–213
Brown, Willie 121
Bruder, Hank, 50–51
Brumbaugh, Carl 56
Brunnel, Mark 202
Bryant, Paul "Bear" 29–31
Buchanan, Junious "Buck" 121
Buchanon, Willie 161
Buckley, Terrell 208
Bucknell University 17
Buffalo Bills 186
Butkus, Dick 90–92, 103, 226
Butler, Bill 148
Butler, LeRoy 157, 222–223

Caan, James 89
Caffey, Lee Roy 81, 146
Cagle, Red 56
Calhoun, George Whitney 36–38
California (state) 43, 148, 180, 185
Cal's Comment 36
Camelot 178, 180
Canadeo, Ruth 65, 67
Canadeo, Tony 5, 61–67, 107; awards-highlights 62; biography 236; career statistics 236–237
Canadian Football League 154
Candlestick Park 203
Cannon, Billy 106
Canton, Ohio 3, 6, 17, 23, 38, 40, 48, 52, 61, 65, 79, 88, 109, 114, 119, 134, 142, 148, 157–158, 160, 172, 174, 187, 194, 222, 224, 225–228
Capers, Dom 218
Capitol Division 147
Carlson, Chuck 5
Carmichael, Harold 158
Carolina Panthers 167
Carpenter, Lew 135, 138
Carr, Joseph 32–33
Carr, Lloyd 215
Carroll, Bob 147
Casey, Bernie 139
Catholic priest 78, 82
Centenary College 23
Central Division 81, 139
A Century of Excellence, 100 Greatest Packers of All Time 4, 34, 69, 196, 228
Chamberlain, Wilt 28, 112
Chandler, Al 112
Chandler, Don 179, 195
Chicago, Illinois 48, 50, 61–62, 85, 174
Chicago Bears 3, 11, 14–15, 18–19, 22, 26, 32, 36, 40, 43, 54, 56, 86, 90, 92, 97, 119, 132, 165, 170, 213, 219

Chicago Cardinals 37, 43, 50, 53, 66
Chicago Daily News 19
Chicago Tribune 58
Chinatown 202
Chmura, Mark 208
Christensen, Jack 159, 162
Christl, Cliff 3, 5, 10, 119, 123, 131, 163
Christy, Dick 87
Cincinnati Bengals 74–75, 154, 186, 208, 215
Cincinnati Reds 32
City Stadium 38, 152
Civil Rights Act, Movement 82, 114, 189
Claridge Hotel 189
Clark, Don 148
Clark, Kristine Setting 5
Clarke, Frank 195
Clarke Hinkle Field 15, 20
Clayton, Mark 28
Clemson University 31
Cleveland, Ohio 54, 200, 209
Cleveland Browns 6, 73–74, 79, 96, 105, 108, 121–122, 124, 130, 133–134, 136, 179, 189, 226
Closing the Gap 5, 151
Coalinga Junior College 148
Coastal Division 81, 139
Cobb, Ty 28
Coffin Corner 51
Coffman, Paul 96, 183–184
College All-Star Game 174, 192
Collins, Nick 215
Colorado 40, 50, 55
Comp, Irv 161
Copernicus 29
Cornelius, North Carolina 197
Cotton Bowl 159
Couch, Tim 168
Covert, Jimbo 158
Creed, Apollo 105
Crosby, Mason 215
Cuozzo, Gary 193
Cumberland Mountains 46
Currie, Dan 79, 81, 86, 88, 90, 174
Curry, Bill 107, 123

Dale, Carroll 81, 88, 99–100, 139, 174, 195
Daley, Art 66, 163
Dallas Cowboys 3, 73–74, 99, 116–119, 183, 193, 203, 210, 212, 226
Dallas Texans 67
Daly, Dan 41
Daniels, Clem 114
Daniels, Dee 155
Darling, Bernard "Boob" 48
Dartmouth University 17
Daugherty, Duffy 112
Davis, Al 148, 207
Davis, Nodie 120
Davis, Sammy, Jr. 128

Index

Davis, Terrell 224
Davis, Willie 1, 3–5, 71, 79, 83, 94, 114, 119–126, 133–135, 137–138, 140, 150–152, 179, 193, 196, 204, 224; awards-highlights 119–120; biography 243; career statistics 243–244
Dawkins, Brian 222
Dawson, Len 152, 212
Dayton, Ohio 38
Deep South 74, 124
DeLamielleure, Joe 147
Delaware River 142
Denver, Colorado 8
Denver Broncos 202, 214
DePere, Wisconsin 58–59
DePere Dickinson School 59
Detroit, Michigan 133, 200
Detroit Lions 34, 59, 90, 111, 115, 132, 134, 161, 173–174, 203, 212, 215
Devine, Dan 96, 208, 224
Dickerson, Eric 108
Dickey, Doug 72
Dickey, Lynn 7, 75, 182, 184
Dickinson College 17
Didinger, Ray 115
Dietzel, Paul 106
Dillon, Bobby, 144, 157–163; awards-highlights 158–159; biography 248; career statistics 248
Dilweg, Laverne "Lavvie" 23, 26, 40, 48, 51, 158, 229
Ditka, Mike 73, 191–192
Doar, Mrs. W.T. 44
Don Hutson Center 28–29
Donels, Ray, 58
Doomsday Defense 119
Dotson, Earl 209
Dotson, Santana 210
Douglass, Mike 182
Dow Chemical 125–126
Dowler, Boyd 78–79, 99–100, 158, 176, 193, 195, 225–226
Drew, Harold "Red" 31
Driver, Donald 61, 168, 223, 229
Duluth, Minnesota 48
Duluth Eskimos 47
Dunn, Joseph "Red" 10, 23, 40, 48, 50, 56
Dunnavant, Keith 98, 101

Earp, Jug 23
Easley, Kenny 222
East 26th Street Liberties 47
East West Shrine Game 17, 173
Eastern Conference 81, 139, 176, 194
Easton, Pennsylvania 142, 147
Electric Company 147
Eller, Carl 68
Elmwood Park, Illinois, 85
Elway, John 99, 202
Engle, Rip 191–192
ESPN 170, 228
Evans, Doug 209

Fanning, Beverly 183
Favre, Brett 6–7, 34, 61, 68, 94, 103, 136–137, 164–171, 207–208, 211, 221, 227; awards-highlights 164–165, 168–169; biography 249; career statistics 249–250; family 167
Fearsome Foursome 120
Feathers, Beattie 66
Fellowship of Christian Athletes 198–199
Ferguson, Howie 143
The Fire Within 5
Fitzgerald, Larry 224
Fitzgerald, Tommy 127
Five O' Clock Club 63
Flanagan, Mike 142, 168
Fleming, Marv 193
Florida A&M University 112, 120
Flynn, Tom 161
Forchette, Jackie 88
Ford, Len 6
Fordham University 77
Forester, Bill 90, 193
Forrest Gregg Award 224
Forrest Gump 223
Fort Wayne, Indiana 45
Forte, Bob 161
Fortmann, Dan 22, 52
Fox, Bob 5, 88, 123–124, 139, 158, 174, 189, 214
Frankford Yellow Jackets 8, 40
Franklin Field 146
Freeman, Antonio 167, 229
Freezer Bowl 74
Fremont, Ohio 215
Fresno State University 218
Friedman, Benny 52, 56
Fritsch, Ted 64
Fullwood, Brent 206

Gabriel, Roman 99, 139
Galbreath, Harry 202
Gandy, Ralph 31
Gantenbein, Milt 51, 56
Garland, Grace 43
Garrick Theater 47
Gator Bowl 191
Geneva College 22, 26
George, Bill 97–98, 119
Georgia Tech University 31
Gifford, Frank 130
Gilchrist, Cookie 114
Gillingham, Gale 158, 224
Glanville, Jerry 207–208
Glasgow, Missouri 23
Gold Dust Twins 108
The Golden Boy 114, 127, 131, 133
Goldenberg, Charles "Buckets" 43
Gonzaga University 62, 64, 67
Gosselin, Rick 163
Grabowski, Jim 108, 195
Graham, Otto 13
Grambling State University 120

282　Index

Grange, Harold "Red" 18, 26, 54
Gray Ghost of Gonzaga 62, 64, 66
Green, Ahman 109
Green Bay, Wisconsin 36–37, 48–50, 114, 131, 135, 151–152, 170, 184, 200
Green Bay Packers 1, 3, 35–36, 61, 63, 67, 76, 86, 94, 103, 111, 118, 132, 134, 138, 148, 157, 162, 177, 180, 188, 190, 194, 204, 217, 221, 226; Board of Directors 61, 63, 66, 125; Executive Committee 43, 61, 63; Hall of Fame 59, 96, 182, 227; Television Network 187
Green Bay Press-Gazette 19, 36–37, 55, 58–59, 66, 163
Green Bay Sweep (also power sweep and sweep) 70–71, 106, 130–131, 144–145, 175–176
Green Bay West High School 8
Greene, George "Tiger" 75
Greene, Joe 134
Greene, Kevin 196
Greenwood, Lee Ann Michalske 59
Gregg, Forrest 3–5, 68–75, 88, 94, 117, 143, 145, 154, 159, 174, 176, 179, 184, 196, 204–205, 225, 228; awards-highlights 69–70; biography 237; career statistics 237–238
Gremminger, Hank 114
Gretzky, Wayne 28
Grier, Rosey 120
Griese, Brian 215
Grimes, Billy 66
Grimm, Dan 72, 224
Groomes, Mel 111
Gros, Earl 146
Gugliemi, Ralph 127
Gunga Din 44
Gutekunst, Brian 228

Hadl, John 96, 208
Hagan's Opera House 44
Halas, George 16, 27, 36, 43
Ham, Jack 188, 195
Hannah, John 68
Hanner, Dave "Hawg" 61, 135, 154, 163
Hannie, Caleb 213
Hanson, Ralph "Sand", 47
Harlan, Bob 43, 65, 202, 205, 207, 226
Harlan, Kevin 187
Harrington, Joey 215
Harris, Al 212–213
Harris, Cliff 157–158, 222
Harris, Franco 195
Harrison, Eliot 70
Harrison, Marvin 224
Hasselbeck, Matt 212
The Hawk 160, 162
Hayes, Bob 195
Haynes, Abner 114
Healey, Ed 22
Hecker, Norb 151
Hein, Mel 22, 24

Heisman Trophy 106, 128–129, 216
Henderson, William 210
Hendricks, Ted 6
Hennepin Avenue 47
Henry, Jack 51
Henry, Wilbur "Fats" 22
Herber, Arnie 7–13, 18, 32, 40, 42, 50, 55; awards-highlights 9; biography 230; career statistics 230
Heritage Trail Plaza 49, 132
Herrock, Ken 207
Hickok, Ralph 5, 21, 189
Highland Avenue 77
Hill, Calvin 117
Hill, Jim 150
Hill, Shaun 214
Hill, Winston 158
Hinkle, Clarke 4, 14–20, 42, 64; awards-highlights 15; biography 231; career statistics 231; family 17
Hodkiewicz, Wes 228
Holland, Darius 210
Holmgren, Mike 167–168, 200, 208, 227, 229
Horner, Sam 90
Hornung, Paul 4–5, 35, 50, 68, 71, 73, 78–79, 81, 88, 90, 99–100, 104, 107–109, 114, 124, 127–133, 146, 174–176, 178, 193, 196, 204, 212; awards-highlights 128–129, 131, 159; biography 244; career statistics 244–245

Hotel Northland 151
Houston Oilers 106, 202
Howard, Desmond 210
Howard High School (Chattanooga, TN) 198
Howton, Billy 135, 143, 159
Huard, Damon 215
Hubbard, Robert "Cal" 4, 21–27, 48, 51, 54, 56; awards-highlights 22; biography 231–232; career statistics 232
Huff, Sam 90–91, 105
Hutson, Don 3–4, 11, 18, 28–35, 41, 42, 49, 51, 55, 64, 68, 92, 109, 185, 223; awards-highlights 29, 33; biography 232; career statistics 232–233

Ice Bowl 5, 73, 81, 99, 101, 139, 147, 172, 195, 224, 226
In Search of a Hero: Life and Times of Tony Canadeo, Green Bay Packers Gray Ghost 5
Indian (later Acme) Packing Company 37
Infante, Lindy 207–208
Instant Replay 2
Iola, Wisconsin 57
Iowa State University 53, 58
Iron Man streak 164–165
Iron Mike 54–56, 59
Ironwood, Michigan 47
Isbell, Cecil 12–13, 41, 64
Ivery, Eddie Lee 184

Index

Jackson, Keith 200, 202, 210
Jacksonville, Florida 191, 202, 210
Jefferson, John 183–184
Jennings, Greg 170, 229
Jeter, Bob 83, 116
Jim Crow laws 111
Johannes, Lee 38
Johnson, Pastor Keith 196
Johnson Controls 126
Joiner, Charlie 121
Jones, David "Deacon" 70–71, 120, 226
Jones, Ed "Too Tall" 21
Jones, Nathan "Tricky" 120
Jones, Sean 202
Jones, Walter 228
Jordan, Henry 4, 76, 79, 134–140, 196, 204, 224; awards-highlights 135; biography 245; career statistics 245–246
Jordan, Montana 173
Joslin, Rick 35
Jurgensen, Sonny 7, 95, 99–100

K-Gun offense 186
Kansas City Chiefs 152–153, 171, 212, 215–216
Karras, Alex 119, 132–133, 158
Kauffman Foundation 125
Kelly, Jim 186, 199
Kelly, John Simms "Shipwreck" 32
Kelly, Leroy 193
Kennedy, Pres. John 79, 176
Kenosha Cardinals 45
Kent State University 88
Kentucky Derby 127, 133
Keytesville High School (Missouri) 23
Kiesling, Walt 6, 22, 52
Kimberly-Clark 20
King, Peter 169–170, 214
Kingdome (Seattle) 167
Kipling, Rudyard 44
Kitna, Jon 215
Klein, Dusty 172
Knoxville News-Sentinel 198
Kopay, Dave 83
Kramer, Jerry 1–5, 52, 68, 72, 77, 79, 85, 88, 97–98, 101, 123, 126, 130–131, 133, 137, 140, 145, 147, 157, 163, 172–179, 204, 224–225; awards-highlights 173, 175; biography 250; career statistics 250
Kramer, Ron 78, 130, 158, 192
Krause, Paul 213
Kremer, Andrea 170
Kuechle, Oliver 38, 43

Lackawanna Express 17
Lafayette College 53
Lambeau, Earl "Curly" 3–5, 8–9, 11, 17, 19, 23–24, 32, 36–43, 50, 64, 66, 204, 225; awards-highlights 37; biography 233; coaching record 233–234

Lambeau Field 73, 94, 108, 170–171, 184, 206, 213, 227
Lambeau Leap 223
Lambert, Jack 88, 92
Landry, Tom 73, 101, 117, 193
Lane, Dick "Night Train" 213
Lanier, Willie 92
Largent, Steve 28
Larson, Lloyd 38
Lary, Yale 159
Las Vegas, Nevada 126
Lasorda, Tom 150
Lawrence Journal-World 58
Layne, Bobby 104
Lea, Bud 38
Leahy, Frank 127–128
Lee, Mark 161
Leinart, Matt 215
Levens, Dorsey 167
Levy, Marv 186–187
Lewellen, Vern 18, 23, 40, 48, 158, 229
Lewis, Ray 92, 103
Lewisburg, Pennsylvania 17
Lewiston Morning Tribune 173–174
Lilly, Bob 74, 134
Linsley, Corey 142
Lisbon, Louisiana 120
Little, Larry 52, 224
Little Falls, Minnesota 225
Lofton, James 4, 75, 180–187, 229; awards-highlights 181–183, 186; biography 250–251; career statistics 251
Lombardi, Hal 83
Lombardi, Marie 72, 79
Lombardi, Vince 1, 3–5, 14, 36, 39. 56, 62–63, 68–69, 72–73, 87–89, 92, 94, 96–99, 106–109, 114, 116–118, 120, 124, 129–131, 133, 135–138, 144–145, 150–152, 160, 162–163, 174–176, 179–180, 187–188, 193–195, 204, 206, 208, 224–227; awards-highlights 76–77; biography 238; coaching record 238–239
Lombardi, Vince, Jr. 83
Lombardi Avenue 77
Lombardi Trophy 219
Lombardi's Left Side 5, 113, 116
Lori Lane 152
Los Angeles, California 42, 88; Coliseum 139; Sunset Strip 127
Los Angeles Dons 6, 66
Los Angeles Raiders 155, 185–186, 202, 223
Los Angeles Rams 88, 111, 120, 139, 174
Los Angeles Times 153, 185
Lott, Ronnie 103
Louisiana State University 105–106, 174
Louisiana Tech University 209
Louisville, Kentucky 128
Louisville Courier-Journal 117
Lowe, Paul 114
Luckman, Sid 13, 65

Index

Lundy, Lamar 120
Lyles, Lenny 120
Lyman, William Roy "Link" 22, 56
Lynch, John 222

Mack, Tom 52
Mackey, John 191–192
Magnificent Screwball 51
Majkowski, Don 206, 208
Major League Baseball 27, 32
Malcore, Paul 102
Mandarich, Tony 206
Mann, Bob 111, 151
Manning, Peyton 216
Mantle, Mickey 127
Mara, Wellington 79
Marchetti, Gino 70, 120
Marine Hospital (Portland) 128
Marino, Dan 170
Marlboro (cigarettes) 127
Marquette University 143
Marsters, Al 17
Martin, Charles 112–113
Martin, Dean 128
Maryland State University 191
Masters, Norm 72, 176
Masterson, Willard 140
Matthews, Clay 229
Mayes, Derrick 211
Mayo Clinic 178
Maywood, Illinois 85
MBA (degree) 124–125, 179
McCarren, Larry 7, 96, 142
McCarthy, Mike 170
McConkey, Phil 184
McCoy, Mike 96
McDonald, Tommy 115
McGee, Max 99, 127, 129–130, 154, 159, 176, 195
McGinn, Bob 200
McHan, Lamar 97
McKenzie, Mike 211
McKenzie, Reggie 147, 211
McLean, Ray "Scooter" 62, 97, 106, 129–130, 174, 204
McMillan, Alvin "Bo" 23, 26
McNally, Johnny "Blood" 4, 10, 23, 26, 32, 40–42, 54, 56; awards-highlights 45; biography 234–235; career statistics 235; family 44
Mecklenburg County Medical Examiner's Office 196
Memorial Stadium 193
Memphis Showboats 199
Mercein, Chuck 101
Meredith, Don 99, 195, 212
Metro-Goldwyn-Mayer 125
MGM Grand 126
MGM Mirage 125
Miami, Florida 72
Miami Dolphins 118, 200, 202, 210, 215, 224

Michaels, Lou 173
Michalske, August "Mike" 4, 23, 26, 40–42, 48, 51–59, 195; awards-highlights 53–54, 59; biography 235; career statistics 236; family 54, 59
Michels, John 211
Michigan State University 54, 79, 112–114, 141, 174, 188
Middleton, Terdell 183
Midwest 48, 124
Miller, Tom 64
Million Dollar Pier 189
Milwaukee, Wisconsin 48, 88, 200
Milwaukee Athletic Club 140
Milwaukee Badgers 47
Milwaukee County Stadium 139, 167, 227
Milwaukee Journal 39
Milwaukee Journal Sentinel 61
Milwaukee World Festival Inc. 140
Minersville Park 47
Minneapolis Tribune 47
Minnesota Vikings 98, 100, 164, 168, 183
Minshew, Gardner 99
Mississippi 169
Missouri 23, 27
Molenda, Bo 23
Monsieur Beaucaire 47
Monska, Pete 191
Montana, Joe 99, 171, 208
Moore, Lenny 193, 195
Moore, Tom 192
Moorestown High School 191
Morrall, Earl 99
Motley, Marion 189
Munchak, Mike 52, 195
Munoz, Anthony 68
Murphy, Mark 148

Nagurski, Bronko 14–17
Namath, Joe 7, 50, 100
National Association of Broadcasters 125
National Broadcasting Company 124
National Football League (also NFL) 3, 7–8, 11, 14, 19, 21, 23–25, 28, 31–32, 36, 38, 42–43, 50, 54–55, 64–65, 71, 73, 79, 81, 96, 99, 109, 111, 115–116, 119, 131, 140, 146, 148–149, 151–155, 161–162, 164–165, 168, 170–172, 182, 184, 188, 192, 199, 202, 217, 221, 224, 227; 50th Anniversary Team 2, 91–92, 172, 175; Films 70, 85, 88, 100, 123; Network 29; 100th Anniversary Team 68, 70, 90–91; Players Association 199; 75th Anniversary Team 68, 70, 86, 91–92
NCAA Track and Field Championships 180
Neenah, Wisconsin 20
Nelson, Jordy 226, 229
Nesbitt, Gerald 173
Nevers, Ernie 47, 50
New England Journal of Medicine 197
New England Patriots 43, 102, 169, 203, 216

Index

New Jersey 188–189, 191
New Orleans Saints 104, 109, 133, 147
New Richmond, Wisconsin 44
New York 47
New York Giants 12, 19, 23, 33, 78–79, 89–90, 105, 111, 122–123, 130–132, 134, 146, 151, 165, 174, 176, 186, 193
New York Jets 74, 164, 168, 171, 183, 205, 207, 211
New York Yankees 127
New York Yankees (football) 40, 53–54, 66
Newsome, Craig 203, 210
Nitschke, Ray 6, 61, 68, 79, 85–93, 103–104, 123, 134, 154, 174, 176, 178–179, 196, 204, 225; awards-highlights 86–87, 91, 178; biography 239; career statistics 239–240; family 85
Nix, JW 161
Nobis, Tommy 90–91
Noll, Chuck 225
North Carolina State University, 86
Norwood, Scott 186
Notre Dame Box 9–10, 12, 43

Oakland Raiders 73, 106, 115, 148, 167, 205, 209, 211, 213–214, 216–217, 224, 226
O'Brien, Jim 117
Oconomowoc, Wisconsin 140
O'Donnell, Bob 41
Ohio River 17
Ohio State University 86, 216
Olejniczak, Dominic 62, 225
Olsen, Merlin 134
Omega Psi Phi fraternity 113
Oneida Avenue 20
Orange Bowl 154
Orr, Jimmy 193
Orton, Kyle 214
O'Toole, Andrew 5

Pace, Orlando 228
Pacific Coast Conference 148
The Packer Way 205
Page, Alan 134
Pain Gang: Pro Football's Fifty Toughest Players 16
Palmer, Carson 215
Parcells, Bill 207–208
Parilli, Babe 159
Parins, Robert 185, 226
Parker, Jim 68
Parks, Rosa 111
Paterno, Joe 192
The Paul Hornung Scrapbook 5
Payton, Walter 108
Pederson, Doug 165
Penn State University 54, 188, 190–192
Pennsylvania 188
Perkins, Don 195
Peter Pan 51
Petitbon, Richie 119

Philadelphia, Pennsylvania 111, 113
Philadelphia Bell 150, 154
Philadelphia Eagles 51, 66, 78, 107, 122, 144, 167, 186, 199, 209
Philipsburg, New Jersey 142
Piccolo, Brian 89
Pine Bluff, Arkansas 29, 31
Pine Bluff High School 29
Pitts, Elijah 99, 130–131, 151–152, 154, 195
Pitts, Ruth 152
Pittsburgh Pirates (football team) 51
Pittsburgh Steelers 88, 119, 189, 195, 203, 218–219, 225
Plum, Milt 115, 212
Polian, Bill 225
Polo Grounds 12, 19, 42
Portsmouth Spartans 38, 50
Pottsville Maroons 38, 40, 47
Presley, Elvis 122
Pro Football Chronicle 41
Pro Football Hall of Fame 1, 3, 8, 10, 17, 21, 27, 33, 49, 52, 55, 59, 61, 79, 88, 92, 134, 140, 148–149, 154, 157, 162–163, 172, 188, 194, 199, 222–223, 225, 228
Pro Football Researchers Association 157, 194, 225; Class of 2011 157; Class of 2016 225
Pro Football's Meanest Men 104
Proviso East High School (Illinois) 85
Pugh, Jethro 147, 172
Pyle, CC 54
Pyle, Mike 92

Quinlan, Bill 130, 135, 138

Raider Nation 167
Raji, BJ 213
Rapoport, Ian 228
Ray Nitschke Field 92
Red Lobster 200
Reeves, Dan 195
Reggie White Sleep Disorders Research and Education Foundation 197
Regis College 8, 40, 50, 55
Reischel, Rob 10
Remmel, Lee 16, 51
Renfro, Mel 74, 117, 195
Resurrection Church 82
Reynolds, Neil 16
Rice, Jerry 29, 224
Richards, Julia 32
Rhodes, Leonard "Bunky" 112
Rhodes, Ray 200
Richter, Pat 192
Ringo, Jim 6, 81, 141–145, 147, 225; awards-highlights 142–144, 147; biography 246; career statistics 246–247
Rison, Andre 168
Rivard, Raymond 50
Roaf, Willie 228
Robinson, Dave 1, 3–4, 6, 81, 83, 92, 188–195,

212; awards-highlights 189–191; biography 251–252; career statistics 252; family 191, 195
Robinson, Eddie 120–121
Robinson, Elaine 152, 189–190
Robinson, Eugene 210
Robinson, Frank 191
Robinson, Jim 125
Rock Island (Illinois) 38
Rockne, Knute 9, 36
Rockwood Lodge 43
Rocky (movies) 105
Rodgers, Aaron 61, 170, 218, 221–222, 226–228
Romo, Tony 218
Ronzani, Gene 66, 143, 159, 225
Rose Bowl 31, 86, 216
Rote, Tobin 143
Rozelle, Pete 132–133
Ruth, Babe 28, 35
Ryan, Frank 99

Saban, Lou 142
Sabol, Steve 100
St. Cecilia High School 77
St. Clair, Bob 21
St. John's University 45, 51
St. Louis Browns 85
St. Louis Cardinals 72–73, 117, 183
St. Louis Rams 171, 213, 216
St. Norbert College 53
St. Petersburg, Florida 27
Samuels, Abe 128
San Diego Chargers 73–74, 150, 154, 183, 192
San Diego State University 182
San Francisco, California 173, 209
San Francisco 49ers 21, 43, 107, 171, 182, 186, 203, 208, 210, 228
Sanders, Barry 164–165, 203
Sandpoint, Idaho 173, 178
Sandpoint High School 173
Sara Lee 125
Sargent, Olive 135, 137
Sayers, Gale 89, 193, 224
Schaap, Dick 2
Schlitz Brewing Company, 83, 125, 189
Schmidt, Joe 90–92, 119
Schneider, John 211
Schneidman, Herb 16
Schwartzwalder, Ben 143
Scott, Ray 61
Seattle Seahawks 167, 212
Seau, Junior 92
Shakespeare, William 44
Sharpe, Sterling 158, 205, 223–224, 229
Sharper, Darren 161
Shaughnessy, Clark 11
Shell, Art 155
Shell, Donnie 158
Sherman, Mike 169
Shields, Will 52

Shinnick, Don 120
Shipnuck, Alan 170
Shofner, Jimmy 173
Shor, Toots 127
Shreveport, Louisiana 23
Siberia (of the NFL) 96, 112
Silverstein, Tom 61
Simmons, Wayne 203, 209
Simpson, O.J. 147
Sisk, Johnny 16–17
Skorich, Nick 144
Skoronski, Bob 143, 145, 229
Slater, Duke 158
Slattery, David 83
Sleep Wellness Institute 197
Smith, Billy Ray 120
Smith, Bruce 198
Smith, Jerry 83
Snavely, Carl 17
Soldier Field 192
South Bend (Indiana) 37, 45
Southeastern Conference (SEC) 31
Southern Methodist University 75
Southern Mississippi University 207
Southwest Conference 159
Speedie, Mac 158
Spokane, Washington 64
Spokane Spook 64
Sport (magazine) 104, 181
Sporting News 68–69, 92
Sports Illustrated 16, 30, 98, 170, 198, 216
Sprinkle, Ed 158
Stafford, Matthew 215, 218
Stahlman, (Dick) 56
Stallworth, John 88
Stanford University 31, 180–182
Stanley, Skip 173
Starr, Bart 3, 7, 61, 75, 77, 92, 94–102, 116, 138–139, 150, 154, 159, 172, 174, 176, 179, 182–183, 193, 196, 204–205, 225–226; awards-highlights 95–96; biography 240; career statistics 240–241
Starr, Ben 97
State Fair Park 19, 42
Staten, Mark 141
Staten Island Stapletons 11
Staubach, Roger 74
Steel Curtain 119
Steel Pier 189
Stenerud, Jan 6
Stram, Hank 153, 212
Strong, Ken 16
Studebaker 45
Sullivan, Dr. Michael 196
Summerfest 140
Super Bowl 75, 88, 92, 96, 116, 118, 123, 155, 167, 170–171, 180, 184, 202, 206, 210, 214, 217–218
Super Bowl I 152, 212
Super Bowl II 73, 115, 157, 224, 226

Index 287

Super Bowl VI 74, 112, 116–118
Super Bowl XVI 74
Super Bowl XVIII 154
Super Bowl XXV 186
Super Bowl XXVI 186
Super Bowl XXX..203, 210
Super Bowl XXXI 124, 168–169, 203, 210–211
Super Bowl XXXVI 216
Super Bowl XXXVII 217
Super Bowl XLV 65, 219
Swann, Lynn 88
Symank, John 161
Syracuse University 142, 191

T-formation 43
Tagliabue, Paul 124
Tampa Bay Buccaneers 182, 217, 222
Tarkenton, Fran 226
Taylor, Jim 4–5, 71, 73, 81, 86, 94, 99–100, 103–109, 114, 129–130, 146, 150, 174–175, 196, 204, 225; awards-highlights 104; biography 241; career statistics 241–242; family 105–106
Taylor, Lawrence 92, 188
Teague, George 209
Texarkana 120
Texas A&M University 26
Texas Tech University 108
Thanksgiving (Day) 81, 114, 161, 176, 215
Theta Delta Chi fraternity 181
Thigpen, Yancey 203
Thomas, Derrick 188
Thomas, Duane 74
Thompson, Darrell 207
Thompson, Ted 170, 211, 227
Thunder and Lightning 106, 108–109, 137
Thurston, Fred "Fuzzy" 72, 130, 145, 175, 224
Timmerman, Adam 210
Titletown 6, 184, 210, 214
Tittle, Y.A. 90, 123
Tomlinson, LaDainian 131
Tony Canadeo Day 67
Toomay, Pat 117
Toronto, Ohio 17
Toronto Argonauts 150, 154
Toronto High School 17
Torre, Joe 150
Trafton, George 22
Tuck Rule Game 216
Tunnell, Emlen 6, 111, 114, 130, 151–153, 159, 163, 213
Turnbull, Andrew 38
Turner, R. Gerald 75
Turney, John 124
Twentieth Century 129
Twin Cities 44

Unitas, Johnny 13, 95, 99–101, 115, 138, 152
United Press 19
U.S. Air Force 97
U.S. Army 65, 77, 122

United States Coast Guard 20
United States Football League 199
U.S. Military Academy 23
U.S. Navy 37
University of Alabama 11, 29–31, 95, 207
University of Chicago 124
University of Colorado 226, 228
University of Georgia 31
University of Idaho 173
University of Illinois 86, 96, 108, 174
University of Kentucky 29
University of Michigan 182, 215–216
University of Minnesota 207, 224
University of Notre Dame 36–37, 45, 47, 127–129
University of Pittsburgh 191
University of Southern California 88, 128, 148, 211
University of Tennessee 31, 72, 159, 198–199
University of Texas 159, 161
University of Utah 193
University of Virginia 134
University of Wisconsin 8, 36–37, 88, 146
Upshaw, Gene 52, 199, 224
Utah State University 193

Vagabond Halfback 46, 50–51
Vagabond Halfback: The Saga of Johnny Blood McNally 5
Vainisi, Jack 62, 79, 114, 158, 163, 174, 204, 225
Valentino, Rudolph 46–47
Van Brocklin, Norm 131
Van Buren, Steve 66
VanderKelen, Ron 192
Van Every, Harold 10
Van Susteren, Greta 170
Veenter, George 58
Vicodin 168
Virginia 47, 134

Wade, Bill 123
Walker, Herschel 199
Walker, Jimmy 31
Walker, Wayne 173–174
Wallace, Mike 219
Waller, Ron 154
Walsh, Bill 181–182
Washington, DC 148, 200, 209
Washington, Kenny 111
Washington, Mark 117
Washington Redskins 29, 64, 82–83, 147, 165, 184, 225
Waterfield, Bob 13
Watt, JJ 190
Waukesha, Wisconsin 182
Wayne, John 127
Webster, Mike 88
Wells, Scott 142
West High School (Cleveland) 54
West Point 23

Index

Western Conference 64, 78, 81, 107, 133, 139, 145, 176
Western Division 132
What's My Line? 90
Whisky a Go-Go 127
White, Reggie 6, 123, 167–168, 196–203, 209, 223, 227; awards-highlights 196–197, 199; biography 252; career statistics 253; family 197–198
White, Sara 197
Whitehurst, David 182
Whitley, David 29
Whittenton, Jesse 152
Willems, Ted 58–59
Williams, A.D. 122, 126, 137
Williams, Aeneas 171
Williams, Billy Dee 89
Williams, Brian 210
Williams, Travis "the Roadrunner" 139
WilsonArt International 163
Winnie, Russ 16, 22
Winning in the Trenches 5, 72
Winters, Frank 142
Wisconsin 35, 45, 92, 203
Witten, Jason 224
Wolf, Ron 28, 36, 136–137, 162–163, 168, 204–211, 226–227; biography 253; drafts as Packers GM 253–254; highlights 205

Wolfe, Thomas 187
Wood, Willie 79, 83, 94, 114–116, 134, 138, 157, 160, 163, 172, 179, 196, 204, 212–213, 225; awards-highlights 150; biography 247; career statistics 248
Woodson, Abe 103
Woodson, Charles 6, 115, 157, 161, 212–219; awards-highlights 213–216, 218; biography 255; career statistics 255
Woodson, Rod 213
World Football League 154
World Series 27
World War II 34, 43, 65

Yaeger, Dennis 162–163
Yankee Stadium 81, 89, 105, 176
The Year the Packers Came Back: Green Bay's 1972 Resurgence 94
YMCA 151
Young, John 113
You Can If You Will 2
Young, Steve 171, 199, 208

Zagorski, Joe 5, 94, 98–100
Zimmerman, David 5, 14, 24, 55
Zimmerman, Paul 16